THE INFLUENCE OF THE AMERICAN BAR ASSOCIATION ON PUBLIC OPINION AND LEGISLATION

A DISSERTATION

IN POLITICAL SCIENCE

PRESENTED TO THE FACULTY OF THE GRADUATE SCHOOL OF THE UNIVERSITY OF PENNSYLVANIA IN PARTIAL FULFILLMENT OF THE REQUIREMENTS FOR THE DEGREE OF DOCTOR OF PHILOSOPHY

M. LOUISE RUTHERFORD

THE LAWBOOK EXCHANGE, LTD.
Clark, New Jersey
2004

ISBN 1-58477-434-7

Second printing 2005

Printed in the United States of America on acid-free paper

THE LAWBOOK EXCHANGE, LTD.
33 Terminal Avenue
Clark, New Jersey 07066-1321

Please see our website for a selection of our other publications and fine facsimile reprints of classic works of legal history:
www.lawbookexchange.com

Library of Congress Cataloging-in-Publication Data

Rutherford, M. Louise (Mary Louise), b. 1892.
The influence of the American Bar Association on public opinion and legislation / M. Louise Rutherford.
p. cm.
Originally published: Philadelphia: [s.n.], 1937.
Thesis (Ph.D.)—University of Pennsylvania, 1936.
Includes bibliographical references and index.
ISBN 1-58477-434-7 (cloth: alk. paper)
1. American Bar Association. 2. Legislation—United States. 3. Public opinion—United States. 4. Pressure groups—United States. I. Title.

KF326.R8 2004
340'.06'073—dc22 2004040927

THE INFLUENCE OF THE AMERICAN BAR ASSOCIATION ON PUBLIC OPINION AND LEGISLATION

A DISSERTATION

IN POLITICAL SCIENCE

PRESENTED TO THE FACULTY OF THE GRADUATE SCHOOL OF THE UNIVERSITY OF PENNSYLVANIA IN PARTIAL FULFILLMENT OF THE REQUIREMENTS FOR THE DEGREE OF DOCTOR OF PHILOSOPHY

M. LOUISE RUTHERFORD

PHILADELPHIA

1937

To

My Husband

JOHN BRISBEN RUTHERFORD

ACKNOWLEDGMENT

The writer wishes to express sincere appreciation to all those who offered advice and suggestions in the preparation and writing of this thesis. It would be impossible to name all those who have given encouragement in undertaking the study. Much indebtedness is due officers and leaders of the American Bar Association, the Pennsylvania Bar Association, the Philadelphia Bar Association, and other groups, members of Congress and State Legislatures, Mr. Charles E. Beardslee, Esq., of the California Bar, Rush C. Butler, Esq., of the Illinois Bar, Louis G. Caldwell, Esq., of the Washington, D. C. Bar, Harry S. Knight, Esq., of the Pennsylvania Bar, Dr. James T. Young, of the University of Pennsylvania, and Dr. W. Brooke Graves, of Temple University, who responded sympathetically to interviews and to letters of inquiry. To the Carnegie Foundation for the Advancement of Teaching through Dr. Alfred Z. Reed; the American Law Institute, first through the late Honorable George W. Wickersham, former President, and later through Honorable George Wharton Pepper, President of the Institute; the Law Library of the Philadelphia Bar Association through Mr. James Carson Baxter; and Dr. John G. Hervey, Associate Dean Temple University Law School, much gratitude is due for fine spirit of cooperation manifested in making data available. To my friends, Miss Isabel Hill and Miss Mary L. Baldwin gratitude is expressed, to the former for assistance rendered in editing the manuscript, to the latter for making interviews in various parts of the country possible. To Professor Clyde L. King grateful appreciation is expressed for his patience and many vital and stimulating suggestions offered relative to the method of organizing the material and completing the study, as well as to its subject matter and style. Finally, to John Brisben Rutherford credit is due for constant encouragement rendered through the months of preparation.

M. LOUISE RUTHERFORD

August, 1937

TABLE OF CONTENTS

TABLE OF CONTENTS

TABLE OF CONTENTS

"Democracy is on trial in the world on a more colossal scale than ever before."—*The Spirit of Democracy*—Charles Fletcher Dole

CHAPTER I

INTRODUCTION—SCOPE AND PURPOSE

"When Law ends, tyranny begins."—William Pitt,
Earl of Chatham.

ONE pressing question is ever before us today: can democratic government adequately function and thus survive, or are dictatorships inevitable? DeTocqueville, that great student and admirer of American democracy, observed with characteristic acumen that the test of the United States democracy would come when the public domain was exhausted.[1] As long as free land was available, adjustments were comparatively easy. Since our frontiers according to leading present-day economists have now gone, democratic government here as well as elsewhere is being challenged. Though the great world war was fought to make the world safe for democracy, it fell short of attaining this goal. It is all too evident that though democracy may not have failed, it is under fire; the capacity of democratic government to maintain and defend itself is being questioned. And why? Among reasons that could be given, two should be noted:

(1) The almost entire absence of machinery to obtain trained, skilled and trustworthy men in government office.

(2) The failure to organize services of voluntary groups, especially those expert in government and law.

---

[1] Quoted, American Bar Association Report, Vol. 33 (1908), p. 831.

In 1886, in a paper presented before the American Bar Association entitled, "The Opportunity for the Development of Jurisprudence," Mr. Johnson T. Platt stated that the group then before him was living in a time when every human institution no matter how venerable was being examined and brought up for judgment. He added, "Events now succeed each other with such rapidity, and changes are so quickly brought about that there is less time for deliberation." [2] How like the present, when every democratic institution is "up for judgment," and usually adverse judgment. One can well ask, "Is democracy possible?" And we may answer, "Yes, if we reject the old and vicious ideology that anyone can serve in any capacity, since to the victor belongs the spoils," and adopt a new ideology that anyone can serve in any capacity if he is trained and has ability. Voluntary services of unbiased experts in government should be evaluated and used. The American Bar Association may constitute one of these voluntary groups, and this study represents an effort to obtain facts in relation to what contribution, if any, the American Bar Association has made and is making in the field of government and public administration. Has it influenced Public Opinion, by what methods, and to what extent?

The Honorable Elihu Root well stated that democracies depend upon the formation and adequate expression of Public Opinion.[3] What is "Public Opinion?" may be asked. Mr. Harold J. Laski in his book, "Politics," at page 125, states:

> ". . . there is rarely such a thing as a general public opinion. What occurs is rather the development of a series of public opinions centering about the issues which arise; and the relative power of these opinions depends upon the knowledge and organization they can command."

---

[2] Ibid., Vol. 9 (1886), pp. 215-227, particularly p. 216.

[3] Ibid., Vol. 46 (1921), p. 568.

And again, at page 91,

"Effective public opinion for purpose of government, in a word, is almost always opinion which is organized and differentiated from that of the multitude by the possession of special knowledge."

If this be true, then it would seem that only through groups organized with an avowed purpose and objective, and methods to effectuate such purpose and objective can an effective public opinion in matters of government be organized. Lawyers, because of their training and acquirement of specialized knowledge, may well be in a position to organize public opinion in matters of government and law. Though governmental problems are difficult of solution, yet quacks and charlatans are not lacking with their ready remedies. Little is accomplished by ballyhoo. There are no panaceas, especially for governmental and legal problems; only knowledge and organization can offer workable solutions. Problems of the present day, as any other day, are solved by taking particular aspects and studying them, and from such study evolving programs, which through action, may bring results.

The American Bar Association is composed of legal technicians, and might be of value on the technical side of legislation, both statutory and judicial. Lawyers form part of the governmental machinery; aside from their numbers in the legislature and on the bench, they are officers of the court, members of the judicial department of government.[4] For this reason, in their organized capacity, they are in a strategic position to influence Public Opinion and bring about the drafting and passage of certain legislation. In private matters, through their presentation of matters before the Court by way of argument, lawyers influence the Courts in their interpretations of the law. Under the Common Law, as is well known, the English judges have formed one of the outstanding subordinate legislatures of the world. The intricacies of the problems of government have

[4] Ibid., Vol. 51 (1926), p. 86.

increased tremendously; since Congress cannot know all the facts, it cannot possibly cope with them. Lawyers, in their organized groups, because many of the problems are within their special knowledge, have command of the facts, and may be in a position to render assistance. Even if Congress were superhuman, which it obviously is not, it could not possibly write all the laws that are enacted, nor should Congress, the Executive or the Judges be expected to grapple with and solve all problems before them. The complexity of modern day civilization and of government organization makes the service of technicians in special fields essential to obtain passage of necessary and proper laws, as well as effective administration of justice.

There is need of perfecting the democratic process, especially in the fields of law making, law enforcement and interpretation. Lawyers are experts in these fields, and it might be well to ascertain what is the relationship of the lawyer, especially in his organized capacity, to government. Perhaps, the layman should know whether the organized bar has rendered or is rendering service, and how adequate and how valuable it has been and is. Can the organized bar be of any assistance in obtaining efficiency in the functioning of democratic government?

Though a lawyer, the author holds no brief for lawyers, individually or as organized in bar associations. The purpose of this study is to gather facts relating to the policies and activities of the American Bar Association with special reference to those adopted to influence the formulation of public opinion and to sponsor the drafting and passage of legislation; that is, to show what contribution, if any, lawyers as a group have made to the effective functioning of our American democratic government. Professor James T. Young, of the Political Science Department of the University of Pennsylvania, regards facts as representing a selective process based on value judgments. Certainly, the effort can be made to keep the selective process as objective as possible. On the basis of factual data, a critical analysis and evaluation will be made of the effectiveness of the American Bar Association in the determination, formulation, declaration and execution of its policies and activities as tested by results, with certain recommendations as to how said policies and activities could be made more effective. There is need of factual data regarding the policies and activities of the American Bar Association because the profession of law represents a public profession, and occupies a strategic position in the government and the society politic.

Professor Young in a radio address on November 6, 1934, emphasized the need for fact and for field rather than desk research. The factual data on which this study is based has not only been collected from the American Bar Association Year Books, but there has been an effort to witness the actual functioning of the organized bar in its multiple activities by attendance at annual and other meetings of the national, state, and county bar associations, as well as those of Sections and Committees, supplemented by interviews with leaders and members of the organized bar, as well as with members of other organized groups, both friendly and unfriendly. Minute investigations of particular subjects that affect current issues or problems are essential, and the effort here is to ascertain how dependent on lawyers we are for the kind of law we have, and its administration and interpretation.

It is proposed to survey the scope and to analyze the significance and possibilities of the different policies and activities of the American Bar Association, together with the programs initiated to effectuate such policies, and the cogency of such programs. Though a purely descriptive study, with an intention to be suggestive rather than exhaustive, the idea is to organize, systematize and classify the organized bar's influence. The study will be confined to the American Bar Association, and the work of state and county bar associations will only be discussed as they affect or are affected by the national association. All activities of the latter association pertaining to aeronautics, admiralty, insurance, international affairs, mineral, patent, trade-mark and copyright law will be excluded, since these represent highly specialized branches of law, and each includes within itself a separate field of study. The main interest is not in the content of laws sponsored by the different subsidiary groups within the American Bar Association, but what the Association did and how. The influence of the American Bar Association will be shown by a presentation of the activities of certain Sections and Committees dealing with matters of a more general nature than those excluded. In any event, nothing is lost for the purpose of this thesis, since the excluded differ from the included groups only in the more highly specialized material with which they deal. This represents a pioneer study of a professional group, and it should be noted that the particular professional group is a part of the government.

The method pursued will be to set forth policies as shown by the facts, the existing machinery for execution of policies, and recommended changes which facts may show desirable. Structural, as distinguished from the functional organization, will first be discussed. Then will follow the influence of the organized bar within its own ranks to uphold the honor of the profession of law and to maintain higher standards of professional service. The policies of the organized bar regarding public relations will be presented. Furthermore, an analysis will be made of the bar's influence on public opinion respecting the Constitution, Judicial Procedure, Administrative Agencies, and Legislation. The machinery used to effectuate policies will be considered, together with evaluation of the machinery and recommendations for its improvement.

CHAPTER II

ORGANIZATION OF BAR, AND PURPOSE

"Let us go on unto perfection." Hebrews VI; 1.

A. HISTORICAL DEVELOPMENT OF BAR ASSOCIATIONS

1. PRE-REVOLUTIONARY PERIOD

BAR organization may be said to have its origin in the gregarious instinct of individuals to band together for mutual protection and benefit. Historically, bar organization began in the medieval guild. The Inns of Court, which in England control one branch of the legal profession, represent a federation of genuine guilds. The origin of these Inns is lost in antiquity, but they or their predecessor organization were in existence as early as the twelfth century, and probably originated as companies or quasi-corporations of lawyers, who owned and resided in the four Inns, patterned after the French College of Advocates. Though it is thought that they existed in their present form in the reign of Edward III in 1327, little satisfactory information is available until the time of Henry VI (1422-1461), when they were considered by Sir John Fortescue, Chancellor, in his "De Laudibus Legum Angliae." After a series of viccissitudes, the barristers, in 1606, by statute, succeeded in organizing the English bar and obtaining a monopoly of the most desirable practice. The other branch of the profession, the solicitors, gradually organized itself similarly into The Incorporated Law Society.[1]

Since the American colonists brought with them the tradition of an organized bar, they, prior to the Revolution, formed a number of colonial bar associations. However, because lawyers were in disrepute in the seventeenth century, there does not appear to be any organization of lawyers until the eighteenth century. The first New York Bar Association existed in New York city from about 1745 to 1770. An association in New Jersey was formed to discuss the Stamp Act in 1765. There were associations in various counties in New England, sometimes comprising several counties.[2]

2. POST-REVOLUTION CIVIL WAR PERIOD

During the Post-Revolutionary Civil War period, the bar, because of external influences, became individualistic, and bar associations were almost extinguished. The era of Jacksonian democracy did not lend itself to bar organization; the whole idea of bar associations as selective groups militated against the then current concept of democracy. With the exception of the Law Association of Philadelphia, organized in 1827, this extreme democratic concept prevented the formation of associations until after the Civil War. The few associations formed in the South during this period, namely, Mississippi in 1825, Arkansas in 1837, Louisiana (Association of the Bar of New Orleans) in 1847 and 1855, Kentucky in 1846, and Massachusetts in 1849, were only exceptions that proved the rule, and they were but weak and feeble organizations. None of these have endured. Two groups, more in the nature of library associa-

[1] Warren, Charles A., History of the American Bar (Little, Brown and Company, 1911), p. 28; Wickser, Philip J., "Bar Associations," Reprint from Cornell Law Quarterly, Vol. XV, No. 3, April, 1930, footnote 4, pp. 3-4; American Bar Association Report, Vol. 35 (1910), p. 812; Ibid., Vol. 38 (1913), pp. 767-774.

[2] Warren, Charles A., Op. Cit., p. 201; Wickser, P. J., Op. Cit., pp. 4-5.

tions, were permanent and are active today, namely, Social Law Library of Boston, organized in 1804, and the New York Law Institute, organized in 1828. Also, the Law Library Company of Philadelphia, organized in 1802, and associated members of the Bar of Philadelphia, organized in 1821, were consolidated in 1827 under the above name of the Law Association of Philadelphia. This association still continues, though in 1931 its name was changed to the more descriptive title "The Philadelphia Bar Association." [3]

3. CIVIL WAR TO DATE

Bar associations, with few exceptions as noted above, having disappeared, did not reappear until the eighteen-seventies. The first of these new organizations, founded in February, 1870, in the days of the Tweed ring, was the Association of the Bar of the City of New York.[4] In the next eight years, seven city and eight state bar associations were organized in twelve different states. The state bar associations included those of New York, the first to be organized; Illinois organized in 1877 and Vermont in 1878; the city bar associations included those of Cincinnati, organized in 1872, Cleveland in 1873, St. Louis and Chicago in 1874, Memphis and Nashville in 1875, and Boston in 1876.[5] The Secretary of the American Bar Association in his report of 1888, stated that a list of bar associations of the country was appended to the 1887 report. By adding to that list the Virginia State Bar Association, formed in July, 1888, and also the Bar of North Carolina, the list would total twenty-seven state bar associations in the country, which represented three-fourths of all the states of

[3] Wickser, P. J., Op. Cit., p. 5, and footnote 7; Law Association Centennial 1802-1902—Philadelphia; and Reed, Alfred Z., Training for the Public Profession of the Law (1921), p. 205.

[4] Wickser, P. J., Op. Cit., p. 7; Reed, Alfred Z., Op. Cit., p. 206.

[5] Webber, Marvelle C., "Origin and Uses of Bar Associations," American Bar Association Journal, Vol. 7 (1921), pp. 297-300.

the union. Although Pennsylvania had not organized a state bar association, it included within its limits a long list of what might be called local bar associations, and Massachusetts also had several of such associations.[6]

B. ORIGIN OF AMERICAN BAR ASSOCIATION

1. REASONS FOR ORGANIZATION

It was perhaps natural that the first bar associations in the United States should be formed in cities, where lawyers would be apt to congregate. With the development of railroad transportation in the eighteen-seventies, the organization of lawyers on a national scale became practical. Such an organization had its beginning at a meeting of the American Social Science Association in 1877, at Saratoga, New York. At this meeting, in a session of a Section or Department of Jurisprudence, Honorable Simeon E. Baldwin read a paper on "Graduate Courses in Law Schools." Out of the discussion that followed came a resolution that the future development of law schools be commended to the care of the legal profession. Judge Baldwin, in January, 1878, brought the matter before a session of the Connecticut Bar Association, of which he was a prominent member, whereupon a committee of three was appointed to consider the propriety of organizing an Association of American lawyers, said committee to have power to issue a circular. In April, 1878, such circular was prepared, which circular was followed by a letter. In June, 1878, a call signed by some of the most distinguished members of the Bar of the United States, including B. H. Bristow, of Kentucky, W. M. Evarts, of New York, Randolph Tucker, of Virginia, and some twelve other gentlemen, summoned members of the bar throughout the country to form a bar association

[6] American Bar Association Report, Vol. 11 (1888), pp. 18-19.

whereby "delegates representing the profession in all parts of the country might meet together annually for comparison of view and friendly intercourse." It was added that such an organization might be of great service in helping to assimilate the laws of the different states, in extending the benefit of true reforms and in publishing the failure of unsuccessful experiments in legislation. The first meeting, called for August 21, 1878, found seventy-three lawyers from eighteen states and the District of Columbia signing the register and organizing the American Bar Association.[7] It has generally been conceded that the origin of the American Bar Association represents largely the work of Simeon E. Baldwin; it is said that he personally wrote to six hundred lawyers in forty states, from which number came those seventy-three men, who organized the Association. A Constitution was drafted, a Committee on Legal Education and Admissions to the Bar was appointed, and the subject of uniform state laws considered.

2. EARLY POSSIBILITIES AS TO ORGANIZATION

Although the American Bar Association was organized as a selective voluntary association, it was immediately appreciated at the time of organization that close relations between this new national association and the older state bar associations were desirable. Before adjourning, the members attending the first meeting adopted a resolution that the Executive Committee should devise measures for establishing close relations between the national and state bar associations. At the second meeting in 1879, the full privilege of membership was extended at any annual meeting to any three delegates from a state association, and where no state bar association existed, city or county asso-

[7] American Bar Association Report, Vol. 1 (1878); Ibid., Vol. 5, (1882), p. 59; Baldwin, Simeon, "The Foundation of the American Bar Association," American Bar Association Journal, Vol. 3 (1917), pp. 658-695; Ibid., July, 1935, p. 452.

ciations were privileged to send two delegates. When the American Bar Association was formed, practically no county associations were in existence. At each meeting, the Secretary reported on delegates from state and local associations; the number of delegates did not average above five until 1888, when there were eighteen representatives.[8]

In 1887 Mr. J. A. Broadhead, who had been the first president of the American Bar Association, attempted to organize a representative national association. Half of the thirty-eight state associations sent delegates to the first meeting, but after a few meetings, the association disappeared, having held its last banquet in 1891.[9] And so, the attempt to form a federated type of organization for the bar never materialized, and the selective voluntary association became the prevalent type, and still is, though there have been attempts at affiliation, notably between state and county groups.[10]

Although the federated type of organization for the bar was never realized, still the idea, having been stressed by Judge Baldwin, never died out. Since 1916, the idea has been more definitely agitated. However, this movement for greater coordination of bar associations will be discussed later.

C. OBJECT OF ORGANIZATION

1. PURPOSE AS EXPRESSED IN CONSTITUTION

The Constitution, submitted by Judge Simeon Baldwin in 1878 and duly adopted, stated the object of the Association in this way:

---

[8] Wickser, Philip J., "Representative Government in the American Bar Association," American Bar Association Report, Vol. 57 (1932), pp. 581-582.

[9] Wickser, Philip J., "Bar Associations," Op. Cit., p. 10. A recent attempt at a representative national association is seen in the development of the Lawyers' National Guild, organized at Washington February, 1937.

[10] Notably Minnesota and Pennsylvania.

"Its object shall be to advance the science of jurisprudence, promote the administration of justice and the uniformity of legislation and of judicial decision throughout the Union, uphold the honor of the profession of the law, and encourage cordial intercourse among members of the American Bar."

This general object, as thus formally stated, continued unchanged until the adoption of the New Plan of Organization in August, 1936, when the object was enlarged by the addition of these words:—

". . . and to correlate the activities of the Bar organizations of the respective States on a representative basis in the interest of the legal profession and of the public throughout the United States."

From the beginning of its organization, the American Bar Association has published annual reports: Volume I, in 1878, numbered 49 pages; Volume 55 in 1930, 1354 pages; and Volume 60 in 1935, 1126 pages. In 1915 the Association initiated the publication of the American Bar Journal. From 1915 until 1920 it was issued as a quarterly; since 1920 it has been published as a monthly publication. Dr. James Grafton Rogers called this Journal one of the most important activities of the Association.[11] Certainly, it is valuable as it has represented the only permanent, consistent, and continuous tie between the governing group and the membership.

2. HOW THE ASSOCIATION FUNCTIONS AND WHAT THE SCOPE OF ACTIVITIES INCLUDES

The American Bar Association up to the adoption of the New Constitution and By-Laws in 1936, functioned largely through its executive committee, together with the standing and special committees, the various sections and allied bodies. The Executive Committee determined policies, which were carried out largely through the sections and committees. This former Executive Committee was re-

---

[11] Rogers, James Grafton, "Fifty Years of the American Bar Association," American Bar Association Report, Vol. 53 (1928), p. 525.

sponsible only to the Convention, which met once a year. In 1935, before the adoption of the New Plan of Organization, there were thirteen standing committees and fourteen special committees.[12]

The sections were not organized until 1893; in that year, the first section, that of Legal Education was formed. Immediately before the adoption of the New Plan, there were thirteen sections.[13]

The American Bar Association in this development of sections and committees, standing and special, may be said to have followed that of Congress. Whenever a new question of legal significance or of public moment arose, a new committee was formed to deal with the subject. As the old problems were settled and passed out of the legal and political horizon, the Committees charged with the consideration of such problems, diminished in importance and were discontinued.

Instead of a New Deal, the American Bar Association, in 1936, developed and adopted a New Plan. Under this New Plan of organization, adopted in August, 1936, the House of Delegates became the policy-determining body of the Association. This House of Delegates may be said to be a representative body, chosen according to a plan to be hereafter discussed. Instead of having policies determined by an Executive Committee responsible only to the Annual Convention, which included about two or three thousand lawyers, or fewer than two per cent of American lawyers, national policies will now be determined by a group representative of the 78,000 membership of state bar associa-

---

12 See American Bar Association Report, Vol. 60 (1935), pp. 19-24 and pp. 25-28.

13 See Ibid., Vol. 60 (1935), pp. 29-55. Note should be made of the Junior Bar Conference movement. The original call was sent out to interested persons in connection with the 1932 meeting; in 1933, issue of an independent organization or one within the American Bar Association arose. Due to the cooperation of the Association's subcommittee, approval of the Executive Committee was obtained for official Conference in 1934, since which time the Junior Bar Conference has been given the status of a Section. Ibid., Vol. 60 (1935), pp. 622-632.

tions and the 28,000 membership of the American Bar Association. The Administrative body, the Board of Governors, is a responsible committee of the House, and in all respects subject to control by the House. (See Article VI, Section 3 of the New Constitution.) The New Plan of organization provides for fourteen standing committees including such diverse activities as the following:

(1) Admiralty and Maritime Law.
(2) Aeronautical Law.
(3) American Citizenship.
(4) Commerce.
(5) Commercial Law and Bankruptcy.
(6) Communications.
(7) Federal Taxation.
(8) Jurisprudence and Law Reform.
(9) Labor, Employment and Social Security.
(10) Legal Aid Work.
(11) Noteworthy Changes in Statute Law.
(12) Professional Ethics and Grievances.
(13) State Legislation.
(14) Unauthorized Practice of the Law.[14]

All of these committees have been functioning under the former organization with the exception of that on Labor, Employment and Social Security, which is a new committee. Twelve sections are also provided for as follows:

(1) Section of Legal Education and Admissions to the Bar.
(2) Section of Patent, Trade-Mark and Copyright law.
(3) Judicial Section.
(4) Section of Public Utility Law.
(5) Section of Bar Organization Activities.
(6) Section of Criminal Law.
(7) Section of Mineral Law.
(8) Section of Municipal Law.

---

[14] See Article X, Section 1 of By-Laws, adopted August, 1936.

(9) Section of Insurance Law.
(10) Section of International and Comparative Law.
(11) Junior Bar Conference.
(12) Section of Real Property, Probate and Trust Law.

These sections also were all functioning at the time of the adoption of the New Plan of organization, with the exception of the Section of Bar Organization Activities, which in part replaces the former Conference of State Bar Delegates. The New Plan coordinates and ties together the work of the Association within by giving the Chairman of the Sections representation in the House of Delegates. The Section Chairman can thus keep section members in touch with policies and decisions of the House.

D. PERSONNEL OF ORGANIZATION

The American Bar Association is an organization consisting entirely of individual members; before 1936, it had little structural connection with state or local associations, and as stated above, carried on its work through Sections and Committees. From 1893, when the first Section was established, a large part of its work program had been carried on through these Sections, which in effect were semiautonomous bodies.[15] In 1878, the Association commenced with seventy-three charter members, which membership steadily increased until the membership numbered 28,228, as of June 30, 1936.[16]

Though the membership was approaching 30,000, and the attendance at annual meetings had reached 3000, the national organization was far from being representative of the legal profession, since the membership represented ap-

15 Wickser, Philip P., "Bar Associations," Op. Cit., p. 8.

16 Letter from Olive G. Ricker, Executive Secretary American Bar Association, dated October 1, 1936. Referendum of membership taken March, 1937, on President's proposal as to federal courts was submitted to 29,616 members. (American Bar Association Journal, April, 1937, p. 271.)

proximately only sixteen per cent of the 175,000 lawyers in the United States. Though the American Bar Association was not adequately representative, yet it should be recognized that it was the only national group which influenced the opinion of lawyers and through which lawyers could voice their opinion.

State and local bar associations numbered in excess of 1,400 associations, and when these were considered, then sixty per cent of the lawyers of the country belonged to some bar association.[17] While at its inception there was an earnest effort to obtain some organic connection between the national bar and the state and local groups, it did not materialize in any definite results until 1936, when the New Plan was adopted. Through the representative organization developed under the New Plan, in addition to greater cohesion within, a definite tie is to be established between the state and local groups on the one hand, and the national association on the other.

E. FRAMEWORK OF AMERICAN BAR ASSOCIATION

1. EARLIER TYPE

The Constitution and By-laws of the Association provided originally for a President, Vice-President from each state, a Secretary, and a Treasurer. The provision regarding the Vice-President was changed in 1933 to provide for a Vice-President from each of the ten judicial circuits, and was further changed in 1936, by incorporating these representatives into the Board of Governors. The Executive Committee was, up to 1936, the policy-determining or governing body of the Association, in which virtually all powers of control including that of the purse were lodged. It was composed of fifteen members, nine elected members and six

[17] Commercial Law Journal, Op. Cit., p. 649; American Bar Association Journal, June, 1935, p. 387.

ex-officio members, including the President, the Treasurer, the Secretary, the retiring President, the Chairman of the General Council, and the Editor of the American Bar Association Journal. Members of the Executive Committee served for a term of three years and were ineligible for reelection. These officers and members of the Executive Committee were nominated by the General Council, consisting of one member from each state, elected by a state caucus of members at the conclusion of one of the sessions of the annual meeting. In addition to this General Council, there was a State Council of five members, formerly a Local Council of five members, including the Vice-President for the state. The members of this State Council were elected by members of each state present at the annual meeting. This State Council was supposed to form, with the members of the General Council for each State, and the Vice-President for the Circuit, the point of contact between the national association and the state and local associations. The members of this State Council had the particular duties of passing on all applications for membership in the national association, of building up the membership and aiming to secure the adoption of legislation approved by the Association. This was the political structure.

In addition, there was a "work group," of Sections and Committees, which constantly functioned to sift out matters of importance to the bar and public, and to bring them to the floor of the meeting of the whole association. Members of the Association then determined whether the resulting recommendations should be accepted or rejected.[18]

When the Association was first organized, seven committees were appointed, and this number had been increased as necessity demanded. The sections were semi-autonomous groups, as stated above, which elected their own officers, a Chairman, Secretary, and Council, the latter composed of eight members elected for four-year terms; these sections with few exceptions made studies of some specialized legal

18 American Bar Association Report, Vol. 45 (1920), p. 25.

problem. Authorization of the Executive Committee had to be obtained before any action could be taken; aside from this, the Sections were virtually free to choose topics, make programs and arrive at conclusions. The first Section of the Association was not organized until 1893, and it seems fitting that this group should have been the Section of Legal Education, since lawyers would naturally be concerned with the standing and capability of members of their profession. The idea of Sections within the American Bar Association encountered some opposition, for in 1894 a resolution was offered that Sections should be abolished. In the discussion that ensued, Mr. B. F. Hughes, of Pennsylvania, stated that he would like to hear some reason advanced why more mischief would result in performing educational work of the bar under the name of "Section" rather than the name of "Committee." The resolution to abolish sections was laid on the table.[19]

2. TRANSITION TO COORDINATION BETWEEN DIFFERENT BAR ASSOCIATION UNITS

As stated above, from the beginning, there has been an attempt to develop contact between the county, state, and national bars by means of representatives or delegates from county and state bar associations to the annual meetings of the American Bar Association. The delegates were few in number, had no real voting power to represent county or state bars, and made no contribution until the establishment of the Conference of Bar Association Delegates in 1916. More effective contact was obtained through functional cooperation to carry out policies of Sections and Committees than through structural changes. Aside from functional contacts between the national and state bar associations to carry through policies of the national bar Sections and Committees, the influence of the national association that seeped down to the state and local bar asso-

[19] Ibid., Vol. 17 (1894), p. 66.

ciations was through three mediums: (1) the Vice-Presidents, originally one for each state, later in 1933, one for each of the ten judicial circuits; (2) the Local Councils originally, later the State Councils; (3) members of General Council. At best, the connection was rather tenuous.

Though the effort to develop structural contact between county, state, and national bar associations was from the time of the organization of the American Bar Association in 1878 almost continuous, it amounted to little [20] until 1916, when a distinctive effort was made to connect local and state bar associations with the American Bar Association. As a result of the activities of the Wigmore Committee appointed in 1913, and under the leadership of the Honorable Elihu Root, then President of the American Bar Association, an invitation was issued to all state and local bar associations to send delegates to meet representatives of the American Bar Association at a special conference at Chicago August 28, 1916, for the purpose of bringing about closer relationship between the American Bar and other bar associations. Two sessions were held, at which were represented fifty-four state and local bar associations.[21]

The first recommendation of the Conference asked that the Constitution of the American Bar Association be amended by a new article, providing for referendum, when demanded by the General Council, though authority to submit questions was limited to the Executive Committee.[22] The second provision was allied, and provided that the President of each state bar association, which accepted, should be a member ex officio of the General Council of the American Bar Association, and that the secretary of such bar association should be a member ex officio of the Local Council of the American Bar Association in that state.[23] Stress at the present time could well be given to a statement of

[20] Note should be made of the Mecartney Resolution for appointment of Committee on reorganization in 1917. American Bar Association Report, Vol. 31 (1907), p. 107.

[21] Ibid., Vol. 41 (1916), pp. 7, 8 and 94.

[22] Ibid., Vol. 41 (1916), p. 590ff.

[23] Ibid., Vol. 41 (1916), p. 592.

the Honorable Elihu Root at this Conference that active interest and real cooperation cannot be obtained unless you give them something to do and some power to do it.[24] The above proposed amendments were approved by the Executive Committee and adopted by the American Bar Association.[25]

The original call had been for a single conference; early in 1917, the President of the American Bar Association called a meeting of the Committee on Cooperation Among State Bar Associations, with the President and former President of the Association, and this group called the second conference in 1917.[26] This second and informal conference in 1917, at Saratoga, was termed successful. By adoption of a resolution, the Conference resolved to become a permanent organization.[27] The Conference met at Cleveland in 1918, and at Boston, in 1919. At this 1919 meeting, the Conference became a Section of the American Bar Association, with the following purpose as noted in Article I of the By-Laws:

> "To create a better understanding between members of the American Bar and to induce a better and more effective cooperation by bar associations of the country in the maintenance, extension and observance of standards set by the American Bar Association."

Membership to the Conference, according to Article II, should "consist of delegates from various bar associations of the country to be selected as follows: five delegates from the American Bar Association, three from each State Bar Association, and two from each Local Bar Association." [28] The Conference had a two-fold function: (1) To collect data from all bar associations of the country relative to the betterment of the administration of justice, and to report conclusions to the American Bar Association and the

---

[24] Ibid., Vol. 41 (1916), p. 593.

[25] Ibid., Vol. 41 (1916), p. 9.

[26] American Bar Association Journal, Vol. 3 (April, 1917), p. 93; (October, 1917), p. 580.

[27] American Bar Association Report, Vol. 42 (1917), p. 438.

[28] Ibid., Vol. 45 (1920), p. 396.

local bar associations; (2) To receive from the American Bar Association suggestions to be brought to the attention of local bar associations.[29]

Having reached the status of a Section, the Conference carried on its work as did every other Section, except that, since its members consisted of representatives of state and local bar associations, it did not have the facility of the other Sections, because its members were not experts working with particular questions and problems in their own specialized field. The Conference initiated many projects,[30] through discussion and propaganda, but as a coordination device, if the pragmatic test was used, it could not be considered as a success. The delegates had no power to commit their association, they only had power to express their own views, and adopt recommendations, which were taken back to the state and local bar associations; sometimes they were adopted, and oftentimes they were not. As Dr. James Grafton Rogers well expressed it, the first two propositions adopted, namely, those for referenda and the making of the president of the state bar association a member of the General Council, ex officio, came to naught; the first though embodied in the Constitution as Article XIII was unemployed and forgotten, and the other after a period of two years was found unsatisfactory and eliminated. What the Conference furnished was mainly a forum for individual expression.[31]

In 1919, representation from state and local bar associations to the American Bar Association, initiated in 1878, was abandoned, since representatives now had a definite group in which they could express their views, namely, the Conference.

---

[29] Ibid., Vol. 47 (1922), p. 42.

[30] Wickser, Philip J., "Representative Government in the American Bar Association," American Bar Association Report, Vol. 57 (1932), pp. 581-592; see especially p. 581.

[31] Rogers, James Grafton, American Bar Association Journal, Vol. 16 (1930), pp. 15ff; Wickser, Philip J., "Bar Associations," p. 10, footnote 18; American Bar Association Report, Vol. 54 (1929), p. 52.

The Conference of Bar Association Delegates had as one of its committees that of Cooperation between Bar Associations, which considered closer cooperation between the American Bar Association and state and local associations. At the 1922 meeting of the Conference, it was stated that while the time was not ripe for complete federation of state associations with the national association, federation was the ultimate goal, as was again stated in 1936. One delegate at this 1922 meeting explained how the Washington State Bar Association had effected a unitary membership with practically all county associations of the state. Out of the discussion came the adoption of a motion which provided for a Committee of Five to "investigate and report on means for better coordination of efforts of Bar Associations and its opinion on the practicability of federating the Bar Associations of the country." Chief Justice Taft made an eloquent plea for bar integration to the end that through the formulation of a real public opinion of the bar, its responsibility for reforms in the administration of justice might be assumed.[32]

At the 1923 meeting, Chief Justice Taft remarked on the importance of the organized bar to advise not only the general public, but also representatives of the public who were gathered in legislative assemblies in those fields in which the bar by reason of professional status and experience was most competent to advise the public, that is, in the field of judicial administration.[33] At this 1923 meeting, the Conference Committee on Coordination of the Bar, acting with a similar Committee created by action of the Executive Committee of the American Bar Association agreed that the election of members of the General Council should emanate from state associations, an idea that precipitated some conflict in 1888. This recommendation of the two committees was adopted by the Conference, but not by the American Bar Association.[34] At this meeting, the matter of coordina-

---

[32] American Bar Association Report, Vol. 47 (1922), pp. 598ff.
[33] Ibid., Vol. 48 (1923), pp. 548ff.
[34] Ibid., Vol. 48 (1923), pp. 42-46; also p. 552.

tion was emphasized by the President, Honorable John W. Davis, who appointed a Special Committee to devise a plan for cooperation. President R. E. L. Saner, the following year, also stressed it, attaching to his annual address a "Memorandum on National Federalization of the Bar." [35] He eulogized the American Medical Association, and held it before his legal group as an example; this eulogy has been consistently indulged in for many years and still endures.[36] Though it is noted that four former Presidents, Honorable Elihu Root, Honorable John W. Davis, Honorable Cordenia A. Severance, and Honorable R. E. L. Saner agreed that the organization of their day was not at all satisfactory in concentrating all organized bar activity into a harmonious whole,[37] yet little real contact between county, state, and national bar association groups was attained until the featuring of the National Bar Program in 1933, and the subsequent adoption of the New Plan in 1936.

At the 1928 meeting of the Conference, with Dr. James Grafton Rogers as Chairman, the policy of eulogy of the Conference and its contribution to the coordination of bar units changed to one of sharp, adverse criticism, perhaps too adverse in the light of its achievements and contributions of the past.[38] There is no doubt that the Conference had certain accomplishments to its credit, which Harry S. Knight, Esq., in 1931, then Chairman of the Conference, listed as being chiefly the enactment of bar organization statutes in nine states, incorporating of the bars of those states, the creation of activity for incorporated bars in other states, and the formation of judicial councils in twenty states.[39] However, as a result of the address of criticism of Dr. Rogers to the Conference of Bar Delegates, and his emphasis on a need for a better organization of the bar of the country, the Executive Committee, the General

---

[35] Ibid., Vol. 49 (1924), pp. 152-173.
[36] Ibid., Vol. 49 (1924), p. 163.
[37] American Bar Association Journal, Vol. 16 (1930), p. 16.
[38] American Bar Association Report, Vol. 53 (1928), p. 527.
[39] Ibid., Vol. 56 (1931), p. 493.

Council, and the Conference of Bar Association Delegates, in October, 1929, each appointed a Committee to devise some plan of reorganization.[40]

The Conference Committee prepared the report, which was endorsed by the other two committees. The report ended with the recommendation that the Executive Committee of the American Bar Association appoint a Special Committee to ascertain from state bar associations, executives, and leaders, their attitude toward some form of affiliation between the national, state and local associations, and also to evolve a plan that would affiliate state bars, in whatever form organized, with the American Bar Association. This Committee, appointed August, 1930, was to report its findings and recommendations to the Executive Committee, by January, 1931, if possible.[41] The report of this Committee on Coordination of the Bar, made at the 1931 annual meeting of the American Bar Association, was said to be a report of information only. It stated that during the year 1930-1931, the Committee had met frequently, and had been in contact by correspondence and otherwise with many lawyers and bar associations of the country, in an effort to secure the opinion of the bar as to the best way of bringing the work of the American Bar Association to them, and as to whether the American Bar Association should be affiliated with the other bar associations either by joint work or some method of closer affiliation. The Committee learned that there was a great desire that the work of the national association be presented to the state associations in a more effective manner, and that the latter be informed of the policies and activities of the former association. On the question as to whether there should be real federation, there was great diversity of opinion. The Committee stated that it was laying out a program which would require four or five years for accomplishment. In pursuance of that purpose, the Committee had made report

[40] Ibid., Vol. 55 (1930), p. 24.
[41] Ibid., Vol. 55 (1930), p. 25.

to the Executive Committee, recommending certain procedure, which report the Executive Committee had referred to the General Council; the General Council did not approve of all the details of the report and made certain suggestions, but did approve of the spirit and effort to bring the national association in closer contact with the lawyers of the country.[42]

The Association Committee was reappointed, and continued its study during the year 1931-1932. It held sessions at Atlantic City in September, 1931, at Charleston, in January, 1932, and at Washington, in May, 1932. The Conference Committee on Bar Reorganization and the Association Committee jointly communicated with every state and local bar association, sent them information, and urged active consideration of bar coordination. Too, these Committees published statements and special articles in the American Bar Association Journal, and were represented on programs of various state and local associations, and at conferences of Committees and leaders. The Committee recommended certain amendments to the Constitution and By-Laws, which were proposed for the improvement of the structure of the Association; these amendments had been approved by the Executive Committee, and were summarized under five headings:

(1) Substitution of one Vice-President for each of the ten federal circuits for the present 53 Vice-Presidents.

(2) Authorization for the Executive Committee to appoint one or more Junior Executives to lay a foundation for a definite, continuous and direct contact with other associations throughout the year.

(3) Establishment of a three-year term for members of the General Council with the idea of building up and expanding the responsibility and representative functions of that body, the Council not to take office until the conclusion of the meeting at which elected.

(4) Change of name of Local Council to State Council.

---

42 Ibid., Vol. 56 (1931), pp. 132-133.

(5) Provisions for payment of expenses of members of General Council in attendance at meetings between annual meetings. More frequent meetings of the General Council would result in benefits to the whole association, and would increase the power of the Council to represent sentiment of the bar of the country. There were also some minor amendments, which were suggested with a view to improving the machinery of the association; it was wisely stated that the future of the organized bar of the United States would begin with local bar associations.[43]

These changes, after two years of research and work by the Committee on Coordination may seem slight, and as the Committee admitted, they only tended to change the structure of the national association.

A transition from this stress on structure to one on a work program to develop coordination among all bar associations was initiated in 1933, with the beginning of what is known as the National Bar Program. During the winter of 1932, the Committee on Coordination submitted recommendations to and conferred twice with the Executive Committee. At the May meeting, plans were authorized for work to be completed before the annual meeting in August, 1933. These plans involved the assumption that coordination as a matter of practical reality could best be achieved in terms of work rather than in the political or theoretical organization of units of associations. Since it was evident that such plans for a work program must, first of all, be laid before the leaders and membership of associations, the Executive Committee, through President Clarence E. Martin, invited the Presidents and Secretaries of all state and certain local associations, delegates to the Conference of Bar Delegates, to meet with the Executive Committee and the General Council of the American Bar Association to discuss a plan for a National Bar Program August 29th, 1933. In the proceedings, this meeting is reported under the heading "Conference of Bar Association Officers."

---

[43] Ibid., Vol. 57 (1932), pp. 543ff, and also pp. 54ff.

The Committee on Coordination with the assistance of the Executive Secretary had made a survey from the Year Books of state associations for three years to ascertain programs which had occupied the attention of bar associations; out of the above Conference of Bar Association Officers in 1933 came the National Bar Program, which represented an effort to promote a functional relationship with state and local associations on four topics or problems of general interest and importance to the profession and the public, as follows:[44]

1. Criminal Law and its Enforcement.
2. Unauthorized Practice of the Law.
3. Legal Education and Admission to the Bar.
4. Judicial Selection.

In furtherance of the program, the American Bar Association offered to place an officer in the field for personal conference with other associations; to establish a bureau for exchange of data at headquarters; to provide a forum for debate at its annual meeting, and to record and publicize sentiment of the profession as it developed in judging concrete proposals for improvement of the administration of justice.

The plan as set forth received vigorous prosecution during the year 1933-1934, and met with widespread acceptance by state and local associations of the country. Over 300 associations cooperated by answering questionnaires, holding meetings for study and action on National Bar Program subjects, and for exchange of data and opinion. As part of the program, over fifty legal periodicals were serviced; the work and findings of the American Bar Association and all coordinated associations were publicized with the lay press; many personal conferences were had and addresses made; the Committee on Coordination met twice during the winter of 1933-1934.

Three of the four subjects listed on the National Bar Program were discussed at some length at the annual meet-

[44] Ibid., Vol. 58 (1933), pp. 185-188, 497 passim and 514 passim.

ing in 1934.[45] It was decided in 1934 to continue the National Bar Program for three years, with an additional subject, "Professional Ethics."

In 1935, the Committee on Coordination, after considerable research, submitted four possibilities of organization for the American Bar Association, as follows:

(1) A continuation of the present organization with slight changes looking to a stronger connection between bar groups.

(2) A continuation of the National Bar Program.

(3) A service emphasis to attract a larger percentage of lawyers to membership in bar organizations.

(4) Federation.

Of these four specific plans, the Association adopted federation. Later, a concrete plan for bringing about a representative and improved organization of the legal profession was evolved. The General Council, the Executive Committee, the Vice-Presidents and many of the Section and Committee Chairmen met with the Coordination Committees in Chicago, January 13 to 15, 1936. Before the sessions in Chicago, there had been an extensive expression of opinion from state and local bar associations and individual lawyers throughout the United States; expressions were related to the first draft of proposed plan sent out under date of November 1, 1935.[46] In May, 1936, the plan was reconsidered and necessary changes made. At the annual convention in August, 1936, the New Plan as submitted was adopted by an overwhelming vote, thus ending a twenty-year struggle for revision of the system under which the association operated. Though originally a small social group, the Association had developed into a large group carrying on all kinds of research projects, and working for the improvement of law and the administration of justice.

---

[45] Ibid., Vol. 59 (1934), pp. 106ff, 153ff, and 224ff.

[46] American Bar Association Journal, February, 1936, pp. 83, passim.

According to the New Plan of Organization, control and administration of the American Bar Association is vested in a House of Delegates. The new system would provide for a House of Delegates consisting of 166 delegates, chosen as follows:[47]

State delegates, one from each state, nominated by petition of American Bar Association members within a state, and elected by mail ballot of American Bar Association members in state or territory.[48]	51	
State bar association delegates chosen by method selected by state bar association, one delegate for every 2000 members of state bar association, 1 additional for every 1000 members, maximum 4 delegates.	70	estimated
Local bar association delegates as may be chosen by and from local bar association. (Such association must have membership of 800 members or more.)	13	estimated
Five delegates chosen from Assembly (Membership in attendance at annual meetings).	5	
Officers of other national organizations, and delegates from affiliated organizations of the legal profession such as the American Law Institute, American Judicature Society, President of National Conference Commissioners, Chairman of National Conference Bar Examiners, Chairman of National Conference Judicial Councils, President Association of American Law Schools, President National Association Attorney Generals.	7	
Attorney General and Solicitor General of United States.	2	
Chairmen of Sections.	12	
President, Secretary, and Treasurer of American Bar Association.	3	
Other ex officio members of the Board of Governors.	3	
	166	

[47] See Article V, Sections 3-7, of New Constitution of 1936.
[48] See Article V, Section 5, of New Constitution.

The state delegates replace the former General Council, but the state delegates are chosen by a method which represents an effort to gain participation and interest of the stay-at-home member. The state and local bar association delegates replace the former Conference of Bar Association Delegates, terminated at the 1936 meeting. Provision for referendum vote on major policies is also provided by Article V, Section 10. A provision for referendum has existed since 1916, though practically never used.[49]

In so far as the 1936 plan of organization represents an attempt to make the Association more representative and to give the stay-at-home member more participation in the affairs of the Association, it is a step in the right direction. While the New Plan was not submitted as perfect, it is an entering wedge in the direction of coordinating the different bar groups by tying in the state and local associations to some extent, and by giving the Sections and affiliated groups some voice in the determination of policies. After more than fifty years of effort, the beginnings of a cohesive bar organization are being realized.

The National Bar program featured in 1933-1934 and 1934-1935, acted as a temporary expedient through which state and local associations functioned with the national association first in four selective fields, and later in five, as stated above. Through that device the state and local associations worked with the national association in the designated fields. Having performed its object, the National Bar program will be continued, but as merged and swallowed up in the New Plan of organization adopted in 1936. The Special Committee on Coordination was continued with a two-fold purpose:

(1) To devise ways and means for the practical working of the New Plan, and

---

[49] Supra, pp. 20 and 22. The new provision for referenda was used in 1937 to determine the stand of the Bar on the proposal to increase the number of justices of the U. S. Supreme Court to fifteen.

(2) To stimulate state and local associations to send their best representatives as delegates.

The latter is obviously vital to the success of the New Plan, for it would seem to be predicated on the representative character of the delegates chosen, and particularly those chosen from state and local associations. Certainly, under the New Plan, state and local bar associations through these delegates or representatives may participate in developing and formulating policies of the American Bar Association. A weakness, however, should be noted in that the state and local bar associations retain their autonomy and their delegates cannot bind such associations in the House of Delegates. (See Article V, Section 2.) The House of Delegates of the American Bar Association also retains the privilege of deciding which state bar association may select delegates if the question should arise as to any state or territory. Perhaps, a short discussion of state bar organization may not be amiss.

According to Mr. Philip J. Wickser, there are three possibilities for organization: (1) Selective voluntary association, the original form of bar organization in this country; (2) Compulsorily incorporated bar, usually termed the integrated bar, a form of organization sponsored largely by the American Judicature Society and the Conference of Bar Association Delegates, and (3) Federated Bar.

The theory of an all-inclusive or integrated state bar was first discussed according to one authority at certain state association meetings in the West in 1914. It envisages an association in which every lawyer of the state would have a voice and vote, and in which the membership was made compulsory by act of the legislature. This discussion was continued by the American Judicature Society, which sponsored the theory and prepared a Model Act providing for an incorporated state bar. In 1919 the principle involved was considered by the Conference of Bar Association Delegates, and a Special Committee was appointed. The report of this Special Committee favoring the incorporated bar was discussed and approved at the 1920 meeting, and state bar associations were urged to consider the matter and take appropriate action. In 1922 only one state, North Dakota, had an incorporated bar; by 1930, seven states had incorporated bars with some seven additional states reporting favorable action on incorporation as soon likely. By 1932, ten states had incorporated bars and some ten or fifteen more states had introduced bills; by 1933, the number of incorporated bars had increased to eighteen with attempts to obtain enactment of bar organization bills in sixteen additional states.[50] It should be noted that in 1927 opposition developed in the East, when the New York State Bar Association repudiated the whole idea.[51]

If a state should have both a voluntary and incorporated bar association, the House of Delegates would decide which state organization was entitled to be represented through its delegates.

It is too soon to estimate the success of the New Plan of organization. A study of the past history of the Association shows that since its inception, the problem of a representative and coordinated bar has been considered, and whenever any plan was proposed, it was adopted with great enthusiasm, for example, note the exuberance when the Conference of Bar Association Delegates was heralded as the mechanism that would bring the desired coordination between the different bar units. Though the Conference of Bar Association Delegates did not give the result desired, nevertheless, it is recognized that the Conference did contribute to the effective functioning of the American Bar Association. Certainly, it furnished the basis on which the present attempt to give representation to state and local bar associations is predicated. No plan is automatic or self-workable; rather, the human or personal element is

---

[50] Journal American Judicature Society, Vol. 19, No. 3, p. 77, October, 1935.

[51] American Bar Association Report, Vol. 57 (1927), p. 448.

important, and the success of the New Plan will depend, in large measure, on the personalities entrusted with its administration and development.

F. FINANCIAL SYSTEM

The American Bar Association is largely financed through the dues of members, which amount to eight dollars per year. The annual dues also include a subscription to the American Bar Association Journal, the publication of the American Bar Association, and its chief instrumentality for keeping in touch with its membership. The dues of state and county groups vary, but in the Pennsylvania State Bar Association, the dues are eight dollars per year, and in the Philadelphia County Bar Association twenty dollars per year. It is thus evident that a Philadelphia lawyer, if he desires to maintain membership in his county, state and national associations must pay annual dues amounting in the aggregate to thirty-six dollars. The dues of the different counties and states vary; the point to be noted is that membership and dues of each association are separate and distinctive.

Committees and Sections of the American Bar Association until 1935 were financed from appropriations made to them by the Executive Committee; in 1935, by an amendment to the By-Laws, the Sections were enabled to assess dues for membership therein; these dues are used for the purpose of financing publications of those sections. Many of these publications such as those of the Section on Public Utility Law are quite elaborate and expensive.

At the 1935 annual meeting, it was announced that the Carnegie Corporation would contribute to the American Bar Association $50,000, to carry out and make effective the National Bar Program. This payment, spread over a three-year period, was then matched by the American Bar Association, which means that the National Bar Program is to have available $100,000 to effectuate its purpose.

Chapter III

GROUP OBJECTIVES AND METHODS TO RAISE STANDARDS OF PROFESSIONAL SERVICE

"The law: It has honored us, may we honor it."—Daniel Webster.

A. Legal Education and Standards of Admission

1. INTRODUCTORY

The question of regimentation for industry and for the individual presents one of the most important problems before the country today. Since law is a profession affected with a public interest, it is not surprising that there has always been regulation in this profession, sometimes by lawyers themselves, sometimes by courts, and sometimes by legislatures. No one has a vested right to follow a public or quasi-public calling or profession.[1] The practice of law is not a "private business but a public trust;"[2] it is not a right but a privilege.[3]

At the present time, it is more than ever realized that for the protection of the public, lawyers should meet the highest educational and character standards for admission to practice; also that they should be required to adhere to the highest standards of ethical conduct. Too, there should

1 American Bar Association Report, Vol. 26 (1903), p. 593.

2 Ibid., Vol. 28 (1905), p. 591.

3 The Legal Intelligencer, Philadelphia, February 29, 1936, p. 4, "On Restricting Admission to the Bar," by Edward Stone and Hirsh W. Stalberg.

be a method of purging the profession of those who do not so conform, and of preventing unauthorized practice by those without proper training. Since justice and its administration are among the prime needs of life, it is important that those who are charged with the administration of law should assume their important duties adequately equipped for the purpose.[4] Standards of admission, which include the whole subject of legal education, are therefore of great importance to the public as well as to the legal profession. Austin Abbott in a paper, "Existing Question of Legal Education," went so far as to state that legal education is an indispensable condition of our national welfare.[5] It has been well said that whether for good or ill, lawyers are and have been from the beginning a dominant factor in the public life of the nation, wherefore it seems then plainly a matter of highest public concern that their training should be exacting and adequate.[6] Our law schools have been recognized definitely as training schools for public life and their proper maintenance, therefore, considered a matter of public interest.[7]

2. HISTORICAL BACKGROUND

(a) Pre-Revolutionary Period

Some historical background of the development of legal education and standards of admission to the Bar is essential before the Bar's policies and activities can be intelligently considered.

In England, legal education has remained rather consistently in the hands of the lawyers themselves. The barrister branch of the English legal profession is controlled by the Bar as organized in the Four Inns of Court, through their control over admission and discipline of their numbers.

---

[4] American Bar Association Report, Vol. 19 (1896), p. 463.
[5] Ibid., Vol. 16 (1893), p. 389.
[6] Ibid., Vol. 20 (1897), p. 518.
[7] Ibid., Vol. 20 (1897), p. 520.

It was in 1235 that parties to a suit were formally permitted to appear by "attorney" on special license of the king. In the reign of Edward I (1275), the First Statute of Westminster recognized and extended appearance by attorney. According to Pollock and Maitland, the legal profession then first began to take definite shape.[8] In the reign of Edward II (1307-1327), and more notably in the reign of James I (1603-1625), the power of appointing "attorneys" was vested in the judges, who were especially charged to appoint people, who were virtuous and learned. After James I, in the reign of George II (1729-1760), a further provision was added to secure properly qualified "attorneys," namely, that they should serve terms of apprenticeship. This second main branch of the English legal profession, that of solicitors and attorneys, is now controlled by the Law Society, established in 1825. In 1877, an act was passed, which exists today, giving the Law Society the power to determine examinations and secure the proper standards of knowledge and learning for admission.[9]

The English Bar is thus organized as an independent and self-perpetuating organization; members are responsible only to their associates for the proper exercise of their privileges. With the establishment of the Joint Council on Legal Education by the Four Inns in the 19th century, the unification of the barrister branch of the profession was completed.[10]

In Canada, responsibility for admission to legal practice is vested in the legal profession through its governing body in each province.[11]

---

[8] Warren, Charles, Op. Cit., p. 23, American Bar Association Report, Vol. 21 (1898), p. 605, American Bar Association Journal, January, 1935, p. 43.

[9] American Bar Association Report, Vol. 50 (1925), pp. 263-274, paper by The Right Honorable Lord Buckmaster, former Lord Chancellor of England, "The Romance of the Law."

[10] Reed, Alfred Z., Training for the Public Profession of the Law (1921), pp. 15-16.

[11] American Bar Association Report, Vol. 22 (1899), p. 584.

Legal education is largely controlled in Continental Europe by the universities. Many factors have caused this, the most important of which was the early discovery of a systematized body of Roman Law, and the cultivation of it by the Medieval Universities. Today, prospective lawyers must study law in a University and qualify through an examination conducted sometimes in cooperation with state officials; this examination constitutes the test of proficiency. However, the Bar itself is not relieved of responsibility, and retains valuable control over the practical and ethical features of a lawyer's education, but exercises this control in a supplementary way.[12]

This country inherited from England the tradition that responsibility both for legal education and for admission to the Bar should be placed almost entirely upon the practicing lawyers and judges, and should not be shared with universities as in Continental countries.[13] The basis for the American system of bar admission is derived from two sources: (1) The fact that English practitioners exercised control during the period when the thirteen original states were English colonies, and (2) The fact that independent influence was exerted by native legislation, which adhered to the idea that the legal profession should not be placed beyond the reach of the average man.

At the time that America was colonized, admission to practice in the English lower courts was granted by judges; later this control was transferred in England to practitioners. The earlier method of admission by judges was extended by legislative process to Colonial courts; though there were variations as to the particular branches of the judicial organization in which the power of admission should be lodged, all systems constituted a subordination of lawyers to the judicial power; the Colonies adopted the English plan used for admission to the lower courts. During

12 Reed, Alfred Z., Op. Cit., pp. 12-13. Dr. Reed's work is especially relied on for the early history of the legal profession.

13 Reed, Alfred Z., Op. Cit., p. 4.

the Colonial Period, judicially admitted practitioners came to be regarded as constituting the Bar. In portions of New England and possibly New York City, judges permitted the county Bars to exercise actual control over their own membership; in New England the practice survived until the revolution. However, the idea of a self-perpetuating class was repugnant to the idea of American democracy, and the legislatures were all too willing to function in admitting individuals by special legislative act. The type of requirements for admission set down by the Bar led to the suspicion that it was fostering a monopoly, and the whole system of bar control was swept away by legislation. Since then the power of admission has been universally regarded in this country as a function of the Bench rather than of the Bar, and is lodged in whichever part of the judicial system is selected by the legislature. The idea of inherent power over admission by the Court is of modern origin.[14]

During the Pre-Revolutionary period, three systems of admission are to be distinguished:

(1) Each court admitted attorneys to its own bar; this system was in vogue in Massachusetts, New Hampshire, Pennsylvania, Maryland, also in Georgia. The higher Court guarded entrance to the Bar more jealously, and thus there grew up a sort of graded Bar.

(2) Judicial comity; admission to one court admitted to all; this system obtained in Rhode Island, Connecticut and Delaware.

(3) Centralized control over admissions, which control was exercised in three ways: (a) The highest court admitted to its bar; in theory the lower courts did the same. However, a license was necessary by an Examining Board of General Court as in Virginia. (b) Full control over admission to all courts was lodged in the Supreme Court, as in South Carolina. (c) Attorneys were technically appointed by the Royal Governor, but appointment was made

---

[14] Reed, Alfred Z., Op. Cit., pp. 35-38.

on recommendations of the judge; this was the method used in North Carolina, New York and New Jersey.[15]

(b) Revolution—Civil War Period.

For some sixty years after the Revolution, the system of allowing each court to admit to its own Bar (separate bar system) was predominant in the Northeastern section of the country.[16] The above three methods of admission to the Bar persisted, for immediately prior to the modern movement to raise the bar admission requirement, the same three methods of locating the admitting power existed.[17]

(c) Post Civil War Period

The general tendency up to the Civil War following the prevalent democratic philosophy of the time was to make admission to the Bar increasingly easy.[18] This democratic impulse prevented the development of a self-determining Bar and the distinction existing in England between the barrister and the solicitor.[19] Since 1890, the control of Bar admissions, in order to develop and maintain higher standards, has moved altogether in the direction of centralization.[20]

On the educational side, to show something of the decline in standards of admission to the Bar before the Civil War, it might be pointed out that in 1800, a definite period of preparation was prescribed in fourteen out of nineteen states, or nearly three-fourths; in 1840, requirements were provided in not more than 11 out of 30 jurisdictions or one-third of the total, and in 1860, a definite period of study was required in only 9 of the 39 jurisdictions or only one-

15 Reed, Alfred Z., Op. Cit., p. 68.
16 Ibid., p. 68.
17 Ibid., pp. 70-71 and 72-73.
18 Reed, Alfred Z., Op. Cit., p. 40.
19 Ibid., p. 38.
20 Ibid., p. 73.

fourth of the total number.[21] The Civil War exerted an influence in restoring educational standards in two ways: (1) Actual conduct of the war taught the meaning and value of efficiency in public life and the need of democracy for experts. (2) Aftermath of corruption made political reforms indispensable.[22] Since the Civil War, considerable organized effort has been attended with partial success to remedy the laxity of the former period.[23]

Dr. Alfred Z. Reed, of the Carnegie Foundation, for the Advancement of Teaching, concedes that the principal contribution to the cause of law reform during the decade 1870-1880 was made by organized bar associations. The new movement first influenced the period of study; in 1860, 9 of the 39 states, or one-fourth, had prescribed periods of study; in 1890, the number had risen to 23 of the 49 states, or nearly one-half; in 1917, 36 of the 49 states, or three-fourths of the total had prescribed periods of study. These organized bar groups also lengthened the period of study; in 1869, 6 jurisdictions required three years; in 1890, 9 states made this a requirement; in 1921, due to the influence of the American Bar Association, 28 states required the three year preparation.[24] A transition was made from law office training to law school training; the importance of the law schools was inevitable because of the growing complexity of the law and the movement since the Civil War to stiffen bar examinations.

It is evident that while the colonies took over the English practice in relation to legal educational standards and admission control, there has not been, as in England, any real concentration of responsibility and control. As to legal education, this was first centered in the law office, and later transferred to the law school; control of admission was lodged in the courts usually under a constitutional or statutory mandate.

---

21 Ibid., p. 86.
22 Ibid., p. 90.
23 Ibid., p. 40.
24 Reed, Alfred Z., Op. Cit., p. 91.

3. POLICIES AND ACTIVITIES OF AMERICAN BAR ASSOCIATION IN THE FIELD OF LEGAL EDUCATION AND STANDARDS OF ADMISSION

The policies and activities of the American Bar Association in the field of legal education and admission to the Bar will be treated chronologically, as far as possible, since this plan of treatment will best show their development.

(a) Preference for Law School Training

One of the initial Committees appointed at the time of the organization of the American Bar Association was a Committee on Legal Education and Admission to the Bar. At the first session, the Constitution of the Association then adopted, provided in Article III, for the appointment of this Committee, which was instructed to report at the following annual meeting some plan of assimilating through the Union (1) the requirements for candidates for admission to the Bar, and (2) the regulation, on principles of comity, of the status of gentlemen, already admitted to practice in their own states. Acting under these suggestions, the Committee prepared its first report. When law office training or the apprenticeship system was the order of the day, the report showed a definite and distinct emphasis on and preference for law school training.[25] In the 1879 report, the Committee recommended that state and local bar associations be requested to suggest the maintenance by public authority of schools of law with certain specific standards. This resolution was amended, and as passed required the states and their local bar associations to recommend and further the maintenance of law schools.[26] As early as 1880, the Committee endeavored through the Vice-President and Council for each state to obtain the facts in regard to qualifications existing by law for admission to the bar and also the necessity of elevating the standards

[25] American Bar Association Report, Vol. 2 (1879), p. 235.
[26] Ibid., Vol. 2 (1879), p. 235, and Vol. 3 (1880), pp. 40-44.

together with the best methods of accomplishing that object. In conformity with power given it by resolution adopted to carry through this policy, the Committee addressed a letter to the Vice-President and Local Council for each state requesting the above mentioned facts. Answers were received from twenty-three states. On the basis of replies received, the Committee was able to submit a tabulated statement of requirements for admission to the Bar in all the states of the union, and in the 1881 report made three recommendations respecting legal standards, which recommendations were adopted as follows: (1) that three years legal training be required, (2) that diploma entitle recipient to admission, and (3) that time spent in law schools be counted as equivalent to time spent in attorney's office.[27] Having shown general sympathy with law schools and presented a recommendation of three years training in a law school, the Committee after making such elaborate reports in the field of legal education and admission to the Bar displayed no activity from 1882 until 1890, and did not even make reports.[28]

(b) Raising Standards of Law Schools in Relation to Both Legal and Pre-legal Education

When the Committee resumed its activities in 1890, its problem was the too rapid multiplication of low grade law schools, and therefore, its first emphasis was on improvement of law schools. In the succeeding nineteen years, it presented nine exhaustive reports dealing primarily with law schools, and including such subjects as law school curriculum, preliminary education, methods of teaching, state law schools and law degrees.[29] In 1890 it initiated a policy of developing a course of study for American law schools, based on courses of study in European and American schools, and thus once more was interest awakened in the

[27] Ibid., Vol. 4 (1881), pp. 27ff.
[28] Ibid., Vols. 5 to 12 (1882-1889).
[29] Ibid., Vol. 34 (1909), p. 777.

subject of legal education and admission to the Bar. While the recommendation of the preceding committee of 1879 that a law school should be established in every state had not been literally attained, yet in 1890 there were fifty law schools in the country or more than one for each state. However, though law schools had increased in number and standards were low, the power of control of admission had, through acts passed in a number of states, passed from courts of first instance to the higher courts. It has been well said that this report of 1890 is worthy of consideration.[30]

In 1891 the Committee made an even more extensive report. In order to carry out the mandate for the betterment of law schools, and hence of legal education, the Committee of 1890-1891 met December, 1890, and upon consultation resolved to execute its policy of improving law schools by collecting the fullest possible information as to the condition of legal education both in the United States and other countries. To obtain information as to the former, a circular of inquiry was sent by President Henry Wade Rogers on behalf of the Committee to the Chief Justice of each state. A large majority favored both changes proposed in preliminary report of 1890, with respect to admission to the bar, namely, vesting power exclusively in the highest court of the state, and providing for a permanent board or commission.[31] It was in 1891, that resolution was adopted, requiring of each student two years study before he presented himself for examination. Pre-legal education was also first mentioned in 1891.[32]

As to modern legal education in foreign countries, the Committee had the assistance of Honorable William T. Harris, Commissioner of Education in this ambitious project. Commissioner Harris sent to all foreign countries, with which the Bureau was in communication, a list of questions prepared by the Committee, which questions covered not

30 Ibid., Vol. 24 (1901), p. 514.
31 Ibid., Vol. 14 (1891), pp. 301-310.
32 Ibid., Vol. 27 (1904), pp. 510-514.

only details of legal education, but also organization and administration of the schools. The Committee felt that this information would be of service in comparing foreign systems with our own. The questions were forwarded in March, 1891, and a large number of replies were received, and were still being constantly received. As the answers were not complete, the Committee felt that the material accumulated should be turned over to the Committee for the next year.[33] Even in 1892, while much information had been assembled, it was far from complete, and many gaps needed to be filled before an intelligent view of the whole subject could be presented. The Committee felt, too, that before considering proper course of study for the American Law School, it was desirable to learn the present condition of legal education in the United States, and the views of leading educators on the subject. It, therefore, addressed a number of gentlemen of reputation as educators and requested their views. The Committee also procured catalogues of nearly all the law schools, including the most important ones in the United States.[34] At this annual meeting in 1892, a recommendation was adopted requiring two years law study and placing power of admission in the highest court of the state, with an examination supervised by a Committee appointed by said court. A proposed recommendation to make the law course three years was lost.[35] It was also in 1892, that a Committee was appointed to prepare plans and issue invitations for a general meeting of those interested in legal education.[36]

Out of this meeting came the organization of the Section of Legal Education in 1893. By adoption of By-Law XIV, this first section of the American Bar Association defined its object to be "the discussion of methods of legal education." It was authorized to make recommendations to the Association, which should be referred by the Asso-

---

[33] Ibid., Vol. 14 (1891), pp. 325-327.
[34] Ibid., Vol. 15 (1892), pp. 317, passim.
[35] Ibid., Vol. 27 (1904), p. 514.
[36] Ibid., Vol. 25 (1902), p. 529.

ciation to the Committee on Legal Education.[37] From 1893 until 1917, when the Council on Legal Education was authorized, there was then in the American Bar Association this cumbersome machinery of a Committee on Legal Education and a Section on Legal Education, both of which were working for the same end, the raising of standards of legal education and admission to the bar. Action taken by the Section had to be reported to Committee and brought by Committee before the Association for final action.[38] The two groups worked in apparent harmony for a time though there seems to have been much overlapping, and a definite conflict developed later in the matter of formulation and adoption of standard rules.[39]

Nevertheless, with the organization of the Section, there was developed a forum in which problems in this field of legal education and admission to the bar could be discussed, and recommendations made for solution. From this time on, it should be noted, too, that there was a definite stress not only on legal training, but also on adequate prelegal education. The Chairman of the Section in 1893 stated that a very small proportion of men entering the legal profession in the United States have had the benefit of a liberal education, and that in this respect the profession in the United States contrasted unfavorably with the profession in European countries.[40] In a review of the state of legal education as found in the law schools of the United States, he said that the report of the United States Commissioner of Education for 1890-1891 gave the total number of law schools in the country as 56, and the number of law schools in operation for the year 1893-1894 as 72. This comparison showed the all too rapid multiplication of law schools.[41]

---

[37] Ibid., Vol. 16 (1893), pp. 366-367.

[38] Ibid., Vol. 31 (1907), p. 67. For summary of Proceedings of American Bar Association in this respect, see Reed, Alfred Z., Present Day Law Schools in the United States and Canada (1928), pp. 22-44.

[39] Infra, pp. 57-60.

[40] American Bar Association Report, Vol. 17 (1894), p. 397.

[41] Ibid., Vol. 17 (1894), p. 391.

The Section in 1895 recorded by resolution its approval of the lengthening of the law school period from two to three years.[42] In 1896 recommendation of the Section for a three-year law school course was referred to the Bar Association, which referred it to Committee, which Committee in 1897 reported in favor of such recommendation. This marks the transition from two to three years of legal training.

To emphasize the lack of preparatory training, a paper read at the 1895 meeting stated that of the 9000 students registered at 73 law schools in 1894, only 2000 were graduates of colleges or universities, and that four-fifths of lawyers were non-college men.[43] At the 1896 meeting, the Section made a determined effort to improve preliminary training by adopting a resolution that the Section request the Committee on Legal Education in its next report to consider the feasibility of adopting a minimum standard for admission to law schools and to a degree, to the end that all schools falling below minimum standards should not be regarded in good standing.[44] In 1897, as part of the proceedings of the Section, a Conference on Legal Education and Admission to the Bar was held, to which representatives from different states reported on their own state requirements. Questions had been sent out two or three years before by Mr. John Hinckley, Secretary of the Association, regarding the usefulness of bar associations in the various states. Each secretary of a state association was asked to submit information about the work of the bar association of his own state and how it could be improved. A representative from each state reported on the admission authority in the state and the work done by the state bar association to raise educational and general admission requirements.[45]

---

42 Ibid., Vol. 18 (1895), p. 406.
43 Ibid., Vol. 18 (1895), p. 429.
44 Ibid., Vol. 19 (1896), p. 450, and Vol. 27 (1904), p. 510.
45 Ibid., Vol. 20 (1897), pp. 433ff, for reports of state representatives.

Recommendations made by the Section endorsing a three-year course of study and a high school education both for admission to law schools and to the Bar were approved by the Committee, and adopted by the Association.[46] The Section in 1897 adopted resolutions that delegates from state and local bar associations to this conference be requested to communicate to associations represented by them the resolutions adopted by the Bar Association relative to legal and preparatory requirements, and also that the Secretary of the Section should be required to send similar communications to associations not represented.[47]

Report was made in 1898 of activities by different state bar associations in lengthening the period of law study and in securing necessary legislation to centralize control of admission in the supreme court of the state.[48]

The Section performed a valuable service in its early years by acting as a clearing house for the exchange of information and ideas among bar examiners and law schools teachers. In 1899 with a view to coordinate all the agencies active in the field of legal education and admission to the Bar, the Section adopted two resolutions of importance: (1) That a Committee of Five be appointed to report on the advisability of state boards of law examiners forming themselves into an organization, and (2) That a Committee of Three be appointed to consider what action, if any, should be taken to bring reputable law schools of the country into closer relations with each other and with the Section of Legal Education, and that Committee have power to invite such law schools to meet in conference with the Section the following year. The former resolution had little immediate influence, for though a Conference of Bar Examiners did have one meeting in 1904, at St. Louis, and efforts were made to revive the Conference in 1911, they came to nothing. Eventually, however, such a Conference was organized in 1931, and is now functioning. Out of the

[46] Ibid., Vol. 20 (1897), pp. 24 and 33-34.
[47] Ibid., Vol. 20 (1897), p. 449.
[48] Ibid., Vol. 21 (1898), pp. 503ff, for state bar reports.

latter resolution came the organization of the Association of American Law Schools, which became a factor in the program for higher standards of legal education. The Committee, pursuant to the resolution adopted by the Section in 1899, sent invitations to all law schools of the country to send delegates to meet in conference with the section; 35 law schools sent delegates, and on August 28, 1900, these delegates organized the Association of American Law Schools, and adopted a Constitution. Standards adopted for admission of law schools into the Association provided for high school preparatory training for entrance, library facilities, and a two-year law course of thirty weeks per year of ten hours average per week; at the end of five years, this last requirement of length of law school course was to be increased to three years.[49] This emphasis on lengthening the period of the law school course to three years had been emphasized by the American Bar Association five years before.[50] In 1901 Mr. Clarence D. Ashley, in a paper presented before the Section, also anticipated the present goal of a college degree.[51] Mr. Ernest W. Huffcut, Chairman of the Section in 1902, in reviewing accomplishments in the field of legal education, stressed the fact that the lengthening of the course of study to three years had progressed rapidly during the past decade. In 1894 only eight law schools had such requirement, while in 1902, from 98 existing law schools, 56 had a three-year course requirement.[52]

Though the Association had gone on record in 1897, as favoring the requirement of a minimum preliminary education of high school, little was done until in 1903, the Committee more definitely directed attention to it. In its report, the Committee called attention to the fact that the Association of American Law Schools required each law school member to maintain an entrance examination equivalent to

[49] Ibid., Vol. 23 (1900), pp. 447ff.
[50] Ibid., Vol. 18 (1895), p. 406.
[51] Ibid., Vol. 24 (1901), p. 525.
[52] Ibid., Vol. 25 (1902), pp. 538-539.

that required for high school graduation, and that 37 of the 104 existing law schools with an enrollment of 8,464 members, through their membership, were adhering to the standards. The report further stated that 9,314 of the 14,127 law students, or nearly 70 per cent were enrolled in schools maintaining the high school entrance requirement. The Committee reported that it had considered the question of what the preliminary training ought to be. To ascertain opinion on the subject, it had addressed a circular letter to a large number of persons, including university presidents, deans of law schools, judges, members of the Bar, and others, in this and other countries, and received a large number of replies, which had been fully considered. From this consideration of replies to the circular letters and other sources of information, the Committee had reached the following conclusion: The lawyer must now get all his non-professional education before he begins the study of law; the purpose of the preliminary education should be two-fold: (1) to give mental power, and (2) to give useful knowledge; both were highly requisite, and the first indispensable.[53] This report was received and filed.[54]

The Chairman of the Section in 1904, Dean James Barr Ames, in expressing a hope that schools would require of students preliminary education equivalent to completion of two years college, recapitulated results in this field as follows: In 1896, only 7 from 76 schools, or less than one-tenth, required a high school course for admission, while in 1904, 51 such schools or nearly one-half had such requirement.[55] It should be noted that the agitation for two years college preliminary training before law school study began to be agitated at this early date.

In an effort to make available statistics in reference to law schools, the Section adopted a resolution that officials of the Section should from year to year prepare and

[53] Ibid., Vol. 26 (1903), pp. 395ff.
[54] Ibid., Vol. 26 (1903), p. 11.
[55] Ibid., Vol. 27 (1904), p. 511.

furnish for publication in the annual report of the American Bar Association a report exhibiting the state of legal education in the United States with respect to certain topics regarding, inter alia, entrance requirements and length of course leading to law degree. However, a resolution that the above be presented to the American Bar Association for approval was not pressed; the Chairman and Secretary of the Section were to try to carry through the project without asking permission of the American Bar Association.[56] Lawrence Maxwell, Jr., Esq., Chairman of the Section in 1905, made the comment in his address that the collection and publication of statistics bearing on the condition of schools and state legal education in the United States is the most important function of the Association, for it would thus furnish data whereby it would be possible to draw conclusions and urge reforms based on actual conditions.[57] At the 1906 meeting, some idea of procedure adopted to gather statistics was obtained from the Section report; a blank form had been drafted and submitted to those interested in legal education; copies had been distributed at the meeting for suggestions. Thus, while part of the work was complete, the principal part, the actual gathering of statistics from all schools, still remained to be done.[58]

In furtherance of its policy to raise standards of preparatory study, the Committee, desiring information in relation to conditions in foreign countries, addressed a communication to Honorable Elihu Root, Secretary of State, and inquired whether the Department would secure, through diplomatic officers of the United States abroad, information concerning legal education and rules governing admission to the Bar in countries to which they were accredited. The Department issued a circular of instruction to ambassadors and ministers requesting them to secure for the Committee

---

[56] Ibid., Vol. 27 (1904), pp. 502-506.
[57] Ibid., Vol. 28 (1905), p. 584.
[58] Ibid., Vol. 30 (1906, Part 2), p. 3.

the desired information. Data from thirty-five countries was thus obtained, the Secretary of State, ambassadors, and ministers of the United States thus rendering a distinct service to the cause of legal education in securing the requested information.[59]

Of the thirteen recommendations submitted in 1907, eight dealt with educational qualifications, general and legal, and their enforcement. A stand was again taken for a minimum of high school preliminary education with a goal of two years college, and three years legal training and the Secretary was directed to send copy of resolution to all state and territorial bar associations and all boards of law examiners. Law schools were urged to insist on high school training for admission, and copy of resolution to this effect was sent to every law school in the United States. The action of certain night law schools in lengthening courses to four years was approved, and copy of resolution to that effect was sent to all night law schools.[60]

Thus, it is seen that in 1908, high school preliminary education was approved as a minimum with the expression of a goal of two years of college training. The preparatory requirement of two years of college was again discussed, and action thereon reaffirmed at the 1909 meeting, as was commendation of action of night schools in making their course four years.[61]

Then in 1918, the Association by resolution approved action taken by many law schools in requiring a two-year college course as a condition of admission to courses of law study; the Association expressed the conviction that this should be the minimum requirement recognized by law schools of the first rank.[62]

---

59 Ibid., Vol. 31 (1907), p. 521.

60 Ibid., Vol. 31 (1907), pp. 588-590. Of the 13 recommendations submitted in 1907, the first 12 were adopted in 1908. See American Bar Association Report, Vol. 32 (1908), pp. 17-23.

61 Ibid., Vol. 33 (1908), pp. 19-23, and Vol. 34 (1909), pp. 512-513.

62 Ibid., Vol. 43 (1918), p. 72.

In 1897, in order to further eliminate low grade law schools, the Section commenced a policy of sponsoring a strict state supervision over the degree conferring power. This problem was referred to the Committee on Legal Education and Admission to the Bar.[63] At the 1898 meeting, the Committee reported that it had given proper consideration to the subject, and advised that the resolution of the Section should be adopted by the Association; the National Association would thus put its stamp of disapproval on the abuse of conferring degrees without proper qualifications. A resolution disapproving the policy prevailing in several states of making it possible for persons to organize law schools and confer degrees without reference to length or course of study was adopted.[64] In 1906 and 1907 the Committee sponsored a Uniform Act to regulate the conferring of law degrees.[65] It advised the Bar Association that in its opinion a distinct and particular service could be rendered to the cause of legal education in the United States by securing the enactment of such an act. The Committee prepared a draft of the proposed law for the consideration of the Association. In urging the proposed law, the Committee stated that it sought to remedy a conceded evil and to remove, so far at least as law degrees were concerned, the reproach with which American degrees were regarded in every European country.[66] The Act recommended by the Committee in 1906 and 1907, with slight change, was annexed to the 1909 report.[67]

A Section Committee on conferring the LL.B. degree was appointed in 1907, to consider and report on whether it was advisable for the Section to adopt a resolution that the LL.B. degree should be restricted to law schools with a three-year course for the first degree in law. It reported its conclusion at the 1908 meeting that such a resolution ought

---

[63] Ibid., Vol. 20 (1897), pp. 59 and 60.
[64] Ibid., Vol. 21 (1898), pp. 28-31.
[65] Ibid., Vol. 29 (1906), pp. 487-492, and Vol. 31 (1907), p. 573.
[66] Ibid., Vol. 31 (1907), pp. 573ff.
[67] Ibid., Vol. 34 (1909), p. 501.

to be adopted by the Section, and also recommended that the Section advise the Association that the right to confer degrees should be regulated by a Uniform Law.[68]

At the 1911 meeting, two resolutions were read: (1) that the Bar Association was of opinion that the privilege of conferring the LL.B. degree ought, in the United States as in England and Scotland, to be restricted to three-year law schools, and (2) that the right to confer degrees should be regulated by a uniform law. Motion was adopted that report be transmitted to members of the American Bar Association, members of the State Boards of Bar Examiners, and Deans of American Law Schools, etc., asking for criticism and suggestions. Both matters included in the resolutions were again discussed in 1912.[69]

Akin to this problem of strict state supervision over the degree conferring power is that of the sale of degrees. The Committee on Jurisprudence and Law Reform in 1903 was requested to inquire as to the abuse of corporate powers vested in any American college or university by the indiscriminate award or sale of honorary degrees in law.[70] To ascertain how far the evil of sale of honorary degrees in law existed, the Committee addressed a letter to several Vice-Presidents of the Association, and received replies from forty states and territories including the District of Columbia, and ascertained that only one man was seeking to sell honorary degrees in law, which gentleman was promptly arrested. The Committee considered that no further action was necessary.[71]

The early practice of admitting graduates of law schools to practice of law without further examination, called the "diploma privilege" was early frowned upon.[72]

---

68 Ibid., Vol. 33 (1908), pp. 775-776.

69 Ibid., Vol. 30 (1911), pp. 638-641, and Vol. 31 (1912), pp. 20, 609-610, and 973-974.

70 Ibid., Vol. 26 (1903), pp. 106-107.

71 Ibid., Vol. 27 (1904), p. 380.

72 Reed, Alfred Z., Training for the Public Profession of the Law (1921), p. 266.

Though in 1881 the issue was dodged, in 1892 the American Bar Association declared against the diploma privilege. In 1901 the Committee on Legal Education and Admission to the Bar referred disapprovingly to admission to practice on law school diplomas.[73] The Association of American Law Schools at its first meeting condemned the practice in a resolution.[74] The Section of Legal Education in 1905, expressed its disapproval of the diploma privilege by resolution.[75]

(c) Sponsoring of Centralization of Control of Admissions.

Centralization of control of admissions was sponsored by the Bar Association at an early date. In 1891 the Committee on Legal Education and Admission to the Bar advised the Association to adopt a resolution recommending that the power of admission to the Bar in each state be lodged in the highest court of the state, and that the examination of candidates be referred to a permanent commission.[76] In 1892 the recommendation was adopted by the American Bar Association.[77] At the time this action was taken, the general practice was for local courts in each state to admit to the Bar. License to practice in the Court, to which the candidates were admitted, carried with it the right to practice in all other courts of the state, the "multiple avenue system," as Dr. Reed called it. In 1901 the Association of American Law Schools at its first annual meeting adopted a resolution that admission to the Bar should be only after examination by the State Board of Law Examiners appointed by the highest appellate court of the state.[78] This action taken by the American Bar As-

---

[73] American Bar Association Report, Vol. 24 (1901), p. 407.

[74] Ibid., Vol. 24 (1901), pp. 580-582.

[75] Ibid., Vol. 28 (1905), pp. 560-580, and Vol. 30 (1907), pp. 561-562 and 589-590.

[76] Ibid., Vol. 14 (1891), p. 349.

[77] Ibid., Vol. 15 (1892), pp. 9 and 20.

[78] Ibid., Vol. 24 (1901), p. 580.

sociation in 1892, and by the Association of American Law Schools in 1901, was regarded as voicing the best judgment of the profession on a matter of great importance to the community, to the Bench, and to the Bar. In 1907 the Committee considered it advisable that the Association should again express its opinion in favor of the creation of State Boards of Law Examiners, and advised the adoption of such a resolution, which resolution was adopted in 1908.[79]

In 1913 the whole stress of the Section turned to the work of the State Board of Bar Examiners, for while it was recognized that the law schools were doing the chief work in legal education, yet there had arisen another very important influence in legal education, namely, the State Boards of Bar Examiners. It was felt that some systematic and continuous effort should be made to bring the Bar Examiners of the United States into touch with the work of the Section. With this in view, the Secretary of the Section wrote the Secretaries of State Bar Associations for addresses of various Bar Examiners and also wrote to the West Publishing Company for a list of State Bar Examiners. The Secretary suggested that as part of the report of the meeting of the Section, there should be published a complete list of the Bar Examiners of the various states; this recommendation was referred to the incoming Executive Committee for consideration and action.[80] At a joint session of the Section with the Association of American Law Schools in 1913, it was pointed out that for several years the Association of American Law Schools and the Section had been discussing proper standards for admission to the Bar, and had agreed at every meeting that standards were too low, and should be materially raised. It was suggested, first, that members of the American Bar Association needed to work with the Bar generally to instil a sentiment in regard to the matter, and secondly, that no matter what the

---

79 Ibid., Vol. 31 (1907), pp. 563-572, and Vol. 33 (1908), p. 19.
80 Ibid., Vol. 38 (1913), pp. 737-738.

standard was, whether it was set by the Court or Legislature, the final, ultimate, and only real standard was that set by the Board of Bar Examiners.[81] The various groups working in this field of legal education and admission to the Bar at this time might well heed both of these valuable suggestions and with profit.

(d) Movement for Standard Rules (1906-1918), and Formulation and Enforcement of American Bar Association Standards, adopted in 1921

In 1906, the movement for standard admission rules was initiated by the appointment in the Section of a Committee on Standard Rules, not discharged until some nine years later. Lucien H. Alexander, Esq., led the movement in the Section, and commented on the great lack of uniformity in the various states with reference to the rules of admission. While some states had excellent rules, others were totally deficient in important particulars. Mr. Alexander intimated that it might be advisable to have a Committee of the Section draft standard admission rules, which when approved could be recommended by the American Bar Association as a guide to states desirous of securing the best system for admission to the Bar. A Committee of seven was duly appointed. The Committee in 1907 reported that it had gathered statistics and data from a number of states, and requested that it be continued.[82]

The Chairman of the Section in 1908 suggested that because the report of the Section Committee on Standard Rules for Admission to the Bar had been received late, and only one member of the Section Committee was present at the meeting, that action be deferred until the next year, namely, 1909.[83] The report set forth that the Committee had gathered, analyzed, and classified rules for admission

---

81 Ibid., Vol. 38 (1913), pp. 885-889.
82 Ibid., Vol. 31 (1907), p. 900.
83 Ibid., Vol. 33 (1908), p. 774.

to the Bar in the various jurisdictions in the United States, and members of the Section were asked to express their opinion on the sixteen rules pending before them.

At the 1909 meeting of the Section, a resolution was adopted that the Section Committee on Standard Rules for Admission to the Bar be continued and directed to send a copy of its report to all members of the State Board of Bar Examiners with request for suggestions and criticisms. Also, prior to May 1, 1910, the Section Committee should submit copy of preliminary draft of rules to (1) each member of the American Bar Association, (2) the Chief Justice of each State Appellate Court, (3) each State Board of Bar Examiners, and (4) the Dean of each Law School. The sixteen standard rules were discussed seriatim, and all approved except the fourth, providing that a lawyer on admission should be designated as attorney and counsellor, and not merely attorney, and the fifteenth as to fees.[84] At this same meeting, Franklin M. Danaher, Esq., in a paper, eulogized the work of this Section Committee in formulating standard admission rules as an aid to those states which had no rules, and for the information of those states whose rules needed strengthening or amendment.[85] During the next year, 1909-1910, the Section Committee on Standard Rules continued to transact its work in accordance with the plan outlined for them, and send out summary of suggestions received by them.

The Section Committee in 1911 presented a lengthy and elaborate report.[86] The 1912 report of the Section resubmitted the 1911 report showing the work of the Committee and a tentative judgment of the Section on each proposition.[87] In 1913, the Section Committee reported submission of the sixteen rules to all members of the Association, all appellate courts and federal judges, members of

84 Ibid., Vol. 34 (1909), pp. 742-767.
85 Ibid., Vol. 34 (1909), p. 785.
86 See Ibid., Vol. 36 (1911), pp. 637, 640-641.
87 Ibid., Vol. 37 (1912), pp. 813-886.

the boards of bar examiners, and law school professors, and discussion of those rules on two different occasions. Motion was adopted that Section Committee be continued, and instructed to prepare final draft for the 1914 meeting in the light of the suggestions received.[88]

It was reported in 1914 that the Section Committee had been aided materially by expressions of opinion from many sources. Committee then submitted for consideration of the Section, draft rules for admission to the Bar, prepared by the New York State Board of Law Examiners, which rules varied in some particulars from the propositions tentatively adopted by the Section. Consideration of the New York draft by the Section was deemed essential before submission of final Committee report. Mr. Alexander further clarified the issue by declaring that the Section Committee had first presented the sixteen propositions some years before, which propositions were adopted in 1909, and had been adopted in different years, had been modified, altered and changed, and stood in the form in which they appeared in the American Law School Review in the spring. The rules proposed by the New York Board were not intended to take the place of work done by the Section Committee, but were merely offered to supplement the Section Committee's work. The Section Committee was asked to consider them in connection with its work.[89]

Seventeen standard rules were finally adopted by the Section in 1916.[90] When the Rules were presented to the American Bar Association by the Section, a motion that propositions be referred to the Bar Association's Committee on Legal Education, that the Committee report on the rules and recommendations in 1917, and that said rules and recommendations be printed in the next issue of the Journal, was adopted.[91]

---

88 Ibid., Vol. 38 (1913), pp. 738-740.
89 Ibid., Vol. 39 (1914), pp. 794-797.
90 Ibid., Vol. 41 (1916), pp. 652-655.
91 Ibid., Vol. 41 (1916), p. 62.

When the Association's Committee on Legal Education and Admissions to the Bar reported on standard rules at the 1917 annual meeting, the seventeen standard rules of the Section had been decreased to ten. On a motion to recommit the matter to the Association's Committee, Mr. Alexander, who had first agitated for the appointment of the Section Committee on Standard Rules, made a plea that if the matter was recommitted, it should be recommitted to the Section. He stated that the Section Committee on Standard Rules had considered the matter nine years before the Section, at which boards of bar examiners and professors from law schools met and debated. When the matter came before the American Bar Association in 1916, it had been referred to the Association's Committee on Legal Education, members of which committee sat in the Section of Legal Education, and opposed some of the provisions by the Section. The report of the Association's Committee included matters advocated by the Section Committee, but defeated in the Section. It was plainly a question of which group was to control, the Committee or the Section, the latter of which had worked with the problem for nine years. The motion that the report be recommitted to the Association's Committee was carried.[92]

After years of work, discussion, and conflict between the Section and the Association's Committee, the first, second, third, fourth, fifth, sixth, seventh, and ninth standard rules for admission to the Bar as recommended in the report of the Council of Legal Education was approved in 1918; the eighth was not pressed, as it would compel every candidate for the Bar to attend a law school and graduate.[93]

As part of the same movement for high standard rules, the Committee on Legal Education and Admission to the Bar and the Executive Committee of the Association of American Law Schools in 1913 requested the President of

---

[92] Ibid., Vol. 42 (1917), pp. 90-95.
[93] Ibid., Vol. 43 (1918), pp. 73-76.

the Carnegie Foundation, Dr. Henry S. Pritchett, to sponsor, through the Foundation, an investigation of legal education similar to the one made on medical education, which study had cost something over $50,000.[94] The hope was expressed that the investigation would not be confined to law schools, but might be extended to the matter of admissions to the Bar in the various states with a view of making known to the entire country the facts relating to the subject. The Foundation, in accepting, explained that it intended that the study should cover not only examination of all law schools of the country, of the various curricula, libraries and facilities for teaching, but also consideration of the relation of the legal profession to the administration of law and its obligations to the social regime.[95]

An effort was also made to overhaul the machinery of the American Bar Association to develop more proficiency in effectuating high standards for admission to the Bar by focusing the activities of three organizations, the Committee on Legal Education, the Section of Legal Education and the Association of American Law Schools. In 1917 the Committee on Legal Education and Admission to the Bar successfully recommended that the Bar Association create a Council on Legal Education similar to the Council on Medical Education, created by the Medical Association in 1905. The Committee in its report expressed the belief that a Council of Legal Education created by and responsible to the American Bar Association could become a competent agency in promoting higher standards both among law schools and state boards of law examiners. It reviewed the activities of the Council on Medical Education of the American Medical Association, and the consequent reduction of medical schools by about forty per cent.[96] By the Fourteenth By-Law, adopted in 1916, the Executive Committee of the Section had been enlarged, and made into a body of seven,

94 Ibid., Vol. 38 (1913), p. 25.
95 Ibid., Vol. 38 (1913), pp. 474-476.
96 Ibid., Vol. 42 (1917), pp. 464, passim.

called the Council on Legal Education, in effect a program-making Committee for the Section. It was recommended that this Committee of the Section should be known as an "Advisory Committee," and that the Council on Legal Education of the whole American Bar Association should consist of five members with seriate tenures of five years, to be appointed by the President.[97] Thus, in 1917 the Council on Legal Education, recommended by the Committee on Legal Education, was created under the American Bar Association.

In 1919 under the new Constitution, the Section was empowered to adopt its own By-Laws subject to the approval of the Executive Committee of the American Bar Association. The Constitution provided for what is the present organization of the Section, namely, a Chairman, Vice-Chairman, Secretary, Treasurer, and a Council of eight members. This Council on Legal Education is successor of the former Council of Legal Education created two years before by the Association on recommendation of the Committee on Legal Education. The Council was created to accomplish for the law schools what the Council on Medical Education had been created to do for the medical schools; it was charged with the duty of considering measures for the improvement of the systems of pre-legal and legal education in the United States, and in particular was to inspect the law schools of the country and to classify them. Hope was expressed that law schools would be brought into harmony with the American Bar Association; this was one object for creating the Council.[98]

When in 1920 the Association of American Law Schools held a special summer meeting with the American Bar Association, the first since 1913,[99] the new policy of militant

[97] Ibid., Vol. 42 (1917), p. 91.
[98] Ibid., Vol. 44 (1919), p. 33.
[99] Ibid., Vol. 45 (1920), pp. 510 and 516. The Law School Association since 1914 abandoned its practice of meeting with the Bar Association and met by itself during Christmas vacation. Reed, Alfred Z., Present-Day Law Schools, etc. p. 35.

action was initiated. This did not represent a definitely new policy nor a complete break with the past, but represented an evolutionary process looking toward the coordination of agencies working for the elevation of standards of legal education and admission to the bar, namely, the Bar Association, with its subsidiary and affiliated groups, the Section and its Council, the Association of American Law Schools and the State Boards of Bar Examiners. The Council at first emphasized the improvement of law schools, and it was not until probably 1931 that more attention began to be paid to the official or state standards of bar admission. The Law School Association in 1920 emphasized that it was not unmindful that its organization in 1900 was the result of a movement initiated in the Section.[100] The necessity for cooperation between the Bar Association, the law schools and examiners was discussed, and the history of the Council was reviewed. The meeting together of the American Bar Association and the Association of American Law Schools in 1920 thus marked an effort at closer cooperation for a constructive program for the improvement of legal education especially in the law schools.[101]

A special committee of the Chairman and six other members was appointed by the Section in 1920; the work and report of this special committee marked the definite change to the militant policy to elevate standards of legal education and admission to the Bar. The Committee, organized by the Chairman of the Section, the Honorable Elihu Root, held its first meeting in New York on March 4, 1921. A questionnaire was sent (1) to deans of every resident law school in the United States, (2) to every Committee on Legal Education of a state or local bar association, (3) to every state board of bar examiners, and (4) to members of the Bar, whose names were obtained from state vice-presidents of the American Bar Association and other sources. The answers were considered helpful. This

[100] Ibid., Vol. 45 (1920), p. 517.
[101] Ibid., Vol. 45 (1920), pp. 522ff.

Committee again met in New York on May 19 and 20, 1921, at which meetings informal addresses were presented, followed by questions and discussions. It was proposed that the Section of Legal Education and the American Bar Association should adopt recommended standards and that the Council on Legal Education and Admission to the Bar should be directed to use the standards in the work of classification. It was admitted that the method of publicity and persuasion by publishing classified lists of law schools would be necessary until proper standards had been set by law. To do this, there would have to be cooperation with state and local bar associations, since they had knowledge of local conditions and could contact those who could put the principles into practice. To further bring the national association into close touch with the state and local associations, the calling of a Conference on Legal Education in 1922 was recommended, to which each of the associations would be invited to send delegates.[102]

The recommendations of the Special Committee, after full debate, were adopted by the Section, and also by the Bar Association in 1921,[103] and are as follows:

(1) Each candidate should be a graduate of a Law School with the following standards:

(a) 2 years study in college (pre-legal requirement).

(b) 3 years full time in law school, longer in part time law school.

(c) Adequate library.

(d) Sufficient number of teachers giving full time.

(2) Examination by public authority to determine fitness.

(3) Publication by Council on Legal Education and Admission to the Bar of names of complying and non-complying law schools.

---

102 Ibid., Vol. 46 (1921), pp. 679ff.

103 Note should be made of the fact that 1206 persons attended the American Bar Association meeting and 700 the Section meeting when resolutions were presented and adopted. Ibid., Vol. 54 (1929), p. 672.

(4) President of Association and Council to cooperate with state and local bar associations to urge adoption of above requirements.

(5) Council to call Conference on Legal Education in the name of the American Bar Association; state and local delegates to unite groups.

The first two recommendations represented direct action, the third represented a direct communication to the public; the fourth and fifth appealed to state and local bar associations. The Section report and resolutions were adopted by the Bar Association in 1921.[104]

Two problems were committed to the Council on Legal Education: (1) to cooperate with state and local bar associations in urging the adoption of recommendations for admission to the Bar; (2) to bring to the attention of intending law students law schools, which had been found to comply with prescribed standards.[105]

In 1922 the Section reported progress in classification of law schools in accordance with standards and also that the Special Conference on Legal Education by Bar Association Delegates had been held February 23 and 24, 1922, in Washington, and that standards for admission to the Bar, adopted by the Conference, had been brought to the attention of state and local bar associations.[106]

The most important work of the Section was to call this Conference of Bar Associations of the country with the purpose of asking endorsement of standards adopted by the American Bar Association in 1921. Thus, it is seen that immediately after the adoption of the standards by the National Bar Association, efforts were made to enlist the cooperation of the state and local association.[107]

---

104 American Bar Association Report, Vol. 46 (1921), p. 47.

105 Ibid., Vol. 49 (1924), p. 621.

106 Ibid., Vol. 47 (1922), pp. 42 and 689. Three hundred and forty-seven delegates attended the meeting, representing 45 state associations, 110 city and county bar associations, 5 foreign bar associations, and 27 universities. American Bar Association Report, Vol. 54 (1929), p. 674.

107 Ibid., Vol. 47 (1922), pp. 38-39.

Since the adoption of standards, the duties of the Section and its Council have consisted in urging that standards be adopted by the law schools and states. The early emphasis was on classification of schools rather than pressure on state boards to raise standards. In 1923 the Council held a meeting, and considered problems of classification of law schools. The Council gathered information as to standards of law schools of the country, first by questionnaire, and second, by various letters for additional information.[108] A tentative list of approved schools and of schools which had announced their intention of shortly complying with standards was published in the November, 1923, issue of the American Bar Association Journal.[109] This original "A" list contained 39 schools and the "B" list 9 schools.[110] A later list of schools complying with standards, published in 1924, contained 41 Class "A" schools, and 15 Class "B" schools.[111]

From the beginning of the campaign to raise standards of legal education and admission to the Bar, the Council or executive group of the Section had more success in raising standards in the law schools than by the admission authorities. This was probably due to the fact that efforts were concentrated on the former rather than the latter. In 1925 it was reported that the officers and Council of the Section during the year 1924-1925 had continued the work of inspecting and classifying law schools and presenting to prospective law students the recommendations of the American Bar Association for proper preparation for the Bar. However, progress made in the adoption of standards by the different state admission authorities was far from satisfactory, and the cooperation of the state bar associations was urged. The Committee on Legal Education of the Conference of Bar Association Delegates worked on the prob-

---

108 Ibid., Vol. 48 (1923), p. 678.
109 American Bar Association Journal, November, 1923, p. 728.
110 American Bar Association Report, Vol. 49 (1924), p. 395.
111 Ibid., Vol. 49 (1924), p. 395.

lem, for in 1925 it reported that it had not been successful in obtaining financial support, and decried the slowness of legislatures in raising requirements in states where better law schools had complied with the American Bar Association standards, because this situation was turning students to inferior schools.[112]

The Council on December 29, 1925, also decided to abolish Class "B" list of law schools, and to list law schools only as "Approved," or "Not Approved." The Council then reported that 64 schools were then on the approved list, and voted that no law school was to be approved until personally inspected.[113] The Council continued the work of endeavoring to bring to the attention of prospective law students classification of schools and standards recommended by the American Bar Association by issuing a pamphlet, which explained briefly the reasons which induced the Bar Association to make the recommendations, and contained a list of approved law schools.

Though much work has been done by the Council in the classification of law schools and in an endeavor to reach prospective law students, still the real work of the Council with the states did not begin until 1927, when another solid foundation for action with results was laid by the appointment of a full-time Director for the Council, to give help to states seeking to advance standards of admission to the Bar by complying with requirements of the American Bar Association. Mr. H. C. Horack, Secretary of the Law School Association, was appointed Adviser to the Council on September 2, 1927,[114] with an appropriation

---

[112] Ibid., Vol. 50 (1925), p. 657. The Conference of Bar Association Delegates had a Committee charged with the duty of conferring with the Section and with similar Sections or Committees of other bar associations for purpose of promoting adoption of standards of legal education and admission to the Bar, approved by the Conference, encourage improvement of legal education, and disseminate information in relation to legal education. American Bar Association Report, Vol. 49 (1924), p. 308.

[113] Ibid., Vol. 51 (1926), pp. 56 and 797ff.

[114] Ibid., Vol. 52 (1927), pp. 111-112, 547.

from the Executive Committee, which made a $15,000 budget possible, and with authority to establish an office to carry on the work contemplated by the Council, namely, to visit law schools, state and local bar associations, boards of law examiners, and others, to promote standards by explaining the desirability of adopting and securing aid from those, who would actively interest themselves in the establishment of the standards in the several states. Since the work of the Council was largely educational in nature, it had of necessity to be carried on largely through these local groups.[115]

As above stated, the list of schools complying with standards published in 1924 contained 43 Class "A" law schools and 15 Class "B" law schools. Class "B" law schools had been abolished, and there were in 1927, 65 approved law schools, located in 37 states and the District of Columbia. However, the most effective work of the Council was directed to state admission authorities. New York was cited as an example of Council pressure on states to raise standards to conform to bar association standards. Application was made to the Court of Appeals, in which control of admission was vested, by various bar associations of New York State, and a hearing was had before the Court on the subject. The Council cooperated with the Bar Association. On June 7, 1927, the New York Court of Appeals amended the rules for admission to practice so as to require from students beginning study of law after October 15, 1929, two years' college work.[116]

With the appointment of the full-time director, the work of the Council for adoption of American Bar Association standards by law schools and states became more effective; this is not surprising if the increased budget is

---

[115] Ibid., Vol. 53 (1928), p. 621. Note the appointment of an independent Committee on Admissions to the Bar, established by the Conference of Bar Association Delegates. Also see Reed, Alfred Z., Present-Day Law Schools in the United States and Canada, pp. 43 and 71, Note 3.

[116] Ibid., Vol. 52 (1927), pp. 338-340.

considered, since from 1921 to 1927 it ranged from $1,500 to $4,500. During these years, since the Council could not have published extensive lists of schools, it listed members of the Association of American Law Schools whose standards for membership were practically the same as those of the Bar Association. In 1921 a questionnaire was sent to the various schools asking about conditions, but it was realized that these answers alone could not be taken as a basis of classification, but would be of use for check when actual inspection was made. A few schools were personally inspected, particularly a year or two prior to 1927. After 1927, with the establishment of a permanent Bureau of Legal Education, a school was only approved after personal inspection.[117]

A slight modification of requirements regarding prelegal work was approved in 1927, because of opposition which had developed to the 1921 standards due to inadequate educational facilities and other reasons. Strict compliance with the two year college requirement was waived, and the new standard provided for prelegal examinations by state universities or boards of examiners for applicants who were obliged to make up the preliminary qualification outside of an accredited institution of learning.[118]

In order to insure a large attendance at the 1928 Section meeting, notice of the meeting was sent to deans of all law schools, approved or unapproved, presidents and secretaries of all state bar associations, all members of state bar examining committees, and delegates to the Conference of State and Local Bar Associations.

In 1929, after eight years' work with the standards adopted in 1921, the Section reviewed results. It was admitted that while the Section and Council had done its

117 Ibid., Vol. 53 (1928), p. 152. For activities of the Conference Committee on Admissions to the Bar, see Ibid., Vol. 52 (1927), p. 70.

118 For change, see Annual Review of Legal Education, 1926-1927, pp. 7-9, American Bar Association Report, Vol. 52 (1927), pp. 111, 545-547.

share, results were really due to the efforts of the Adviser, Mr. H. C. Horack. Mr. Horack at this meeting reported that the number of states which had increased educational requirements so as to demand at least two years college work as preliminary to law school study, had almost doubled in two years; that thirteen states had such requirements, while definite advance had been made in others.[119]

The groups on which the Council used pressure differed in the various states, for in some states it was the Bar and Court rather than the public that needed to realize the changed conditions which made higher and different requirements necessary. In some states, the control of admissions was vested in the legislature, while in others it was vested in the courts; in the former, bills were introduced into the legislature or hearings arranged; in the latter, the matter was submitted to the Court.[120] Where power of control was vested, that is where the Council used its pressure, though in 1932, the Council called attention to the fact that progress during the year 1931-1932 in raising standards for admission to the Bar occurred almost entirely through the adoption of Rules of Court.[121] The Courts, where given the rule-making power by the legislature or where they had exercised it as an inherent right, were much more responsive to demands of the Bar.[122] The Council also developed another field of service by making surveys of legal education in cooperation with local bar associations and boards of law examiners in states where definite efforts were being made to improve legal educational conditions; such a survey had been made in Pennsylvania.[123]

It was also reported at the 1929 meeting that, since the creation of the position of adviser, 64 law schools had

---

119 American Bar Association Report, Vol. 54 (1929), p. 607.
120 Ibid., Vol. 54 (1929), p. 681.
121 Ibid., Vol. 57 (1932), p. 658.
122 Ibid., Vol. 57 (1932), p. 68.
123 Ibid., Vol. 54 (1929), p. 686.

been visited, that much assistance had been given to schools, and as a result of the work of the Council since September 1, 1927, over a half million dollars had been added to library, equipment, and quarters in various schools,[124] that during the year 1928-1929, the Council had prepared a new questionnaire which was sent to all law schools in America because it desired to secure a fair picture of the character of each school and the manner in which it was being conducted. The questionnaire was returned by approved and unapproved schools; only six schools refused to furnish information as to structure and activities.[125]

Two resolutions were adopted at this 1929 meeting, namely, (1) that the Section reaffirmed its belief that public interest required adherence to standards of legal education and admission to the Bar as now promulgated by the American Bar Association,[126] and (2) that the law schools should not be operated as commercial enterprises, and that compensation of any officer or members of the teaching staff should not depend on the number of students or on fees received.[127] Dean William Draper Lewis said in an address at this very meeting that no more important duty confronted the American Bar Association and the Section than the duty to cooperate with the courts, bar examiners, and state and local bar associations, to get at facts, educational and financial, concerning commercialized schools and create a just public demand for their elimination.[128]

The 1930 Council report continued to show favorable results. While in 1921 no state had required applicants to have more than high school education and only 35 law schools or 24 per cent required two years' college training, in 1924 43 Class "A" law schools were listed, in 1930 ap-

---

124 Ibid., Vol. 54 (1929), p. 679.
125 Ibid., Vol. 54 (1929), p. 684.
126 Ibid., Vol. 54 (1929), pp. 644 and 656.
127 Ibid., Vol. 54 (1929), pp. 658 and 663.
128 Ibid., Vol. 54 (1929), pp. 664-669.

proved schools had increased their number during the year from 65 to 74. During the three years since the appointment of the adviser, 82 law schools had been personally inspected. States requiring two years college training had increased during the year from 11 to 15; in 16 other states, state bar associations had approved standards and recommended adoption. Mr. H. C. Horack, having resigned as adviser in the Fall of 1929, Mr. Will Shafroth had been appointed adviser January 1, 1930.[129] It was in 1930 that the Council decided that with the approval of the Executive Committee a small Bulletin would be published from time to time; at the meeting, it was reported that two issues had appeared, and had been mailed to a large selected list including state boards of bar examiners, state committees on legal education and admission to the bar, state supreme court judges, officers of local bar associations, American Law Institute and the Conference of Bar Association Delegates and like groups.

During the next year, 1930-1931, five law schools were inspected by the adviser, and three were placed on the approved list, making the total number 77. States requiring two years college training previous to law school study had been increased to 17.[130] The publicity work in connection with standards of legal education was vigorously pursued. Since the previous annual meeting, four issues of "Notes on Legal Education" had been printed and distributed to a selected mailing list of 6500; articles had appeared in many publications.[131] The same publicity schedule was adhered to the following year.[132] The adviser also cooperated with the Bureau of Education of the United States Department of the Interior, and a pamphlet on "Law as a Career," containing, among other things, a summary of American Bar Association standards, had been

[129] Ibid., Vol. 55 (1930), pp. 31-33, and 618-625, passim.
[130] Ibid., Vol. 56 (1931), pp. 614-616.
[131] Ibid., Vol. 56 (1931), p. 607.
[132] Ibid., Vol. 57 (1932), p. 656.

printed, and some 50,000 copies were being distributed among various high schools and preparatory schools of the country.[133] These standards were to convey to the prospective student the information that there was an approved and unapproved list of law schools.

After the regular meeting of the Section in 1930, an informal Conference of Bar Examiners was called at which members of some sixteen boards were present, and it was decided to organize a separate Conference of Bar Examiners in 1931. A Committee was appointed by the Chairman of the Section to arrange for the Conference. A series of bulletins and articles on subjects of general interest to bar examiners was published by the adviser's office, and sent out during the year with the purpose of stimulating interest in mutual problems preparatory to the Conference.[134] Under the leadership of the Section, the Conference of Bar Examiners was organized September 16, 1931, and plans for a permanent organization formulated.

The address of the Chairman of the Section, George H. Smith, Esq., in 1931, gave a comprehensive idea of the progress made in the improvement of standards for admission to the Bar. He presented the 1921 figures that only 35 law schools or 24 per cent required two years' college training for entrance,[135] and 138 law schools had a course of three years or longer, and contrasted this situation with that of 1931 when 122 law schools or 68 per cent required two years' college preparatory work and 96 per cent or all but 7 schools had a law course of three years or more. The record for the states was as impressive, for in 1921 no state required for admission to the Bar more than a high school education,[136] while in 1931, 17 states required the equivalent of two years' college for admission to study law.[137] The Council in its next report in 1932

133 Ibid., Vol. 56 (1931), pp. 607.
134 Ibid., Vol. 56 (1931), pp. 608ff.
135 Supra, p. 71.
136 Supra, pp. 71-72.
137 American Bar Association Report, Vol. 56 (1931), pp. 614ff.

declared that 19 states, in which 53 per cent of the lawyers of the United States practiced, had a two-year college preparatory requirement or the equivalent, that 16 states had standards approved by state bar associations, and only 9 states had no requirement of general education.[138]

The second annual meeting of the National Conference of Bar Examiners was held October 10 and 11, 1932. It was announced that through the generosity of The Carnegie Foundation, and through contributions made by the several states, it had been possible to set up a permanent office for the Conference, publish a monthly magazine, "The Bar Examiner," send out bar examination questions, and act as a clearing house for the exchange of useful information by the Boards.[139] The conference continued its work of securing and publishing accurate statistics on admissions to the Bar.[140]

The campaign to emphasize professional ethics was aided by the National Conference of Bar Examiners when it adopted a resolution recommending the examining boards of the several states to include the subject of professional ethics in tests or examinations. In pursuance of the same campaign, the Chairman of the Section communicated with deans of all law schools of the country, and from information received found that less than thirty had failed to adopt the suggested course.[141] The campaign for teaching professional ethics has been conducted by the Section, the Committee on Professional Ethics and Grievances, the Association of American Law Schools, the National Conference of Bar Examiners and the Executive Committee of the American Bar Association.[142]

A new enterprise was undertaken by the Council in 1933, in promoting and managing a series of fifteen radio broadcasts under the title, "The Lawyer and the Public,"

---

[138] Ibid., Vol. 57 (1932), p. 655.
[139] Ibid., Vol. 57 (1932), pp. 71 and 657.
[140] Ibid., Vol. 58 (1933), p. 92.
[141] Ibid., Vol. 57 (1932), p. 70.
[142] See, infra, pp. 91-92.

made possible by the cooperation of the National Advisory Council on Radio in Education. Approximately 150,000 announcements of the broadcasts were distributed; notices of the series appeared in almost every law journal of the country. The response of the Bar was considered favorable, for state and local bar association officials sent 700 letters expressing interest and registering approval of the program, and listeners also sent many letters and questions.[143]

In paving the way for the adoption of the National Bar Program, the new instrumentality or machinery, organized in 1933 and destined to be one of accomplishment, Honorable Clarence E. Martin, in an address before the Conference on "The Necessity for Coordination," [144] decried the fact that public opinion was not sympathetic to high legal professional standards. In calling attention to the long and tedious journey to raise standards for admission to the Bar, he pointed out that of the several committees authorized by the Bar Association Constitution in 1878, the one on Legal Education and Admission to the Bar headed the list, and a prominent position had always been given to the subject. Nevertheless, despite efforts of the Association, only 19 states had adopted minimum standards, and 16 state bar associations had urged adoption. Because the Association had seemed to lack sufficient strength to influence public opinion, the necessity for the National Bar Program had arisen. Since the initiation of the National Bar Program in 1933, the policy of the Association membership, especially of most of its leaders, has been changed from one of superlative congratulation on accomplishment to one of positive condemnation for lack of such accomplishments.

With the organization of the National Bar Program, the Council on Legal Education became even more defi-

---

143 See, infra, p. 113.

144 American Bar Association Report, Vol. 58 (1933), p. 500.

nitely active. It declared that it had now reached the point where it believed that a considerable amount of pressure should be applied to the non-complying schools. Through the National Bar Program an opportunity was presented to secure more active support of Bar Associations all over the country.[145]

In 1934 the Section of Legal Education met jointly with the Conference of Bar Association Delegates, in order that delegates might further stimulate the work of the state and local organizations.[146] Maps were displayed which showed pictorially the progress made in raising standards of legal education and admission to the Bar. These maps showed the country at the time when the Association approved the standards in 1921, thirteen years before. At that time Kansas alone had the requirement of two years' college preliminary education, while in 1934 the map showed that 24 or one-half of all the states of the Union with 63 per cent of the population of lawyers and general population were living in states which had adopted the two-years' college educational qualification. The report stressed the difficulty of having standards adopted, because of the fact that there were forty-eight separate jurisdictions, each with its own system of admission control, with power sometimes lodged in the Court, sometimes in bar examiners, and sometimes in the legislature. The Council concentrated its efforts on the group in which power was lodged, with the remarkable results as shown by the maps on display.[147] The Council of the Section was authorized to publish with its list of approved law schools a list of unapproved law schools, with four classifications.[148] In 1935 the number of states adopting the two-years' college pre-

[145] Ibid., Vol. 58 (1933), p. 612.

[146] Ibid., Vol. 59 (1934), p. 206.

[147] Ibid., Vol. 59 (1934), pp. 205-207, and 672.

[148] Ibid., Vol. 59 (1934), p. 677.

requisite or its equivalent had reached 26; by November, 1935, that number had been increased to 28 states.[149]

There is little doubt that the reorganization of the Section with its Council on Legal Education in 1919, and the adoption of the Standards for Admission to the Bar in 1921, with its consequent militant policy and program of action, has been effective in raising standards of legal education and admission to the Bar. However, it should be noted that the Council has been more effective with the law schools than with the admission authorities of the states. This is accounted for by the fact that coercion of law schools was first sought through classification of law schools and pamphlets circulated among prospective law students. About 1931, the policy of stressing the coercion of state regulatory authorities was initiated. If the legislature had power over admissions and expulsions, the Council concentrated its efforts on the legislature to have the state requirements for admission to the bar raised; if this power of admission and expulsion was centered in the Courts, then the Council used its efforts on the Courts to have passed the necessary rules of court providing for higher standards of admission to the Bar. The purpose of the Council's efforts were first, last, and always, high standards for the legal profession, and since this is a sine qua non of a successful and enduring democratic government, because the legal profession is so tied to the development of law, especially in its interpretative aspects, the efforts of the Council are to be commended.

The standards of the American Bar Association and Association of American Law Schools are almost identical. For example, the Annual Review of Legal Education for 1935 reported that 81 law schools had qualified for membership in the Association of American Law Schools; 114 law schools still did not appear on this honor roll. Of the

---

[149] Ibid., Vol. 60 (1935), p. 123. Letter of Will Shafroth dated April 7, 1936, stated that Indiana had just passed the two-year college requirement making the number of states 29.

114, 7 had been approved by the American Bar Association, making a total of 88 approved by the Association.[150] Since standards for membership in the Association of American Law Schools and those for approval of the Council of Legal Education of the American Bar Association are similar, one might conclude that credit for the movement for higher standards should be given to the law school association. Aside from the fact, however, that the Association of American Law Schools owes its existence to the parent body, the American Bar Association, the Law School Association, while effective in keeping undesirables out of its own ranks, was not at all effective in rendering assistance to the lower grade law schools or in raising official or state standards of legal education or admission to the Bar. When the American Bar Association adopted in 1921 the legal standards proposed by the Special Committee appointed in 1920, it took care to organize machinery for having the standard for admissions adopted. Through its Conference of Bar Delegates in February, 1922, it enlisted the cooperation of the state and local bar associations, and thus was able more effectively to execute its policy of using pressure, first on law schools, and then on legislatures and courts, to have standards adopted and enforced.

Preservation of high standards of the Bar and its efficiency as an indirect but essential agency of government requires a high standard of fitness, not only of legal learning, but of education generally, and moral stamina as well. It should be noted that aside from the stress made on the teaching of ethics, there is a decided lack of emphasis on character qualifications.[151] The emphasis for more general education and better legal training is all very well, but

---

150 Annual Review of Legal Education for 1935, p. 31.

151 Cf. American Bar Association Report, Vol. 50 (1925), p. 793, where the Section urged the Supreme Court of the United States to promulgate uniform rules for investigation of character and fitness of applicants to practice before the district courts.

there is need for greater consideration of character and integrity as well as of legal training. One reason for this lack of emphasis might well be that the matter of character has been the particular duty of the county board; however, the National Bar Association should give leadership in this important field as in others. It did in 1915 make a much-needed emphasis on "Moral Character," when the Section adopted a resolution requiring in addition to certificate as to moral character personal examination of each applicant for admission to the Bar. The qualification of "certificate as to moral character" proved ineffective in excluding undesirables, and many county boards are now adopting the practice of a personal examination.[152]

At the 1935 meeting the Bar Association adopted resolution recommended by the Section of Legal Education that the Association approve the plan of character examination used by the National Conference of Bar Examiners to investigate the character and record of migrant attorneys applying for admission to various states on a comity basis and recommending the use of this investigation service by the several states. This plan, originated by the Conference, subsequently endorsed by the Association, and adopted by a number of states, is now available to states, which may call for the history of a lawyer applying for admission in that state on the basis of his previous admission in another state.[153] This may go far in solving the migratory problem; it is to be hoped that the National Bar Association will soon give adequate leadership in the whole field of character standards to the end that the bar and bench will have in its personnel none but those of the highest integrity.

---

152 Philadelphia County and other counties in Pennsylvania, since 1928, have had Committees on Character which give a personal examination before the student is admitted to study, and another before he or she is admitted to practice.

153 American Bar Association Report, Vol. 60 (1935), pp. 126 and 639.

(e) Judicial vs. Legislative Control Over Admissions

The movement for the incorporated bar, initiated in 1914, for the purpose of making the organized Bar more effective in raising standards, purging the profession of undesirables, and developing a more efficient administration of justice, has precipitated a discussion as to which branch of the government has inherent control over admissions, the judicial or the legislative. Proponents of the incorporated Bar are prone to insist that inherent control over admissions lies with the legislature, while those of an individualistic Bar contend that control lies with the judiciary.[154]

In a series of articles which appeared in the Journal of the American Bar Association for September, October, and December, 1933, and January and February, 1934, Charles A. Beardsley, Esq., of the California Bar, presented the case for the integrated Bar and legislative control. Amos C. Miller, Esq., of the Illinois Bar, presented the case for judicial control. In these articles, there appeared to be some confusion of three distinct powers, namely: (1) incorporation of the Bar, (2) admissions, and (3) discipline. From a consideration of the cases, it would seem that while the legislature doubtless has the power to incorporate the Bar or any other group desiring so to incorporate, still the judiciary has control over admission to its own court, and over exclusions therefrom. In American Law Report (Annotated) 66 A.L.R., page 1512, in a discussion of the power of the legislature respecting admission to the Bar, where the scope of the discussion was limited to cases involving statutes regulating admission to Bar, which are questioned as being infringements of judicial power, the majority rule was said to be generally conceded that the legislature may in the exercise of its power

[154] Cf. American Bar Association Report, Vol. 28 (1905), pp. 626-627, and Vol. 30 (1906), pp. 29-30.

prescribe rules and regulations for admission to the Bar, which courts will follow, but such rules and regulations must not be unreasonable or deprive the courts of inherent power to prescribe rules and conditions of admission to practice. This appeared to be the rule in the United States, California, Connecticut, Kansas, New York, North Carolina, Ohio, Oregon, Washington, West Virginia, and Wisconsin courts. The minority was then noted: some cases hold that the legislature may not regulate admission to the Bar in any manner on the ground that the courts have the sole right to prescribe the qualifications of those who are to become their officers, and to prescribe rules and regulations for admission, without interference from either of the other branches of government. This is the rule in Illinois, New Jersey, and Pennsylvania.[155] Even in California, which has an integrated Bar, it was held in Spears v. California, 294 Pacific 697 (1930), that while the powers of the Committee of Bar Examiners are merely recommendatory and not binding on the Court, nevertheless, the Committee of Bar Examiners was expressly created by statutory enactment for the definite purpose of relieving the Court of the onerous duty of examining applicants for admission and investigating legal and moral fitness to practice law in California. The Court for this reason will refuse to exercise its power in contravention to the adverse recommendation of the Committee of Bar Examiners unless convincing evidence is presented by the applicant to the Court as proof that such adverse recommendation is not based on sound premises and valid reasoning.

It would seem that though inherent power of admission may, from the cases, be in the Court, still the Court welcomes action from an efficiently organized state bar association. From an address delivered by Mr. Beardsley, and printed in the Missouri Bar Journal, it would appear

[155] See In re Petition of Joseph P. Splane, 123 Pa. 527 (1889), Hoopes v. Bradshaw, 231 Pa. 485 (1911).

that the integrated California Bar Association has become a more effective instrumentality for raising and maintaining high standards of service for lawyers than was the former voluntary association. He stated that during the seventy-seven years of existence of the voluntary state bar association, there were twenty-seven disbarments or suspensions, and that during the four years that the incorporated Bar had functioned, there had been eighty-four disbarments or suspensions, and in addition twenty-four private reprovals administered by the Board of Governors and forty-nine public reprovals, making seventy-three reprovals in all.[156] The point that is made by Mr. Beardsley is an impressive one: that by concentrating power and responsibility in the organized Bar, it is in a position, nay, is forced to retain in its ranks only those who have the integrity and training to serve clients and public adequately.

While the American Bar Association of itself and working in cooperation with state and local bar associations has, in the past, as shown above, made certain contributions in raising and maintaining professional standards of service, additional measures are still necessary if the Bar is to maintain its personnel on a high plane.

The problem of standards for admission to the Bar, educational and character, remains with us, and it would appear to be a problem for the ages, and not for any particular generation. However, a particular generation can and must lay a solid foundation looking toward solution, and that is what the American Bar Association, working with its coordinate and subsidiary groups, has consistently done.

When in 1899 and 1900, the American Bar Association took action out of which came the organization of the Association of American Law Schools, it helped the cause of higher professional standards, on the educational side

---

[156] Missouri Bar Journal, May, 1932, Vol. 3, No. 5, pp. 67ff.

at least. The Bar Association's great mistake was not to keep the close contact thus established. The two Associations, the organized Bar Association and the Law School Association, did not work in any concerted way until 1921, when the standards for admission were formulated and adopted. It has been well stated that the Section and Committee on Legal Education helped to improve the quality of law schools and advance qualifications for admission to the Bar not only by direct recommendation, but also indirectly by bringing about the Association of American Law Schools and the Conference of State Boards of Bar Examiners, each of which met for the first time in 1900.[157]

Another development that slowed down accomplishments was the much deplored conflict that evolved between the Section and the Committee on Legal Education in 1917, when the Standard Rules were in process of being drafted and adopted.[158]

Even when the 1921 standards for admission were adopted, little was accomplished until the permanent Council staff was organized. It was a mistake to have used pressure at first on the law schools only, for if pressure had also been used on the official or state groups with power to admit to practice, then the law schools would have been forced to raise their standards to conform to the state requirements or go out of business. Perhaps the Council chose the easiest road first, since through its contact with the high grade law schools, it had an instrumentality available for pressure, and there is little doubt but that the Council did do a great deal to bring many of the low grade and border-line law schools into the approved group. To reenforce this conclusion, reference should be made to the 1905 report where the idea is presented that arguments for higher standards for admission to the Bar should be directed not to law schools but to legislatures

---

157 Ibid., Vol. 27 (1904), p. 514.
158 Supra, p. 60.

and bar examiners. Let the standard for admission to the Bar be placed higher and the standard for admission to law schools will follow.[159]

With the purpose of insuring a high grade Bar, one recommendation is now being urged, namely, to limit the number of lawyers in a particular county and state.[160] This is anathema to both those who believe in the old idea of democracy, as well as those who abhor regimentation. Anything so arbitrary as this should not be approved until after thorough investigation and study of the problem.[161]

A divided Bar, such as exists in England in its differentiation between barrister and solicitor, has also been proposed. In England, however, the distinction developed at an early date and is a matter of tradition. If these distinctions are created arbitrarily, they are not apt to survive the pragmatic test. The proposal that well-trained lawyers should handle the more important legal controversies, and those trained at the lower grade law schools should handle the smaller cases, would not help the situation. If there should be any differentiation, it would seem that the better trained lawyers should handle the smaller cases, since the largest percentage of the public only contact the lower or so-called inferior courts. It is most important in a democracy such as exists in this country, that there should be a public opinion created that is favorable to the courts and law, and since this is the particular responsibility of the legal profession, it should assume the responsibility of seeing that all of its members are well trained, capable, and scrupulous.

---

159 American Bar Association Report, Vol. 28 (1905), p. 567.

160 Such proposals go back as far as 1707. See Legal Intelligencer, June 4, 1936, p. 4. See also American Bar Association Journal, January, 1936, pp. 42-46; Philadelphia Legal Intelligencer, February 29, 1936, p. 4; Philadelphia Inquirer, October 9, 1935, p. 2.

161 Survey of the Wisconsin Bar has been made by L. K. Garrison, Dean of the Law School, University of Wisconsin, which showed that the Wisconsin Bar was not overcrowded. For survey, see 10 Wisconsin Law Review, pp. 131-169; for discussion, see American Bar Association Journal, May, 1935, pp. 264-266. The New York County Lawyers Association is also in process of making such a survey.

Standards for admission to the Bar should be high, though it is recognized that high standards, to be permanent and effective, must be the result of a slow, gradual, but steady development. The Bar Association could well adopt a program now which would require of prospective lawyers the minimum of a four-year college training, three years of legal instructions in an approved law school, and in addition, a one-year interneship in an approved law office or some branch of the public service, for example, in a legal aid office.

More attention should, perhaps, be given by the steering groups interested in making legal education adequate, namely, the courts, the bar examiners, the law schools, the Bar Association and practitioners, to inculcate something of a social viewpoint in the lawyers of the future. In 1906, this arresting statement was made:

> "There can be no doubt that the proper education of our judges and of our practicing lawyers is a matter of public concern, and one in which our universities and especially our state universities, could well be engaged. There can be no doubt that lawyers should be taught to look upon their profession as one in which they can be of real social service. . . . Our lawyers and judges are, of all public servants, those in whose training the public should take the greatest interest. . . . we need not only practicing lawyers, but lawyer citizens." [162]

An alert, effective state bar association, with affiliated local groups, is essential to getting standards of the American Bar Association adopted by the courts, legislatures, and law schools. A comparative study could, with profit, be made of the different types of state bar organizations, namely, the voluntary, affiliated, and integrated, as to cogency in maintaining high standards of professional excellence. There is much armchair philosophy current at the present time as to relative effectiveness of the different types of state bar organization. Conclusions, therefore, are apt to be prejudiced.

---

[162] American Bar Association Report, Vol. 33 (1908), p. 830.

One concession can be made to the organized bar, namely, the necessity for standards has always been recognized, though success in enforcement has not been attained. The chief weakness of the organized bar here has been its antipathy to change and the lack of adequate emphasis on character standards. There has been, however, an emphasis on high standards to be enforced for the protection of the public. It was well stated in 1903,

> ". . . admission to the Bar is an important matter of civil service and not of philanthropy." [163]

B. MAINTENANCE AND ENFORCEMENT OF CANONS OF ETHICS

By raising and maintaining high professional standards, the organized Bar has endeavored to take preventive measures to keep in its ranks only those who have the integrity and training to give clients and the public adequate service. In spite of the fact that standards, both educational and moral, have been continuously and consistently raised by the American Bar Association's policies and activities since its organization, charlatans and shysters have managed to secure admission to the Bar. This is partly due, as mentioned above, to the fact that admission standards are not high enough and sufficient emphasis has not been placed on moral or character qualifications. The Bar, when undesirables have entered the profession, has taken measures to rid the profession of such miscreants and rogues. While the power of disbarment is a judicial function, still the organized Bar, knowing its own personnel better than the courts, usually congested and overburdened, has assisted the Court in this function. And the Courts cooperate with the Bar in applying the penalty when the Bar's investigation has shown the need. Thus, the organized Bar has endeavored to defend the profes-

---

[163] Ibid., Vol. 26 (1903), p. 403.

sion by preventing the admission of the incompetent and unworthy. Failing in this, it has endeavored to expel from the profession those already admitted, who have shown themselves incapable of realizing their privileges and responsibilities and who have shown themselves to be unwilling to live up to standards. These standards after 1908 were available in Canons of Ethics, developed and adopted by the American Bar Association in that year.

The movement for the adoption of these Canons of Ethics shows something of the thoroughness of the American Bar Association in the determination and execution of its policies. The policy was initiated in 1905 by a resolution presented by the Chairman of the Executive Committee, and adopted. This resolution created a Committee of Five of which the retiring President was chairman, to report to the following meeting in 1906, upon the advisability and practicability of the adoption of a Code of professional ethics.[164] This Committee in 1906 reported favorably on both points,[165] and successfully recommended the appointment of nine from Bench and Bar to report for consideration and action at the 1907 meeting a series of canons of professional ethics in the form of a code for adoption and promulgation.[166] The Committee corresponded with all states having bar associations, and collected canons of such states as had adopted them, twelve in number. Louisiana had a code in its charter, which consisted of eight short rules; the associations of the other eleven states had codes, which followed the code prepared in 1887 by Judge Thomas Goode Jones, then Judge of the United States District Court for the middle District of Alabama. Judge Jones had prepared this code for the Alabama State Bar Association, and it had been substantially adopted in ten other states. The report then presented gave the Alabama code and variations made by the ten associations.

---

[164] American Bar Association Report, Vol. 28 (1905), p. 132.
[165] Ibid., Vol. 29 (1906), pp. 600-604.
[166] Ibid., Vol. 29 (1906), p. 35.

The Committee made several requests, namely, that the Committee should be increased in number, and that authority should be given the Committee to send to every member of the American Bar Association and to each of the Associations that had adopted codes of ethics a copy of its report, and also that, if the Executive Committee approved the expense, the Committee should send a reprint of Sharswood's work on "Legal Ethics," with request for suggestions and comments.[167] This was to be completed by December 1, 1907, in order that the Committee might prepare Canons of Legal Ethics, circulate draft before May 1, 1908, with further request for suggestions, and prepare code for final submission at the 1908 meeting. A resolution to this effect was adopted.[168]

The Committee held its first meeting in the City of Washington, which lasted three days and was attended by ten members of the Committee. It made draft which it entitled a code, and also draft of form of oath, which was printed and sent out to all members of the Association, committees on Professional Ethics of state bar associations if such committees existed, and secretaries of all state bar associations, with invitation for criticism. Over 1000 letters were received in reply; these were tabulated by the Secretary. The Committee next met in New York City to review the Canons in the light of suggestions received. A number of changes in the way of simplification were made. Later, after considerable correspondence, the Committee met again in New York. The report presented at the 1908 meeting represented the final work unanimously recommended by Committee members.[169] The Canons were submitted with a recommendation that if approved by the Association, they be adopted and printed annually in the reports of the Association, and also that they be reprinted

---

167 This was done by printing Sharswood's Ethics as Vol. 32 (1907) of the American Bar Association Reports.

168 American Bar Association Report, Vol. 31 (1907), pp. 61-64.

169 Ibid., Vol. 33 (1908), pp. 55-57.

forthwith in pamphlet form and two copies forwarded to each member of the Association, and ten to the secretary of each state bar association. The Committee also recommended that the subject of professional ethics be taught in all law schools, and that all candidates for admission to the Bar be examined thereon.[170] This matter of requiring a knowledge of professional ethics was again agitated in 1931 and years subsequent thereto. The foundation of the Canons of Ethics, adopted by the Bar Association in 1908, was the Code of Ethics adopted by the Alabama State Bar Association December 14, 1887, formulated by Judge Thomas Goode Jones,[171] who was made a member of the American Bar Association Committee in 1907.[172] The rapid adoption of these Canons of Ethics by State Bar Associations is shown by the fact that in 1910 it was reported that twenty-two states had already adopted them.[173]

While the American Bar Association thus furnished leadership in this important matter of adopting high ethical standards[174] as promulgated in the Canons of Ethics, enforcement was dependent on local associations. In 1921 the Committee on Ethics of the American Bar Association sought the instrumentality of the Conference of Bar Association Delegates for the purpose of securing a consideration and discussion of ways in which standards of the Bar Association might be made more effective in different localities of the country.[175] By resolution adopted, the Conference welcomed the cooperation of the Committee on Professional Ethics of the American Bar Associa-

[170] Ibid., Vol. 33 (1908), pp. 567-573.

[171] Supra, p. 87.

[172] American Bar Association Journal, Vol. 8 (1922), pp. 111-113.

[173] American Bar Association Report, Vol. 35 (1910), p. 53. The 22 states adopting the Canons of Ethics included Arkansas, Florida, Illinois, Indiana, Iowa, Kansas, Louisiana, Maine, Minnesota, Montana, Nebraska, New Jersey, New York, North Dakota, Ohio, Oklahoma, Pennsylvania, South Dakota, Tennessee, Vermont, Virginia, and Washington.

[174] Cf. Address of Charles A. Boston, American Bar Association Report, Vol. 39 (1914), p. 839.

[175] American Bar Association Report, Vol. 46 (1921), p. 568.

tion, and recommended that Canons be adopted in those states where they had not yet been adopted, and that each state and local bar association be urged to aid, through appropriate committees, the maintenance of high standards of professional conduct.[176]

In 1921 the subject of professional ethics was agitated with special reference to counsel of trade associations. In that year, the Committee on Commerce, Trade and Commercial Law considered the problem, and noted that trade associations were playing quite an important part in economic life and that there were more than one thousand of these associations, whose activities were either national in scope or touched subjects of national importance not to mention many others which were either state-wide or local. In view of the fact that counsel for these associations were usually attorneys for members of Associations, many interesting questions of professional ethics were presented when conflicting interests arose. The Committee on Professional Ethics of the New York County Lawyers Association had prepared an interesting document thereon, and had considered it in open public meeting May 4, 1921. Too, the Commerce Committee had since taken up the matter in conjunction with the Bar Association's Committee on Professional Ethics. Resolution was adopted that the Committee give further consideration to the matter.[177]

In 1922 the Committee reported that at its meeting there had been extended discussion pro and con on the topic of legal ethics of trade associations. Argument by representatives of the National Credit Men's Association for the organization known as "Adjustment Bureau Work," could not meet contention that such an organization would eliminate the close and personal relationship existing between lawyer and client. Resolution was adopted that personal relations between attorney and client should be ob-

176 Ibid., Vol. 46 (1921), p. 569.
177 Ibid., Vol. 46 (1921), pp. 312 and 52-54.

served, that there should be no division of fees by a lawyer with a layman, and that the Association disapproved of the organization of adjustment bureaus wherein lawyers' services were furnished by Associations to members.[178] In reporting on the legal status of trade associations and their functions in 1923, the Committee acknowledged valuable suggestions from parties interested, who spoke before it. Resolution of the Committee presented recommendation (Appendix D), for guidance of trade associations, which statement was practically the same as announcement made by the New York County Lawyers Association through the Committee on Professional Ethics and Committee on Unlawful Practice of Law. The Commerce Committee also reported on the bonding of the integrity of a lawyer in his professional capacity, and recommended a resolution condemning the bonding of attorneys in the faithful performance of duties as attorneys. Both recommendations were adopted by the Bar Association.[179]

In 1924, pursuant to resolution adopted on recommendation of Standing Committee on Legal Ethics and Grievances, a Special Committee on Canons of Ethics was appointed.[180] In 1924, on its recommendations, supplemental Canons were adopted, and in 1933, further changes were made.[181]

At the present time there appears to be forty-six canons of Professional Ethics,[182] and thirty-four canons of Judicial Ethics.[183]

In 1929 the American Bar Association, without recourse to its Section or Council, after a discussion of character requirements for admission to the Bar from the point of view of the judge, the lawyer and the law school, adopted a resolution concerning a compulsory law school course in

---

178 Ibid., Vol. 47 (1922), pp. 289 and 291.
179 Ibid., Vol. 48 (1923), pp. 284, 291-292.
180 Ibid., Vol. 49 (1924), pp. 466ff.
181 Ibid., Vol. 59 (1934), p. 588.
182 Ibid., Vol. 60 (1935), pp. 683-696.
183 Ibid., Vol. 60 (1935), pp. 697-705.

professional ethics, thus placing itself on record as favoring such a course. In 1931 the Association approved the action of the Section and Council in negotiating with law schools and boards of bar examiners for adequate instruction in professional ethics and examination on the subject.[184]

Where the Canons of Ethics have been adopted by state and local associations and been made rules of court, their enforcement is apt to be more effective than if not recognized by state and local groups. The real work of enforcement should probably be done by the County Bar groups. The American Bar Association Committee on Professional Ethics and Grievances functions as an advisory body on ethical problems, and as a clearing house for suggestions for improvements.

In 1935 the National Association announced the publication of a survey of present methods of disciplinary proceedings, which though not complete, might well form the basis for obtaining needed uniformity and a more effective enforcement of the Canons.[185]

The Canons of Professional Ethics having been drafted and adopted in 1908, and thus laying a basis upon which conduct of lawyers could be judged, a movement was initiated for drafting canons of professional ethics for the judiciary, by a resolution which proposed the appointment of a Committee of not less than eleven members; this resolution was referred to the Executive Committee in 1909.[186] Action on these canons did not progress quite as rapidly as those for the legal profession generally. In 1923 it was reported that the proposed Canons of Judicial Ethics, printed in the February issue of the American Bar Association Journal, had been distributed to 1300 or

---

[184] Annual Review of Education, 1930, p. 2; Ibid., 1934, p. 69, notes 3 and 4; American Bar Association Report, Vol. 54 (1929), pp. 38-41, 118-120, 145-148, 188-225; also Vol. 56 (1931), pp. 306-307, etc.

[185] American Bar Association Journal, April, 1935, p. 201.

[186] American Bar Association Report, Vol. 34 (1909), p. 88.

1400 newspapers and magazines throughout the country, and had received gratifying consideration by the press.[187] These Canons were adopted by the American Bar Association July 9, 1924; the Committee, which finally prepared the Canons as adopted, was appointed in 1922.

C. CONDEMNATION AND REPRESSION OF UNAUTHORIZED PRACTICE OF THE LAW

The Committee on Unauthorized Practice of the Law has well stated its belief that the practice of law as a profession with all the safeguards now developed is vital to the true administration of justice. It has been seen that lawyers, in order to secure a license to practice, are compelled to adhere to higher and ever higher standards of conduct and proficiency. As has been stated, it is a public profession, and therefore its standards, educational and moral, should be high. Since the lawyer is and should be highly trained, it naturally follows that those who do not have the training, or who are not amenable to discipline for breach of the profession's high ethical standards, should not be permitted to engage in unauthorized practice of the law. In addition to purging its group of its own undesirables, the organized Bar has also endeavored to protect the public by waging campaigns against unlawful practice by corporations and laymen.

It is thought by the public generally that this movement of the organized Bar to repress unauthorized practice of the law is of quite recent development, dating from the depression in 1929. The truth of the matter is that the organized movement against unauthorized practice, excluding local developments in New York,[188] was first agi-

187 American Bar Association Journal, Vol. 9 (1923), p. 161.

188 1913, Committee on Unauthorized Practice was created in the New York County Lawyers' Association, J. H. Cohen, Chairman. 1925, the Association of the City of New York created a similar Committee. American Bar Association Report, Vol. 59 (1934), p. 155.

tated as many other matters were, in the Conference of Bar Association Delegates in 1919. At one of the Conference sessions in 1919, the subject of the relation of trust companies to the practice of law was discussed. A motion was adopted that it was the sense of the Conference that definition should be given to the practice of law, to be placed in the Code of Professional Ethics or enacted into law in the different states, and a Committee was appointed to prepare such a brief.[189]

This Special Committee reported at the 1920 meeting, and the brief containing definition of the practice of law, that is, what constitutes practice of law, and what constitutes unlawful and improper practice of law by laymen and lay agencies, was ordered sent to all state and local bar associations with the request that they urge its adoption into the laws of their states.[190] In the roll call of the delegates at the 1921 meeting, it was noted that resolutions submitted at the previous meetings of the Conference had had marked effect in many localities, especially in the matter of curbing unlawful practice.[191]

The Conference, having agitated the matter among the state and local associations, seems to have dropped the subject after 1922, when report was made of activities in California. The matter was revived in 1930 by the Standing Committee on Professional Ethics and Grievances, as the result of pressure from the outside. This Committee had for a number of years received complaints of encroachments of corporations and other lay organizations, and had also been frequently called on to express opinions regarding the conduct of lawyers, who acted as attorneys for patrons of employer intermediaries. (See Opinion 8, American Bar Association Report, 1925, page 518, and Opinion 10, American Bar Association Report 1927, page

[189] American Bar Association Journal, Vol. 6 (1920), pp. 19-31.

[190] American Bar Association Report, Vol. 45 (1920), pp. 55, 395, and 397.

[191] Ibid., Vol. 46 (1921), p. 572.

357.) The Committee had ruled that it was improper for a lawyer while serving a lay intermediary as a salaried employee to act as attorney for employers' patrons; an attorney must be free to exercise independent judgment. The principles on which the opinions were based were later affirmed by the Association's adoption in 1928 of Canon 35 on Intermediaries, and Canon 34 on Division of Fees. Lay encroachments were cited as indicating an increasing commercialization of the practice of law, which was considered as a decided menace to the usefulness of the profession. The Committee recommended that a general investigation should be made of the extent of unauthorized practice, and of activities, if any, to check it. It was suggested that a Special Committee of five on Unauthorized Practice of the Law be appointed for the purpose of investigating such practice, and when the investigation was completed, this Special Committee should join with the Committee on Professional Ethics and Grievances to consider what action should be taken to protect the public against such improper practice, and report to the Association.[192]

Pursuant to resolution, the Special Committee was appointed January 30, 1931, held two meetings with the Standing Committee on Professional Ethics and Grievances, and agreed on its duties as set forth in the above purpose. The Committee proceeded with its investigation of unauthorized practice by sending to all known bar associations in the country a letter and questionnaire, copies of which were annexed to the 1931 report of the Committee. A large number of replies were received, representing a vast amount of material. Examination of replies made to the Committee established beyond question that unauthorized practices were general and increasing. Types of unauthorized practice as disclosed by the replies to questionnaire were listed.[193] The questionnaires also disclosed

---

[192] Ibid., Vol. 55 (1930), pp. 476ff.

[193] Ibid., Vol. 56 (1931), p. 471.

that penal statutes forbidding practice of law by corporations and lay individuals were lacking in some states and were inadequate in others. Since this fact was disclosed, it was seen that the problem was one that could be best handled by state and local bar associations. In states where there was no law making it unlawful for laymen to practice law, the Committee suggested that the state bar association should endeavor to secure appropriate legislation. Committee believed that the best policy was to have legislation making it unlawful for anyone to practice law, who was not admitted to practice, and to leave it to the courts to determine what constituted the practice of law, thus wisely differing from the former policy of the Conference.[194] Wherever feasible, resort to an amicable method of persuasion and agreement was recommended, but since it was recognized that discussion and negotiation would not eliminate all unlawful practices, appropriate proceedings should be made possible. The Committee agreed that interest in its work was widespread, and appeal was made to it for advice and information from lawyers and bar associations from all parts of the country.[195]

The Special Committee continued to act as a clearing house and to stimulate and coordinate activities of the state, district and local associations. On February 13, 1932, the Committee sent to the bar associations of the country a circular letter reporting developments since the 1931 circular letter, and asking for further statements of fiduciary activities. The replies indicated a marked improvement in relations between fiduciaries and members of the Bar since the circular letter and questionnaire in 1931. Agreements were still recommended, which agreements should not define what constituted the practice of law.[196] In 1933 the Special Committee was made a Standing Committee. During the year 1932-1933 bar associations and individual law-

194 Supra, p. 94.

195 American Bar Association Report, Vol. 56 (1931), p. 117.

196 Ibid., Vol. 57 (1932), pp. 157 and 566.

yers displayed increased interest in the work of the Committee. Many requests were received for bibliography, information and advice with regard to agreements, declarations of principles, proposed legislation and conduct of lay agencies. The subject of greatest concern was that of collection agencies and law lists.[197] The Committee reported that it was convinced that statutes imposing a penalty on corporations and unlicensed individuals undertaking to practice law were desirable, and should be enacted in states where they did not exist. It was also important that statutes should not be emasculated by exceptions or a definition of the practice of law. Whether a particular course of conduct did or did not constitute practice of law should be left to the courts. The Committee requested the active cooperation of all bar associations, and requested that reports and decisions be sent to the American Bar Association Committee in order that efforts could be coordinated.[198]

Some idea of the technique of the American Bar Association on Unauthorized Practice of Law was given in its 1934 report. Complaints that came to the national committee were referred to the local committees for investigation and prosecution. These local committees in turn sent up to the national committee requests for authorities, forms, bibliography and advice on problems of many varieties.[199]

The National Bar Program, initiated in 1933, had as one of its four subjects, "The Unauthorized Practice of the Law." In furtherance of this National Bar Program, the Committee reported (1) that it had prepared and circulated among bar associations of the country a pamphlet, entitled, "Notes on Unauthorized Practice," to which was appended a bibliography, designed to be not only informative, but to express conviction of the Committee that the proper point of departure for consideration of the ques-

---

197 A Special Committee on Law Lists was appointed in 1935.
198 Ibid., Vol. 58 (1933), pp. 182 and 477-483.
199 Ibid., Vol. 59 (1934), p. 530.

tion of unlawful practice is the public interest and not self-interest; (2) that this pamphlet had been followed by a questionnaire, requesting each association to undertake serious consideration and discussion of unauthorized practice, to appoint a committee if none was in existence, and to report its views and findings to the American Bar Association, and (3) that members of the Committee had also delivered addresses and written articles. A book of statutes, decisions, and bibliography, compiled by Professor Frederick J. Hicks, Yale Law School, assisted by Mr. Elliott R. Katz of the Connecticut Bar, had been published by the American Bar Association. Committee announced its objective to be the maintenance of law as an independent profession in the interest not so much of constituent members as of the public. One whole session of the 1934 annual meeting was concentrated on the subject, "The Effect of the Unauthorized Practice of Law on the Administration of Justice." The whole history of the movement against unauthorized practice was reviewed together with policies and activities of the national committee. Two very definite results were noted: (1) that interest and activity among state and local associations had greatly spread and increased, and (2) that there had been a decrease in certain unlawful practices, most notably in the fiduciary field.[200]

Charles A. Beardsley, Esq., of the California Bar, at this session presented facts and figures to show the efficacy of the integrated bar of California,[201] in winning out in its battle against the bankers. If the public is to be aligned on the side of the organized Bar, the organized Bar must, as it did in California, give constructive service to the public, service along the line not only of raising educational standards of the Bar to higher levels, but service along the line of improving the administration of justice.[202]

---

200 Ibid., Vol. 59 (1934), pp. 153-156.

201 Supra, pp. 81-82.

202 American Bar Association Report, Vol. 59 (1934), pp. 167-172.

In 1935 the Committee emphasized that the problem can best be handled by state and local associations, but that these associations are looking to the national association for guidance, leadership, suggestions, and help, all of which were being furnished. Almost 200 associations had Committees on Unauthorized Practice of the Law, and the monthly pamphlet, "Unauthorized Practice News," was being forwarded to a mailing list of 1600.[203]

Since members of the Bar are held to a rigid course of training before admission, and to considerably higher standards of ethical conduct than other individuals, the public should be protected from the practice of law by unauthorized persons, which endangers the personal and property rights of the public, and interferes with the proper administration of justice. If a man acts as his own lawyer, or engages the services of those who are not properly trained, more business is created for the lawyers by mistakes made by such unskilled practitioners. Whether this is true or not, both the lawyer and the public should combine in their common cause to eliminate unlawful practice of the law. Let the public realize that the practice of law is a public calling which requires rigorous training, and that the lawyer is rightly held to the most exacting standards of conduct, because the public must be protected from chicanery and fraud. If these were practiced by the lawyer, the public has redress, for the lawyer can be made to suffer the penalty of disbarment; if they are resorted to by the layman or trust company, the public has no redress, unless in the case of the layman, the type of fraud would be sufficient to constitute a crime. In the case of the trust company, there is no redress, for as it has often been said, "A corporation is an entity with no body to be kicked, and no soul to be damned." [204]

---

[203] Ibid., Vol. 60 (1935), pp. 143, 521ff, also American Bar Association Journal, May, 1935, p. 307.

[204] This comes from the well-known quotation from Sir Edward Coke, "They (corporations) cannot commit treason, nor be outlawed nor excommunicate, for they have no souls." Case of Sutton's Hospital, 10 Rep. 32.

CHAPTER IV

DEVELOPMENT OF FAVORABLE PUBLIC RELATIONS

"Equal and exact justice to all men, of whatever state or persuasion, religious or political."—First Inaugural Address, Thomas Jefferson.

A. EMPHASIS ON SERVICE

1. ADOPTION OF HIGH PROFESSIONAL STANDARDS

One of the most effective means of creating a favorable public opinion is through the performance of a necessary and competent service. "If thou doest well, shalt thou not be accepted?"[1] might well be heeded. The organized Bar, as shown above, has since its beginning adhered to a consistent policy of maintaining and raising standards of legal education and admission to the Bar, maintaining high ethical standards for those in the legal profession, and developing adequate machinery for purging the profession of undesirables, and unauthorized practitioners.[2] As has been emphasized, in many respects the organized Bar has not fully succeeded in carrying through all its responsibilities. There is need for even higher standards for admission and more adequate and uniform machinery for ridding the profession of unethical practitioners. However, through its National Bar Program,

---

[1] Genesis 4: 7.

[2] Supra, pp. 42-99.

merged in the New Plan of organization, the American Bar Association may be said to be in process of developing adequate machinery for handling these very difficult problems. While the organized Bar has done a great deal to insure a high type of personnel in its own ranks, it should be noted that the public at large knows little of the self-regulation and self-disciplining of members of the Bar. The organized Bar has not until quite recently developed any machinery of its own for making its accomplishments in this field known to the public, and it would seem that too much emphasis has been given to the unethical practitioner and the lawyer criminal and not enough to the constructive service of the lawyers and the organized Bar.

2. FOSTERING AND SPREADING LEGAL AID

(a) Brief Historical Background of Legal Aid Movement

The first Legal Aid Society was organized in New York March 8, 1876. The movement was initiated and set on foot by a group of private individuals led by Arthur von Briesen, a philanthropic leader of the New York Bar.[3] From 1876 to 1900, legal aid work grew slowly; in 1886 there were two legal aid societies, but by 1910 the number had grown to fourteen. The next four years, between 1910 and 1914, the number doubled to twenty-eight, and in 1917 there were forty-one organizations in existence.[4]

These legal aid groups differ in organization, namely, they may be private or public, and also differ in their source of maintenance, sometimes being financed by private agencies, sometimes by Bar Associations, and sometimes by municipalities. Kansas City, early in 1910, created a public legal aid organization.[5]

---

[3] Annals of American Academy of Political and Social Science, March, 1926, p. 4.

[4] American Bar Association Report, Vol. 45 (1920), p. 224.

[5] Ibid., Vol. 45 (1920), p. 225.

(b) Development of Bar's Activities in This Field

Legal Aid has a definite and close relationship to the administration of justice, and it would seem that lawyers, either individually or in their organized groups, would be essential to the successful development of any such movement. Mr. Reginald Heber Smith, author of the standard work on Legal Aid, "Justice and the Poor," has well stated that the "essence of legal aid work is providing lawyers' services to the poor, either freely or at a nominal charge." [6] In other words, a legal aid organization is a poor man's law office.

Though legal aid organizations had been in existence since 1876, it was not until 1920 that the American Bar Association took an active interest in this work. As early as 1906, Dean William Draper Lewis, Chairman of the Section on Legal Education, in a paper delivered by that Section, entitled "Legal Education and the Failure of the Bar to Perform Its Public Duties," remarked that it never occurred to bar associations that legal aid was their problem, and that they owed a duty to the community to try and solve it.[7] Nevertheless, nothing was done until 1920 when the American Bar Association appointed its first legal Aid Committee, which Committee felt that its greatest service could be rendered not only by contacting the legal aid groups already in existence, but by establishing a definite relationship between those groups and the Bar Association. To effectuate this relationship, it was proposed to bring legal aid work within the number of activities fostered by the Bar Association.[8]

And thus, though organized legal aid work began in 1876, and in 1878 the American Bar Association was formed, and notwithstanding the fact that the two agencies

[6] Ibid., Vol. 45 (1920), p. 217.
[7] Ibid., Vol. 30 (1906), Part II, p. 41.
[8] Ibid., Vol. 46 (1921), p. 494.

had already shared a common interest in striving to make more perfect the administration of justice, yet for over forty years the two organizations existed side by side without contact, without mutual recognition, and without joining hands. In 1920 the organized Bar accepted definite professional responsibility for the proper upbuilding and conduct of legal aid work, and played no small part in its record of advancement.[9]

Nevertheless, it should be noted that mention of legal aid was made in a bar program in 1917. In that year, the Conference of Bar Association Delegates by resolution stated, "It is the sense of this Conference that Bar Delegates, State and Local, should be urged to foster the formation and efficient administration of legal aid societies for legal relief work for the worthy poor, with the active and sympathetic cooperation of such Associations, and that attorneys generally be urged to give such societies their moral and financial support." [10]

In 1919 Reginald Heber Smith's book, "Justice and the Poor," gave a new impetus to the cause of legal aid and stimulated the interest of bar associations and the Bar generally, as is shown by the fact that in 1920 the Association conducted a symposium on legal aid work, out of which came the appointment of the Special Committee on Legal Aid.[11] In 1921 the Association amended its Constitution to create its Standing Committee on Legal Aid work. The reasons assigned for the Standing Committee were given as follows:—

(1) The Bar has a direct responsibility to see that every cause has its day in court.

(2) This responsibility is best met by the organized Bar.

(3) The large city job can best be done by legal aid organizations.

---

[9] Ibid., Vol. 56 (1931), p. 410.
[10] Ibid., Vol. 42 (1917), p. 437.
[11] Ibid., Vol. 45 (1920), pp. 147 and 217-258.

(4) There should be a direct relationship between the American Bar Association and legal aid work.

(5) This relationship should be recognized by the creation of a standing or annual committee to report to the Association as to progress, needs, advantages and shortcomings of legal aid work in the United States.[12]

In 1922 a resolution was passed calling on state and local bar associations to provide Committees on Legal Aid work, and this resolution was transmitted in November, 1922, to state associations by the Conference of Bar Association Delegates, the point of contact between the national and state groups.[13]

The Committee for the year 1922 reported that during its first year it had confined its work to two main lines of effort:

(1) It had cooperated wherever possible with organized legal aid work. Several of its members had visited legal aid societies and bureaus. Three members of the Committee had attended the Convention of Legal Aid Organizations in Philadelphia in March, 1922.

(2) It had considered what practical things the Bar could do for legal aid work.

The Committee sent a letter to the secretary of every bar association in the country to determine how far the organized Bar had given support to legal aid. Its aim, in which it claimed to be successful, was to convince the Bar, as a matter of professional responsibility, that it had an obligation of encouraging and supporting legal aid work.[14]

Report was made in 1922 that much interest had been displayed by different local groups. Pursuant to the request of the Conference of Bar Association Delegates in 1919, the Bar of the City of New York had appointed a Special Committee on Legal Aid, which filed its report in

---

[12] Ibid., Vol. 46 (1921), p. 493.

[13] Ibid., Vol. 47 (1922), p. 402. Conference reported that it had brought to the attention of the American Bar Association and local associations the cause of legal aid. Ibid., Vol. 47 (1922), p. 42.

[14] Ibid., Vol. 47 (1922), p. 403.

1919.[15] Then, in 1920, the New York State Bar Association appointed its Special Committee on Legal Aid, which filed its report January 16, 1920. It sent questionnaires to sixty-one bar associations, and found that in most communities little interest in legal aid work was being shown. The directors of the New York County Lawyers' Association adopted a resolution which approved the request of the Legal Aid Society for the cooperation of bar associations, and which commended to the general membership the furnishing of aid and services. In 1920, in Philadelphia, with municipal aid, the law association furnished a special committee to cooperate in organizing the bureau and defining policies. In 1920, in Rhode Island, the Legal Aid Bureau was created through the efforts of the president of the state bar association. In 1921, the Essex County Bar Association assumed responsibility for raising funds for work in Newark. The Louisville Legal Aid Society was created by the Louisville Bar Association, which formally endorsed the idea, and through a committee of its own drafted articles of incorporation, raised necessary funds, and saw that work was begun.[16]

The 1923 Committee reported that progress had been extraordinary. Over thirty associations had taken definite action of some sort, and among the thirty, the great bar associations of the country were included. An example of what the Bar may accomplish was afforded by Illinois and New York. In Chicago, the Special Committee of the Bar Association sat with the Directors of the Legal Aid Bureau. In the rest of the state, a cooperative plan was evolved by the Special Committee of the Illinois Bar Association, under which in any city or town local charities may refer cases to competent attorneys for attention.[17]

Other local activities included New York and Pennsylvania. During the year, the Executive Committee of the

---

15 Ibid., Vol. 47 (1922), p. 405.
16 Ibid., Vol. 47 (1922), pp. 406-407.
17 Ibid., Vol. 48 (1923), p. 374.

New York City Bar had sent a letter to each of its members stating that "legal aid is primarily the obligation of the legal profession." The Pennsylvania State Bar Association had discussed legal aid at the 1922 and 1923 annual meetings. The Philadelphia Law Association had a Committee on Legal Aid, which studied the operations of the Philadelphia Municipal Legal Aid Bureau, and made its first report to the Association in 1922.[18]

As to the policy of developing friendly contact and relationship between the Legal Aid organizations and Bar Association groups, definite progress was shown by the 1923 report, in that the National Association of Legal Aid Organizations had created a Committee to confer with the American Bar Association Committee on certain questions long troublesome in the field.[19]

There are two methods of attacking the problem of inability of the poor to employ counsel: (1) Free service through legal aid societies, and (2) simplifying legal machinery so that lawyers' services are unnecessary, such as the development of the small claims courts, industrial accidents courts, domestic relations courts, and conciliation procedure.

This second aspect of legal aid was noticed by the Bar Association when it sponsored a Poor Litigants Statute, the purpose of which was to insure to any man his day in Court, even if too poor to pay court costs and fees. Note was made of the fact that it could not be uniform throughout the states, because details of application should be flexible enough to suit different court structures of various states. The Committee in 1924 produced a draft that embodied the necessary fundamental controlling provisions, which were to be distributed to bar associations, legal aid organizations, etc. Final draft was to be submitted in 1925.[20]

---

18 Ibid., Vol. 48 (1923), pp. 381-382.
19 Ibid., Vol. 48 (1923), p. 377.
20 Ibid., Vol. 49 (1924), p. 384.

This second draft of the Poor Litigants Statute was presented in the 1925 report. The original draft, submitted in 1924, had been prepared by Professor John M. Maguire, since which time the procedure of other countries and other suggestions had been submitted; the second draft embodied the suggested revisions.[21] The draft with a brief running commentary covered six closely printed pages.[22] The Minnesota State Bar Association had also been active in securing passage of a Small Claims and Conciliation Court act.[23]

The Legal Aid Committee recognized a very definite function of maintaining a continuing study of the administration of justice as it affected poorer people, especially those who lived in large cities. Little change was considered necessary in substantive law, but such change for better procedure and court organization was found to be requisite.

From studies made by the Committee, it was ascertained that a large proportion of legal aid work involved payment of wages. In 1925 it was learned that legal aid organizations in the United States received upwards of twenty-five thousand claims for wages each year. The small claims courts received as many. Most states had labor bureaus or labor commissions, where complaints were filed. Few states were successful in meeting the situation. The 1925 Committee proposed to study the plan in detail, with the hope that it could draft a statute that could be enacted throughout the country. In this effort it had the cooperation of the International Association of Government Labor Officers, the National Association of Legal Aid Organizations, and the United States Commissioner of Labor.[24] In 1927 the Committee, in order to show the magnitude of the wage-claim problem, stated that out of

21 Ibid., Vol. 50 (1925), p. 453.
22 Ibid., Vol. 50 (1925), pp. 456-462.
23 Ibid., Vol. 48 (1923), p. 380.
24 Ibid., Vol. 50 (1925), p. 453.

an average of fifty consultations a day in the Buffalo Legal Aid Bureau, one-quarter were wage claims.[25] The draft presented was not considered ready for action or even discussion. Somewhat flamboyantly, it was stated that the unpaid wage earners of the country had one champion willing to spend time and money to see that they obtained equal protection of the laws, and that champion was the American Bar Association.[26]

The Conference of Bar Association Delegates discussed conciliation procedure, and received reports from a Special Committee which found that conciliation procedure was successfully used in other countries, notably Norway and Denmark. The Conference asked the Legal Aid Committee to make a study to determine why conciliation procedure was not utilized by American administration of justice.[27] Mr. F. H. Randall, Graduate Student of the Harvard Law School, was employed to study the history of conciliation in Anglo-American Law. He found that the right to attempt to bring about conciliation appeared to remain an inherent power of American courts. The total absence of conciliation in American procedure was due to a misapprehension. In the light of Mr. Randall's research, it was considered that the Judicial Section of the American Bar Association might, with profit, conduct an investigation. Conciliation was found to exist in legal aid offices. For example, the New York Legal Aid Society was fifty years old, and only ten per cent of cases had been brought to court. "In America, thanks to Legal Aid, we have this voluntary domestic precedent of conciliation procedure, which settled two poor men's cases out of three." [28] It would seem that there is little conciliation in our law, though legal aid is showing the way.

---

25 Ibid., Vol. 52 (1927), p. 114.

26 Ibid., Vol. 52 (1927), p. 115.

27 Ibid., Vol. 53 (1928), p. 460.

28 Quoted from "The Lance of Justice," by Professor John MacArthur Maguire, American Bar Association Report, Vol. 53 (1928), p. 461.

(c) Usefulness or Value of Work Done

Legal aid work is important in allaying unrest, removing suspicion of the integrity of our institutions, and in promoting good citizenship. For the American Bar Association to be a leader in the work is not only a help to legal aid organizations, but redounds to the credit and advantage of the Association itself.

What has the Bar to offer? Generally, it may be said that it has given financial support, rendered assistance, served on boards of directors, and given time and loyal interest. Particularly, it may be added that the Denver Legal Aid Society owed its existence largely to the efforts of its bar association.[29]

The work of legal aid organizations grew more rapidly after the appointment of the first committee on legal aid by the American Bar Association. In 1920 there were forty-one legal aid societies and bureaus handling ninety thousand cases; in 1924 there were seventy-two legal aid offices caring for one hundred and twenty thousand clients.[30] In 1929 one hundred and seventy thousand people came into legal aid offices, and in 1934 there were some eighty legal aid organizations throughout the country, handling upwards of three hundred thousand cases.[31]

Although legal aid work has thus grown steadily, the organizations entrusted with its administration are, like most other organizations, feeling financial strain during the depression. At the 1934 meeting of the American Bar Association, it was reported that a Special Committee of the National Association of Legal Aid Organizations had asked the American Bar Association Committee to consider a plan in which the American Bar Association, state and larger county and city bar associations would make small

29 American Bar Association Report, Vol. 51 (1926), p. 127.
30 Ibid., Vol. 50 (1925), p. 454.
31 Ibid., Vol. 59 (1934), p. 104.

grants directly to the National Association of Legal Aid Organizations. In pressing the point, the Chairman of the American Bar Association Committee stressed a matter which he considered merited the earnest attention of the Association, namely, the Bar's increasing awareness that it has a public relations problem on its hands. He suggested that financial support of legal aid was the only practical way to develop proper public relations, for the Bar has the definite obligation to see that no man is denied justice through an inability to employ counsel.[32]

Legal aid officers act really as outposts, carrying on quietly every day effective work for sound American citizenship. When the Bar supports legal aid, it is not only living up to the ethical obligation of the profession, but is enabling the administration of justice in the country to be impartial, thereby making direct contribution to the safety and security of the nation.[33] To deny service increases distress and despair, also susceptibility to communism and dole. The best and most positive Americanization work would be sympathetic consideration and efficient enforcement of rights of people needing legal aid, thus creating confidence in the administration of justice. Legal aid can be likened to the good Samaritan that rendered realistic service.[34]

From the foregoing review of the Bar activities in the legal aid field, it is obvious that the organized Bar did do much to accelerate and spread legal aid. While the American Bar Association did not begin its activities in the field of legal aid work until 1920, still the movement itself was initiated by a philanthropic lawyer, Arthur von Briesen. The work seemed to proceed slowly until the entrance of the organized bar into the field. In four years, from 1920 to 1924, legal aid organizations almost doubled. It would appear that the organized Bar should be given some

32 Ibid., Vol. 59 (1934), pp. 496-497.
33 Ibid., Vol. 55 (1930), p. 106.
34 Ibid., Vol. 57 (1932), p. 161.

credit for work done in accelerating and spreading legal aid. On the other hand, the organized Bar has not assumed its full duty of seeing that legal advice and a fair hearing are available to everyone, even the poorest. It is conceded that legal aid is inadequate. The Bar has the responsibility to sponsor and obtain adequate and well-staffed legal aid organizations in all communities. If one does not exist in a particular community, it is the duty of the organized bar of that community to ascertain the reason, and see that one is organized. It is necessary to make law understandable, and our courts and institutions understandable and acceptable to the people. Failure to do this tends to unrest and disquiet.[35]

Perhaps it is not extravagant to state that the public is suspicious of the Bar. People should be educated to appreciate the Bar and the services rendered by it. All organizations need increased prestige. The legal aid organization offers a great opportunity to increase the prestige of the bar in the minds of the people of the country.

The Bar could increase general respect for law if it could point out that justice was not too expensive for even the poorest. The administration of justice is a matter of public concern. Some states have done much in the way of eliminating costs in indigent cases. There should be in every section of the country a group of the local Bar, preferably composed of leaders, who would publicly announce that they are ready to hear and advocate or defend in courts, if necessary, any meritorious cases where the person aggrieved is unable to employ counsel. This phenomenon would contribute more than any to inculcate respect for law and to promote within the comprehension of the masses of our citizens confidence in the legal profession.[36]

The legal aid society as a piece of machinery in the public relations field of the Bar has been and is recom-

---

[35] Ibid., Vol. 54 (1929), pp. 134 and 135.
[36] Ibid., Vol. 48 (1923), p. 634.

mended.[37] Clients who experience effective legal aid service will become the friends of the legal profession. According to the late Mr. John Alan Hamilton, as quoted in the 1934 Committee report, "The Bar in this country needs legal aid as badly as an aristocrat in Russia needs calloused hands." [38]

As previously stated, legal aid work can be organized and operated by independent private legal aid societies, public legal aid organizations or legal aid groups acting under or with bar associations. It is difficult to state which system is the best, but since it is the Bar's own obligation to furnish effective judicial machinery and necessary access to it, the conclusion is inevitable that bar associations should continue to play an ever-increasing role in legal aid work. If legal aid work is carried on by independent, private, or public agencies, there can be little disciplining by the organized Bar, and abuses may spring up, such as the reference of profitable cases to particular law firms. If legal aid is operated under bar associations, or in connection with bar associations, then there can be proper regulation by such bar associations to insure the reason for the existence of legal aid work, namely, fairness and justice to all.

B. PUBLICITY

1. RADIO PROGRAM

In 1933 the American Bar Association through the cooperation of the National Advisory Council on Radio in Education sponsored a series of fifteen broadcasts, to be given every Sunday night commencing February 12, entitled "The Lawyer and the Public." The purpose of these

[37] Ibid., Vol. 58 (1933), p. 189.
[38] Quoted in American Bar Association Report, Vol. 59 (1934), p. 497.

broadcasts can be gleaned from a consideration of their purpose, namely, to promote a better understanding of the lawyer on the part of the public.[39]

As stated above, 150,000 announcements of the broadcasts were distributed, notices of the series appeared in almost every legal journal of the country, and the response of the Bar was considered favorable, for state and local bar association officials sent 700 letters expressing interest and registering approval of the program. Listeners also sent letters and questions.[40]

The merit or demerit of the radio in interpreting persons and causes to the public has never been estimated. So far as the lawyer and the organized Bar are concerned, it would seem that the fifteen technical lectures could have had little effect in interpreting the lawyer to the public. Perhaps the failure to present the number of lay listeners that sent letters and questions, while listing the fact that 700 state and local bar association officials had written letters of commendation, is significant.

2. NATIONAL BAR PROGRAM

Apparent is the fact that the National Bar Program, organized in 1933 for the purpose of coordinating the different units, namely, the national, state and county bar associations, has also been developed as a means of interpreting the lawyer to the public. As stated above, the National Bar Program is important because it represents

---

[39] The fifteen lectures, presented by leaders of the organized Bar, included such subjects as "The American Bar, its Past Leaders and its Present Aim," "Training for the Bar," "Shall I Become a Lawyer?" "The Lawyer's Influence upon Public Opinion," "Pitfalls Along the Legal Education Road," "Should the Public Distrust the Lawyer?" "The Lawyer and Business," "What is the Bar Doing to Improve the Administration of Justice?" "Reforming the Law Through Legislation," "Hurdles in the Path of a Candidate for Admission to the Bar," "The Lawyer Looks at His Responsibilities," "How the Law Functions," "Restating the Law: an Attempt at Simplification," "How Far Is a Judge Free in Rendering a Decision," and "Selecting Judges."

[40] Supra, p. 75.

not only talk but a type of work which has accomplished a great deal by giving to the local bar associations necessary leadership in the important fields of raising professional standards, selecting judges, and administering criminal law. The emphasis on functional coordination is commendable, for it represents a strengthening of machinery already in process of development since the date of organization. The choice of five subjects, after proper and sensible investigation and study, is also praiseworthy. The subject of "Legal Aid," should also be included, for it represents a possibility for an effective public relations program for the organized bar. Campaigns of propaganda are of little value. A city transit company may spend thousands of dollars to build up favorable public relations, only to have such favorable opinion vanish in one stormy day when estimable members of the public are compelled to wait on some cold corner for the trolley car that does not come. Efficient service is the keynote of any effective public relations; nothing will commend the legal profession to the public more quickly than a realization that it is through the efforts of the organized bar that legal remedies are placed within the reach of the poorest, and that the Bar is doing its part to develop an effective administration of justice in all branches of the law.

CHAPTER V

INFLUENCING PUBLIC OPINION ON THE UNITED STATES CONSTITUTION

"He who preserves or rescues the Constitution from threatened violation deserves more glory than the victor of a hundred battles."—Thaddeus Stevens.

A. ORIGIN OF POLICY TO DEVELOP KNOWLEDGE AND RESPECT FOR THE CONSTITUTION

1. INTENSIVE CAMPAIGN OF EDUCATION

The post-war period brought many problems, not the least of which was the challenge to so-called fundamental principles of American government. The Bar looked with disfavor on the skepticism expressed regarding the Constitution, called the bulwark of American liberties. This attitude was to be expected, since lawyers in order to qualify for admission to the Bar to practice law must take an oath to defend the Constitution as must the President of the United States. In 1922 the American Bar Association by the appointment of a Special Committee on American Citizenship initiated a policy to stand firm for this oath to defend the Constitution,[1] and to struggle for constitutional traditions. Since the World War, various organizations had been formed for the purpose of Americanization work. The Bar Association, in considering the lack of respect for the

[1] American Bar Association Report, Vol. 47 (1922), p. 420, and Vol. 53 (1928), p. 525.

Constitution and fundamental institutions, recognized certain lines of service peculiarly belonging to them.[2] If the constitutional form of government bequeathed by the founding fathers was to be preserved, need for activity on the part of members of the Bar was felt.[3] Lawyers as exponents of the law should unite as civic leaders for the preservation of the Constitution. If such a goal was to be achieved, there must be unity of policy and a definite program[4] to counteract the subversive influence of the reds and pinks, the ignorance of the foreign vote, and the general apathy of the intelligent American.[5]

On January 8, 1922, a Special Committee on American Citizenship was appointed "to devise ways for promoting the study of and devotion to American institutions and ideals." Lawyers were to cooperate with every patriotic society and organization in an effort to stem the tide of radical attack on the Constitution, laws, courts, law-making bodies, executive and flag.[6] This Special Committee recommended the appointment of a Standing Committee on Citizenship, with a definite policy.

An ambitious program was formulated with the express purpose of influencing public opinion in defence of the traditions of constitutional government by reaching the schools, of organizing oratorical contests and of distributing printed material. In its first year, the Committee was given just a nominal appropriation from the Association's treasury to carry on its work, but in the second year, it was given an appropriation that was the largest that the Association had ever in its history, up to that time, devoted to any single department.[7]

---

[2] Ibid., Vol. 48 (1923), p. 442.
[3] Ibid., Vol. 48 (1923), p. 443.
[4] Ibid., Vol. 48 (1923), p. 445.
[5] Ibid., Vol. 49 (1924), p. 257.
[6] Ibid., Vol. 47 (1922), p. 416.
[7] Rogers, James Grafton, American Bar Leaders, p. 224.

2. OBJECT AND PURPOSE OF EDUCATIONAL PROGRAM

The main objective of the Bar Association was the education of the public with reference to the nature and ideals of our government as embodied in its basic law, the Constitution of the United States. In the language of the Association, the purpose was thus expressed, "To reestablish the Constitution of the United States and the principles and ideals of our government in the minds and hearts of the people." [8] The Committee on Citizenship was designated as the permanent instrumentality to stimulate and guide civic activities among members of the Bar.

B. TECHNIQUE THROUGH WHICH BAR ASSOCIATION INFLUENCED PUBLIC OPINION ON THE CONSTITUTION

1. COMMITTEE ON CITIZENSHIP OF AMERICAN BAR ASSOCIATION WITH COMMITTEES ON CITIZENSHIP OF STATE BAR AND COUNTY BAR ASSOCIATIONS

The American Bar Association, since it is a national association, can only be instrumental in reaching the people through the state, county and community units. In order for the state and county bar association activities to be effective, they needed to be coordinated.

To carry out its policies, the National Association first appointed a Special Committee on American Citizenship in 1921, which Special Committee in 1922 was made a Standing Committee. In 1923 this Committee published its periodical, "The Story of the Constitution," which was widely distributed. In 1924 the late Josiah Marvel, Chairman, sensed the necessity of local agencies in the state, and spent a year in formulating and organizing committees on American Citizenship in most of the state bar associations. The

[8] American Bar Association Report, Vol. 48 (1923), p. 442.

National Committee on Citizenship was instrumental in coordinating the service of local and state bar associations for united action in furtherance of the formulated purpose, by preparing and distributing to all state bar associations suggested by-laws for the creation of standing committees on American Citizenship,[9] and by stimulating the creation of standing committees in local associations. If the object of the Association was to be attained, it was important for the American Bar Association Committee to reach all lawyers, and this was to be accomplished by a federative system beginning with the counties, then the states, and culminating in the central national body.[10] Thus the Committee on Citizenship of the American Bar Association assisted in organizing a state citizenship committee in connection with state bar associations in every state with the result that in 1925, such an organization existed in forty-two states, and it was expected that the remaining six states would be completed before the 1926 meeting.[11]

The attempt to operate directly on the Bar constituted a gigantic task. The mailing list of fifteen thousand names with which the Committee was in immediate touch represented hardly ten per cent of the Bar of the United States.[12] In order to quicken lawyers in this line of activity, the National Committee on Citizenship sent circular letters to every member of the American Bar Association in April, 1925, outlining its purpose and setting forth some of its activities.[13]

Evidently the circular letter did not produce the desired results, for in 1927 the Executive Committee made certain changes in the machinery for carrying out the organized bar's program to develop knowledge of and inculcate respect for the Constitution. The first system of com-

---

9 Ibid., Vol. 48 (1923), p. 448.
10 Ibid., Vol. 49 (1924), p. 262.
11 Ibid., Vol. 50 (1925), p. 335.
12 Ibid., Vol. 49 (1924), p. 262.
13 Ibid., Vol. 50 (1925), p. 336.

mittees proved inadequate because of the lack of coordination gained between the National Committee and the local committees.[14]

The organization of the committees on citizenship in the state and local associations had been a valuable work, but as an adjunct to the American Bar Association Committee on American Citizenship, it proved weak. At each meeting of the state bar associations, a change of Committee was made, of which fact the American Bar Association was not informed. The mailing list was thus useless within a year. In addition, a majority of the committee members in the state and local groups were not members of the National Association, and took no interest in the National Association Committee work. From the files, it was ascertained that only ten per cent of non-members were active, while seventy per cent of the American Bar Association members functioned.[15]

2. CHANGE IN ORGANIZATION; COMMITTEE ON CITIZENSHIP OF AMERICAN BAR ASSOCIATION WITH SUBCOMMITTEE OF AMERICAN BAR ASSOCIATION IN STATES

In 1927, on the suggestion of the Citizenship Committee, the Executive Committee of the American Bar Association approved a new plan. A special committee on American Citizenship was to be established in each state, composed of members of the American Bar Association, selected by the Vice-President of the National Association for that state, with the advice of members of the Local Council, the Vice-President of the state being ex officio a member of the Committee. The Council decided the size of the Committee for each state. These state committees were not to supersede the local committees of the state bar associations, for each state naturally had its own citizenship problems, and with these the state bar associations

[14] Ibid., Vol. 53 (1928), p. 325.
[15] Ibid., Vol. 52 (1927), pp. 75-76.

must deal through their own committees. The National Committees in the States had for their purpose and aim the teaching of the Constitution, the carrying forward of the educational program of the National Bar Association. The idea of the new machinery was a real federated organization working for a common end, the local committees to handle special problems, and the Standing and Special Committees to deal with national problems. "Education! this is our job!" constituted the motto.[16] The old system, in addition to its looseness, worked jerkily and spasmodically, and the new structure was considered necessary in order to gain continuity.

As an indication of the inclusiveness of the new machinery, it was reported at the 1928 meeting that forty-three states had committees, two states had their own committees coordinating with the American Bar Association, and that only three states had no committees. In effect, there was a Committee on American Citizenship of almost five hundred members, covering almost the entire country. Members of the Committee were appointed until the work was relinquished, insuring a coherent and continued organization.[17] By 1929 the organization of a special committee in every state but two had been completed.[18] In 1933 it was reported that there were "about four hundred and ninety members of local committees with state chairmen in forty-five states, a stable, continuing and loyal body" to consummate policies.[19] During 1933 and 1934, deeming it the special work of colleges and universities to develop an educated citizenship, the Committee addressed some five hundred and ninety-three questionnaires to colleges and universities throughout the United States, to which it received three hundred and thirty-six replies. The composite picture of the replies, according to the Committee, was

[16] Ibid., Vol. 52 (1927), pp. 238-239.

[17] Ibid., Vol. 53 (1928), pp. 325-326.

[18] Ibid., Vol. 54 (1929), pp. 82 and 301.

[19] Ibid., Vol. 58 (1933), p. 337.

disconcerting and surprising, namely, that the study of the Constitution in the colleges was mostly an elective and a mere incident to the study of civil government.[20]

3. PRESSURE ON LAW SCHOOLS AND STATE BOARDS OF BAR EXAMINERS

Recognition was made of the fact that the law schools could not be reached directly. It was recommended that state bar associations note and insist that no candidate be admitted to the Bar, who did not have a thorough knowledge of the fundamental instrument of his government.[21]

In the 1927 report, it was recommended that appeal should be made to members of the boards of law examiners of the various states for a revision of questions to test the candidates' knowledge of the Constitution.[22] In 1928 the Committee recommended that the law schools should require strict preliminary examination on the Constitution. If board of law examiners of the different states would take up the subject and impose an examination on the Constitution, the law schools would be forced to teach it.[23]

4. COOPERATION WITH ALLIED PATRIOTIC ORGANIZATIONS

The American Bar Association, through its Committee, early realized that it could render one important service in the development of knowledge of the Constitution by giving leadership in coordinating the various forces at work in the field. In 1925 the Association instructed the Committee on Citizenship to contact civic associations, religious societies and meetings of citizens for all civic purposes.[24] A plan was evolved to work with and coordinate

[20] Ibid., Vol. 59 (1934), pp. 64-65.
[21] Ibid., Vol. 49 (1924), p. 262.
[22] Ibid., Vol. 52 (1927), p. 238.
[23] Ibid., Vol. 53 (1928), p. 328.
[24] Ibid., Vol. 50 (1925), p. 336.

efforts of every society in America competent and willing to work, namely, the American Legion, patriotic societies, such as the Sons of the Revolution, Masonic Service Association, Knights of Columbus, Chamber of Commerce, the Rotary, Lions and Kiwanis Clubs, the Association of Teachers, and other important influences.[25]

The Committee to make its work more effective distributed pamphlets and cartoons, and arranged for radio addresses on the Constitution and fundamental institutions.

C. EFFECTIVENESS TESTED BY ACCOMPLISHMENTS AND RESULTS

1. SPONSORED LAW REQUIRING THE TEACHING OF THE CONSTITUTION IN THE PUBLIC SCHOOLS

From the outset, the paramount concern of the Committee was the proper teaching of the Constitution in the schools, and its efforts were consequently centered on the public schools. The mind of the child was to be reached while it was still in a plastic state.[26] To accomplish this aim, emphasis was placed on the passage of a law requiring the teaching of the Constitution in the various states, and as far as this activity was concerned, the result was one of apparent, continued effectiveness and achievement. In 1923 it was reported that due to the Committee's efforts, twenty-four states had passed a law, requiring the teaching of the Constitution in the schools; in five states a bill had been presented but had not passed, and in only nineteen states had no law been presented or passed.[27] The passage of the law alone had a fine moral effect, for in the absence of very definite requirements, the Constitution was indifferently taught. Of course, the passage of the law alone

25 Ibid., Vol. 49 (1924), p. 260.
26 Ibid., Vol. 49 (1924), p. 260.
27 Ibid., Vol. 48 (1923), p. 446.

did not cure the deficiency of teachers.[28] In 1924 it was shown that thirty-one states then had a definite law requiring the teaching of the Constitution, an increase of seven during the year.[29] In 1925 the number had been increased to thirty-three,[30] and in 1927 to thirty-seven, leaving only eleven states in which there was no such law.[31] The number in 1928 still remained at thirty-seven, with one additional state requiring the teaching of the Constitution by legislation, and two other states attempting to secure its passage.[32] In 1929 it was reported that two more states, Texas and North Dakota, had adopted the suggested act, requiring the teaching of the Constitution in the schools, making thirty-nine that then required it.[33] In 1930 and 1931, the number of states requiring instruction had reached forty-three.[34]

From the foregoing survey, it would seem that the Bar's avowed aim to obtain the enactment of a law in every state, which law required the teaching of the Constitution in the public schools, was almost an accomplished fact.

2. ORGANIZED SUMMER CONFERENCES ON THE CONSTITUTION AT COLLEGES

The Committee early initiated a policy of contacting colleges to include in their summer school conferences methods of teaching the Constitution in the various schools, because they found an apparent lack of knowledge of the Constitution on the part of teachers. After a year's activity on the part of the Committee, forty-two colleges and universities definitely reported that they would undertake to organize such conferences.[35]

---

28 Ibid., Vol. 48 (1923), p. 446.
29 Ibid., Vol. 49 (1924), p. 263.
30 Ibid., Vol. 50 (1925), p. 335.
31 Ibid., Vol. 52 (1927), p. 236.
32 Ibid., Vol. 53 (1928), p. 327.
33 Ibid., Vol. 54 (1929), p. 302.
34 Ibid., Vol. 55 (1930), p. 44, and Vol. 56 (1931), p. 334.
35 Ibid., Vol. 48 (1923), p. 447.

3. FORCED TEACHING OF CONSTITUTION IN LAW SCHOOLS

The knowledge of the Constitution on the part of lawyers was found to be deficient. Efforts were, therefore, made to have the law schools include the proper courses on the Constitution. To bring pressure on the law schools to act, appeal was made to boards of law examiners of various states to revise questions to test the law school student's knowledge of the Constitution.[36]

4. ORGANIZED AMERICANIZATION COMMITTEES

Sixty Americanization Committees were organized in fifty-three judicial districts. District judges in seventy-eight districts cooperated. Aliens were to be made Americans in mind before they were made such in fact.[37]

5. STRESSED CELEBRATION OF NATIONAL HOLIDAYS

The Committee successfully established the celebration of national holidays, such as Constitution Day, Patriots Day, Memorial Day, Independence Day, etc. Constitution Day was even expanded into Constitution week.[38] Thanksgiving Day was emphasized as a National holiday, for the Committee claimed that through its efforts on Thanksgiving Day, 1928, the clergy in a thousand communities, in enumerating the blessings for which people should give thanks, made particular note of the American form of government and its benefits.[39] Through its publication, the American Bar Association Journal, an appeal was made to the American Bar for an appropriate celebration on February 4, 1934, of the 133d anniversary of the accession of John Marshall to the Chief Justiceship. Some thousands of these

---

36 Ibid., Vol. 52 (1927), p. 238.
37 Ibid., Vol. 50 (1925), p. 336.
38 Ibid., Vol. 48 (1923), p. 447.
39 Ibid.. Vol. 54 (1929), p. 301.

appeals were mailed to the Bench and Bar of the nation, with encouraging results.[40] The Committee also advocated preparations for a fitting celebration in 1937, of the 150th anniversary of the formulation of the Constitution; to this end, the Chairman of the Citizenship Committee for 1933-1934 offered a Bill in the House, providing for a Commission of fifteen men, which had been favorably reported, but had not passed; action was hoped for in the seventy-fourth Congress.[41]

6. DISTRIBUTED PAMPHLETS AND CARTOONS ON CONSTITUTION

The Committee wrote many pamphlets and furnished various items including cartoons, which were widely circulated.[42] In 1924 it was reported that more than one hundred and thirty thousand pamphlets on the Constitution had been circulated.[43] In 1927, it was said that the demand for the Committee's pamphlets had broadened, and that they went into every state in the union.[44] In 1931, in a supplementary report, the Committee proclaimed that it had aroused interest in the real study of the Constitution. Interested people and organizations had received 5246 copies of the Declaration of Independence and the Constitution, 3685 copies of the Story of the Constitution, 4549 copies of the Handbook of the Constitution, and 3933 copies of suggestions for observation of Constitution week.[45]

7. COOPERATED IN ORGANIZING ORATORICAL CONTESTS

Entirely outside the Bar organization, a group of patriotic newspapers instituted contests for addresses on the

---

[40] Ibid., Vol. 59 (1934), p. 423, and American Bar Association Journal, January, 1934, pp. 15-17.

[41] American Bar Association Report, Vol. 59 (1934), p. 424.

[42] Ibid., Vol. 48 (1923), p. 449.

[43] Ibid., Vol. 49 (1924), p. 263.

[44] Ibid., Vol. 52 (1927), p. 238.

[45] Ibid., Vol. 56 (1931), p. 53.

Constitution among pupils of high schools, and offered prizes of substantial value. By a process of selection and elimination, they prepared for final contests in Washington. The Nebraska Bar Association, impressed with the procedure, carried through a contest, and proposed as soon as neighborhood bar associations undertook the work, to have interstate contests from year to year.[46]

The Committee in 1928 acknowledged with appreciation the efforts of the leading newspapers in carrying on this work of national oratorical contests on the Constitution. It was admitted to be valuable work, but the comment was made that it should reach the junior high schools, especially the eighth grade, as well as the senior high schools.[47]

8. ARRANGED RADIO ADDRESSES

Radio addresses on the subject of American Citizenship were broadcast over Station WEAF on Tuesday nights during June, 1925. Responses by letters and telegrams addressed to speakers and committees showed great interest.[48] Two years later, it was reported by the Committee on Citizenship that short radio talks on the Constitution by distinguished lawyers were received with interest.[49]

In 1928 there was a note of discontent, as far as the national bar itself was concerned. The Committee, in recalling the fact that in 1926 a series of radio addresses on the Constitution had been broadcast, said that the program had been a failure, except in two or three of the largest cities, of which New York was one, and that the failure was due to the difficulty of obtaining competent lawyers to speak. The New York Bar radio program from March 6 to June 12, 1928, included a series of addresses by leaders of the New York Bar and one by President Silas H. Strawn.[50]

---

46 Ibid., Vol. 49 (1924), pp. 260-261.
47 Ibid., Vol. 53 (1928), p. 328.
48 Ibid., Vol. 50 (1925), p. 336.
49 Ibid., Vol. 52 (1927), p. 238.
50 Ibid., Vol. 53 (1928), p. 326.

In 1930 report stated that arrangements with fifty-five broadcasting stations had been made, that the number would doubtless be increased in the next four weeks and that with two exceptions, all stations in the country had given their facilities without charge.[51] In 1931 the Committee had had a series of broadcasts every day for one week through the courtesy of the National Broadcasting Company.[52] John Marshall Celebration on February 4, 1934, furnished the occasion for radio addresses. Prophets of ballyhoo are utilizing the radio with seemingly positive results. But it is to be doubted whether either constitutional principles or any of the other technical material handled by the Bar Association can be successfully transmitted to the public via radio.

D. EVALUATION AND CRITICISM

Even a cursory glance at the policy and program of the Bar Association through its Committee on Citizenship shows an earnest effort to develop respect for the Constitution. The Bar recognized the responsibility of the legal profession for its preservation, and appealed to the organized Bar in the several communities to support its basic principles. To this end, great stress was placed on the passage of laws in the various states, requiring the teaching of the Constitution in the public schools. While the Bar Association might be said to have effected its purpose in this respect, since over forty states require such teaching of the Constitution, yet doubt has been expressed about the effectiveness of this educational program, due to the type of text books and the teachers.[53] However, though poorly taught, any presentation would, at least, bring to the im-

---

51 Ibid., Vol. 55 (1930), p. 41.

52 Ibid., Vol. 56 (1931), p. 53.

53 Ibid., Vol. 59 (1934), pp. 64 and 428.

mature youth of the elementary schools the historic background of the Constitution, and thus might create an interest in those events which led up to its adoption.

The organized Bar's emphasis on fundamentals may be a healthy one as long as the constitutional framework is adequate for the solution of social, economic and political problems. Since government is a dynamic one, necessary adjustments make changes inevitable. With respect to changes, the organized Bar has consistently emphasized that these must be made in accordance with constitutional principles, and this, after all, is essential for stability.

There are two forces in society requisite for its welfare and existence: (a) the conservative force to preserve what is worth preserving; (b) the progressive force to prevent stagnation. From its policies and activities, the organized Bar must be classified in the former group for it consistently has upheld the Constitution, and what it calls fundamental principles and institutions.

A consideration of the policies and activities of the organized Bar respecting amendments to the Constitution might not be amiss. In 1911, among four resolutions referred to the Committee on Jurisprudence and Law Reform, one referred to legislation in behalf of equal suffrage (woman suffrage). The Committee reported its conclusion that it did not deem the subject a proper one for the Association to consider, since political discussions were taboo, and the subject was not included in the objects of the Association.[54]

In 1918 a strong protest was voiced against the Prohibition Amendment. The Committee on Jurisprudence and Law Reform in its report expressed its belief that constitutional changes in the National Constitution were unnecessary at that time, and urged Congress and the legislatures to note that proposed suffrage and prohibition amendments were propositions of the kind which should not at any time

---

[54] Ibid., Vol. 36 (1911), p. 384.

be embodied in the national Constitution. After much discussion, the report of the Committee was indefinitely postponed.[55]

The general policy of abstaining from political and economic questions and limiting itself to legalistic and juristic questions and problems was early adhered to. However, though a social and economic question, the Bar Association has taken a stand on the Child Labor Amendment, yet it has taken its stand against the amendment on the general ground that too great power should not be transferred to the federal government. Though the Child Labor Amendment was passed by Congress in 1924, it has not been ratified by the requisite number of states. Quite recently, about 1933, it was once more revived as a vital question, and the Amendment is being ratified by an increasing number of states. In 1933 the Executive Committee of the American Bar Association took a stand in opposition to the Child Labor Amendment, which stand was ratified by the whole Association at the following annual meeting. A Special Committee was appointed in pursuance of a resolution adopted by the Executive Committee, and approved at the 1934 annual meeting, to oppose on its behalf ratification of the Child Labor Amendment. The Special Committee submitted a most exhaustive report presenting arguments against the amendment, which report was presented in the American Bar Association Journal for January, 1935.[56]

At the 1936 meeting the Assembly by a vote of 233 to 109 favored continued opposition to the Child Labor Amendment. Action on the part of the Bar Association relative to the Child Labor Amendment was opposed on the ground that the question being a political one was outside the purview of the Bar Association. The Committee, nevertheless, was continued by the above overwhelming vote.

---

[55] Ibid., Vol. 43 (1918), pp. 45 and 67.

[56] American Bar Association Journal, January, 1935, pp. 11ff.

The Bar has quite consistently opposed centralization of authority in the Federal government, and has thus sponsored a federal scheme which would give a minimum of power to the central government and leave a maximum of power in the states. The recommendation of the Committee would leave the affair of child labor with the states, for it cited with approval, the sponsoring of the Uniform Child Labor Law by the Bar Association.[57]

[57] Conference of Commissioners on Uniform State Laws formulated a Uniform Child Labor Act, which was adopted by the Conference and the Bar Association in 1912. American Bar Association Report, Vol. 35 (1910), p. 1154, Vol. 37 (1912), p. 26. In 1929 the Conference, after consideration of third tentative draft of the Child Labor Act, approved it in 1930; in 1935 it was reported as enacted in one state. American Bar Association Report, Vol. 55 (1930), p. 60, and Vol. 60 (1935), p. 733.

Chapter VI

PROMOTING CHANGES IN JUDICIAL ADMINISTRATION TO ELIMINATE CONGESTION AND EXPEDITE PROCEDURE

"The Law hath not been dead though it hath slept." Measure for Measure—Shakespeare.

A. Court Organization

1. PASSAGE OF LAW PROVIDING FOR CIRCUIT COURT OF APPEALS TO LESSEN CONGESTION IN SUPREME COURT OF THE UNITED STATES

It has been truly said that the administration of justice is the highest and most sacred function of government. If there is one branch of the government that should be free from so-called "politics" or "favoritism" it is the judiciary. Since no democracy is possible unless there is an efficient administration of justice because of their familiarity with legal proceedings, lawyers should take the lead in measures calculated to secure the best administration of justice.[1]

The American Bar Association early in its history considered the problem of delay of justice caused by congestion in the Supreme Court of the United States. In 1881, by resolution adopted, a Special Committee, consisting of the President of the Association, his successor, and seven other members, was appointed with instructions to inquire into

[1] American Bar Association Report, Vol. 57 (1932), p. 564.

what adequate remedy could be provided for elimination of delays now incident to final determination of suits pending in the highest court of the United States, and with power to prepare and in its discretion to print report with all possible speed.[2] This Committee became known as the Committee on Relief of the Supreme Court. After careful consideration of the subject, though all members of the Committee agreed that there was an imperative necessity that Congress should in some manner provide an adequate remedy for delays incident to the final determination of causes in the United States Courts, still the Committee could not agree on the solution, and thus both majority and minority plans were submitted. The majority plan provided for the establishment of intermediate appellate tribunals between the present Circuit Courts and Supreme Court, and the minority plan provided for a division of the Supreme Court into subdivisions, sections and committees.[3] The majority plan was embodied in a bill then pending in Congress known as the "David Bill," which had been passed by the Senate May 12, 1882. The majority report was adopted by the Association.[4] The Committee continued in existence until the adoption of the Act of March 3, 1891, which created the Circuit Courts of Appeals.[5]

The report for 1891 gave much information as to the movement for the establishment of the Circuit Court of Appeals. It recited that the report of the Committee presented at the 1890 meeting had been received and approved. The resolution submitted by the Committee was adopted by the Association, which resolution again urged Congress to provide a remedy for delays in determining causes in the Supreme Court of the United States by establishing intermediate Courts of Appeals in each circuit according to the recommendation of the Association. The Committee was

---

[2] Ibid., Vol. 4 (1881), p. 84.
[3] Ibid., Vol. 5 (1882), pp. 23, 343, and 363.
[4] Ibid., Vol. 5 (1882), p. 101.
[5] Ibid., Vol. 14 (1891), pp. 54 and 377; for the act, see Vol. 138, U.S. Rep. 709.

directed to continue its efforts to that end.[6] At that time two bills were being considered: (1) H. R. 9014, which had passed the House April, 1890, and (2) a substitute, reported to the Senate August 5, 1890, by Senator Evarts. The adjournment of Congress had prevented further action by the Committee. During the following session, copies of the resolution adopted by the Association were transmitted by the Secretary to the Judicial Committees of both Houses, and the matter was earnestly pressed on the attention of Senators and Representatives both in person and by correspondence. The Act establishing the Circuit Court of Appeals, as finally passed March 3, 1891, was the Evarts Bill. The nine Circuit Courts of Appeal were duly organized June, 1891.

The American Bar Association's part in moulding and influencing professional and public opinion to that end was attested in more than one Congressional debate.[7] The Bar's effectiveness here cannot be questioned. Since the Circuit Court of Appeals is the court of last resort for a large class of cases, the congestion in the Supreme Court was lessened to that degree, at least.

In 1897 the Association received a telegram from Senator Hoar, Chairman of the Judiciary Committee of the United States Senate stating that the Association would confer a great benefit by appointing a Committee to consider the present constitution of the United States Circuit and District Courts as to whether they might be consolidated or their present distribution of jurisdiction improved.[8] A motion was adopted that a Special Committee of five be appointed to consider the question of harmonizing and rendering consistent the organization of Courts of the United States subordinate to that of the Supreme Court. As stated hereafter, through the efforts of the Committee to Suggest Remedies and Formulate Proposed Laws to Prevent Delays

---

[6] American Bar Association Reports, Vol. 13 (1890), pp. 31, 33. 40, and 43.

[7] Ibid., Vol. 14 (1891), p. 377.

[8] Ibid., Vol. 20 (1897), pp. 60ff.

and Unnecessary Cost in Litigation, the Circuit Courts were consolidated with the District Courts and thus abolished by Act of March 3, 1911.[9]

2. DIVISION OF EIGHTH CIRCUIT AND ORGANIZATION OF TENTH JUDICIAL CIRCUIT TO DISTRIBUTE MORE EVENLY THE WORK OF THE CIRCUIT COURTS OF APPEALS

Because of the unequal distribution of work in the United States Circuit Courts of Appeals, a resolution was adopted in 1925, that the American Bar Association's Committee on Jurisprudence and Law Reform be requested to consider and report to the Association its recommendation as to the advisability of a revision of the judicial circuits of the United States. The Committee on Jurisprudence and Law Reform promptly proceeded to investigate conditions in the several circuits throughout the country. It first ascertained the view of members of the Supreme Court and senior circuit judges. From these sources the Committee obtained much information and a free expression of view. The question whether justice was being administered promptly and at such time and places as to serve the convenience of litigants and members of the Bar required a consideration of present and prospective population and manner of distribution. The Committee felt that the subject was big enough to be dealt with by a Commission appointed by Congress or a duly authorized Committee of that body, but felt, however, that a useful function might be performed by a continuation of its investigations. Suggestions made by members of the Judiciary were set forth in the report. Little investigation was needed to show that work among the several Circuit Courts of Appeals and for the several circuits was unequal. The Committee of the Association of the Bar of the City of New York had recommended that "naturalization" as a judicial function should

---

9 Infra, p. 162, fn. 7.

be transferred from courts to some executive agency. It also recommended that minor offenses should be handled by special tribunals of officials.[10]

The Committee on Jurisprudence and Law Reform continued its investigation, and after consultation with lawyers and judges of federal courts, gathered an additional body of statistics, and recommended that its conclusions, embodied in legislation then presented to the Association, should be approved. The proposed bill was made a part of the report, and provided for the amending of Section 116 of the Judicial Code (being Section 211 of the United States Code), to provide for ten judicial circuits. The division proposed on east and west lines was not approved by the circuit judges or members of the circuit, and was not pressed.[11] At its April meeting in 1928, the Executive Committee authorized a volunteer committee of eighth circuit lawyers, organized at the 1927 meeting, to become a Special Committee to examine and report at the 1928 annual meeting on the advisability of dividing the eighth judicial circuit, and recommend a plan for such division if deemed advisable. This Committee became known as the Committee on the Division of the Eighth Circuit. A bill, H. R. 13,567, introduced in the House by Congressman Newton of Minnesota, had been submitted to members of the Committee, and they had been requested to consider the bill, and submit it to state bar associations as well as to judges and lawyers of the respective states.[12] The Special Committee unanimously reported in favor of this Newton Bill. Another bill known as the Thatcher Bill had been introduced and a hearing held to consider it. Many letters opposing this bill were written to the Judiciary Committee of the House, and the Chairman of the Special Committee of the Bar Association appeared before the House Judiciary Committee to oppose passage. After consultation with circuit judges and a number of district judges, the Newton

---

[10] Ibid., Vol. 51 (1926), pp. 431ff.
[11] Ibid., Vol. 52 (1927), pp. 303ff, and Vol. 53 (1928), p. 136.
[12] Ibid., Vol. 53 (1928), pp. 135-136 and 394.

Bill was prepared to provide for the new tenth circuit with four circuit judges. This Newton Bill had the approval of the late Judge Sanborn, and was endorsed by Bar Associations of Arkansas, Kansas, and Minnesota. At a meeting of the Special Committee, held July 26, 1928, nine members of the Committee voted in favor of the Newton Bill. Other members of the Committee expressed approval. At another meeting, where there were about forty, eighth circuit, lawyers present, in addition to members of Committee, the bill was unanimously endorsed. The Committee submitted with its report a copy of letter written by Judge Stone on behalf of himself and other judges endorsing the bill, and also submitted copies of favorable resolutions passed by the Minnesota and Arkansas state bar associations, as well as the South Dakota and New Mexico bar associations. Report of the Special Committee was approved, and the resolution endorsing the Newton Bill was unanimously adopted.[13] In 1929 it was reported that the Newton Bill had been passed by Congress and signed by the President February 28, 1929; that the Circuit Court of Appeals of the Tenth Circuit had been organized shortly after the passage of the bill. The report was accepted, and Committee discharged.[14]

Commendation is due to the Committee for its wise and effective procedure in obtaining the view and support of those residents of the eighth circuit, who knew the problem, were interested in its solution and influential enough to attain results. This probably was the reason that the objective was obtained so expeditiously, though singleness of purpose of the Special Committee should also be noted. In any event, the division of the eighth circuit represents effective work on the part of an organized group.

---

[13] Ibid., Vol. 53 (1928), pp. 135ff.

[14] Ibid., Vol. 54 (1929), p. 339.

3. SUPPORT OF THE UNITED STATES BOARD OF TAX APPEALS

The United States Board of Tax Appeals was created by the Revenue Act of 1924, largely through the efforts of the Bar Association Committee according to assertions of tax experts on the Committee, though nothing written can be found regarding this fact. The sixteen board members are experts on tax questions. The creation of such a board proposed to provide a tribunal within the executive branch of the government which should be independent of the Treasury Department for the hearing and determination of controversies between taxpayers and the Bureau of Internal Revenue. This formerly was done by the Treasury Department, but was not found to be satisfactory, since it was a party in interest in the matter at issue before it. The Board of Tax Appeals is a judicial tribunal of limited jurisdiction with power to review decisions of the Commissioner of Internal Revenue with respect to income and profit, estate, and gift taxes.[15] Its limited jurisdiction is due to the fact that it only hears and decides on questions of deficiencies, and does not have jurisdiction over refund claims, though the Bar Association Committee of 1933 advocated such extension of jurisdiction.[16] The board holds hearings at various points throughout the country wherever the volume of business warrants, thus obviating the necessity of journeys to Washington.[17]

From the time of the board's creation, the American Bar Association through its Committee on Federal Taxation has continued to concern itself with increasing the efficiency of the board as a functioning tribunal. No one is especially interested in this except the board itself, the United States

---

15 Korner, J. G., U. S. Board of Tax Appeals, Journal of American Bar Association, October, 1925, p. 642.

16 American Bar Association Report, Vol. 58 (1933), pp. 115, 460.

17 Ibid., Vol. 55 (1930), p. 514.

Treasury Department and the American Bar Association.[18] The Bar Committee's chief concern has been the extension of the Board's jurisdiction with a definite emphasis on speeding up action. To this end of expediting the disposition of cases in the United States Board of Tax Appeals, the Committee was successful in securing the following legislation:

(1) That the board be relieved from making findings of fact in every case; incorporated in Act of 1928.

(2) That burden of proof of fraud be placed on the Commissioner of Internal Revenue instead of the taxpayer; incorporated in Act of 1928.

(3) That bar of the Statute of Limitations should not only operate to bar the remedy but should extinguish it. The Committee consistently opposed any attempt to revive taxes extinguished or barred by the Statute of Limitations.[19]

The Committee with a view to eliminating congestion and technicalities recommended the following amendments to Revenue Act, but they have not been adopted:

(1) That the Board of Tax Appeals be authorized to appoint special masters for taking of testimony and reporting findings thereon for consideration of the board.

(2) That the expiration of a period of limitation against the government should not be considered as constituting jeopardy, permitting the making of a jeopardy assessment calling for payment in ten days or the posting of a bond. (Though not adopted, the Treasury Department indicated that it would not make any further jeopardy assessments of such a nature.)[20]

(3) Section 280 of the Revenue Act of 1926, permitting assessment against transferees of assets of taxpayers was not repealed as recommended by the Committee; how-

---

18 Morris, George M., "Tax Law Revision Recommendations of the American Bar Association," National Income Tax Magazine, October, 1927, pp. 373-375.

19 American Bar Association Report, Vol. 53 (1928), p. 400.

20 Ibid., Vol. 53 (1928), p. 400.

ever, the burden of proving liability of the transferee was placed on the Commissioner of Internal Revenue in the Revenue Act of 1928.[21] The Committee is still working for a provision in the law, which will give relief to transferees of taxpayers.[22]

During the short session of Congress in 1929, the Bar committee attempted to secure legislation extending the jurisdiction of the United States Board of Tax Appeals to proceedings for recovery of taxes based on claims that taxpayers were entitled to special assessment on their excess profit taxes.[23] No further report is made of this very definite project, but it may be interesting to note why the matter was dropped. According to the statement of a member of the Committee, the Commissioner of Internal Revenue in order to stop the pressure to transfer responsibility in respect to special assessments to the Board of Tax Appeals, agreed to be fairer and more liberal in the matter of special assessments.

Though there is some criticism of the board, because of congestion of cases, still prevalent in spite of the Committee's efforts, and especially as compared with the English system which disposes of tax cases in the year in which the tax is due, there is no doubt but that the new procedure in the Board of Tax Appeals is quite superior to that of the old procedure where the taxpayer had to pay his tax as fixed by the Collector of Internal Revenue, and then appeal to the court. The Committee always expresses itself as completely satisfied with the performance of the board. At the 1933 meeting it emphasized its satisfaction in this way: "That institution (the board) in the nine years of its existence has demonstrated an adequate capacity to interpret, as a specialized tax court, the multitude of everchanging federal tax laws which began in 1913, and have played so important a part in the business life of the country ever since. In

21 Ibid., Vol. 53 (1928), p. 400.
22 Ibid., Vol. 58 (1933), p. 459.
23 Ibid., Vol. 54 (1929), p. 341.

these nine years the independence of the board's judgment, as against mere administrative determinations, is indicated in many respects. The surest indication of this independence is the reduction of aggregate deficiencies proposed by the Commissioner of Internal Revenue in excess of $1,300,000,000 to approximately $400,000,000. The records show that less than 12 per cent of appealable decisions of the board have actually been taken, that the board has been affirmed in whole or in part by the Circuit Courts in more than 70 per cent of its decisions, and that its record before the Supreme Court is even better." [24]

The 1935 report continued its eulogy of the Board of Tax Appeals by citing agreement of members of the Bar that the board has successfully speeded up the procedure for bringing cases to a hearing. It added that the preservation of the board is construed as a project peculiarly within the province of a Committee created to deal with procedure and practice in federal tax administration. The Committee was empowered to continue to present to the courts, the Treasury Department and the Board of Tax Appeals, suggestions for improving tax administration and procedure.[25]

4. CONSIDERED CREATION OF FEDERAL COMMERCIAL COURT

Because the extension of federal power had been far-reaching, great congestion had resulted in the United States District Court; the Committee on Commerce, Trade and Commercial Law, in 1921, therefore, considered the matter of the creation of a Federal Commercial Court along the lines of the English Commercial Court. The Committee was empowered to give further consideration to the subject.[26] In 1922 the Committee reported that it had been unable during the year to give much consideration to the subject,

---

[24] Ibid., Vol. 58 (1933), p. 466.
[25] Ibid., Vol. 60 (1935), pp. 238 and 581.
[26] Ibid.. Vol. 46 (1921), pp. 312 and 354.

but that the matter was important, and should be considered further; the Committee was again empowered to further consider the subject.[27] In 1923 the Committee reported that as a result of its study it had ascertained that strictly speaking there was not a Commerce Court in England, but that there was a "short cause" or "speedy list" in Kings' Bench Division of the High Court of Justice, popularly known as "Commercial List" procedure, based on "Rules of Court." Jury trials were abolished or curtailed, and pleadings reduced to a minimum.[28] The Committee was again given further time to consider the English system of Commercial Courts.[29] The opinion of the Committee, expressed in its 1924 report, was that it would not be possible or desirable to establish a general system of commercial courts, but the Committee called for the enactment of the bill sponsored by the Bar Association through its Committee on Uniform Judicial Procedure, which would give the Supreme Court of the United States full authority to make and amend rules of Court governing procedure in common law cases, and also in cases before the Interstate Commerce Commission, the Court of Claims, and other tribunals.[30] Here, the Bar Association through its Committee on Commerce, Trade and Commercial Law, showed itself alert to the ever-present problem of congestion in the Court.

---

27 Ibid., Vol. 47 (1922), pp. 288 and 293.

28 Ibid., Vol. 48 (1923), p. 294.

29 Ibid., Vol. 48 (1923), p. 285.

30 Ibid., Vol. 49 (1924), pp. 288-289; infra, pp. 228-239.

B. COURT PERSONNEL

1. OPPOSITION TO JUDICIAL RECALL

(a) History and Extent of Judicial Recall

Judicial recall, as differentiated from "Recall" generally, may be defined as the removal of a judge from office by popular vote, and the movement, dating from 1908, with the adoption of judicial recall in Oregon, represented one of those waves of extreme democracy, as distinguished from constitutional democracy, which waves sweep the country periodically, and against which the organized Bar consistently arrays itself. California was not far behind Oregon, for in 1911, it declared its advocacy of judicial recall. The movement in agitation was from west to east.

The high spot of the movement may be said to have been in 1912, 1913, and 1914. During the year 1912-1913, recall of judges was made a Constitutional provision in the states of Arizona and Nevada, and was voted on by the legislatures of Kansas and Minnesota, to be submitted as a constitutional amendment for adoption by the people. In Colorado, constitutional amendments for both recall of judges and recall of judicial decisions were initiated by the people under the initiative and referendum, and were adopted. In Arkansas, the constitutional amendment for recall of judges, initiated by the people, was passed at the 1912 election, but the Supreme Court held that it had not been properly submitted, and therefore had not been adopted. Sentiment in the legislatures of Wisconsin, Illinois, Ohio and other states showed itself strong for the principle of judicial recall. Even as far east as Massachusetts, a constitutional amendment was urged, authorizing recall of judicial decisions. Quite in keeping with the popular wave for judicial recall, there was activity in Congress respecting the popular election of judges. In April, 1913, a joint resolution was presented in Congress, proposing to states the election of all federal judges, with a tenure of twelve years, and providing for recall of judges. In December, 1912, a Senate Joint Resolution was introduced proposing a constitutional amendment providing for veto of Supreme Court decisions by Congress. In 1913 the provision for judicial recall had been adopted in various states, listed as follows: Oregon (1908), California (1911), Colorado (1912), Arizona (1912), and Nevada (1913).[31] During 1914-1915, only one state, Kansas, was added to the foregoing list, thus showing some abatement of the movement.[32]

(b) Reason for Bar's Opposition

The American Bar Association opposed judicial recall because it militated against a principle always upheld by the organized Bar, namely, the independence of the judiciary. If the people by popular vote could remove a judge, simply because he had rendered an unpopular decision, what would become of the certainty and stability of our laws and government? The Bar looked upon the whole movement as extremely socialistic, a struggle against the institution of individual property rights, and it vigorously organized to combat the movement and safeguard the maintenance of our judicial system with its free and independent judiciary.[33]

The plan adopted in 1911 to fight the judicial recall movement represented the definite entry of the Association into the field of national opinion. In later years, Rome G. Brown, Esq., Minnesota, took over the work, and through a period of ten years "silenced the sentiment for the recall after the most significant and daring campaign the Association has undertaken in its history." [34]

---

31 American Bar Association Report, Vol. 38 (1913), pp. 579, passim, and Vol. 47 (1916), p. 553.

32 Ibid., Vol. 49 (1915), p. 519.

33 Ibid., Vol. 43 (1918), p. 85.

34 Rogers, James Grafton, Op. Cit., p. 124.

(c) Plan and Purpose of Campaign

In view of limited means at the disposal of the Committee to carry on the campaign, it was deemed best that the work should be done principally through local bar associations. The Committee appointed under the resolution adopted to oppose judicial recall was directed to "take such steps as it may deem best to expose the fallacy of judicial recall." [35] To this end, it was proposed:

(1) To carry on as widely as possible, consistently with limited means at disposal, a campaign of education throughout the United States, opposing judicial recall, and

(2) To direct or assist, by special work through this Committee, the various local campaigns in different states and by their legislatures in opposition to these measures.[36]

(d) History of Bar's Activity

When the danger of the judicial recall movement was presented to the American Bar Association August 30, 1911, at a session of its annual meeting, a Committee was appointed to formulate and present to the Association a minute on Recall of Judges. The problem was considered of such significance that six former presidents of the Association were appointed, with Francis Rawle, Esq., of Philadelphia, as Chairman. The minute was presented August 31, 1911, and the following resolutions were adopted: (1) That judicial recall would make decisions rest not on the law of the land, but on transient public sentiment, and would not be a government of laws, but of men; (2) That members of the Bar in every state be urged, through existing organizations or others to be formed, to present to the people reasons well understood by the legal profession why recall should not be made applicable to judges; (3) That

[35] American Bar Association Report, Vol. 37 (1912), p. 574.
[36] Ibid., Vol. 38 (1913), p. 579.

Committee representing each state and territory be appointed by the President, of which Committee the President shall be honorary chairman, and which Committee shall take such steps as it may deem best to expose the fallacy of judicial recall.[37]

The Committee appointed in August, 1911, consisted of one member from each state, but a subcommittee or executive committee was appointed, consisting of six members of which Mr. Frank B. Kellog, of Minnesota, was chairman.[38] Later, this subcommittee met at Chicago for the purpose of formulating a plan of action. It was decided that letters should be sent by the Chairman of the Committee to the member of the Committee in each state, recommending a special meeting of the state associations to take action on the subject of judicial recall, if no regular meeting had been scheduled. Also, where it was practicable, county and city bar associations should take the same action. At the meeting, opportunity for full discussion should be given, and then definite action on judicial recall taken, with the widest publicity in order that general public interest be stimulated. In this way, the interest of individual members of the national, state, county, and city bar associations would be aroused, and the people generally would receive the benefit of the discussion and action taken.[39] At the 1912 meeting, it was reported that under this plan of action, the bar associations of many states had taken action, and such action had been universally opposed to the principle of judicial recall. However, since few legislatures had been in session, no action of such bodies was reported.[40] The Committee did report that in addition to Oregon and California, where judicial recall existed, it understood that the only states which had taken action looking to adoption were the states of Arizona, Colorado, Nevada, and North

[37] Ibid., Vol. 36 (1911), pp. 8, 50-51, and 59-61.
[38] Ibid., Vol. 37 (1912), p. 52.
[39] Ibid., Vol. 37 (1912), p. 575.
[40] Ibid., Vol. 37 (1912), p. 575.

Dakota.[41] In Arizona, an effort had been made to diffuse general information among the electors; over twenty-five thousand copies of speeches of various senators, representatives and other public men had been sent to the entire electorate. In North Dakota, the campaign against judicial recall had been carried on by correspondence and personal interviews with members of the Bar, and had brought about much favorable discussion of the subject of opposition to judicial recall.[42]

In 1913, it was reported that the work of the Committee had been extensive that year, because forty state legislatures had held annual sessions during that year. In many of the forty or more states, legislatures, which had just adjourned, had presented measures for constitutional amendments providing for judicial recall. In some states while not successful, the measure had received surprisingly strong support; for example, in North Dakota, it had lost by only one vote.[43]

In 1914, the Committee in reporting a perceptible change in sentiment toward judicial recall, and noting its own effective work of three years, called attention to the fact that the discussion of the subject had theretofore been too much confined to forums of the American Bar, and had been expressed too much in the parlance of lawyers, who did not really need the instruction, since they could immediately perceive the fallacy of judicial recall. However, the average voter might be led astray, and it was this average voter who should be converted by arguments, which would bring conviction of the real merits of the issue, and that arguments must be formulated with that object in view.[44]

By 1915, the movement showed signs of contraction, for it was reported that during the year 1914-1915 there

---

41 Ibid., Vol. 37 (1912), p. 576.
42 Ibid., Vol. 37 (1912), p. 576.
43 Ibid., Vol. 38 (1913), p. 582.
44 Ibid., Vol. 39 (1914), p. 607.

had not only been no advance, but the Committee had been compelled to meet in only a few instances, and in those had successfully resisted any activity from the other side. Though judicial recall was agitated in fifteen or sixteen out of the forty legislatures in session, reports from states sounded an encouraging note to opponents of the measure. In Kansas, a constitutional amendment was adopted for recall of public officials, including judges, submitted under proposal of the legislature of 1913, for adoption by people at the general election in November, 1914, but this was the only state to be added during the year to those on the judicial recall list.[45]

In Minnesota, the constitutional amendment for recall of public officials including judges, proposed by the Legislature of 1913, was defeated at the election in November, 1914. An intensive campaign had been waged by the Bar Association, and prize arguments of a law school student and a high school student widely and effectually used. A bill, providing for a constitutional amendment for judicial recall, was introduced into the 1915 Massachusetts legislature, and it had received substantially no support. In North Dakota, the 1915 legislature had introduced a bill on judicial recall, which was killed in the House, quite a different result from that of two years before. In Colorado, there became apparent a large and growing sentiment in favor of repealing the constitutional amendment adopted in 1912, providing for recall of judges and recall of judicial decisions. The movement for judicial recall in Nevada had been turned into a movement to revoke recall of judges. In Illinois, the sentiment for judicial recall was expressed rather succintly in this way: "We have got done doing that sort of thing." The matter was not mentioned in the Montana state legislative assembly. New York presented a united front in opposition to judicial recall. Kentucky reported that it believed that judicial recall was dead. West

[45] Cf. supra, p. 143.

Virginia reported that criticism of courts had not yet led to demand for radical change of judicial recall, but for less drastic remedies. Missouri summarized the present situation in the country by commenting that no legislation had been passed and no attempt made at legislation in favor of judicial recall. The Committee concluded that though the issue was not dead, it was no longer dangerous.

Consternation was expressed at this time at the proposals of the American Judicature Society. Not only was the abolition of the election system of judges proposed, but the present method of retirement of judges through impeachment was to be supplemented. Right of removal was to be held not only on charges made and adjudicated by the state legislature and judicial council, but also on vote of the electorate after submission.[46]

By 1916, the strenuous work of the Committee seemed over. No measure providing for judicial recall had been passed by a state legislature during the year 1915-1916, and no proposal for such a measure had been submitted to the electorate of the state during that year. The effectiveness of the American Bar Association's program of education was apparent from the general understanding that seemed to prevail of the viciousness of judicial recall.[47]

The status of judicial recall legislation in 1917 remained as it had been; no further direct judicial recall measures either by legislative acts or constitutional amendments had been passed in any states nor had any of the existing acts or amendments been repealed.[48]

The Association at the 1917 meeting adopted a motion opposing the passage in Congress of the Federal Judge Retirement Bill, introduced by Senator Smith of Georgia. The bill provided in substance that if any federal judge at the age of seventy years, and with ten years previous service, did not resign on full pay as now allowed, the Presi-

---

[46] American Bar Association Report, Vol. 40 (1915), pp. 523-524.
[47] Ibid., Vol. 41 (1916), p. 555.
[48] Ibid., Vol. 42 (1917), p. 440.

dent could arbitrarily retire him and supplant him by appointment of another judge. The Bar here contended that this act infringed the federal constitutional provision that federal judges should hold their office during good behavior; that it was dangerous to introduce a phase of judicial recall by arbitrary power of the executive. At this same meeting, the Committee to oppose judicial recall expressed itself as opposed to the so-called "usurpation" view of judicial function to declare statutes unconstitutional, and also to the proposition that more than a majority of the members of a court must join in any decision invalidating an unconstitutional statute.[49]

It will be seen that the Committee, having successfully combated the judicial recall fallacy, endeavored to enlarge the scope of its activities. At the 1919 meeting, it claimed that during 1917, 1918, and 1919, it had fought all anti-constitutional and socialistic measures. The question arose as to whether these activities might not be outside the scope of the Committee's duties.[50] Whereupon, the Committee tried to get through a resolution condemning socialism in every form, but on opposition the blanket condemnation was not adopted, and the resolution as adopted read as formerly that organized opposition to judicial recall and allied measures be continued by maintenance of the Special Committee for that purpose.[51] With the danger of the spread of judicial recall averted, and the inability to enlarge its scope at the 1919 meeting, the activities of the Committee ceased.

(e) Machinery Used to Carry Out Program

Because of the urgency of the problem of judicial recall, and because it was widespread, the Committee appointed in August, 1911, consisted of one member from each state. However, a subcommittee or executive committee of

---

49 Ibid., Vol. 42 (1917), p. 442.
50 Ibid., Vol. 44 (1919), p. 65.
51 Ibid., Vol. 44 (1919), p. 89.

six was appointed.[52] The primary object of the Committee from its inception was to invite and procure the greatest degree of public discussion of the question of judicial recall, both by members of the Bar, and the public generally.[53]

A great number of addresses were delivered by prominent men, and afterwards published; many articles and pamphlets were written; by distribution through the press, these speeches and pamphlets were given wide publicity. Great public interest was evidenced by the fact that there was a great demand for literature. Many of the addresses were sent to members of the Committee, members of the American Bar Association, and legislators in certain states.[54]

Special campaigns were promoted wherever necessary. The writing and publication of various discussions in leading magazines, periodicals, and newspapers were encouraged and procured. Public discussion arose on numerous occasions and at various points in the United States. Where a direct contest was evident in a state or in a legislature, the Committee promoted and organized opposition, and in most instances it did this successfully. Various printed discussions were distributed throughout the United States and sent to leading newspapers, lawyers, citizens, libraries, officers, state and federal, and all federal and state judges and members of the legislature; three hundred and fifty thousand pamphlets were circulated. Beside covering all libraries in the United States, the Committee as part of its propaganda supplied anti-judicial recall literature to every student in every law school in the United States. It also furnished speakers and debaters before university groups, law schools, bar associations, economic clubs, and business men's associations.[55]

Concentration was placed on state legislatures, a strategic spot. It was emphasized that the fight in each case

[52] Ibid., Vol. 37 (1912), p. 52.
[53] Ibid., Vol. 37 (1912), p. 575.
[54] Ibid., Vol. 37 (1912), pp. 576ff.
[55] Ibid., Vol. 38 (1913), pp. 580ff.

must be made in the state legislature, where it was more practicable to demonstrate the fallacy of judicial recall by education of the representative few than to depend on a campaign before the entire electorate.

An instance of the manner in which the policy of the National Bar Association was adopted by the state and county groups is shown in the action taken in New York state. The New York Bar Association on request of the National Association called a special meeting April 13, 1912, at Albany, at which resolutions were unanimously adopted to condemn the doctrine of judicial recall. To secure action by the Bars of each county, a state committee of fifteen was appointed. This Committee began work at once by sending to the president of the county bar associations, to county judges and prominent lawyers, a letter reciting the action of the American Bar Association and the New York State Bar Association, and urging that something be done. The state committee of fifteen made report to the state bar association, and attached to report copies of resolutions passed in each county, and copies of local papers of each county containing full report of meeting and action taken. Necessity for publicity was stressed, and was appreciated as evidenced by mass of newspaper clippings attached to the reports. Greene County was among the counties that carried out its program in a masterly fashion, and its set of resolutions evidenced the effectiveness of the local bar association as guide-posts to public opinion. The Bar in thirty-two counties of New York state was persuaded to undertake the work which was publicized in such a way that the public knew that the lawyers were opposed to the attempt to cripple the judicial system.[56]

The object of all this activity was the spreading of a general propaganda of education to promote study and discussion of the arguments for and against judicial recall, and to show that judicial recall measures were subversive of our constitutional democracy.[57]

---

[56] Ibid., Vol. 38 (1913), pp. 589ff.
[57] Ibid., Vol. 39 (1914), p. 607.

The Chairman of the Committee acted with almost crusading zeal in addressing various legal and economic associations, personally initiating prize contests in law schools and high schools of Minnesota for the best arguments against judicial recall. These prize essays were published in full in leading papers in Minnesota.[58]

The campaign of the Committee against the judicial recall measure was a campaign of education through the distribution of literature and wide publicity by the press.[59] Through this active propaganda of education for a period of six years, the Committee claimed to have successfully combated all judicial recall attacks.[60]

To sum up, it may be said that the National Committee, working through the state and local associations, initiated and carried through a forceful program of education, by means of addresses, pamphlets, high school and college debates, newspaper articles, and other vehicles of propaganda, to the end that the popular wave for judicial recall might be checked.

(f) Results With Evaluation and Conclusions.

Dr. James Grafton Rogers in 1928 voiced the opinion that one of the great achievements of the American Bar Association was the war of Rome G. Brown and his committee against the movement for judicial recall during the years 1911-1919.[61] Certainly, in 1912, with Theodore Roosevelt as its standard bearer, the movement seemed sufficiently vigorous to sweep the entire country. Indeed, activity looking to adoption of judicial recall was found even in the conservative state of Massachusetts. In spite of all this, the Bar Association, through its effective technique of state and local committees with their corp of speakers, writers, and legislators, succeeded in checking and weakening the movement.

---

[58] Ibid., Vol. 39 (1914), p. 608.
[59] Ibid., Vol. 41 (1916), p. 554.
[60] Ibid., Vol. 42 (1917), p. 441.
[61] Ibid., Vol. 53 (1928), p. 525.

One constructive result of the organized bar's activity was the disclosure of defects in the administration of justice. In carrying through its campaign against judicial recall, it was early recognized that this movement must have had its origin somewhere, and this source was seen to be in evident defects in the administration of justice, such as delays and expense incident to trials in federal and many state courts. That the Bar felt its duty to take action on these defects is displayed by the fact that the Committee reported its belief that the Bar was taking an active part in remedying the defects, namely, judges of the Supreme Court of the United States had taken steps to reform rules of practice in the federal courts, and had called on the Bar of the country for suggestions; bar committees throughout the country had recommended simplification of practice so as to expedite business and save expense to litigants.[62]

Another salutary effect of the Bar's campaign against judicial review might be noted. Through publication of essays and the general school debates, a thorough and careful study of the subject had been induced among a large number of citizen voters.[63] In this campaign, the Bar showed itself true to its consistent policy of upholding the independence of the Judiciary and its potency in combating what it considered a dangerous popular movement.

2. SUPPORTED IMPROVEMENT IN PERSONNEL IN THE FIELD OF LAW ENFORCEMENT

Through its Section on Criminal Law, many projects for improvement of personnel in the field of law enforcement have been discussed. In 1927, in an address before a meeting of the Section devoted to psychiatry, Mr. William A. White recommended, inter alia, that district attorneys and judges should serve interneships in psychiatric clinics

62 Ibid., Vol. 37 (1912), p. 578.
63 Ibid., Vol. 38 (1914), p. 608.

and prisons.[64] Dr. Calvin Goddard, in an address before the Section in 1930, held up Germany and other European countries where the public prosecutor, after he receives his law degree, takes a year's post graduate work in legal medicine and in scientific police methods. Dr. Goddard suggested that similar training could be followed in this country with effective results.[65] Mr. Joseph A. Gerk suggested that the American Bar Association could be helpful in weeding out unethical and unscrupulous underworld lawyers.[66] The Joint Committee Report of 1931 submitted that the law schools could perform a useful function in the solution of the crime problem by informing law students of factors which contributed to present conditions and by considering means for correction or elimination.[67]

In recognition of inefficiency in the public service all down the line, including police, prosecuting attorneys, magistrates, jury commissioners, jurors, trial judges, prison officials, etc., the Section in 1931 recommended the establishment by the American Bar Association of a Committee to formulate practicable plans for the improvement of the personnel by which criminal law was administered.[68] When this recommendation was presented to the Bar Association, it was referred back to the Section.[69]

However, such a Committee on the Improvement of Personnel in Criminal Law Enforcement was organized in the spring of 1933. One meeting was held, at which members of the Committee, as individuals, felt that as a preliminary they might profitably study the desirability of establishing under state bar associations continuing commissions operating with judicial councils to study and report methods and defects in the enforcement of criminal law and means of improving administration. The Committee

---

64 Ibid., Vol. 52 (1927), p. 508.
65 Ibid., Vol. 55 (1930), pp. 567ff.
66 Ibid., Vol. 56 (1931), p. 500.
67 Ibid., Vol. 56 (1931), p. 518.
68 Ibid., Vol. 56 (1931), p. 524.
69 Ibid., Vol. 56 (1931), p. 309.

also encouraged the creation of local committees of associations of laymen, as well as lawyers, to foster better administration of existing law. Pending the recommendation of something more definite, the Committee suggested that the Association could inform the public of the value of trained administrators, upon whom law necessarily depends for operation.[70]

Mr. Charles L. Chute, Secretary of the National Probation Association of New York City, in 1932, presented as the greatest need of probation work, as well as of the entire court organization, a properly selected, trained, and non-political personnel, and advised that competitive examination in the hands of a competent civil service commission or other disinterested board was the only known means of avoiding politics.[71] It is only too evident that if probation and parole are to accomplish objectives to prevent delinquency and crime, something should be done to obtain well-trained social service workers as probation workers and officers.

The foregoing represents some effort on tne part of the organized Bar to study the vital, but difficult problem of obtaining a trained personnel for the administration of criminal justice.

3. REFORM IN JUDICIAL SELECTION AND TENURE

Aside from the need of the civil service for trained personnel, there is one branch of government that demands training of the highest type, and that is the judiciary. It is unfortunate that the judiciary should be under fire or that the administration of justice should be under criticism. Proposals for modernizing justice usually include unification of state courts, transfer of the rule-making authority to the courts, judicial councils, and reform in judicial selection and tenure. The records of the American Bar Associa-

---

70 Ibid., Vol. 58 (1933), pp. 526-527.
71 Ibid., Vol. 57 (1932), p. 606.

tion tend to show that all these proposals have been considered. That popular election of judges is in disrepute, and that judges are often chosen because of their availability rather than their capability are facts that are being more generally recognized. In an effort to sever partisan politics from the judiciary, appointment as the only possible method of selection is being advanced by the legal fraternity.

Organized bar activity in the field of the selection of judges dates back to 1921.[72] Since this problem is largely a local one, it is fitting that most of the activity should have been agitated and carried through by the Conference of Bar Association Delegates. In 1921 a resolution was adopted that the Conference recommend to state and local bar associations that they investigate the work of the New York, Detroit, St. Louis, and Kansas City bar associations in securing the nomination and election of fit judges.[73] Delegates from these associations and also from the Chicago Bar Association reported significant work in reference to securing better judges in their localities. The subject of the duty and responsibility of the Bar in the selection of judges was made the subject for discussion at one meeting in 1921. Mr. William D. Guthrie of New York explained how the New York legislature that year had repealed the law, which for ten years had provided for direct primaries for nomination of justices of the court of appeals and the supreme court. Mr. Amos C. Miller of Chicago presented the great victory of the Chicago Bar Association on June 6, 1921, when twenty judges of the circuit court, approved by the association, were elected against the opposition of the political faction. Mr. Miller, who was chairman of the bar committee, reported that the committee spent about $75,000, and used the money mainly in sending circular

---

72 Note, however, should be made of the fact that in 1913 the Committee on Jurisprudence and Law Reform considered methods of selection. See American Bar Association Report, Vol. 38 (1913), p. 469. Also, Ibid., Vol. 43 (1918), pp. 567-572.

73 Ibid., Vol. 46 (1921), p. 570.

letters to the voters. As a member of the Illinois Constitutional Convention, Mr. Miller had led a movement to avoid what was termed the absurdity of popular election of judges.[74]

In 1922 the scope of the Conference activities was extended by two resolutions, the first of which provided for a committee of five to assemble data to reveal methods by which bar associations might aid in securing the nomination and election of fit judges.[75] This Committee reported that it had found it difficult to secure data, doubtless owing to the fact that generally throughout the country state associations lacked the necessary solidarity and continuity of action necessary to influence judicial nomination and election effectively. Though only seventy-five associations had responded to the Committee's inquiries, it was concluded that the large city associations had done most of the pioneering in the field.[76]

In 1924 the Committee of the Conference made its second report setting forth considerable data concerning practical methods of selecting judges in New York, Cleveland, Detroit, Chicago, St. Louis, and other cities. The data showed how local bar associations assisted voters in choosing proper judicial candidates in primaries and election. This report was published in the American Bar Association Journal for November, 1924. The Committee, from the data which it had collected, understood that popularly elected judges were admitted in many instances to yield unsatisfactory results in large cities, and it was felt that no present prospect of improvement could come from any other source than the bar; where popular election operated satisfactorily, its success was due to the fact that the bar's influence was preponderant. The recommendation was adopted that the Committee be continued to gather more information and disseminate facts.[77] To this end, the Chair-

---

74 Ibid., Vol. 46 (1921), pp. 573-576.
75 Ibid., Vol. 47 (1922), p. 597.
76 Ibid., Vol. 48 (1923), p. 550.
77 Ibid., Vol. 49 (1924), pp. 574-575.

man of the Conference appointed a delegate from each state bar association who would work with the Committee on Judicial Selection of the Conference to the end that there would be established in each state association a committee on judicial selection.[78] It should be noted that this was one of the earlier developments of machinery that made the later National Bar Program of 1933 possible.

In 1926 the Chairman reported that he had succeeded in adding to his Committee a member from each state bar association as a step toward inducing state and larger local associations to create committees on the subject, and enter actively on the work of guiding voters in respect to judicial elections; that several associations had already acted.[79] In its report for 1927, it submitted the state of affairs throughout the country, which indicated that there was a steady trend toward the assumption by the organized Bar of a duty of aiding voters in the selection of judges. In 1932 a resolution was adopted that the Conference through its Committee should report on various ways of selecting judges now in use or proposed, and indicate its preference. A debate on the subject of the best method of selecting judges was staged at the 1933 conference. Mr. Julius Henry Cohen of New York spoke in favor of the executive appointment of judges; Mr. Joseph F. O'Connell of Boston presented the matter of direct election of judges. The effect of bar primaries on the selection of proper judicial candidates was the subject of a paper, on which there was informal debate. As stated above, the subject of selection of judges was listed as one of the four subjects of the National Bar Program in 1933, and again listed in 1934 and 1935. The 1935 January issue of the American Bar Association Journal announced the publication of a Handbook on Judicial Selection, but upon application being made for a copy, reply was received that "The printing and distribution of The Handbook on Judicial Selection has been un-

---

78 Ibid., Vol. 50 (1925), pp. 656 and 79.
79 Ibid., Vol. 51 (1926), p. 674.

avoidably postponed." The Pennsylvania State Bar Association in December, 1935, through its Judiciary Committee, reported that it was then engaged in a study of the methods of selecting all judges learned in the law in the courts of Pennsylvania.

At the 1936 meeting of the American Bar Association, the Assembly asked the House of Delegates to create a Special Committee on the subject of Selection of Judges, and the House promptly complied. The Assembly also reaffirmed Canon 28 relating to standard of judicial conduct, and the House unanimously adopted the measure.[80]

Though activity of the Bar Association in this field of selection and tenure of judges dates back to 1921, it does not appear to have progressed beyond the stage of study and investigation, though interest in the problem is unquestionably increasing. Some local bar associations have developed some degree of effective control,[81] and others, stimulated by the National Bar Program, are in process of facing and acting on the problem.[82] Because the courts and court personnel are being criticized, the organized Bar would show wisdom in more definitely shouldering the responsibility and attempting a solution.

When one studies the Bar's influence in this field of selection and tenure of judges, one is amazed that so little has been done on an acute problem where the lawyer's influence could and should be positive and decisive. The surprising thing is not that, with the standards and machinery developed for selection of judges, the resulting personnel should be deficient, but that it is not worse. Though the judiciary leaves much to be desired, it is the one branch of government where training of some kind is found; exception should be noted in the case of the minor judiciary,

---

80 Legal Intelligencer, October 21, 1936, p. 4 (Vol. 95, No. 94).

81 For example, in Cleveland. See 12 Journal American Judicature Society, p. 178 (1929).

82 For example, California passed a Constitutional Amendment recently providing for appointment of Judges by Governor with confirmation by Board and subsequent check by the electorate. See American Bar Association Journal, May, 1935, p. 308.

where little training is required. However, as stated above, the judiciary is the one branch of government which demands the highest training and absolute divorce from politics. Most of the studies reveal, and all debates revolve around two possibilities for selection of judges: (1) popular selection, seemingly in disrepute with lawyers of the present day, and (2) appointment,[83] often called undemocratic and un-American. Sometimes, as in the case of Cleveland and other large cities, local bar associations aid by submitting lists of those considered fit candidates. Since both of these methods for the selection of judges have been condemned, a middle course is submitted that a judicial council of impartial experts in the administration of justice be utilized not only to develop rules of practice and procedure, but to assume also the responsibility of obtaining the highest type of well-trained and efficient judges for judicial office, either by nomination from a list submitted by the Bar Association, or from an initial list of its own. Standards for the Bench should obviously be higher; the candidate for judicial office should not only have the training of the lawyer, but he should have supplementary training in government and law. Popular selection could no longer endanger the soundness and integrity of the Bench, if popular selection was circumscribed to a list submitted by the judicial council. Nomination could be made by the judicial council, assisted if found necessary, by the state or local bar association. The recommendation of appointment from selected lists furnished by the judicial council has been made in Dade County, Florida. The recommendation here is for selection by the electorate from judicial council lists.

While trained personnel in all departments of government is essential, it is indispensable in that of the judiciary. There should also be longer tenure of office to insure in-

---

[83] For ramifications of appointment, see article by Paul H. Sanders, "Appointment of Judges—an Analysis of Current Proposals," American Bar Association Journal, February, 1936, pp. 131-136.

dependence; all connection of the judiciary with politics or even the suspicion of such connection should be severed. No democratic government is possible without an efficient administration of justice, and this cannot be achieved unless there is a highly trained Bar and a more highly trained Bench. Judges should be selected by those who know something of the character and capacity of those chosen and of the problems involved in a fair and effective administration of justice. The new concept of democracy should be put into practice; the electorate should no longer be asked to do something which it can only do in theory and which in practice is done by the political organization, sometimes corrupt. This new concept of democracy would leave power of control in the electorate, but to a limited degree. To free judges from political control election by the people could be continued, but selection would be limited to lists submitted by a trained group such as the judicial council. Tenure should be lengthy, probably life. There is need for a highly trained and independent judiciary if legal problems of the present and future are to be solved, and constitutional government is to survive.

C. PRACTICE AND PROCEDURE

1. GENERAL LEGISLATION

Practice and procedure is the particular province of lawyers, and in this highly technical field, the organized Bar should be able to make a real contribution to the solution of the many problems. The American Bar Association has consistently favored the enlargement of the powers of judges and courts, and just as consistently opposed any attempt on the part of Congress to curtail the powers of judges and courts. The work in this field of procedural reform has largely been done by the Committee on Jurisprudence and Law Reform, which was first appointed in 1878 at the organization meeting of the Association. Later, in 1919, it absorbed the Special Committee to Suggest Remedies and Formulate Proposed Laws to Prevent Delay and Unnecessary Cost in Litigation, which latter Committee, created in 1907,[84] had, according to report made in 1923,[85] worked for the improvement of civil procedure, and had many judicial reforms to its credit.[86]

---

84 American Bar Association Report, Vol. 52 (1927), pp. 293, passim.

85 Ibid., Vol. 48 (1923), pp. 325ff.

86 For Example: (1) The Technical Errors Bill, which became law by Act approved February 26, 1919, C. 48 (Barnes Federal Code Supplement, Section 1043, p. 63), recommended by Committee in its first report in 1908, and fully considered in reports of 1910-1912. A bill similar in form has been adopted in 25 states.

(2) The taking of testimony in equity cases in open court, which practice had already been adopted in many circuits in admiralty cases and the Supreme Court; by Equity Rule 46, the practice was adopted in equity cases.

(3) Abuse of taking an appeal from a final decision in cases of habeas corpus, and thus causing delay in the execution of criminal sentence, was in 1907 a serious grievance. The 1908 and 1909 reports urged allowance of appeal by the Court by which final decision was rendered or by a Justice of the Supreme Court. This was required by Act of March 10, 1908, C. 76, 35 Statutes 40; recommendation cited that certificate be required in all cases of appeal to the Supreme Court in habeas corpus proceedings. The Act adopted was limited to cases where detention was through process of state court.

(4) Reduction of Fees for Record on Appeal. Report of 1909 dealt with this; it recommended an act reducing the charge for certifying records on such appeals. Bill was amended in Congress, and as amended was signed February 13, 1911, C. 47, Barnes Federal Code, Section 1395.

(5) Distinction between law and equity, and delay and injustice caused by attorney bringing suit on wrong side of court. Another cause of delay and expense was requirement that equitable defense to action at law could only be set up by filing bill in equity. Reforms in these respects were recommended by the Committee in every year from 1909 to 1912; both reforms were effected by Act of March 3, 1915, C. 90, 38 Statutes 956. The Act added 3 sections to the Judicial Code numbered 274-a, 274-b, and 274-c.

(6) In 1911 the Committee recommended that authority to the Supreme Court to review judgments of state courts in constitutional cases should be extended; this was done by the Act of September 6, 1916, C. 448 (39 Statutes 726, Barnes Federal Code, Section 1002).

(7) In 1909, the Committee recommended consolidation of the district and circuit courts; in 1910 Dean Roscoe Pound, then a member of the Committee, gave an admirable statement of rules which should regulate reform of practice. One of these rules was the con-

From its inception the American Bar Association seems to have adhered to a policy of opposing any movement or legislation which tended to abridge or limit the discretionary powers of the United States federal court judges in any way. In 1916, 1918, and 1920, the Committee on Jurisprudence and Law Reform dealt with bills pending in Congress, which would take from the trial judge the right to express an opinion on or deal in any way with questions of fact. A bill restraining the power of federal judges was introduced in Congress [87] and passed the House. The bill was considered by the Judicial Committee of the Senate, and reported adversely by that Committee. The Bar Committee was informed that further action by the Senate was improbable. A similar bill [88] was introduced into the Senate, and referred to the Judiciary Committee; both bills were reported adversely to the Senate April 12, 1920.[89]

In 1916, a bill was pending which would have taken from the judges of the federal courts the right to appoint clerks of court; the Bar Committee was instructed to oppose the bill, and did so successfully.[90] In 1924 this Committee reported that most emphatic efforts had been made by it in opposition to the bill to abridge the power of the

solidation of the courts into one court; the consolidation of the circuit court and district court was effected by Chapter I of the Judicial Code, approved March 3, 1911.

(8) Great reform in business of administration was effected by the Act of September 14, 1922, C. 308, Section 2 (42 Statutes 838, Barnes Federal Code, Supplement, p. 64). The act provides for a conference the last Monday of September in Washington or at such other times and places in the United States as the Chief Justice may designate. The act as finally passed was drawn by the Chief Justice.

(9) In 1909, the Committee recommended that all official fees in the administration of justice should be paid into the Treasury and not retained by officials; reform as far as it related to the fees of clerks in the United States courts, was adopted by Act of February 26, 1919, C. 49 (48 Statutes 1182, Supplement Barnes Federal Code, p. 65). Under the act, the clerks were paid salaries in lieu of fees.

(10) Committee recommended the removal of cases from state to federal courts; conflict of decisions serious. See American Bar Association Report, Vol. 48 (1923), pp. 325-331.

87 H.R. 3171, 1920.

88 Bill S. 228.

89 American Bar Association Report, Vol. 45 (1920), pp. 265-268.

90 Ibid., Vol. 48 (1923), p. 335.

United States judges in the conduct of jury trials. In 1925 the Committee reported that until 1924, its opposition had been successful in preventing the adoption of these bills in either House; that before the last annual report, the Caraway Bill had been favorably reported by the Judiciary Committee of the Senate and passed; that in the House, the Judiciary Committee made a substitution for the Senate Bill, and then reported the measure to the House under the Senate number; that only the crowded condition of the calendar prevented the bill from being passed in the House.[91] In 1926 the Committee reported that several bills, differing somewhat from the Caraway Bill [92] in detail, but predicated on the substantial curtailment of the power of judges, were introduced into the Senate. Hearings were accorded representatives of the Bar Committee before the subcommittee of the Judiciary Committee; from information received, the Committee believed that the bill would not be taken out of that session of Congress.[93] In 1927 the Committee was instructed to oppose the Caraway Bill or similar measures.[94] In 1928 the Committee was again instructed to oppose the Caraway Bill [95] or any bill having the same purpose.[96] In 1929 the Committee reported that it had continued its opposition to all legislation radically limiting the jurisdiction of the federal courts or decreasing its power; that it had prevented the enactment of the Caraway Bill,[97] limiting power of the federal judges to comment on the testimony in jury trials.[98]

Under the policy of opposing any limitation of the jurisdiction and power of courts, the Committee on Jurisprudence and Law Reform was authorized by resolution of the Executive Committee, adopted April 24, 1928, in the name

[91] Ibid., Vol. 50 (1925), p. 410.
[92] S. 455, H.R. 3918.
[93] American Bar Association Report, Vol. 51 (1926), p. 430.
[94] Ibid., Vol. 52 (1927), p. 308.
[95] S. 1094.
[96] American Bar Association Report, Vol. 53 (1928), pp. 102, 424.
[97] S. 1094, S. 374, 71st Congress.
[98] American Bar Association Report, Vol. 54 (1929), p. 374.

of the Association to oppose the passage of any bills intended to diminish the power and to limit the jurisdiction of the federal courts. Under the power granted, the Committee opposed the passage of three bills:

(1) The Caraway Bill, limiting the power of trial judges, discussed above and opposed by the Association for many years.

(2) Norris Bill,[99] which sought to amend paragraph (1) of section 24 of the Judicial Code (section 41, United States Code), by taking from the United States district courts jurisdiction in diverse citizenship cases. Committee under authority vested in it by resolution of the Executive Committee deemed it necessary to record its opposition to the bill by transmitting to each member of the Senate, (a) copy of resolution of the Executive Committee; (b) resolution of this Committee as part thereof, and (c) statement setting forth in detail the damaging effects of the proposed amendment; copy of said resolutions and statement were printed in full in the Congressional Record for May 8, 1928, and was annexed to Committee's report as Appendix A. This Norris Bill evoked from all parts of the country many protests from the bar and press.

(3) Shipstead Bill, the purpose of which was to limit the scope of injunctions in labor disputes. On this, the Chairman of the Committee addressed a letter to the Chairman of the Judiciary Committee of the United States Senate, which letter was attached to report as Appendix B.[100]

Opposition to all legislation radically limiting jurisdiction of the federal courts or decreasing their powers was continued.[101] In 1930 Committee reported that, according to instructions of the Association, it had advised the Judiciary Committee of the Senate of its opposition to the so-

---

[99] Norris Bill, S. 3151.

[100] American Bar Association Report, Vol. 53 (1928), pp. 420 and 424-428.

[101] Ibid., Vol. 54 (1929), pp. 373-374.

called Norris Bill taking away jurisdiction of the federal courts in cases of diverse citizenship.[102] In 1931 the Committee reported that no legislation opposed by the Bar Association had been enacted by Congress; that the Committee had opposed and would continue its opposition to all legislation radically limiting the jurisdiction of the federal courts or decreasing power thereof, adhering to the 1929 and 1930 instructions; that several bills had been introduced in the recent Congress taking away right of removal to federal courts on the ground of diverse citizenship, and that such bills had attracted considerable attention and aroused bitter opposition. One bill, vouched for by Attorney General Mitchell, provided that a corporation doing business in one state should not be entitled to remove a suit between itself and citizens of the state where it carried on business to the federal court on the ground of diversity of citizenship, although organized under the laws of another state. This amendment to section 24 of the Judicial Code, suggested by the Attorney General,[103] was introduced January 19, 1931. In order that careful study might be made of this proposition to limit jurisdiction of the federal courts, a subcommittee was appointed. The subcommittee thus appointed, after study, was divided in its opinions, the majority opposing the bill of the Attorney General, and the minority favoring such legislation; the majority opinion was adopted, and the Association declared its initial policy of opposing any limitation of the jurisdiction of the federal courts.[104]

The Committee in 1932 reported that, in obedience to orders of the Association formally embodied in official resolution, it had been compelled to devote substantially all its available time and energy in an effort to preserve federal jurisdiction in controversies between citizens of dif-

---

102 Ibid., Vol. 55 (1930), pp. 455 and 456.

103 Embodied in H.R. 16344.

104 American Bar Association Report, Vol. 57 (1932), pp. 99-117, 506-511.

ferent states. The Chairman of the Committee at the personal request of the President of the American Bar Association appeared before the subcommittee of the Judiciary Committee of the Senate in opposition to the enactment of legislation destroying or impairing jurisdiction of the federal courts. Nevertheless, the bill,[105] eliminating entirely federal jurisdiction in controversies between citizens of different states, was unanimously and favorably reported to the Senate, was then on the calendar, and would come to a vote during the short session that winter. Similar bills restricting the power of the federal courts were introduced in the House. At the request of the Committee, the Judiciary Committee of the House granted a hearing on all bills of similar character as well as upon bill increasing the jurisdictional amount in removal cases from $3,000 to $7,000. The Chairman and one other member of the Committee appeared on behalf of the American Bar Association in opposition to these bills. The hearing lasted the entire day and the Judiciary Committee of the House refused a favorable report on all the bills. Separate briefs were prepared and filed with the Judiciary Committees of the Senate and House.

At this 1932 meeting, because of the great conflict of opinion that existed among the members of the Association, the resolution giving the Committee the power to oppose "all" legislation radically limiting the jurisdiction of federal courts or decreasing the power thereof, despite the fact that such power had been given since 1928, was referred back to the Committee for further consideration. However, the Committee was empowered to oppose particular bills or measures, namely, the Norris Bill destroying federal jurisdiction in diverse citizenship cases, the bill increasing the present jurisdictional amount of $3,000 in diverse citizenship cases, the Attorney General's bill respecting corporations, and the bill [106] taking away from

[105] S. 939.
[106] S. 3243.

federal district courts jurisdiction to interfere by injunction with orders of state administrative boards affecting rates chargeable by public utilities.[107]

The Committee in 1933, in the Association's restatement and declaration of its established policy, was once more given a blanket authorization to oppose any and all legislation limiting the power of the federal courts.[108] This same resolution was adopted in 1934. At this meeting and in 1935, a resolution was also carried to oppose laws which seek to increase requirement of jurisdictional amount of federal court from $3,000.[109]

Resolutions were also adopted that restrictions of the jurisdiction of the United States district court on claims brought by holders of policies of insurance under the World War Veterans Act be abolished; that when the federal government has entered into business, and contracted with citizens of the United States, the federal district court should be the proper place to settle all disputes; that the Association urged the repeal of all portions of the National Economy Act of March 20, 1933, which limited the jurisdiction of the United States district courts over contracts of insurance.[110]

In addition to this movement in Congress to limit the jurisdiction of the federal courts in cases of diverse citizenship, there has been another to limit the power of the court to grant injunctions. The subject of injunction was dealt with by the Committee on Jurisprudence and Law Reform in 1913 and 1914.[111] On January 31, 1922, a bill [112] was introduced by Mr. Bacharach of New Jersey, and referred to the Judiciary Committee of the House. The action that

---

107 American Bar Association Report, Vol. 57 (1932), pp. 506 and 101.

108 Ibid., Vol. 58 (1933), p. 107.

109 Ibid., Vol. 59 (1934), p. 73, and Vol. 60 (1935), pp. 215 and 489.

110 Ibid., Vol. 59 (1934), p. 486.

111 Ibid., Vol. 38 (1913), pp. 555, 561, and 575, also Vol. 49 (1914), pp. 578-585.

112 H.R. 10,212.

the Committee took to oppose this bill was approved by the Association. Three hearings had been held on the bill; at the first, Mr. Harriman, a member of the Association Committee, attended, and pointed out objections; the Chairman also presented a similar statement.[113] In 1923 it was reported that under instruction of Association, the Committee had opposed successfully several bills prejudicial to the administration of justice.[114] In 1928 Committee was instructed to oppose the so-called Shipstead Bill,[115] limiting the scope of injunctions in labor disputes, the effect of which would be to limit equity jurisdiction of the federal courts so as to prohibit them from issuing injunctions except for damage to property, and then only when property was tangible and transferable, and to oppose any bill of similar import.[116]

The Committee, in 1929, reported that up to that time it had prevented the enactment of the Shipstead Bill[117] as amended.[118] However, just three years later (1932), the Committee reported that when Congress had under consideration the so-called Anti-Injunction Bill, taking away from federal courts the power to issue injunctions in labor disputes in certain cases, it had submitted a formal written statement of the position of the American Bar Association in opposition to legislation of that character; that the method used had not been satisfactory or adequate, as the bill had been passed, and was then a law.[119] One cited weakness called attention to the fact that, when amendments or changes were made in the original bill, the Committee had not been able definitely to state that the Bar Association had taken action on the particular bill, and could simply call the attention of the Judiciary Committee

---

113 American Bar Association Report, Vol. 47 (1922), pp. 360-362.
114 Ibid., Vol. 48 (1923), p. 335.
115 S. 1482.
116 American Bar Association Report, Vol. 53 (1928), p. 420.
117 S. 1482.
118 American Bar Association Report, Vol. 54 (1929), p. 374.
119 Ibid., Vol. 57 (1932), p. 506.

of the Senate and House to the opposition of the Association to the general principle of restricting federal court jurisdiction in certain matters; that this had definitely weakened whatever influence the Association had with the Committees and Congress.[120]

In the field of public utilities, there was another movement, which sought to curtail the jurisdiction of the federal courts, but this will be discussed later under the particular heading of "Public Utilities." [121]

Although the Association had thus consistently opposed all efforts to curtail powers of the federal courts, it has also taken a positive stand in relation to simplification of practice and procedure. As an example of this, its efforts to carry through a reform to simplify procedure on appeal to the Supreme Court by abolishing writs of errors and thus limiting right of review to appeal (review as of right) or certiorari (review permitted and allowed by Court) should be considered.

The Committee on Jurisprudence and Law Reform in 1920 began a study of the right of review, whether sought by writ of error, appeal, or certiorari, but in view of the passage of the Act of February 26, 1919 (Technical Errors Bill), drawn and sponsored by the Association, it hoped that the Supreme Court would find a way to adopt a Rule of Court to remove grievances. Until the Court had had an opportunity to deal with the subject, the Committee did not desire to recommend legislation.[122] In 1921 the Committee reported that on the frequent occasions on which

---

[120] Ibid., Vol. 57 (1932), p. 99. Another source of weakness might be noted. The Philadelphia Bar Association at a special meeting held March 18, 1932, defeated recommendation of its Committee that the Association oppose the Norris-LaGuardia Bill, which proposed, inter alia, to limit effect of yellow dog contracts and curb injunctive powers of federal courts in labor disputes. Action of the Association was sent to the President and the Attorney General. Minutes, Philadelphia Bar Association, pp. 261-265 (H11578). By this action, the Philadelphia Bar Association, a strong county association, did not support the American Bar Association in its opposition to the Anti-Injunction Bill.

[121] Infra, pp. 217-220.

[122] American Bar Association Report, Vol. 45 (1920), p. 263.

the Supreme Court had been called on to decide whether or not writ of error, appeal, or certiorari was the proper remedy to obtain review, the Court was disposed to look on the subject as determined by statute, and not subject to modification by Rule of Court, and therefore the Committee had concluded that further legislation was necessary, which proposed legislation was appended to the report as Bill F.[123] In 1922, report was made that bill, abolishing writs of error and giving remedy by appeal in cases where there was a right of review, had been amended by the Judiciary Committee of the Senate, and as amended had been favorably reported; copy of bill was annexed to report as Exhibit "C." [124]

The Committee in 1923 reported that since the adoption of the Judiciary Act early in our history questions had arisen as to when review should be sought by writ of error and when by appeal. The Committee had recommended in 1921 and 1922 that writs of error be abolished and only appeal used. The Act of September 14, 1923, provided that when appeal or writ of error was taken to or issued out of the wrong court, it should not be dismissed but should be transferred to the proper court. The Committee admitted that this was a reform, but did not accomplish the result at which the Committee aimed, and it therefore renewed its recommendation in favor of the bill for abolition of writs of error and substitution of the remedy by appeal, said bill being attached and marked "B." [125] In 1924, the Committee reported that such a bill [126] had been introduced into the Senate by Senator Walsh, and had passed the Senate May 15, 1924; in the House, the bill [127] had not yet been reported.[128] In 1925 it was reported that the bill had passed the House, but before being sent to the President,

[123] Ibid., Vol. 46 (1921), p. 396.
[124] Ibid., Vol. 47 (1922), p. 356.
[125] Ibid., Vol. 48 (1923), p. 332.
[126] S. 2693.
[127] H.R. 5566.
[128] American Bar Association Report, Vol. 49 (1924), p. 342.

the Chairman of the House Judiciary Committee had the measure recalled to the House.[129] On April 26, 1926, the Bar Committee submitted a substitute measure before the Senate Committee. Then without the knowledge or cooperation of the Bar Committee, the bill in its original form [130] unexpectedly passed both Houses of Congress and was signed by the President. After its enactment, numerous difficulties were suggested, which difficulties would have been obviated if Committee's substitute measure had been enacted. The Committee sought to correct the situation by a bill [131] and were successful in securing its passage.[132]

In 1920 the Committee on Jurisprudence and Law Reform commenced its long campaign for the passage of a Federal Declaratory Judgments Act, which would provide for a decision in a controversy before violation of the contract or suit for damages. Activities for the passage of this act show something of the way a technical piece of legislation is drafted and passed. The Committee in 1920 recommended the adoption of an act by Congress amending the Judicial Code by adding after 274-c a new Section providing for declaratory judgments, which recommendation was approved.[133] In 1921 it was reported that the Conference of Commissioners on Uniform State Laws had taken up the subject of a Uniform Declaratory Judgments Act for the states.[134] In drawing the federal bill, recommended to the Association August, 1920, the language of the English act had been followed, which act had been in force upwards of fifty years. The argument was presented that the jurisdiction of the federal court was more strictly defined and limited by the Constitution and Statutes than the English Court of Chancery was restricted, and that,

---

[129] Ibid., Vol. 50 (1925), p. 409.

[130] S. 1801.

[131] H.R. 12,441.

[132] American Bar Association Report, Vol. 51 (1926), pp. 429-430, also Vol. 52 (1927), p. 308, and also Vol. 53 (1928), p. 423.

[133] Ibid., Vol. 45 (1920), p. 260.

[134] Ibid., Vol. 46 (1921), pp. 311, 349-353.

therefore, the bill should insert an affirmative grant of power. The bill recommended to the Association in 1920 had been amended and introduced in the present Congress, and annexed to the 1921 report and marked "C." No hearing had been had on the bill, but it had been referred to a subcommittee. The Committee on Jurisprudence and Law Reform recommended that the bill should be so amended that it would take the form appended as "D," and thus only apply "in case of actual controversy." [135] An amended bill [136] was annexed to the report in 1922 as Exhibit "A." It was introduced in the House, and also considered at hearings before the Judiciary Committee of the Senate February 29, 1922, and before the Judiciary Committee of the House the following day. Some of the Senators pointed out that by legislation in some states or by local practice, some of the objects of the bill could be obtained under existing practice. The Bar Committee showed the Senators the many beneficial purposes subserved under the Declaratory Judgments Act not now available; brief statement of the benefits were annexed to report and marked "B." [137] The 1923 report annexed a list of cases in which English courts had given relief, and also annexed bill approved in 1922. It was noted that the bill had been carefully drawn so as to guard against the objection that the courts of the United States had no power to render judgments in purely hypothetical cases. Hearing had been held on the bill, but no vote taken. The recommendation was adopted that the Committee be continued to advocate the passage of the bill.[138] In 1924 the Committee reported that it had caused to be introduced into Congress five bills, one of which authorized the federal courts to render declaratory judgments in all cases of actual controversy as to legal rights of the parties before actual breach had occurred giving cause of

---

[135] Ibid., Vol. 46 (1921), p. 386.

[136] Embodied in H.R. 10143.

[137] American Bar Association Report, Vol. 47 (1922), p. 356.

[138] Ibid., Vol. 48 (1923), p. 333.

action. The House Bill,[139] introduced by George S. Graham, Chairman of Judiciary Committee, had not yet been reported in the House; in the Senate, fear was expressed that the measure might be perverted to monopolistic purposes. Thereupon, the Committee drafted an additional clause that the act should not be construed to give the court jurisdiction to determine whether or not a proposed contract or combination was illegal under the Anti-Trust laws.[140] At the 1925 meeting, it was reported that sometime prior to the former annual meeting, the Association had had a hearing before the Judiciary Committee of the Senate and House. A majority of the Bar Committee attended this hearing. After a thorough discussion, no opposition developed except before the Senate Committee where the necessity for the measure was questioned. The Bar Committee had continued its efforts to procure the passage of bill by submitting briefs and by correspondence, but appeared to have made no progress, as the bill had remained in the two Judiciary Committees. Report was made, however, of progress in the states. Since the adoption of the Uniform Declaratory Judgments Act in 1928 by the Conference of Commissioners on Uniform State Laws, seventeen states had passed such legislation.[141] The Bar Committee received authority to promote the passage of the federal bill authorizing declaratory judgments.[142] In 1926 report was made that bill[143] authorizing declaratory judgments had been advocated by a member of the Bar Association's Committee before the Judiciary Committee of the House at a hearing March 25, 1926; that bill had since been favorably reported. A similar bill[144] had been in-

---

139 H.R. 5194.

140 American Bar Association Report, Vol. 49 (1924), pp. 71-72 and 341.

141 Ibid., Vol. 50 (1925), p. 103, for list of states; by 1935, 25 states had approved the act; Pennsylvania passed the Uniform Declaratory Judgments Act in 1923.

142 Ibid., Vol. 50 (1925), pp. 106 and 408.

143 H.R. 5365.

144 S. 615.

troduced in the Senate, and on April 29, 1936, a hearing had been held before the subcommittee of the Judiciary Committee of the Senate, at which seven members of the Committee appeared in support of the measure. Authority was given to continue to promote the passage of the bill.[145]

In 1927 it was reported that since no progress had been made in the Senate, and no action had been taken in the House after favorable report of its Committee, the bill had to be reintroduced.[146]

In 1928 report was made that bill [147] had passed the House; that hearing on the bill had been held before a subcommittee of the Judiciary Committee of the Senate April 27, 1928, which hearing was attended by a number of members of the Bar Committee. This subcommittee was convinced of the utility of the proposed measure, but doubted that the Courts could be vested with authority to render declaratory judgments under the Constitution.[148]

In 1929 it was reported that the Bar Committee had consistently urged the passage of the law; that former Chairman of the Committee, H. W. Taft, Esq., on April 27, 1928, made argument in favor of the bill [149] before the Judiciary Committee of the Senate, and was supported by other members of the Bar Committee, namely, Governor Montague and Professor E. M. Borchard of Yale. However the bill failed of passage. The Committee was empowered to continue work for its enactment. No report was made in 1930, except that the Committee recommended the enactment of the Declaratory Judgment Law in cases of actual controversy.[150] No further bar association reports were made in reference to action on the Declaratory Judgments Act, but an act of Congress, authorizing fed-

145 American Bar Association Report, Vol. 51 (1926), pp. 108 and 428.

146 Ibid., Vol. 52 (1927), p. 307.

147 H.R. 5623.

148 American Bar Association Report, Vol. 53 (1928), pp. 422-423.

149 H.R. 5623.

150 American Bar Association Report, Vol. 55 (1930), pp. 66 and 454.

eral courts to render declaratory judgments, after passing the House four times, was adopted by the Senate June 6 and 9, 1934, and approved by the President, June 14, 1934.[151]

The Association not only opposed curtailment of the jurisdiction of federal courts and of the power of judges, but also objected to the limitations of lawyers' activities and fees. In 1934, through its Committee on Jurisprudence and Law Reform, the Association went on record as opposed to the enactment of a bill [152] which proposed to prevent lawyers from appearing in claims against the government or any of its administrative bodies and from charging a fee in excess of $5,000 or 20 per cent of amount recovered. The bill required the lawyers to file with a government official their fee contract, and provided a fine for violation.[153]

The Committee on Jurisprudence and Law Reform and its predecessor, the Special Committee to Suggest Remedies and Formulate Proposed Laws to Prevent Delay and Unnecessary Cost in Litigation, appear to have been largely concerned with legislation respecting judicial administration.[154] In one year, 1927-1928, it was reported that twenty-

---

[151] Borchard, E. M., Declaratory Judgments, p. 246 (1934).

[152] S. 2805 and H.R. 8170.

[153] American Bar Association Report, Vol. 59 (1934), p. 486.

[154] In addition to activities enumerated, the Committee on Jurisprudence and Law Reform in 1886 approved a bill providing for preparation of a Federal Code of Procedure to regulate both civil and criminal procedure. (American Bar Association Report, Vol. 9 (1886), pp. 75, 81, 551, and Ibid., Vol. 10 (1885), pp. 28 and 315-320). Note should be made of an early effort at codification of the law, known in bar association circles as the great fight on codification. In 1884 a Committee on Delay and Uncertainty in the Law was appointed on which Committee Hon. David Dudley Field, ardent proponent of codification, served. In 1885 it was reported, inter alia, that the law should not be made by judges. The remedy proposed was embodied in a resolution: "The law itself should be reduced as far as possible to the form of a Statute." Action on the resolution was postponed. American Bar Association Report, Vol. 8 (1885), pp. 83 and 323-364. In 1886 after extended debate the Resolution was amended thus: "The law itself should be reduced so far as its substantive principles are settled to the form of a statute." The amended resolution was adopted, and as John Hinckley, former Secretary of the Association, aptly put it, "Peace prevailed, and nothing more was done." Ibid.,

four bills had had the attention of the Committee. The Committee found it possible to become involved in all this intricate legislation because it had one member residing in Washington, who made it his business to follow such bills as were introduced in Congress affecting the Bar of the country either advantageously or to the contrary.[155] The consensus of opinion, expressed in 1932, was that the American Bar Association should establish a closer contact with the great law committees of Congress, with a view to securing the best possible legislation.[156]

The great obstacle encountered in Congress in pressing bills recommended by the Association was reported to be indifference. Cooperation of every member of the Association in urging members of Congress to heed repeated recommendations of the Association was continually asked. It was stated that lawyers were unjustly censured for defects in administration of justice, and yet no profession had done as much for its improvement.[157]

Vol. 9 (1886), pp. 11-74, and American Bar Association Journal, July, 1935, pp. 454-455.

The Committee on Jurisprudence and Law Reform also sponsored legislation to provide for removal of causes to the District Court of United States for the proper district when defendant or defendants are nonresidents of a state: (American Bar Association Report, Vol. 45 (1920), pp. 59 and 259; Ibid., Vol. 46 (1921), p. 384; Ibid., Vol. 47 (1922), pp. 357 and 366; Ibid., Vol. 48 (1923), p. 329). Also to provide for removal of case from state to district court. (American Bar Association Report, Vol. 53 (1928), pp. 419 and 428; Ibid., Vol. 54 (1929), p. 376.) Committee also advocated the appointment of an official stenographer in the federal court. (American Bar Association Report, Vol. 34 (1909), pp. 585, 605, 608; Ibid., Vol. 35 (1910), pp. 622-623; Ibid., Vol. 47 (1922), p. 358; Ibid., Vol. 48 (1923), p. 333; Ibid., Vol. 50 (1925), p. 408; Ibid., Vol. 51 (1926), p. 429; Ibid., Vol. 52 (1927), p. 307; Ibid., Vol. 53 (1928), p. 423; Ibid., Vol. 54 (1929), p. 375; Ibid., Vol. 55 (1930), pp. 67 and 454.)

In 1927, the Committee promoted passage of a bill authorizing registration of judgments from sister states and giving them full faith and credit in the state of registration. (American Bar Association Report, Vol. 52 (1927), pp. 292 and 294-303; Ibid., Vol. 53 (1928), p. 424; Ibid., Vol. 54 (1929), pp. 373-374; Ibid., Vol. 55 (1930), pp. 67 and 454.)

155 Ibid., Vol. 53 (1928), p. 101.

156 Ibid., Vol. 57 (1932), p. 101.

157 Ibid., Vol. 49 (1924), p. 349.

In 1932 some idea of procedure of the Committee of Jurisprudence and Law Reform was presented; the present plan under which it operated resulted in sending to the Chairman and each member of the Committee a copy of all bills directly affecting the judicial code, the judiciary, and many other changes in substantive law. The Committee had given attention to bills which it deemed important; it was not considered advisable to make detailed reports to Association on the hundreds of bills which were referred to it. Weaknesses were pointed out by the Committee in the whole procedure, namely, the fact that the Association met only once a year; that the Committee took its orders and obtained authority from the Association; that the Association would direct the Committee to oppose a certain bill, referred to by number pending in Congress; that subsequent to annual meeting the bill was changed by amendment or amended and reintroduced with a new number. The Committee was thus without authority to act as to the amended bill; in one or two instances this action had tended to destroy the force and effect of opposition of the Bar Association. The Committee suggested that the Association should delegate full authority to the Executive Committee to favor or oppose legislation upon which the Association had not had opportunity to pass; such action of the Executive Committee should bind the Association as if adopted at an annual meeting, for that would permit the Association to speak with authority at all times instead of once a year.[158]

2. LEGISLATION IN PARTICULAR FIELDS

(a) Criminal Law. Attempt to Meet the Crime Problem

The problem of crime is always with us; it ebbs and flows in accordance with the emphasis given to it by the

---

158 Ibid., Vol. 57 (1932), pp. 508-509. This authority is now vested in the House of Delegates.

newspapers. As was well stated by Mr. J. B. Winslow, in his Presidential address before the American Institute of Criminal Law and Criminology in 1912, "If there be any questions of greater importance to society than the questions which cluster around the criminal law and its due enforcement, I know not what they are." [159] However that may be, in attempting to meet the problem, there is hostility between those who would urge the protection of society on the one hand, with those who would plead for justice to the accused on the other; that is, the clash between those who stress protection of society and those who stress protection of the accused. With the traditions of this country against tyranny, the emphasis has been on the latter, and the accused has been surrounded with all kinds of safeguards. As early as 1913, at the fifth annual meeting of the American Institute of Criminal Law and Criminology, lawyers, through Moorfield Storey, commenced to advocate the need of innocent members of society for protection against crime, to insist that innocent citizens no longer needed protection against tyranny, and to call on the members of the legal profession to recognize their duty of furnishing protection against crime.[160] Justice Holmes was quoted in an address presented before the Criminal Law Section of the American Bar Association in 1925, as stating that there was much more danger today that criminals would escape justice than that they would be subject to tyranny; that concern should be not so much that some innocent man might be convicted, but that no guilty man would escape.[161]

A consideration of the crime problem includes: (1) a study of conditions of heredity and environment and (2) a reference to criminal procedure, including police, prosecution, courts, penal institutions, probation, and parole. The first might be said to be the special province of the home, the school, and the social agency; the latter, the re-

---

[159] Ibid., Vol. 37 (1912), p. 1204.
[160] Ibid., Vol. 38 (1913), p. 1094.
[161] Ibid., Vol. 50 (1925), p. 701.

sponsibility of the organized Bar. As a matter of fact, it will be seen that the Bar's influence has been mostly in the field of law enforcement, and perhaps this is due to the fact, as Justice Stone said, that of all the law enforcement agencies, the most important is the Bar.[162] And since the crime problem is largely a local one, the need to develop some functional connection between the different organized Bar units has always been recognized. The need for limitation of activities was well expressed by Dean Justin Miller in 1928 in his address before the Section, when he stated that though members of the American Bar Association should understand the nature and extent of the problem, they should make their contribution in that field for which their training has best qualified them, that is, in substantive and procedural criminal law. It will be observed that the bulk of the organized Bar's activity has been in the realm of procedure.

The American Institute of Criminal Law and Criminology was organized in June, 1909.[163] Its object was thus defined, "to further scientific study of criminal law and procedure, to formulate and promote measures for solving the problems connected therewith and to coordinate the efforts of individuals interested in the administration of certain, speedy justice." [164] The proceedings of the Institute were printed in the American Bar Association Year Books from 1911, the third meeting of the Institute, until 1919, the eleventh meeting inclusive. A study of the personnel of the Institute discloses the fact that many of the officers and executive board members were leaders in the American Bar Association, namely, Dean John H. Wigmore was the first president, and Mr. Nathan William MacChesney was the third. The meetings of the Institute were held immediately before the annual meeting of the American Bar Association.

---

[162] Ibid., Vol. 49 (1924), p. 198.

[163] Ibid., Vol. 36 (1911), p. 962.

[164] Ibid., Vol. 42 (1917), p. 722; see also Vol. 38 (1913), p. 1081, and Vol. 43 (1918), p. 581.

As early as 1911, it was reported that the Institute had then practically a definite relation with nearly all organizations interested in the subjects it was considering, including the American Bar Association, which had at its meeting recognized the Institute officially, appointed delegates to attend the meeting, and instructed the secretary thereafter to include the program of the Institute in the American Bar Association program, and also to include in the annual volume of the American Bar Association a summary of the Institutes' proceedings.[165]

Scope of Policies and Activities. The American Bar Association's Committee on Jurisprudence and Law Reform had since 1885 included in its program a consideration of many of the problems in the realm of criminal law, and the Institute continued some of these activities. For example, the Institute appointed a Committee on Criminal Procedure and one on Intermediate Sentence and Release on Parole. The Institute in turn set the mould for the future Section of Criminal Law of the American Bar Association. For example, the Section either continued or supplemented work in the field of Insanity and Criminal Responsibility, Judicial Probation and Suspended Sentence, Classification and Definition of Crimes, Criminal Statistics, Sterilization, etc.

The Section of Criminal Law of the American Bar Association was organized in 1920. The early emphasis was on elimination of delays and technicalities in criminal trials; speedy trials and certainty of punishment was the keynote.[166] In 1926 it was decided to create a Council for the Section, composed of officers and five additional members, appointed by the Chairman.[167] Committees of the Section presented their reports to the Section, which then submitted them to the Council; if approved by the Council, recommendations of the Committee were submitted by the Sec-

---

165 Ibid., Vol. 36 (1911), p. 971.
166 Ibid., Vol. 46 (1921), pp. 584ff.
167 Ibid., Vol. 51 (1926), p. 677.

tion to the whole Association. In 1927 the name of the Section was changed to "Section of Criminal Law and Criminology," a development which was considered as a reflection of a changed point of view. Instead of casual functioning, a policy of all-year-round program was followed through, whereby the Section sought to discover causes of crime, to determine more accurately the scope and purpose of criminal law, and to devise appropriate methods of relief.[168]

As will be seen, the Section's activities, in spite of remarks to the contrary, were confined entirely to the law enforcement aspect of the crime problem. It was iterated and reiterated that it was in this field that lawyers, because of their training, could perform their best work and make a contribution. In 1927, Hon. Oscar Hallam, in an address before the Section, stated that there were three types of agencies dealing with crime: (1) Those relating to detection and arrest; (2) Those relating to legal procedure, embracing courts and prosecutors; and (3) Those relating to punishment. This classification showed the lawyers' typical viewpoint, which only included law enforcement agencies, and ignored entirely such potent agencies as the home, school, social groups, etc. However, on another occasion the Juvenile Court and the Probation System were recognized as the first line of defense set up by the state when the home, school, and normal social agencies had failed.[169] It was also stated in the presentation of report in 1933 that the fundamental principle in the Section was that lawyers' interest in the crime problem was not or should not be limited to changing criminal procedure; that the work of the American Law Institute in preparing the Code of Criminal Procedure was a contribution, but after all, it was only a small part of the problem and of the lawyers' responsibility.[170]

---

[168] Ibid., Vol. 54 (1929), pp. 529, and Vol. 55 (1930), pp. 26-27.

[169] Ibid., Vol. 52 (1927), p. 454; and Ibid., Vol. 57 (1932), p. 602.

[170] Ibid., Vol. 58 (1933), pp. 64 and 65.

Formulation and Execution of Policies. The policies and activities of the American Bar Association in respect to problems in the field of criminal law were first formulated and carried through by its Committee on Jurisprudence and Law Reform, though after 1920 they were executed mainly by the Section on Criminal Law. It is to be noted that the activities of the Committee on Jurisprudence and Law Reform sometimes overlapped those of the American Institute of Criminal Law and Criminology and the Section of Criminal Law of the Bar Association. The organized Bar's activities will be considered in this field under the appropriate headings of Police, Court Procedure and Penal Institutions, Probation and Parole.

Police. State Police Organization v. Local. The police constitute the first line of defense against the criminal, and, for no other reason than that, ought to be most effectively organized. But a Committee of the American Institute of Criminal Law on Metropolitan and State Police reported at its 1919 meeting that a discussion of the subject of state police inevitably brought out the fact of the weakness and inefficiency of rural constables as agents for prevention of crime.[171]

Bureau of Identification. As early as 1907, a resolution was adopted that the American Bar Association recommend to the Conference of Commissioners for Uniform State Laws that they draft a law to establish a state bureau of identification of criminals.[172] In a paper by Mr. Forrest Brader before the Criminal Law Section in 1923, attention was called to the fact that the International Association of Chiefs of Police had established a National Identification Bureau at Washington, which was supported by about 180 police departments. However, it was noted that a voluntary organization such as that was wholly inadequate, and the

---

171 Ibid., Vol. 44 (1919), p. 519. Note of the work of the Pennsylvania State Constabulary, organized in 1905, and that of the New York State Police, in 1917, was made.

172 Ibid., Vol. 31 (1907), p. 669.

Committee on Law Enforcement of the American Bar Association had recommended that there should be organized a certain place to which all reports should be made. The bureau should be attached to the Department of Justice, and the Association of Chiefs of Police had considered the matter with the Attorney General. There was need for a central bureau acting as a clearing house for criminal information.[173]

Third Degree. The American Bar Association, early through the Committee on Jurisprudence and Law Reform, took a stand against the third degree and adopted a resolution submitted by the Committee that no confession should be received in evidence unless made voluntarily and in the presence of three persons.[174] The resolution regarding "third degree" had been submitted to the Committee in 1910, and the Committee had reported itself as opposed to the "third degree." The original resolution, considered in 1910 and 1911, dealt with the admissibility of evidence in all criminal prosecutions. A resolution considered in 1913 provided that persons accused of crime and under arrest should not be examined in private, and not even in public unless informed that they were entitled to have counsel present, that they need not answer, and that if they did, the statements would be taken in writing and used as evidence on the trial. While the Committee considered that the many evils prevalent in this field were reprehensible, it was of opinion that since the problem was local, the remedy should be local, and stated that the Committee was not prepared to recommend any changes.[175]

Another resolution required the Committee to ascertain the law respecting innocent witnesses in every state. Letters were addressed to members of the General Council; from replies received from the forty-eight states, it was found that 18 states detained and imprisoned innocent wit-

---

173 Ibid., Vol. 48 (1923), pp. 587-588.
174 Ibid., Vol. 36 (1911), pp. 379-380.
175 Ibid., Vol. 37 (1912), pp. 30-31 and 431-433.

nesses long enough to take deposition, 21 states provided for detention, and 7 states forbade such detention. Thus it was found that 39 states permitted the involuntary detention of innocent witnesses. The Committee was asked to condemn the practice and sponsor a law preventing the detention of witnesses under any circumstances; the Committee concluded that the principle of the common law permitting such detention had better be followed.[176] The matter was again considered in 1913, and the Committee again reported adversely to the adoption; after much parlimentary maneuvering, the Committee action was adopted.[177]

Following an address by Mr. E. W. Camp, of California, in 1929 before the Section of Criminal Law, a Committee was appointed to study the subject of "Lawless Enforcement of Law," including the use of the third degree and other methods of violating the constitutional rights of citizens, ostensibly for the purpose of securing law enforcement. The Committee presented an elaborately annotated report in 1930; after discussion, the Committee was continued for another year for further study of the problem.[178] In 1932 the one resolution recommended by the Section asked that the American Bar Association commend to police and law enforcement agencies the use of modern scientific methods such as were being developed by way of scientific crime detection laboratories, as tending to replace certain methods known as the "third degree." [179]

Bureau of Investigation. In its 1930 report, the Committee on Jurisprudence and Law Reform recommended the enactment of a bill to establish a Bureau of Investigation under the jurisdiction of the Department of Justice. At the session it reported that a bill providing for the establishment of the Bureau had become law.[180]

---

176 Ibid., Vol. 37 (1912), pp. 32 and 431-433.
177 Ibid., Vol. 38 (1913), pp. 468-469.
178 Ibid., Vol. 55 (1930), p. 28.
179 Ibid., Vol. 57 (1932), p. 65.
180 Ibid., Vol. 55 (1930), pp. 67 and 454.

Courts, with Special Reference to Procedure. In matters of purely judicial procedure, it is only appropriate that lawyers take the initiative.[181] A Special Committee on Federal Code of Criminal Procedure was appointed in the American Bar Association as far back as 1893.[182]

In 1922 the Section of Criminal Law adopted a resolution urging the preparation of a Uniform Code of Criminal Law and Procedure, and suggesting that the Section cooperate with the National Conference of Commissioners on Uniform State Laws and the American Institute of Criminal Law and Criminology. In the meantime, the Section was to draft or procure the drafting of laws to put certain principles into effect respecting pleas of guilty, habitual offenders, indeterminate sentences, probation and parole.[183] This movement for uniform laws regulating criminal procedure was commended by Hon. Oscar Hallam and Wade H. Ellis, Esq., in addresses before the Criminal Law Section in 1923.[184]

In 1925 the Section adopted for submission to the American Bar Association a resolution calling attention to the need for a comprehensive survey of the administration of criminal justice, and requesting the Association to provide funds and designate directors for carrying on such a survey. Hon. Oscar Hallam, in a paper before the Section, stated that he would concur in the recommendation of the Committee on Law Enforcement of the American Bar Association that steps be taken to formulate a standard code of criminal procedure for all states, and one that would require that prosecution be speeded and procedure simplified.[185]

In August, 1930, the American Bar Association adopted the following resolution: Resolved by the American Bar

---

181 Ibid., Vol. 49 (1924), p. 182.

182 For details, see Ibid., Vol. 16 (1893), p. 61; Ibid., Vol. 18 (1895), p. 23; Ibid., Vol. 20 (1897), p. 54; Ibid., Vol. 21 (1898), p. 32; and Ibid., Vol. 25 (1902), pp. 25-32.

183 Ibid., Vol. 47 (1922), p. 609.

184 Ibid., Vol. 48 (1923), pp. 604 and 632.

185 Ibid., Vol. 50 (1925), p. 659; and Ibid., p. 677.

Association that the Section on Criminal Law and Criminology be authorized to appoint a Committee to confer with the American Law Institute on lines of possible cooperation for the improvement of criminal justice. The invitation was accepted by the Institute, and representatives of the two organizations met as a joint committee on November 22, 1930. After general discussion, a subcommittee was appointed to prepare and submit report to the Joint Committee outlining program of work for the improvement of criminal justice. On December 31, 1930, the Association of American Law Schools authorized its Special Committee on Survey of Criminal Procedure and Administration of Criminal Justice to cooperate with the Joint Committee of the American Bar Association and the American Law Institute. The subcommittee met frequently, and its members had numerous interviews and considerable correspondence with members of the Joint Committee and other interested and qualified persons. The report was considered in detail after which draft of report was referred back to the subcommittee for redrafting; as redrafted, the report was submitted as the Report of the Joint Committee on the Improvement of Justice before the Section of Criminal Law and Criminology in August, 1931, which report outlined a program of work and called for the aid of all those working in the field of criminal law and criminology.[186]

---

186 Ibid., Vol. 56 (1931), pp. 25, 513-514. The American Law Institute constituted one important group working in the field of Criminal Law. Immediately upon organization on February 23, 1923, certain of its members urged that the Institute should devote attention to the enforcement of Criminal Law. Since the institute could not then undertake the work, a Special Committee of the National Crime Commission was organized, which drafted and put out an outline Code of Criminal Procedure. In May, 1923, the American Law Institute appointed a Committee to prepare and present a draft of a survey and statement on defects of criminal justice. In April, 1925, the Committee made a comprehensive report. The Model Code of Criminal Procedure was urged by the American Bar Association, the Association of American Law Schools, and the American Institute of Criminal Law and Criminology, whereupon with $117,000 contributed by the Laura Spelman Rockefeller Memorial to carry on the work, the drafting of the Code was begun in 1925, and published in June,

Pursuant to recommendations contained in report by Section Committee on Cooperation with the American Law Institute, two new Committees of the Section were set up in 1931; one to examine and report on the Code of Criminal Procedure, prepared by the American Law Institute, and the other to study the problem of the training and selection of personnel in the administration of criminal justice.[187] In 1932 the work of these committees had not progressed far enough to call for action.[188] The above Committee, appointed by the Section to Examine and Report on the Code of Criminal Procedure, suggested in 1933 that the Section should take such steps as were within its power to cause the code to be made the subject of comparative study in all states, and to be urged for adoption in so far as it was pertinent and an advantage.[189] To this end, the Section adopted the following resolutions:

(1) That the Criminal Law Section urge on the American Bar Association that it develop a program calling for detailed examination in each state of the Code of Criminal Procedure of the American Law Institute and advocate and support proposed statutes or court rules incorporating such portions of the Code as are desirable of enactment in each state.

(2) That this be accomplished through the appointment of active committees of state bar associations representing county and local bar associations where possible.

1930, since which time Bar activity has been concentrated on its adoption by the states. The Code epitomizes what the consensus of expert opinion regards as the most advanced procedure which could reasonably be expected to receive the approval of the profession and the sanction of the legislators; it is concerned with trial procedure, the efficiency of court process, and such efficiency is the prime requisite in the effective administration of criminal law of the country. (American Bar Association Report, Vol. 58 (1933), pp. 520-521.) The Institute has also been requested by the Association of American Law Schools and the American Bar Association to undertake a Restatement of Substantive Criminal Law, which is to be a basis for a Model Code of Criminal Law.

187 Ibid., Vol. 57 (1932), p. 64.

188 Ibid., Vol. 57 (1932), p. 64.

189 Ibid., Vol. 58 (1933), p. 523.

(3) That such state bar association committees when organized be urged to avail themselves of expert service of the American Law Institute.

(4) That the American Bar Association consider ways and means of assisting in financing attendance of experts of the American Law Institute.

(5) That state bar association committees be urged to secure the adoption of principles of the code through the exercise of the rule-making power of the courts, rather than through formally enacted statutes.

(6) That the Special Committee of the American Bar Association be established to carry out the provisions of the resolutions.

Such a Special Committee on the Code of Criminal Procedure was appointed late in 1933, and in its report in 1934, it stated that it was a Committee appointed for the adoption of a piece of legislation, and that few if any of the state legislatures had been in session since its appointment. That it was also a Committee of Propaganda, but propaganda costs money, and no appropriation had been made to the Committee. However, the Chairman reported that it had given aid to bar associations interested in making a study of the code.[190] The Committee concluded that the Institute had accomplished its work of preparing the code, that it was not its business to provide the propaganda for adoption of the code, but that this was the business of the Bar Association.[191]

Bench Warrants. A particular aspect of a procedural problem was also considered, namely, bench warrants. In 1905 a motion was adopted that Committee on Jurisprudence and Law Reform consider federal bench warrants

---

[190] For example, in Illinois, the Chairman of the Committee being also President of the State Bar Association, had appointed a Committee to Cooperate with the President of the American Bar Association in the general program of criminal law and its enforcement, and charged the Committee with the study of the Code of Criminal Procedure in Illinois; the Committee hoped to present the Code to the General Assembly in 1935.

[191] American Bar Association Report, Vol. 59 (1934), p. 110.

in criminal cases. It appeared that there was no provision in the case of persons indicted for crime for extradition from one judicial district to another.[192] On this question, the Committee reported in 1906 that the question before the Association was whether it should recommend to Congress the enactment of a law making an indictment conclusive evidence of facts therein alleged, the indictment being only prima facie evidence of the existence of probable cause. The Committee reported that it felt that the recommendation of the American Bar Association of proposed legislation should be given rarely and then with great caution and circumspection; that the voice of the American Bar Association should, if possible, carry conviction; that it should never seek to influence Congressional legislation except in matters of gravest concern, and then only in cases where it spoke with substantial unanimity; and that it did not deem it necessary to express an opinion on the merits of the bill, and advised against recommendation by the Association. The report was accepted, and the recommendation against recommending the bill was adopted.[193]

Jury Service, Challenges, and Disqualification of Witness. In 1910 report was made on resolution referring in 1908 to Committee on Jurisprudence and Law Reform certain proposed legislation respecting service on grand or petit jury, peremptory challenges, and disqualification of witness for perjury or subornation of perjury. While the Committee stated that it might well be that the legislation proposed was desirable, it considered that recommendations should only be made by the American Bar Association to Congress on rare occasions, and then only in matters of gravest import. The report was received, and the recommendation accepted.[194]

The conservatism of this Committee on Jurisprudence and Law Reform at this early date should be noted; it was

---

192 Ibid., Vol. 28 (1905), p. 8.
193 Ibid., Vol. 29 (1906), pp. 15, 481-483.
194 Ibid., Vol. 35 (1910), pp. 11 and 493-496.

long on study, short on action. The Bar Association in the execution of its National Bar Program has progressed far from its former timid policy of inaction to one of action.

In its 1930 report, the Committee on Jurisprudence and Law Reform recommended the enactment of a bill to amend Section 649 of the Revised Statutes providing for waiver of jury in certain jury cases; this act was also reported as having been enacted into law at the time of the presentation of report at the annual meeting.[195]

In 1922 Senator Nelson introduced a bill respecting pleas of guilty, which he requested the Committee to consider. After such consideration, the Committee reported that it was of opinion that the bill embodied a desirable reform.[196]

Expert Testimony. The difficult problem of expert testimony, particularly with reference to trial of cases where insanity is a defense, was referred, before the 1915 meeting, to the Committee of Jurisprudence and Law Reform for consideration and report. The Committee considered the bill to regulate expert testimony which had been presented by the Committee on Insanity and Criminal Responsibility of the American Institute of Criminal Law and Criminality, and unanimously adopted by the Institute October 22, 1914. After due consideration, the Bar Committee recommended its approval with the exception of Section 3, where certain changes were suggested.[197] The Institute itself reported in 1916 that the bill as approved by the Institute had been introduced into several legislative bodies and freely discussed, but had not been passed; that the Institute's committee now felt that the bill was too comprehensive and recommended revisions.[198] In the American Bar Association, the bill to regulate expert testimony, approved by the Institute in 1914, was postponed for a

195 Ibid., Vol. 55 (1930), pp. 67 and 454.
196 Ibid., Vol. 47 (1922), p. 358.
197 Ibid., Vol. 40 (1915), p. 374.
198 Ibid., Vol. 41 (1916), p. 842.

year.[199] Then in 1926, the subject of "Opinion Evidence and Expert Witness" was considered, and certain concrete suggestions were made by the Section of Criminal Law, but no legislation was proposed.[200] In 1927 the Section reported that it would make no further recommendations for improving the unsatisfactory conditions prevailing, but deemed it important to keep alive interest in the subject to the end that ultimately public opinion might force a solution of the difficult problems involved; that the American Medical Association had recently devoted considerable attention to the subject, and appointed a Committee. The Bar Committee invited the Medical Association Committee to attend a conference in December, 1926, which invitation was accepted. The discussion gave no results except to emphasize the difficulty of the subject. The Medical Committee stated that it proposed to draft a bill on the subject of expert medical testimony in the federal courts, and also to coordinate bills in the several states; that passage would first be urged in the national legislature, and then in the states. All proposals provided for the appointment by the court of eminent and disinterested experts for enlightenment of the court. An effort to remove some of the objectionable features of expert testimony in judicial proceedings was reported for the year in Ohio, in which movement Mr. Howland, a member of the American Bar Association Committee, was active. The growth of the movement was noted, and the Committee believed that it could be useful in keeping the Association advised on the subject.[201] In 1928, the Committee reported that it had continued to give consideration to the subject, and that the Chairman had had some correspondence with the President of the American Society of Civil Engineers, who had promised cooperation.[202]

---

199 Ibid., Vol. 41 (1916), p. 18.
200 Ibid., Vol. 51 (1926), p. 435.
201 Ibid., Vol. 52 (1927), pp. 304-306.
202 Ibid., Vol. 53 (1928), p. 421.

In 1934 the Committee on Jurisprudence and Law Reform reported that it had received a letter suggesting cooperation between medical men of New York and the American Bar Association. Some subjects that were listed for discussion were:

(1) Whether appointment of expert witnesses should be delegated exclusively to the Judge so that in criminal cases experts would be impartial.

(2) Whether the McNaughton formula for determining individual responsibility in a criminal act should be changed.

(3) Whether it is advisable to fix legal standards for qualification of expert witnesses in criminal cases, and

(4) Whether in states where law permits appointment of lunacy commission, it should be mandatory that one member be a qualified psychiatrist.

The Committee further reported that the doctors had not crystallized their plans; when they did, either the Criminal Law Section or the Committee on Jurisprudence and Law Reform would be glad to aid in any proper way in the adoption of laws in conformity with decision of joint conference.[203]

Comment by Court and Prosecutor That Defendant Did Not Testify. In the field of simplification of pleading and elimination of technicalities and of tearing down some of the safeguards which were erected to protect the accused in an earlier era, the Bar Association has conducted a continuous campaign to empower the Court and prosecuting attorney to comment on the fact that defendant refused to testify. As early as 1914, the President of the American Institute of Criminal Law and Criminology suggested the advisability of eliminating from the Constitution and statutes that provision which prevented comment on the fact that defendant had refused to testify.[204] In 1925 in listing suggestions for reform in criminal procedure through state

[203] Ibid., Vol. 59 (1934), pp. 488-489.
[204] Ibid., Vol. 39 (1914), p. 1110.

action, Charles Burdick, Esq., recommended that comment should be permitted. He pointed out that on the subject of self-incrimination, Professor Wigmore had stated that the rule against self-incrimination is not the product of common law, but is statutory in origin; that Professor Wigmore and Moorfield Storey had urged that federal and state constitutions be amended to allow the defendant to be called to the witness stand by the state. Mr. Burdick considered that if laws did not go that far, they should, at least, permit comment if defendant did not testify, and yet it was forbidden in most states.[205] In 1931, after long debate, a recommendation of the Section was carried that comment by the prosecution be permitted on the fact that defendant did not take stand as a witness.[206] This same principle with the addition that the Court should also be permitted to comment was embodied in the Model Code, which provisions of the Model Code were, with others, approved at the 1934 meeting.[207]

Psychiatric Service. The clash of interest between law and medicine is not new, says Herman M. Adler, and since he is a psychiatrist, one might glean that by "medicine," he means the particular branch of medicine now called "psychiatry." [208] Yet, in 1927, the Section of Criminal Law and Criminology set aside a session to be devoted to psychiatry, a fact which was considered most important and significant.[209] After all, it should be recognized that lawyers and psychiatrists desire the same ultimate objective, namely, the furtherance of the social weal.[210] Out of this meeting, devoted to psychiatry, came the appointment of a Section Committee to cooperate with similar committees of the American Psychiatric Association and the American Medical Association to study the problem called

[205] Ibid., Vol. 50 (1925), p. 684.
[206] Ibid., Vol. 56 (1931), pp. 29 and 137-159.
[207] Ibid., Vol. 59 (1934), p. 130 (IV-c)-141.
[208] Ibid., Vol. 47 (1922), p. 632.
[209] Ibid., Vol. 52 (1927), p. 497.
[210] Ibid., Vol. 52 (1927), p. 496.

psychiatric jurisprudence.[211] In 1929, the American Bar Association received the report of the work of the Committee, and adopted a resolution recommending use by courts and other official agencies of such facilities of psychiatry as are available to them in their respective communities.[212] During the year 1929-1930, the Committee went further with the work; it presented not merely a report of progress, but an address of Dr. W. Overholser, suggesting the desirability of a study of the practical value and results of the operation of psychiatric clinics. The Section adopted a resolution that such a survey was desirable, and that this desirability be suggested to the Social Science Research Council.[213] Though the Social Science Research Council was unable to make the survey, the Section later reaffirmed the resolution.[214] In 1932 a resolution was adopted that the Section take steps during the year 1932-1933, in the direction of bringing to the attention of state and local bar associations the resolution adopted by the American Bar Association in 1929, relating to psychiatric service, with urgent request for its consideration on the programs of such associations.[215] Dean Justin Miller listed the adoption by the American Bar Association of the Section resolution recommending psychiatric services in the courts as the most outstanding single achievement of the Section.[216]

Criminal Statistics. The first step toward the improvement of the administration of criminal laws, which the legal profession could and should encourage, is the establishment of an adequate and uniform system of gathering statistics of the administration of justice in the United States, to the end that this statistical data might be available to those bodies and organizations seeking the improvement of law administration, said Justice Harlan F. Stone, in a

---

211 Ibid., Vol. 55 (1930), p. 27.
212 Ibid., Vol. 54 (1929), p. 55, and Vol. 55 (1930), p. 27.
213 Ibid., Vol. 55 (1930), pp. 27, 594-612.
214 Ibid., Vol. 58 (1933), p. 517.
215 Ibid., Vol. 57 (1932), p. 594.
216 Interview January 20, 1936.

paper delivered before the Section of Criminal Law in 1924.[217] That this was a real challenge may be gleaned from the fact that the American Institute of Criminal Law in 1911, through its Committee on Statistics emphasized the need for a long campaign of education before court records could be made respectable sources of criminal statistics.

One aim of criminal statistics, according to Dr. Thorsten Sellin, is to furnish the public administrator with a rod by which he may measure the effectiveness of his own work. From statistics, the broad social aspects of the crime problem, the geographical distribution of criminality, its movement and nature, and the extent of social injury may be gleaned. All these factors represent information necessary for corrective or preventive social policies.[218]

In 1923, Hon. Oscar Hallam made caustic comment on the scarcity of data as to crime and criminal procedure, the lack of accurate or comprehensive state statistics of crime, and the entire absence of any uniform system.[219] Dean Justin Miller, Chairman of the Criminal Law Section, in an address before the Section in 1928, reported that various efforts were under way to secure on a comparative basis reliable statistics concerning the extent of crime; such work had been undertaken by the United States Census Bureau; the International Association of Chiefs of Police, and the National Crime Commission.[220] Since the great weakness of criminal statistics was the lack of uniformity which prevented comparison, the classification of Crimes developed by the International Association of Chiefs of Police for Police Statistics and by the Census Bureau for Prison Statistics had in part removed the defect.[221]

Penal. Discrimination Between the Professional and Nonprofessional Criminal. As early as 1882, a resolution was adopted that the Committee be requested to consider

[217] American Bar Association Report, Vol. 49 (1924), p. 196.
[218] Ibid., Vol. 56 (1931), pp. 505-506.
[219] Ibid., Vol. 50 (1925), p. 660, and Vol. 51 (1926), pp. 677-680.
[220] Ibid., Vol. 53 (1928), p. 536.
[221] Ibid., Vol. 56 (1931), pp. 508-512.

and report on the proper method and criterion for discriminating between the professional and nonprofessional criminals and for protection of society against the former. The report submitted in 1885 cited the Massachusetts probation system, and suggested that probation in lieu of imprisonment should not be used in the case of habitual criminals, but that probation after and in addition to imprisonment should be used. Three resolutions were proposed: (1) For records of criminals; (2) For police supervision of persons twice imprisoned, also disenfranchisement; and (3) For drafting state laws by committee and pressure for adoption by local councils. Since opposition developed, the report was received, and action postponed until the following year.[222] No further action was ever taken on the report.

Whipping Post as Mode of Punishment. In 1885 resolution was adopted that the Committee on Jurisprudence and Law Reform consider and report whether the whipping post or other similar mode of punishment is a legitimate form or instrument for punishment of crime consonant with proper objects of criminal law.[223] The opinion in 1886 reported at length on the need of a punishment that would actually punish, and recommended that the interests of society would be promoted by the general use of the whipping post as a mode of punishment for wife beating and other assaults.[224]

Deprivation of Civil Rights. In 1921 the Committee on Jurisprudence and Law Reform sponsored a bill, introduced into Congress, proposing to amend Section 335 of the Penal Code in such a way as to affect judgments of conviction for minor offenses in federal courts. The Committee presented arguments favoring the bill, because it considered it unwise to leave to the discretion of either the

---

[222] Ibid., Vol. 8 (1885), p. 26.

[223] Ibid., Vol. 8 (1885), p. 66.

[224] Ibid., Vol. 9 (1886), pp. 286ff. The whipping post is still being considered as a mode of punishment. See American Bar Association Journal. January, 1935, p. 64.

judge or jury the question as to whether or not in each case deprivation of civil rights should form part of punishment for crime committed, and stated that it was clear that in cases where punishment actually inflicted was imprisonment for a year or less, there should be no deprivation of civil rights.[225] In 1922 it was reported that the bill recommended by the Committee in 1921 had been introduced into both Houses, and the Committee had had a hearing, but no action had been taken by either House.[226] In 1924 it was reported that the bill had been introduced by Senator Walsh and reported to the Senate May 4, 1924, but had not been reported to the House. In 1925 the Committee reported that it had pressed for the passage of this bill, that it had been passed by the Senate, and that in the House it had been referred to the Judiciary Committee, but no action had been taken on it by that Committee.[227] In 1926, it was reported that hearing had been held by the Judiciary Committees of both Senate and House, at which members of the Bar Committee had advocated the measure, but that no reports had yet been made by either Committee.[228] In 1927 it was reported that the bill had been favorably reported to and passed by the Senate; that it had been referred to the House Committee on Judiciary, but that no action had been taken by that Committee.[229] In 1928 it was reported that the bill had not been vigorously opposed, but that neither House had pressed for its passage, and that congestion of business would prevent its passage.[230] No further action appears from the reports.

Sterilization. By way of prevention, the Section in 1928 considered the question of sterilization. This question had been formerly considered by a Committee on Sterilization of the Institute of Criminal Law and Criminology from 1914 to 1917. It was discharged in 1917, because its

225 Ibid., Vol. 46 (1921), p. 389.
226 Ibid., Vol. 47 (1922), p. 357.
227 Ibid., Vol. 50 (1925), p. 409.
228 Ibid., Vol. 51 (1926), p. 429.
229 Ibid., Vol. 51 (1926), pp. 307-308.
230 Ibid., Vol. 53 (1928), p. 422.

studies disclosed that in states which had passed the law it was either found to be unconstitutional or else was not enforced.[231] At the 1928 meeting of the Section, papers were presented by Mr. Otis H. Castle and Mr. Paul Popenoe.[232] Mr. Castle stated that what he intended to present was a work of information only and not one of propaganda. The paper presented a comprehensive recital of the law in this country in respect to human sterilization.

Parole and Indeterminate Sentence. The problem of parole and indeterminate sentence was early tackled when the Committee on Judicial Administration and Remedial Procedure was instructed in 1885 to inquire into the subject of indeterminate sentences of convicted criminals, and to report upon its extent and make recommendations.[233] Nothing appears to have been done by this Committee, but in 1897 a resolution was adopted providing for the appointment of a Committee of five to report at the following meeting which states had adopted acts for parole or indeterminate sentences of persons convicted of crime, and whether such acts had proven beneficent in their execution, together with such general information as in their judgment might be of public interest on these and kindred subjects.[234] In 1899 this Committee on Parole and Indeterminate Sentence reported that the Chairman of the Committee was then in England studying the subject.[235]

A resolution that the Association favored the establishment in the Department of Justice at Washington of a laboratory for the study of the criminal, the pauper, and defective classes was referred to the Committee on Penal Laws and Prison Discipline, formerly the above Committee on Parole and Indeterminate Sentence.[236] In 1903 the Committee reported favorably on such a laboratory.[237]

---

231 Ibid., Vol. 42 (1917), p. 721.
232 Ibid., Vol. 53 (1928), pp. 556-573, and pp. 575-581.
233 Ibid., Vol. 8 (1885), p. 85.
234 Ibid., Vol. 20 (1897), pp. 63-65.
235 Ibid., Vol. 22 (1899), p. 39.
236 Ibid., Vol. 25 (1902), pp. 29-36.
237 Ibid., Vol. 26 (1903), pp. 95-96.

The Committee was also requested to report to the Association at its next meeting as to the proper punishment of professional criminals.[238] In 1904 approval was given the Committee recommendation that study of delinquents be continued.[239]

In 1913 in comments on the fact that the reports of standing Committees of the American Institute of Criminal Law were filled with information, attention was called to the reports of the Committee on Indeterminate Sentences and Parole as giving substantially all laws in each of the states of the Union on that topic with a summary covering the whole field of experience.[240]

The problem of release is still a vital one. As was said by Charles C. Butler, Esq., in a paper before the Criminal Law Section in 1926, the indeterminate sentence and the parole system are not the fruits of maudlin sentiment but of wise statesmanship, which recognizes that the protection of society is the primary object of criminal administration and that the reformation of the prisoner, where practicable, is a desirable means to an end.[241] Criminals who are released without any supervision are apt to prey on society and resume their careers of crime. Studies show that most criminals are released after short terms. As Honorable Charles E. Hughes well pointed out, the Wickersham reports on Penal Institutions, Probation and Parole showed that from a study of the prison and reformatory population of the United States as a whole, 97 per cent of the inmates were subject to release, and the average time served in prison was a little over two years.

Cooperative Movement With Other Groups Grappling With the Crime Problem. When the National Crime Commission was appointed in 1925, its main function was said to be education leading to the formation of state crime

---

238 Ibid., Vol. 26 (1903), pp. 96-97.
239 Ibid., Vol. 27 (1904), pp. 47-51.
240 Ibid., Vol. 38 (1913), p. 1082.
241 Ibid., Vol. 51 (1926), p. 726.

commissions, since crime is chiefly a local problem.[242] The Missouri Crime Survey, the first application of scientific methods on a state-wide basis to determine defects in criminal law and its administration, originated in 1924 with the Missouri Bar Association.[243]

In 1927 Dean Justin Miller, in his annual address before the Section, reported a galaxy of crime commissions and committees; in thirteen states commissions for a survey of crime conditions or for revision of criminal laws had been created.[244] Accomplishments of the Commissions were listed, from which the conclusion was inevitable that Commissions were largely successful in the research field, but were not, on the whole, very successful in getting recommendations enacted into law, not to mention the bigger problem of enforcement and administration of the laws after they are passed. By 1929 it was recognized that no short-lived commission could hope to parallel the work of long-time laboratory-conditioned scientific experiments. Crime commissions and law enforcement commissions had their place, but their work could be little more than initiatory in character.[245]

If one delves at all into the field of criminology, one is impressed with two things: (1) The great amount of work that has been done in an endeavor to solve the crime problem and the infinitesimal amount of accomplishment; and (2) the individualistic character of groups and organizations working in the field, and the lack of a functioning cooperative program.

It is all too obvious that the first is naturally the result of the second, and therefore, the policy of developing cooperation with other groups working for some solution of the crime problem, initiated by the Section of Criminal Law and Criminology in 1927, seemed a wise one. It was in 1927 that the Section decided to name a Committee of three

[242] Ibid., Vol. 53 (1928), p. 534.
[243] Ibid., Vol. 51 (1926), pp. 218 and 743.
[244] Ibid., Vol. 52 (1927), pp. 466-471.
[245] Ibid., Vol. 54 (1929), p. 54.

members to work with a Committee of the American Psychiatric Association to study proposals of the latter Association with regard to medico-legal problems, and report back the following year.[246] Three members were also appointed from the Section to represent the Association at a meeting of the National Crime Commission in Washington, D. C.[247] Dr. Karl A. Menninger, in an address before the Section that year, stated that he regarded it as significant that the legal and medical professions were having a get-together to talk over a thing which in the past had been a matter of misunderstanding and acrimony.[248]

This Committee on Psychiatric Jurisprudence in 1928 reported progress in its work and recommended that it be continued, which recommendation was approved. Report was also made regarding the work of the National Crime Commission, and resolution was adopted by the Section recommending the appointment of a Committee to again cooperate during the next year with the Commission. In addition, report was made regarding the work of the Social Science Research Council, and resolution was adopted by the Section recommending the appointment of a Special Committee to cooperate with the Council. The Section also adopted a resolution calling attention to the wide scope of the crime problem as well as the large number of agencies engaged in combating it, and suggesting that efforts be made to determine the nature and character of programs being undertaken by responsible national bodies, to invite some of them from time to time to participate in programs of the Section, and then to join with them in devising ways and means of solving problems.[249]

Dean Justin Miller, in his address before the Section that year, called attention to work that was being done in the field of criminal law and criminology by the American Law Institute, the National Probation Association, the

---

246 Ibid., Vol. 52 (1927), p. 451.
247 Ibid., Vol. 52 (1927), p. 450.
248 Ibid., Vol. 52 (1927), p. 496.
249 Ibid., Vol. 53 (1928), pp. 62-63.

American Prison Association, the International Association of Chiefs of Police, the American Institute of Criminal Law and Criminology, the American Psychiatric Association, etc., and pointed out that the American Bar Association had been cooperating with several of these groups.[250]

Some reason for the development of its policy of cooperation was given in 1929, when report for that year was presented. The Chairman stated that the Section two years before, in order to get under way some preliminary thinking relative to the establishment of research institutes and laboratories of the kind needed for the purpose, had asked and received permission to establish joint, cooperative committees representing the American Bar Association and other responsible associations interested in the problem of crime. Pursuant to such authorization, committees to cooperate with the American Medical Association, the American Psychiatric Association and the Social Science Research Council had been appointed by the Section.[251] By 1930 four such cooperative committees were listed, namely, Committee to Cooperate with the American Law Institute, Committee to Cooperate with the American Prison Association, Committee on Medico-Legal Problems to cooperate with the American Medical Association, and one on Psychiatric Jurisprudence to cooperate with the American Psychiatric Association. After an address by Dr. Calvin Goddard a resolution was adopted by the American Bar Association that the Section be authorized to cooperate through its Medico-Legal Committee with the International Association of Chiefs of Police in a study of the problems of law enforcement and criminal prosecution. By 1932 the Committee to Cooperate with the International Association of Chiefs of Police was listed as a Section Committee.[252] In 1931 the same four cooperating committees above cited were listed.[253] That same year the report of the Joint Com-

[250] Ibid., Vol. 53 (1928), p. 535.
[251] Ibid., Vol. 54 (1929), p. 54.
[252] Ibid., Vol. 57 (1932), p. 22.
[253] Ibid., Vol. 56 (1931), p. xx.

mittee specified that the time had arrived for the three participating legal organizations of national scope, the American Bar Association, the American Law Institute, and the Association of American Law Schools to consider problems for the improvement of criminal justice and to help coordinate the work now being done by agencies and groups devoted to special phases of work.[254] In 1932, of the nine committees of the Section listed, six represented cooperating committees.[255] In 1933, another cooperating committee was added, namely, Committee on Cooperation with the American Legislators Association.[256]

Since a great need in the field of criminal law and criminology is that of cooperation among groups struggling with the crime problem, the development and execution of this policy by the Section on Criminal Law represents a significant development. It is only through such cooperation among these groups that any gains can be achieved. Public opinion should be mobilized behind any movement to meet the crime problem; isolated groups working here and there can accomplish little. Law and its enforcement can only be as effective as the people desire it to be. The Association through its Section's policies to develop cooperative leadership has performed a real service.

It should be noted that at first the Association's activities were confined to isolated resolutions pertaining to some particular aspect of procedure or punishment, such as discrimination between professional and nonprofessional criminals, the whipping post, bench warrants, etc.[257] Later, and especially in the Section of Criminal Law since 1925, there has been a tendency to develop a broad comprehensive program. It should also be noted that the Association was formerly loath to recommend legislation, and adhered to a narrow policy of avoiding entirely anything that savored of politics.

---

254 Ibid., Vol. 56 (1931), pp. 515-516.
255 Ibid., Vol. 57 (1932), pp. 21 and 593.
256 Ibid., Vol. 58 (1933), pp. 21 and 516.
257 Supra, pp. 189, 196-197.

The present policy of the Section has been considerably widened under the stimulus of the National Bar Program begun in 1933, although even in 1931 the Section's activities were so sweeping and progressive that of the eleven resolutions presented to the Bar Association, seven were referred back to the Committee, three were disapproved, and only one was approved.[258]

The Section subordinated all its other activities in 1933-1934 to program prepared by the Committee on Coordination, and designated as the National Bar Program. In pursuance of this program, a comprehensive questionnaire on the subject of criminal law and its enforcement was sent to the various bar associations of the United States, some thirteen hundred in number. The large response was encouraging.[259] From answers and studies, the Section of Criminal Law formulated a four-point program, with important and definite recommendations; these recommendations were deemed of such importance to the Association and the various state and city associations which furnished the information to compile them, that it was considered wise to have them first presented to the Executive Committee of the Association. The Executive Committee, having approved the recommendations, presented them through the Honorable William L. Ransom to the whole membership of the Bar Association at the 1934 meeting. Then they were again presented by the Chairman of the Section, and one by one were unanimously adopted. The recommendations included the following public measures:

I. (a) The American Bar Association recommends to the governor of each state the establishment of a permanent Committee on Criminal Justice, composed of lawyers and laymen; the committee should maintain close contact with committees of state and local bar associations. (Approved, p. 122.)

---

258 American Bar Association Report, Vol. 56 (1931), pp. 24-30.
259 Ibid., Vol. 59 (1934), p. 111.

(b) The American Bar Association recommends to each state and local bar association the establishment of a Committee on Reform of Criminal Procedure, and also a Committee on Police and Prosecution. The Committee on Procedure should be charged with serious consideration of the adoption of the Model Code of Criminal Procedure approved by the American Law Institute in 1930. The Committee on Police and Prosecution should deal with criticisms and improvement in personnel, qualifications, training, methods of police and prosecuting staff; the committees should work with the Section on Criminal Law and also the International Association of Chiefs of Police. (Approved, p. 124.)

II. The American Bar Association recommends the creation in each state of a State Department of Justice, whose duty will be to direct and supervise actively the work of every district attorney, sheriff and law enforcement agency. The Department should include a central criminal bureau equipped with records and investigators, similar in character and qualifications to those now attached to the Federal Department of Justice. The American Bar Association recommends that Committee on Uniform State Laws be requested to outline an act for the establishment of such State Department of Justice. (Approved, p. 126.)

III. The American Bar Association recommends that state and local bar associations concentrate actively on ridding the profession of dishonest and unethical practitioners, investigate complaints, and where facts warrant, institute disciplinary process with cooperation of the courts. The American Bar Association suggests the subject of disciplinary proceedings as part of the National Bar Program for the ensuing year. (Approved, p. 129.)[260]

IV. The American Bar Association recommends to each state bar association that it formulate improvements

---

[260] Note action of the Philadelphia Bar Association in February, 1935, in investigating improper practices of lawyers in certain criminal cases, which investigation resulted in tying certain lawyers to the "Number Racket," and their consequent suspension or disbarment.

in criminal law and process and submit them to courts, legislatures and people, and that state associations work for promulgation of Rules of Court, where that method is available, and for the enactment of laws and amendment of Constitution, when necessary.

Then follows a series of recommendations, specific and procedural in character:

(a) Improvement of Criminal Procedure contained in Model Code. (Approved, p. 129.)

(b) Criminal defendant offering defense claim of alibi or insanity shall be required to give advance notice to prosecution. (Approved, p. 130.)

(c) Permit Court and Counsel to comment to jury on failure of defendant in criminal case to testify in own behalf. (Approved, p. 141.)[261]

Since the above recommendation was made relative to State Departments of Justice, California has adopted an amendment to its Constitution which unifies the work of its most important law enforcement agencies by placing them under the control of the state attorney general. Legislative activity looking to creation of such departments was cited in at least eight states, namely, Massachusetts, New York, South Dakota, Ohio, Nebraska, Texas, West Virginia, and North Carolina. Commissioners on Uniform State Laws are engaged in the preparation of a bill for the creation of such departments.[262]

It is obvious that all the recommendations presented at the 1934 meeting were in the field of law enforcement, and that none of the recommendations could be said to be in the field of prevention or rehabilitation. The Chairman in his presentation of the report stated that the function of the American Bar Association, the Section on Criminal Law, and the Committee on Coordination may become one of clearing information and of providing assistance to local associations by way of speakers, drafts of legislation, com-

---

[261] Ibid., Vol. 59 (1934), pp. 111-114.

[262] American Bar Association Journal, April, 1935, p. 204.

mentaries and arguments. He further stated that the national organization should not take the place of the state and local associations any more than the federal government should take the place of the local governments in local law enforcement.[263]

It is readily seen that there is no easy solution of racketeering or any phase of the crime problem. It would seem that a great amount of intensive study, research, and work has been done in this field, but with a modicum of results. However, that need not be at all discouraging. Lack of results should present a challenge. Nevertheless, one has to take cognizance of the fact that activity in the field of procedure may reduce but will never eradicate crime. As stated above, the Bar Association in its early days, though it worked on particular problems in the field of criminal law and criminology, did little more than pass resolutions, and perhaps make studies. There was little, if any success in making any of its proposed reforms a reality, and yet there is no doubt that the early activity in the Association prepared the way for the present-day elaborate program of work, which would appear to present a two-point program:

(1) A short-term program, such as building up machinery to get the provisions of the Model Code of Criminal Procedure adopted in the states or such of its provisions as would represent advances in particular states, and

(2) A long-term program, such as state centralization of law enforcement agencies, psychiatric service in all agencies of law enforcement, employment of laboratory methods in detection of crime, transformation of prisons into laboratories for studies of human behavior, etc.

The idea is constantly being stressed that if the crime problem is to be dealt with in a practical and effectual fashion, two things are essential: (1) Facts must be gathered, and (2) Public Opinion must be aroused to compel

---

263 Ibid., Vol. 59 (1934), p. 119.

adoption of legislative and administrative remedies.[264] That the legal profession is equipped to make a contribution in this field was recognized by Attorney General William D. Mitchell in an address before the American Bar Association in 1932, when he stated:

"It may be that those who are skilled in research are not always endowed with training, or sense of proportion, or practical experience with legislative bodies, which enables them to translate their general conclusions into a statute, and that members of the profession, who are active in its practice or on the bench, are the ones who must take hold of these problems, where our institutes and foundations for research leave them, and carry them on to practical achievement." [265]

But it would seem that the Section for some reason has built up rather cumbersome machinery for effectuating its policies, for subjects are first referred by the Section to a Committee, which in turn, after study and formulation of recommendations, submits them to the Section, which refers them to its Council for consideration and report; the Council reports back to the Section, and if favorable to Committee's recommendations, the Section presents them to the American Bar Association. This is probably all very well for the long-term program where the greatest care should be taken at each step, but in a matter where speedy action is necessary and desirable, it is to be regretted. It is evident that the Section's greatest contribution to date is the attempted tying together of all the different groups working on the crime problem. Though different techniques of crime prevention need to be tried, still the greatest necessity is seen to be more cooperation among all agencies working in the field, and it is just here that the Bar has given noted assistance. It is to be hoped that, after proper coordination among the different agencies is assured, the vital leadership that is necessary to the solution of this difficult problem will be forthcoming.

---

264 Ibid., Vol. 51 (1926), p. 201.

265 Ibid., Vol. 57 (1932), p. 297.

(b) Public Utilities

Though the Interstate Commerce Act was passed in 1887, there was little progress in the field of regulation until 1906, when the act was amended and its scope increased.[266] In 1907 the New York Public Service Commission, the first of the state commissions, commenced to function. By 1927, "Public Utility Law" was already noted as an important branch of our jurisprudence.[267]

It was in 1917 that the American Bar Association in its Executive Committee report authorized the establishment of the Section of Public Utility Law, with the provision that the by-law for the purpose should follow in every respect the by-law under which the Section of Legal Education was established.[268]

Hon. William L. Ransom, in an address in 1931, quoted the purpose as contained in the by-laws of the Section as follows:

". . . to bring together for better acquaintance and mutual advantage those members of the Bar, who are interested in the law governing the public services. . . . to hold meetings, conduct discussions, make studies, surveys and analyses, as to law of public utilities under private or public operation; and to formulate and submit to the Section and the Association such report and recommendations as might be deemed useful to the profession and advisable in the public interest." [269]

Frank A. Reid, Esq., Chairman of the Section 1931-1932 in an address defined one of the chartered purposes as declared in the by-laws as:

". . . to provide a common meeting ground and impartial forum for those members of the Bar who are engaged in dealing with problems of Utility Law in any capacity." [270]

---

266 American Bar Association Report, Vol. 45 (1920), p. 450.

267 Ibid., Vol. 52 (1927), p. 68.

268 Ibid., Vol. 42 (1917), p. 27.

269 Ibid., Vol. 56 (1931), p. 734.

270 Ibid., Vol. 57 (1932), p. 767.

The importance of public utilities may be gleaned from an address in 1918 by the first Chairman and founder of the Section, Nathaniel T. Guernsey, Esq., of New York, when he said:

"The statisticians advise that roughly, one-seventh of the wealth of the United States is invested in its Public Utilities, including railroads."

Mr. Guernsey in this address also declared the policy of the Section when he stated that principles underlying and controlling regulation must be worked out through courts, and under the direction of members of the Bar; the Bar had relied too much on engineers. The Section was to follow the consistent policy of the American Bar Association in recognizing the importance of the Courts in our governmental system. He presented as justification for the Section the fact that through meetings by way of papers and discussion, the resulting interchange of views between members might contribute to the correct solution of some of the many questions then affecting public utilities; that the Section must offer an open forum, and welcome free discussion of every mooted question.[271]

The idea of an open forum was inaugurated at the 1919 meeting, and was established in 1920 as a standing feature of the meetings.[272] J. B. Sanborn, Esq., Chairman, in an address before the Section in 1923, quoted the first chairman, Mr. Guernsey, on the need of the open forum, and in turn emphasized the value of discussion. The first chairman had, however, hinted that the Section might do something more than discuss, for he spoke of recommendations and conclusions. Only once down to 1923 had the Section come to a conclusion, and that was in 1922 when it took action in opposition to the Bacharach Bill. Certainly, there were mooted questions of public utility law on which the Section might come to a conclusion and offer a recommendation, namely, (1) rule of valuation, the fundamental

---

[271] Ibid., Vol. 43 (1918), pp. 523-530.
[272] Ibid., Vol. 45 (1920), pp. 445-446.

question of public utility law, (2) the extent to which decisions of the Commissions might be reviewed in court, etc. Conclusions should not be reached after merely a vote of those who might be present at the meetings of the Section. Suggestion was made that these specific questions be referred to the Council or Special Committees of the Section, that such Committees report their conclusions and recommendations, and that further discussion be then had in the Section. Resulting conclusions might then be of value not only to public utility lawyers, but also to the whole public.[273]

Aside from the forum aspect and more in line with a direct action policy, a Special Committee to recommend future action by the Section reported in 1923: (1) That Council of the Public Utility Law Section is hereby authorized and requested by the Section to take action from time to time for the furtherance of approved measures and policies respecting the law of public utility regulation; (2) That Council is hereby authorized and requested to make constructive studies and formulate recommendations concerning the law of public utility regulation and to appoint a Special Committee or subcommittees from the Section or Council.[274]

Hon. William L. Ransom, in an address before the Section on "Going Value," again stressed the importance of discussion when he suggested that the Section might help clarify the problem of "Going Value," for the benefit of courts and Bar, as other Sections and Committees had done with respect to other phases of the law. He added that the Section was the logical place for thought and leadership; that it was the only forum in which legal representatives of companies, commissions, municipalities, investment concerns and other lawyers interested in this branch of law, met in a friendly, open-minded fashion and felt free to act wholly in the interests of an orderly development of

---

[273] Ibid., Vol. 48 (1923), pp. 638-643, passim.
[274] Ibid., Vol. 48 (1923), p. 636.

law. In defining the scope and point of view of the discussions in the section, he stated that it should undertake no advocacy of any contention beyond the one that the bar should try to fulfill its traditional function of leadership and clarification of one of the most difficult phases of the law of private property devoted to public use.[275]

By 1927, the Section had become noted as an open forum. State commissioners, representatives of the Interstate Commerce Commission, attorneys for carriers, and legal representatives of utilities attended the sessions.[276]

Carl D. Jackson, Esq., Chairman of the Section in 1927, in his address, said that review of questions discussed by the Section in the past would show that the Section had keenly realized the importance of all phases of public utility law, that the discussion had been frank and often represented opposing views, and that such an attitude represented ideas of the founders of the Section, namely, the establishment of an open forum for the presentation of views, facts, and arguments bearing on public utility law, which had become one of the most important branches of our jurisprudence.[277]

John G. McLane, Esq., Chairman in 1928, pointed out that discussion in the open forum of the Public Utility Section was largely concerned with the economic and legal principles under which regulation must function, namely, the "rate base" and means of its ascertainment, "rate of return," "depreciation" and its treatment, "railroad valuations" by the Interstate Commerce Commission, and their correspondence or dissimilarity to valuations of other utilities by state commissions, etc.[278]

In 1930, pursuant to custom, the Section conducted an open forum for discussion of the highly controversial subjects relating to public utility law. The first Standing Committee was then appointed to prepare for presentation at

[275] Ibid., Vol. 49 (1924), pp. 681-701, passim.
[276] Ibid., Vol. 52 (1927), p. 69.
[277] Ibid., Vol. 52 (1927), pp. 636ff.
[278] Ibid., Vol. 53 (1928), p. 679.

the following meeting of the Section a report reviewing developments in public utility law, both statutory and judicial, state and federal.[279]

In 1931 the Section had expanded its activities by the appointment of six Committees to report as follows:

(1) Developments in public utility law.

(2) Boundaries between state and federal regulatory powers over public services.

(3) Law of valuing utility property taken under the exercise of eminent domain.

(4) Nature of the functions of state commissions, etc.

(5) Scope and standards of accounting regulations prescribed for railroads and other public utilities by federal and state authorities.

(6) Applicability of anti-trust laws to public utilities.[280]

Thus in 1931, for the first time, the Section had before it a number of well-considered reports, worked out with care by committees during the year and dealing with vital phases of public utility law.[281]

Notwithstanding the reports of the six committees, the Section had no resolutions or recommendations to place before the Association for action because the matters, which the Section through its Council and Committees had been actively studying for the year, had not reached the stage either of adoption by the Section or of recommendation to the Association for expression of opinion thereon.[282]

Hon. William L. Ransom, in an address before the Section in 1931, again emphasized that the Section of Public Utility Law represented an impartial forum and clearing house for constructive ideas and approved experience of those who were wrestling with problems of public utility law.[283] Through work of its six committees, the Section

---

279 Ibid., Vol. 55 (1930), p. 38.
280 Ibid., Vol. 56 (1931), p. xxv.
281 Ibid., Vol. 56 (1931), p. 716.
282 Ibid., Vol. 56 (1931), pp. 39-40.
283 Ibid., Vol. 56 (1931), pp. 726ff.

had obtained some clarification of these subjects, and had made a contribution to an informed, professional opinion concerning them.[284]

At the Section meeting in 1931, it was decided to send an address made by Colonel William J. Donovan and the report of the Committee on the Law of Boundaries between State and Federal Regulation of Public Utilities to the governor of each state, members of each Commission, Senate and House Committees on Interstate Commerce in the United States Congress.[285]

Four Committees were listed for 1932-1933, to report as follows:

(1) Developments during the year in the field of public utility law.

(2) Regulation of holding companies and of relations between holding companies and affiliated operating companies.

(3) Legal aspect involved in cases where the utility charges different rates for different classes or kinds of service, certain of which result in a loss or inadequate profit.

(4) Extent to which the states and the federal government respectively may regulate contract carriers on the highways and waterways.[286]

It was recognized that the reports of Committees constituted a genuine contribution in the field of utility law, and should help to stimulate sound development in the field. The reports were printed and distributed to all members of the Section. Again the fact was stressed that the Section had successfully established itself as "a common meeting ground and impartial forum for those members of the Bar, who were engaged in dealing with problems of utility law in any capacity." [287] The formal reports were

---

[284] Ibid., Vol. 56 (1931), p. 735.
[285] Ibid., Vol. 56 (1931), p. 720.
[286] Ibid., Vol. 57 (1932), pp. 26-28.
[287] Ibid., Vol. 57 (1932), p. 77.

said to be the result of extensive study and research, and had assumed an authoritative aspect resulting in a country-wide demand for the printed text. Formal reports were presented most carefully and at length, and discussion developed a divergence of views, especially pronounced in those fields of law in which actual experience and judicial construction and pronouncement had not clearly mapped the way, economically or legally.[288]

In the discussion at the 1932 meeting, some idea of the policy of the Section was gleaned when Hon. William L. Ransom, former Chairman of the Section, called attention to the fact that much of the time of the Section was then given to economic and public policy questions, the development of the public interest side of legal problems.[289]

A note of doubt as to the value of the open forum provided by the Section on Public Utility Law was sounded when Mr. Joseph B. Eastman, in his address of welcome in 1932, stated that he questioned whether most fruitful discussion could be obtained collectively from either lawyers or commissions, since they were largely responsible for the present procedure, and the father is not always the best exponent of the merits or demerits of his offspring. He granted that the recognition of a need for discussion might well mark the first step toward solution.[290]

Whether the open forum afforded by the Section has been fruitful or not, there is no doubt that the forum did and continues to influence professional opinion, at least in the field of utilities. The personnel of the Section as set forth at most of the meetings included state commissions, professors of law, and counsel for state and federal commissions, for municipalities, and for public utilities. It is readily seen that these represent the very men who are both presenting and deciding the public utility legal questions of the day.

---

288 Ibid., Vol. 57 (1932), p. 752.
289 Ibid., Vol. 57 (1932), pp. 757-758.
290 Ibid., Vol. 57 (1932), pp. 763-764.

In 1934 the Section adopted a resolution suggesting to the Council that it consider the advisability of holding a midyear Conference in Washington, D. C., similar to the midyear meeting conducted by the Commerce Committee and others in the Bar Association.[291]

William Chamberlain, Esq., President of the Section in 1926, in his address, sounded the keynote of the Section's influence when he stated that many of the most important questions formed the subject of papers presented to the Section before these questions were authoritatively passed on by the courts; the value of the papers to those engaged in the cases could not be overestimated.[292] So, year by year, in increasing ratio, the Section has played its part in the formulation of law. Few cases reach the higher courts for decision in a period of less than two years; therefore, full discussion can be had before the Section.[293]

This cursory picture of the development of the Section gives some idea of the way lawyers influence public utility law, not so much statute law, but case law, for it is apparent that in the field of public utilities, most of the law that governs is case rather than statute law. Even when a statute does govern, it follows the law as developed through decisions.

Opposition of Public Utility Section to Limitation of Power of Federal Courts. In 1922 the Section Chairman was empowered to appoint a Committee of five to report views of the Section on the so-called Bacharach Bill and similar legislation, which proposed to inhibit the taking of jurisdiction by the lower federal courts in a case where injunction was sought against the action of state boards or commissions. A resolution in opposition to the Bacharach Bill or any similar legislation tending to limit equitable

---

291 Ibid., Vol. 59 (1934), p. 683.

292 Some idea of the timely and technical character of discussion in the Public Utility Section can be obtained from a reference to papers presented in the Section, as listed in American Bar Association Report, Vol. 55 (1930), p. 866.

293 Ibid., Vol. 51 (1926), p. 815.

powers of the United States courts over orders of commissions was unanimously adopted by the Section, which joined with the Committee on Jurisprudence and Law Reform. The report received approval of the Association.[294]

In 1928 it was proposed that space should be given on informal program to the proposed curtailment of powers of federal courts. It was stated that there had appeared in many forms Congressional proposals to so limit the jurisdiction of the federal courts as to prevent utilities from protecting, by recourse to those courts, their constitutional rights against invasion by state action with respect to rates. Such proposal, presented by Representative Bacharach of New Jersey, was largely discussed at meeting in 1922, and was then the subject of resolution. Agitation was revived in 1928, when at least four proposals of the same kind were presented; in varying forms, they all proposed the same thing, namely, to amend Section 266 of the Judicial Code in order to deny altogether, or limit to such an extent as to render valueless, the right to appeal to the federal courts in the first instance in cases involving alleged confiscatory rates.[295]

As stated above, the Committee on Jurisprudence and Law Reform followed a consistent policy of opposing all measures which proposed to abridge the powers of the federal court. In 1929, through Committee recommendation, the Association adopted a resolution to continue opposition to enactment of the Wagner Bill, which provided that all public utility matters must be tried in the state courts, thus endeavoring to take away jurisdiction of the federal district courts, and to discriminate against public utilities.[296] This action was continued in 1930, when the Committee on Jurisprudence and Law Reform recommended

---

294 Ibid., Vol. 47 (1922), p. 635.

295 Ibid., Vol. 53 (1928), pp. 93 and 682.

296 Ibid., Vol. 54 (1929), pp. 93, 373-374.

the defeat of discriminatory laws taking away from federal courts the power to pass on public utility questions. Said recommendation was duly adopted.[297]

After 1930, when the Committee on Jurisprudence and Law Reform seemed to concentrate most of its efforts on this particular policy of opposing legislation proposing to limit the federal courts, it included the public utility phase; at least, no reports relative to such bills were made before the Section of Public Utility law, so far as written records show.

At the 1932 meeting, report was made by the Committee on Jurisprudence and Law Reform that the Johnson Bill had been introduced, which bill would take away from the federal district court jurisdiction to interfere by injunction or otherwise with orders of state administrative boards affecting rates chargeable by public utilities, where jurisdiction was based solely on the ground of diverse citizenship. This bill was favorably reported to the Judiciary Committee of the Senate against Committee's opposition, but was not reported by the Judiciary Committee of the House.[298]

In 1933 the Committee reported that the Johnson bill had been opposed by Mr. E. W. Everett of Chicago, speaking for the Bar Committee; that division among members of the Bar Committee had developed, and that a strong minority did not believe that the Johnson bill represented any serious or improper invasion of judicial power of the federal courts. The majority of the Committee felt that the Johnson bill was but the beginning of an effort to limit federal jurisdiction step by step. In 1932 it was upon recommendation of this Committee that an identical bill was opposed. The Judiciary Committee of the Senate was informed that a few members of the present Committee did not believe that there was any undue invasion of juris-

[297] Ibid., Vol. 55 (1930), pp. 69 and 455.
[298] Ibid., Vol. 57 (1932), pp. 101 and 507-508.

diction of the federal courts in the bill, thus weakening the influence of the Committee. A resolution was carried that the Association again oppose the enactment of any law which would divert or substantially abridge the jurisdiction of any federal court in litigation based on diversity of citizenship, or which would impair jurisdiction of the federal courts in controversies arising under the Constitution and laws of the United States.[299] Nevertheless, in spite of Association's position, the Johnson Act became law May 14, 1934. At the 1934 meeting, the Committee recommended that the Association urge the repeal of this act, and again the Committee was empowered to oppose the enactment of any law which would divert or abridge the jurisdiction of the federal courts.[300]

Uniform Public Utility Law. In 1923 the Section initiated a movement for a uniform public utility law. In that year, a Special Committee of five members of the Section was appointed to make study and report on the advisability of attempting to establish a uniform utility act. Committee reported to Section on a proposed form for the act.[301] A brief outline and discussion of some of the features of the proposed act, such as Rate Making Section, Review and Appeal, and Terminable Permit were submitted.[302] Resolution was adopted that the report of the Special Committee be referred to the Council of the Section, and that the Council be requested to confer with Committee on Uniform Laws of the American Bar Association; that after Conference the report should be amended as seemed desirable, and that amended report should then be filed with the National Conference of Commissioners on Uniform State Laws for consideration.[303].

In 1923 it was reported that the Association, at the suggestion of the Section of Public Utility Law in 1924, had

299 Ibid., Vol. 58 (1933), pp. 378-380 and 107.
300 Ibid., Vol. 59 (1934), pp. 73-74 and 485.
301 Ibid., Vol. 49 (1924), p. 480.
302 Ibid., Vol. 49 (1924), pp. 723-731.
303 Ibid., Vol. 49 (1924), p. 628.

referred the proposed Uniform Act for regulation of public utilities to the National Conference of Commissioners on Uniform Laws; the Section had offered its services in connection with consideration of the act, and reported progress.[304] Mr. John H. Roemer, before reading Mr. Floyd B. Odlum's paper at the 1925 meeting, urged on the American Bar Association and each and every member the necessity for uniformity in the laws of the several states of the United States in dealing with the subject of public utilities.[305].

In 1926 it was reported that proposed Uniform Public Utility Act was still in process of consideration, and that no action had as yet been taken on it.[306]

In 1927 report was made that the Conference on Uniform State Laws had tentatively adopted a Uniform Public Utility Law concerning which the Section of Public Utility Law had a committee, which had met with the Conference; the probabilities were that it would come up for final action at the following year's meeting.[307]

In 1928 the Section noted with satisfaction the completion of the labors of the Commissioners with respect to the proposed Uniform Public Utilities Act.[308] Up to 1935 the Uniform Act had not been adopted by any state.[309]

Study of reports of the Public Utility Section shows something of the difficulty and intricacy of public utility problems. People talk glibly of these problems and their solutions, but this will not solve problems in the field. Though the Bar Association Section may not have completely solved any problems, yet its policies and activities demonstrate that it is only by study, discussion and constant work on particular aspects of problems that even partial solution can be obtained.

---

304 Ibid., Vol. 50 (1925), p. 77.
305 Ibid., Vol. 50 (1925), p. 814.
306 Ibid., Vol. 51 (1926), p. 64.
307 Ibid., Vol. 52 (1927), p. 634.
308 Ibid., Vol. 53 (1928), p. 93.
309 Ibid., Vol. 60 (1935), p. 733.

That the Section offers a forum for the exchange of views must be conceded. The question might well be asked, "What views?" If the papers and resultant discussion are consulted, it will be found that they center pretty much around the most vital question in the field, the valuation base. The valuation base as laid down in Smythe vs. Ames is approved; public ownership is naturally anathema. The personnel of the Section has been commented on. Aside from its role as a forum, the Section has had little influence on legislation, except to record its opposition to the Bacharach-Wagner-Johnson bills and bills of similar import, and its effort toward uniformity. It may well be, however, since law in this field of utilities is not, on the whole, statute law but decision or case law, and since the group meeting in the public utility forum is one, which formulates this decision or case law, that the Section has had a real influence on the development of law in the field. Such a theme may well furnish material for another study, and hence can only be suggested here.

(c) Taxation.

It is interesting to note, in order that some idea may be obtained of the size of the problem on the administration side of taxes, that in 1923 there were on the docket of the Treasury Department probably about 200,000 cases involving two or three billion dollars.

While the Revenue Act of 1913 represented substantive law, it is included here because the Bar's action on it was to list twenty-five defects in the field of procedure and administration. When the first of the modern income tax laws was passed in 1913, the Bar Association evidently had an energetic chairman of the Standing Committee on Taxation in Professor Ernst Freund. After calling attention to the fact that the introduction of such a system of national taxation, new to that generation, was likely to remain a permanent feature of the tax system, Professor Freund listed twenty-five technical defects in the legal, administrative, and procedural phases of the law.[310] Nothing was ever done toward putting the suggestions contained in this elaborate report into an amended act, and in 1916 the Standing Committee on Taxation went out of existence, though it was succeeded in 1921 by a Special Committee on Federal Taxation. Certain recommendations of the latter Committee were embodied in the Revenue Acts of 1921, 1924, 1926, 1928, and 1932, or amendments thereto.

Claims for refunds presented several problems in procedure and administration, which were duly noticed and solved through the pressure of the Special Committee on Federal Taxation.

(1) On the question of extension of time for filing claims for refunds, confusion arose under the provisions of the Revenue Act of 1921, relative to time limitation on the filing of and suing for refund or credit claims. The Committee resolved that the attention of the Secretary of the Treasury should be directed to the intolerable situation existing. With the aid of the Secretary's staff, a bill to correct the defect was drawn up, and, with the endorsement of the President of the Bar Association, was passed by Congress on March 4, 1923, in spite of great congestion. By this act, claims for refunds under the Act of 1917 were extended two years.[311] The Association, through its Committee, adopted the principle that when the Commissioner of Internal Revenue asked for a waiver of the taxpayer's right to have the tax assessed within a limited time, the equivalent extension of time should be given the taxpayer for filing claims by him for credit refund. Due to this policy, the Committee drafted and had passed successive acts providing for additional time within which refund or credit claims could be filed, the Act of March 4, 1923, being the first of these. Later, through the efforts of the same

[310] Ibid., Vol. 39 (1914), pp. 533-557.
[311] Ibid., Vol. 48 (1923), pp. 121, 438-440.

Special Committee on Taxation, the Act of March 13, 1924, was passed, providing that a taxpayer, who had filed on or before June 15, 1924, a waiver of his right to have income tax assessed within five years after the return was filed for the years 1917 and 1918 should be granted an extension of time within which to file a credit or refund claim.[312] The effect of these two acts, both secured through the efforts of the Special Committee on Federal Taxation, was to give to the taxpayers of the country an additional time within which to file refund or credit claims, thus securing for them something in return for their forced surrender of their rights to limit the period within which the Commissioner of Internal Revenue could assess taxes found to be due. Later, the Act of March 3, 1925, was passed through the efforts of the Committee to protect further the interests of taxpayers who had given waivers.[313]

(2) In February, 1927, the Committee successfully opposed the McKellar amendment to Deficiency Bill, which would have required refund claims allowed by the Commissioner of Internal Revenue to undergo further scrutiny by the Comptroller General.[314] The opposition to this measure arose from the fact that the Committee recognized that the Comptroller General was not a tax authority, and reference to him of tax questions would only hamper the administration of tax matters.

(3) The Committee also worked effectively on the restoration of the interest rate from 4 per cent to 6 per cent. When the rate of interest on refunds of federal taxes was cut from 6 per cent to 4 per cent, the Committee immediately at the 1932 meeting was authorized to secure the passage of legislation reinstating the 6 per cent rate. At the 1933 meeting, it was reported that the 6 per cent rate had been reinstated retroactively by Repeal Act of the

---

312 Ibid., Vol. 49 (1924), pp. 90, 310.

313 Ibid., Vol. 50 (1925), pp. 81, 392.

314 Ibid., Vol. 52 (1927), p. 263.

Post Office Treasury Appropriations Act.[315] Since the American Bar Association was the only representative of the general public which concerned itself with this great error, credit should be given to them for the passage of this act. Since the taxpayer is required to pay 6 per cent interest on failure to pay a tax, it seems fair that the government should also be required to pay 6 per cent on refunds. Not only this, but many taxpayers had, on advice of counsel, paid a tax, which they questioned, with the expectation of a 6 per cent interest rate on refunds when made. This may seem a small matter, but when one considers that the average case involved $15,000, and one office in Washington had a tax matter involving one and a half million dollars, it is readily seen that it represents a rather serious question, to the taxpayer at least.

(4) Through the efforts of the Committee, legislation was also passed providing for the payment of 6 per cent interest to date of payment of refund instead of to date of allowance.[316]

(d) Rule-Making Power of the Court and Judicial Councils.

The movement for uniformity of judicial procedure through the rule-making power of the courts represents a worthy effort to bring about more efficient administration of justice, and in line with this movement is the more modern development of the Judicial Council. This development represents machinery for accelerating necessary and adequate reforms in judicial administration.

The first effort to gain uniformity of judicial procedure on the part of the American Bar Association dates from 1895 to 1899. Stimulated by the Society of Comparative Legislation in England,[317] the American Bar Association considered it desirable that the Association inquire

[315] Ibid., Vol. 58 (1933), p. 449.
[316] Ibid., Vol. 53 (1928), p. 400.
[317] Ibid., Vol. 19 (1896), p. 23.

into and collate facts relative to the movement then in progress to further uniform system of legal procedure and to study comparative legislation throughout the English speaking world. Accordingly, a Committee of five on the Uniformity of Procedure was appointed for that purpose.[318] The Committee so appointed decided that discussion as to the relative merits of the different systems of legal procedure adopted in this country and abroad was not within its province; that it was not so much concerned with the question of which was the better system of practice as with the problem of assimilating prevailing methods of procedure to a common standard; that the purpose of the Committee was to take up the study of comparative legislation relative to procedure in the English speaking world, as authorized by the resolution. A brief examination of the subject was sufficient to show that it would be impossible to accomplish more than gather some facts and make observations on procedure in state and federal courts. To obtain facts, a circular letter containing twelve questions, relative to the nature of procedure of different states, was sent to the vice-president of the association in each state, members of general and local councils, and to the presidents of the state bar associations. The inquiry was responded to, and the one hundred answers placed accurate information before the Committee. In addition to inquiries, investigation had been made in other directions by examination of codes of procedure, practice acts, statutes, and rules of court. Committee also availed itself of a report recently made by the Revision Committee of the State of New York, and containing much information relating to the topic under consideration. The Committee thought that too much power and control in the legislature relative to court rules and regulations was matter of regret. It, accordingly, recommended the passage of an act of Congress to authorize judges of the higher federal courts to

[318] Ibid., Vol. 18 (1895), pp. 32-34.

select from the Bar of a county a limited number of lawyers familiar with procedure in this and other countries for the purpose of drafting and presenting to Congress and to the federal courts such statutes and rules as should tend to simplify procedure in the courts of the United States, render it uniform, and eventually tend to assimilate practice in the supreme courts of the states to a common standard.[319]

The Committee was continued in 1897,[320] and in 1898 it reported its opinion that the adoption of a uniform system of procedure by the federal government would by its influence on the several states bring about better results both as to time and methods than could be accomplished by action on the part of states separately. If a clear, concise, and practical system was adopted by the federal courts, it would be an object lesson to the Bar throughout the Union, and tend to influence public opinion in favor of the best methods of practice. Committee renewed its 1896 recommendations.[321] The recommendation was laid on the table, and in 1899, the Committee was discontinued.[322]

In 1906 Dean Roscoe Pound presented a paper entitled "Causes of Popular Dissatisfaction with the Administration of Justice." After heated discussion, the subject matter of the paper was referred to a Committee to continue study and recommend changes.[323] This development is usually cited as the beginning of the movement for uniform judicial procedure, though it was not until August, 1912, that the Bar Association appointed its Committee on Uniform Judicial Procedure on the advice of the Honorable William Howard Taft, who stated in his official message to Congress December 6, 1910: "I am strongly convinced

---

319 Ibid., Vol. 19 (1896), pp. 411-424, passim, pp. 23-26.

320 Ibid., Vol. 20 (1897), p. 57.

321 Ibid., Vol. 21 (1898), pp. 454-465, passim.

322 Ibid., Vol. 21 (1898), pp. 33-36, and Vol. 22 (1899), p. 33.

323 Ibid., Vol. 29 (1906), pp. 11, 12, 55 and 395ff.

that the best method of improving Judicial Procedure at law is to empower the Supreme Court to do it through the medium of Rules of Court as in Equity." [324]

It was believed that, if Congress would confer on the Supreme Court the rule-making power on the law side as it had on the equity side, such uniformity in the federal courts would act as a stimulus to the states to go and do likewise, and thus uniformity of procedure with consequent simplification would be accomplished. The Committee proposed to induce Congress to enact legislation which would bring this about.

The Amercan Bar Association's Procedural Bill was introduced in the House December 2, 1912. In 1913 the work of the Committee was endorsed, and a Conference of Judges organized. Out of this Conference came the creation of a Judicial Section of the Association, authorized by By-Law 17.[325] Then began the long battle of the Committee for the bill to authorize the Supreme Court to prescribe forms and rules and generally to regulate pleading, procedure and practice on the common law side of the federal courts. In 1914 it began its presentation of a long series of reports, always optimistic and hopeful, though reporting failure to attain its object. The 1914 report showed that several representative members of the Association, including the Chairman of the Committee, Thomas W. Shelton, Esq., had appeared before the Committee on Judiciary of the House of Representatives, and that full discussion of the Bar Association's program had been followed by unanimous report of the Judiciary Committee in favor of the Bar's Procedural Bill.[326] The Committee made one request, namely, that members of the Association communicate with Congressmen and Senators, and urge necessity for adoption of measures recommended. The report was

[324] Ibid., Vol. 46 (1921), Appendix B, p. 470; see also American Bar Association Journal, November, 1936, p. 784.

[325] Ibid., Vol. 38 (1913), pp. 70 and 152.

[326] Ibid., Vol. 39 (1914), p. 571.

received and filed.[327] In 1915 sentiment of the American Bar Association was reported unanimously in favor of proposed procedural reform. Forty-two state bar associations had endorsed it, and many had special state Committees working with the national bar committee. Progress with Congress was reported, for the Senate had adopted a resolution authorizing a subcommittee of the Judiciary Committee to consider in vacation a composite bill, passed by the House of Representatives in the preceding session. The Bar Committee would appear before the subcommittee for the purpose of impressing principles underlying the Bar Association program.[328] The opposition of Senator Thomas J. Walsh, who did not agree with the idea that courts ought to make rules, was noted. The basis of opposition was the inconvenience that the change in pleading and procedure would cause the lawyer.

In 1916 the Committee reported that the Senate had enacted the bill, and that within three or four days the House would probably pass it.[329] In 1917 Committee reported that it had urged on Congress the adoption of the act, which had met the approval of many other associations.[330] The Committee in 1918 reported that while the Committee had no specific request to make, it did need help at Washington; that though the Bar Association measure had been endorsed by the Association, many state bar associations, leading lawyers all over the country, the President of the United States, and the Judiciary Committee of the Senate, and though ninety-five per cent of the House of Representatives were committed to the measure, it was prevented from being passed by three Senators, and possibly one.[331] The Committee continued with the aid of the state associations to sponsor its bill.[332]

---

327 Ibid., Vol. 39 (1914), pp. 45-46.
328 Ibid., Vol. 40 (1915), p. 503.
329 Ibid., Vol. 41 (1916), p. 35.
330 Ibid., Vol. 42 (1917), pp. 87-88.
331 Ibid., Vol. 43 (1918), pp. 87 and 88.
332 Ibid., Vol. 44 (1919), p. 35, and Vol. 45 (1920), p. 71.

In 1921 the Committee commenced to present quite elaborate reports of purposes and arguments for the bill and of activities during the year. The bill proposed to give to the Supreme Court of the United States authority to make rules governing the entire procedure in cases at law to the same extent that it then had power to regulate procedure in equity, admiralty, and bankruptcy. The bill would set judges and lawyers free to perfect machinery of the courts, for which they were held solely responsible by laymen; it would mean centralization of power with consequent responsibility and would conduce to uniformity since the simple, scientific, correlated system of rules, such as would be prepared and promulgated by the Supreme Court for use in the field of the district courts, would prove attractive models for states to adopt for their courts. Difficulty with procedure was due to the fact that coordination between the two departments of government had been destroyed by exclusive legislative control; the legislature should only provide what the courts may do, and the judiciary should regulate how they should do it. Report was made that the bill was held in Committee; if it could be reported out, favorable action would follow. State bar associations which had not already appointed Committees to cooperate for action on the Procedural Bill were asked to do so. Only individual opposition in the Senate was delaying favorable action on the bill.[333]

The Executive Committee in January, 1922, adopted a resolution condemning the suppression of the bill in Committee, and pointed out that the Association had for nine years endorsed the Procedural Bill; that the bill had been introduced into each Congress, and referred to the Judiciary Committees of the Senate and House, and that the bill with one exception had been held in Committee. The Executive Committee requested the Judiciary Committee of the Senate to make report on the bill, and sent copies of

[333] Ibid., Vol. 46 (1921), pp. 461-469.

resolutions to the President of the Senate, the Speaker of the House, and to each member of the Judiciary Committee of the Senate and House. Following this, hearings were held before the Judiciary Committee of the Senate and House, but the bill was, due to the influence of a few senators, still held in Committee. Pressure was considered essential to force bill out of Committee. Members and state committees were asked to continue activity for passage of the bill.[334]

In 1923 report recited that the Committee had been coming before the Association for ten years or more to make reports of progress on adoption of the Procedural Bill. The opinion was expressed that the bill would pass if it could be reported out of the Senate Committee, since eighty-seven Senators were ready to cast favorable votes, and that one Senator had been responsible for suppressing the bill in Committee. It was also reported that United States Circuit Judge Woods, when Chairman of the Judicial Section, had sent out a questionnaire and had ascertained that all but three of the United States circuit judges favored the measure. Members of the association were asked to communicate with Senators and Congressmen.[335] In 1924 it was reported that at the beginning of the session, Senator Albert B. Cummins had introduced the Procedural Bill, on which a subcommittee after public hearing had returned a favorable report; that bill had been reported out of Committee and was on the calendar No. 668. Members were requested to communicate with their two Senators. Questionnaire had been sent by the vice-presidents of the American Bar Association to all Senators and Congressmen, and replies had shown a large majority favored the measure, as was found to be the case among the circuit court judges when Judge Woods had sent out his questionnaire. Vice-presidents were requested to send another questionnaire to every Senator in October asking whether he

334 Ibid., Vol. 47 (1922), pp. 80-82 and 370-381.

335 Ibid., Vol. 48 (1923), pp. 114-116.

favored the bill, and if not, reasons for opposition.[336] The Committee on Commerce, Trade, and Commercial Law took a stand for this law in 1924; in reporting negatively on the feasibility of a system of United States commercial courts on the lines of the English commercial courts, and also on the wisdom of the Bar Association in appointing a Special Committee on Procedure and Practice before the Interstate Commerce Commission, it recommended that the Association in all proper ways further the enactment of the federal law giving the United States Supreme Court full authority to make and amend rules of court governing procedure in common-law cases, and also in cases before the Interstate Commerce Commission, the Court of Claims and other tribunals. If proper rules were adopted, speedy lists could be established, speedy trials had and much good accomplished. A resolution to this effect was adopted.[337]

In 1925, because of the decision of a few men, the bill had again been suppressed in the Judiciary Committees of the Senate and House; members of the Association were urged to communicate with Senators, and state bar associations were requested to continue their independent campaigns for the passage of the bill.[338] In 1926 report disclosed that there was no change in the situation in Washington; that the influence of Senator Walsh had been sufficient to hold the bill in Senate Committee in spite of a majority in favor of the bill; that the House Committee had also continued its obstinate refusal to act. Note was made that response to Senator Walsh's criticism had been published in the Bar Association Journal, sent out in advance, and published in all the leading newspapers of the country. The vice-presidents were commended for their effective work in getting favorable responses from eighty-five to eighty-six per cent of the House and Senate.[339] In 1927 report revealed that the Senate had reported the measure

---

336 Ibid., Vol. 49 (1924), pp. 483-496 and 93-100.
337 Ibid., Vol. 49 (1924), pp. 53, 280, and 289.
338 Ibid., Vol. 50 (1925), pp. 539-552.
339 Ibid., Vol. 51 (1926), pp. 119-122 and 505-506.

out, though vote had not been reached; that a majority of the Senate Committee and ninety-two Senators expressed themselves as favoring the bill; in the House, Chairman George S. Graham and a majority of the House Committee opposed it; however, it was felt that the bill should not be suppressed, since eighty per cent of the members had written to the vice-president of the Bar Association that they would vote for it. Fourteen years before, it was never dreamed that a few men in the Senate and House would have power, largely through Senatorial courtesy, to prevent vote on the bill. Report cited that the bill had gone through a period of education; that work done by the Association Committee had been supplemented by the aid of seventy-five per cent of the members of the Association; that every state association had investigated and passed it; that every state bar association and every governor had been contacted in an effort to ascertain whether there was any association that had not endorsed the measure.[340]

During these years 1925, 1926, and 1927, the Special Committee also had the cooperation of the Committee on Jurisprudence and Law Reform. In 1925 the latter committee joined with the Special Committee in felicitating the Association on the passage of a highly important procedural bill defending the status of courts of appeal and the Supreme Court, and making provision by which appeals to the Supreme Court might be so limited as to enable that tribunal to devote itself more exclusively to important questions of law brought before it on certiorari. Regret was expressed that the procedural bill providing for rule-making power on the law side had again failed of passage.[341] In 1926 the Committee on Jurisprudence and Law Reform noted its cooperation with the Special Committee in its effort to get the procedural bill enacted into law.[342] Then in 1927, the Committee commented optimistically in its re-

[340] Ibid., Vol. 52 (1927), pp. 119-125 and 396-401.
[341] Ibid., Vol. 50 (1925), p. 414
[342] Ibid., Vol. 51 (1926), p. 431.

port that the project for regulating procedure by rules of court had become so well understood that a Special Committee of the Association and a Committee of one of the affiliated bodies now had the subject in charge, and eventual adoption seemed assured.[343]

In reporting in 1928, the Committee, with some justification, it would seem, stated that the principle of rules of court had secured such a firm hold on the Bar of the country that almost every man understood what was meant by uniform judicial procedure; that thousands of letters had been sent all over the country inviting lawyers to aid by influencing Congressmen and Senators to vote for the bill adopted and approved by the American Bar Association fourteen or fifteen years before; that the majority of the Senate and House favored it, and such conclusions were not conjecture, as the vice-presidents had written and received replies to that effect; that its non-passage was due to the opposition of Senator Walsh.[344] In 1929 an adverse change in the personnel of the Senate Judiciary Committee resulted in an unfavorable report on the bill. Though a favorable report was desired, it was stated that any report was a long step forward. The bill would not again be introduced until the convening of Congress in regular session, when it would be pushed for immediate committee action so as to find a place on the calendar of the Senate. In the meantime, communications would again be sent by state vice-presidents to Senators and Representatives. Concerted aid of all members was urged to create public sentiment. Members of the Committee had gone to thirty bar associations and explained the difficulties, and the manner in which associations could aid; state bar associations had given aid, as had also state vice-presidents. Report was also made that nearly every state had adopted the principles of rules of court and judicial councils advocated by Committee.[345]

---

[343] Ibid., Vol. 52 (1927), p. 293.
[344] Ibid., Vol. 53 (1928), pp. 138-141.
[345] Ibid., Vol. 54 (1929), pp. 129-132, 514-524.

In 1930, General Nathan William MacChesney became Chairman of the Committee in place of Thomas W. Shelton, Esq. Though passage of the bill was considered unlikely, in order to keep the matter before Congress, the bill was reintroduced, but nothing further was to be done until the situation for its passage seemed more propitious. An effort was made to have the proposed legislation incorporated in the recommendations of the National Commission of Law Observance and Enforcement, but the Chairman of the Committee on Courts stated that since the Committee had not reached the consideration of civil matters, it was not prepared to include it. The Committee was continued, subject to order and regulation of the Executive Committee as to its scope of duty.[346]

In 1931 it was reported that no further action had been taken, though Committee had kept in touch with the general situation, and through the Chairman had discussed the matter on several occasions in Washington. The Committee was still of opinion that conditions in the Senate were not favorable to conferring additional power of the nature sought by the Committee upon the United States Supreme Court, but felt that the matter should be continued from time to time in accordance with recommendation made, namely, that the Committee continue to have bill introduced, though not undertaking any active campaign for its passage, but that the campaign of education be continued. The Committee had been advised by George M. Morris, Esq., Chairman of the Committee on Relations with the American Bar Association of the Bar Association of the District of Columbia, that at the meeting of the American Law Institute, Mr. Chief Justice Hughes had presented an important project, namely, the Conference of Senior Circuit Judges was endeavoring to secure legislation authorizing it to recommend changes in practice and pro-

---

[346] Ibid., Vol. 55 (1930), pp. 90-92 and 521-562, passim.

cedure in the federal courts. Committee was authorized to confer with the Chief Justice with reference to the matter.[347]

The Committee met in Washington on February 18, 1932. As matters then stood in the Judiciary Committee of the Senate and the House, nothing could be accomplished on the bill sponsored by Bar Committee. By direction of the Committee, the Chairman had interviewed members of the Senate and House Judiciary Committees, and had ascertained that Congress as then constituted was unfavorable to the passage of the act. There was prevalent in Congress a feeling against the federal courts and their jurisdiction, and the Bar Association could do no more at the time than to stop legislation which attempted to limit the federal courts.[348]

A portion of the reform sought by the Association for almost twenty years was attained when the bill was passed in 1932, authorizing the Supreme Court to make rules for practice in criminal cases after verdicts of guilty. The Hon. William D. Mitchell, then Attorney General of the United States, in an address before the Association on "Reform in Federal Procedure," commented that the bill endorsed by the Bar Association to authorize the Supreme Court to establish rules of practice and procedure in civil cases had long been pending in Congress; that the bill in relation to criminal procedure dealt only with proceedings after verdict. The bill applicable to civil cases had met objection in the Senate because of the claim that it would destroy conformity between practice in federal courts and in state courts in the respective states.[349]

In 1933 after proponent and opponent of the Procedural Bill had both died, Judge McClintic, Chairman of the Committee on Uniform Judicial Procedure, declared himself

[347] Ibid., Vol. 56 (1931), pp. 488 and 128.

[348] Ibid., Vol. 57 (1932), pp. 575-576. Note also how the Committee on Jurisprudence and Law Reform concentrated its activities on this very policy—supra, pp. 163-170.

[349] Ibid., Vol. 57 (1932), pp. 295-296.

opposed to the bill; he also declared that he considered it unnecessary to keep the Special Committee unless there was more sentiment among the states and members of Committees of the two Houses. In the absence of a motion to continue, the Special Committee lapsed.[350]

In 1934 the Procedural Bill was sponsored by the Administration through Attorney General Homer S. Cummings, and was enacted into law June 19, 1934 (48 Stat. 1064), in the form proposed by Mr. Taft and approved by the American Bar Association. On June 3, 1935, the Chief Justice appointed an advisory committee of fourteen to assist the Court in the drafting of such rules as would represent the best rules of court practice and procedure of the states. This advisory Committee is serving without compensation. Pursuant to instructions, the Advisory Committee prepared a preliminary draft of rules of civil procedure, which was submitted to an open forum session of the American Bar Association August 26, 1936. In the ten judicial circuits more than one hundred federal judges, five hundred practicing lawyers, and many law teachers and research scholars had participated with the great project. Many suggestions and criticisms had been received from bar associations, patent attorneys, and governmental officers, and a mass of material was assembled. The preliminary draft of rules of civil procedure was submitted for discussion, and criticism and suggestions were again invited. In the Fall of 1936, the Advisory Committee again met, and considered criticisms. The original plan called for a second draft in December, 1936, which was to be sent to Congress under the provisions of the act in January, 1937. The task was such a gigantic one that the redraft of the rules was not completed by December, 1936. The Advisory Committee is planning to issue a redraft of rules as soon as can be done, consistent with careful workmanship.[351]

---

[350] Ibid., Vol. 58 (1933), pp. 108-110.

[351] American Bar Association Journal, July, 1935, pp. 398 and 431, also November, 1936, pp. 783-786, and American Bar Association Report, Vol. 60 (1935), p. 385.

As was well stated by Edgar B. Tolman, Secretary of the Advisory Committee, there has never been such a nation-wide participation of the Bar in the formation of procedural law and no such cooperation between the Bar and the Court. Thus, the passage of this Procedural Bill and the assumption by the Supreme Court of the rule-making power marks the successful culmination of this definite movement in the direction of making more uniform and efficient the procedure in the courts of the country. The mere discontinuance of the Bar Association Committee before the passage of the act vesting in the Supreme Court the right to adopt rules of civil procedure does not mean that its twenty or more years of work and effort were in vain, for there can be little doubt but that the battle waged by Thomas W. Shelton, Esq., played an important part in the adoption of the bill. Such a highly technical reform could not have been attained without the previous program of education.

With so much time and effort given to the passage of the Procedural Bill and without apparent result, there would seem to be some weakness indicated in the Bar Association machinery for effectuating policies. Did Senator Walsh have sufficient strength in the Senate to suppress the bill, or was its suppression and non-passage due to the weakness of the Bar Association with only a vice president and four members of the local council in each state to exert pressure? Was the general membership made to feel the importance of the rule-making power? It would seem from the reports that the membership was approached, both directly and through state associations. It may well be that Henry W. Taft, Esq., of New York, struck the keynote of the whole matter when he spoke of the inertia of the legislature regarding law reform; that the Bar did its duty in formulating and presenting matters of reform, but when they reached the legislature, nothing happened; it was necessary to fight for law reform through pressure of public opinion.[352] To reach even professional opinion on a matter as technical as this Procedural Bill offered great difficulty. Note should be made of the fact that in addition to the unselfish viewpoint of the Special Committee in working for this constructive reform of Uniform Judicial Procedure, there was also the other selfish viewpoint, but this whole development shows an instance of where an unselfish reform in judicial procedure, sought for many years and seemingly not attained, was realized when least expected. Leaders in the Bar Association sometimes cite this as an example of Bar Association ineffectiveness, but it should rather be cited as an instance of the difficulty of obtaining reforms in the technical field of judicial administration and procedure through the legislature. Few know the need for reform and care less. If they are to be efficient and that would mean the elimination of delay, expense and uncertainty, then practice and procedure should, in the main, be governed by rules of court.[353] Perhaps, it is not amiss to comment that the passage of the Procedural Act marks the adoption of the principle that rules of pleading and practice should, as to their details, at least, be formulated by the Courts and not by the legislature.

Judicial Councils. Placing the rule-making power in the highest courts of the states is generally associated with judicial councils, an official body charged with the responsibility of keeping the judicial machinery in the states adequate and abreast of the times. The Merchants Association of New York in its comprehensive study of judicial councils in 1931 opened its report with a quotation from an article, entitled "A Ministry of Justice" by Justice Benjamin N. Cardozo, appearing in the Harvard Law Review of December, 1921, to the effect that the absence of a continuing body to study the working of the courts was one of the anomalies of our legal institutions. In like vein, Harold J. Laski, in his book "Politics," stated that a permanent com-

---

[352] Ibid., Vol. 49 (1924), pp. 97-98.

[353] American Bar Association Journal, Vol. 7 (1921), p. 121.

mission on law reform in which judges, lawyers, and laymen alike participate is one of the most urgent needs of the time.

Dean Sunderland credits the organization and promotion of the movement for judicial councils to the legal profession.[354] Since Justice Cardozo wrote his article suggesting the formation of a Ministry of Justice, twenty states have established judicial councils, the first of which was established in Ohio in 1923. As the "raison d'etre" of the judicial council is to have a permanent official body studying rules of practice and procedure to secure a more efficient administration of justice, it has been conceded that if they are to be effective, there must be a restoration of the rule-making power to the courts. The American Bar Association through its Conference of Bar Association Delegates sponsored judicial councils in 1926, and at the same time linked them with the rule-making power of the courts (state courts). Though in 1926 the Conference appointed two Committees, one on Judicial Councils and the other on the Rule-Making Power of the Courts, by 1927 it had merged the two Committees into one.[355]

At the 1927 meeting of the Conference, the Chairman of the Committee on Judicial Councils explained the need of councils, the method of work, and reported on legislation in ten states where councils had been created. In 1927 acts had been adopted in four states. The Chairman emphasized the great benefits that had accrued through unifying the judicial departments of the states.[356] In the presentation of the Conference report to the whole Bar Association, the opinion was expressed that if power were given to court and courts exercised it, a speedier and more efficient administration of justice would result. The assumption of that power would develop in Bench and Bar a feeling of responsibility that they should manage and con-

---

[354] Pennsylvania Bar Association Report, Vol. 41 (1935), p. 397.
[355] American Bar Association Report, Vol. 52 (1927), p. 448.
[356] Ibid., Vol. 52 (1927), p. 447.

duct the affairs appertaining to the judicial department of government.[357] In other words, by a concentration of power in the hands of Bench and Bar, responsibility would be placed on them to produce a speedy and efficient administration of justice. As an example of the effectiveness of judicial councils, Judge H. A. Hollzer, Executive Secretary of the California Judicial Council, organized in 1928, told of the creation and operation of this body, and what it had accomplished in one year in relieving the court calendars of congestion and in improving details of practice and court administration.[358]

The Committee of the Conference during the year 1927-1928 attempted to disseminate information in reference to the rule-making power of the courts, and also endeavored to develop some action. The result of its activity was recited; five states had passed statutes giving courts power to make rules, some of these rules with the force of law, and seven states had created judicial councils with varying powers and duties. Over thirty states had active committees, which were considering the subject for the purpose of reporting during the winter, when the different state associations would have annual meetings. This interest displayed in these matters was encouraging for two reasons: (1) Because great merit attached to the rule-making power of the court, and (2) Through the assumption of responsibility by courts of prescribing rules of practice and procedure, the Bench and Bar would be made to feel individual responsibility for the administration of justice. The Committee was of opinion that the exercise of the rule-making power by the courts rather than by the legislatures would lead to many reforms and would arouse in the minds of the American lawyer in every state a feeling that the Bench and Bar constituted the third department of government. It was considered that when the Bench and Bar showed a willingness to assume responsi-

[357] Ibid., Vol. 52 (1927), p. 70.
[358] Ibid., Vol. 53 (1928), pp. 516-517.

bility, there was no doubt but that the legislature would give power, and many other reforms pertaining to the administration of justice would be accomplished.[359]

In 1929 part of the discussion on the floor centered around the topic of the growth of judicial councils in the United States. It was noted that the Committee that year had reported an elaborate review of the development and operation of judicial councils, for nearly twenty states, clearly in excess of seventeen, had created judicial councils in various forms under legislative sanction. The councils were made up of practicing lawyers and judges; practically all had come into existence since 1923. Judicial councils were deemed the most significant single development in the machinery of American justice up to that time.[360]

In 1930 a report stated that during the year the Conference had fostered the National Conference of Judicial Councils.[361]

Personnel and functions of judicial councils may be gathered from a consideration of some of the most outstanding of the councils. Steps leading to the creation of the Massachusetts Council, created in 1924, were set forth by Hon. Oscar Hallam, in an address before the Criminal Law Section in 1926. A Judicature Commission was created by the legislature in 1919, which in 1921 recommended the creation of a judicial council in Massachusetts. In 1922 Attorney General Allen in his annual report again recommended the creation of a judicial council as a permanent body, and in 1924 the necessary legislation was secured. The judicial council in Massachusetts is composed of five judges and four members of the Bar, all appointed by the governor. Its function is to make a continuous study of organization, rules, and methods of procedure and practice of the judicial system of the Commonwealth.[362]

---

359 Ibid., Vol. 53 (1928), pp. 96-97.

360 Ibid., Vol. 54 (1929), pp. 51-52.

361 American Bar Association Journal, Vol. 16 (1930), pp. 750-751.

362 American Bar Association Report, Vol. 51 (1926), p. 683.

Dean Justin Miller, in an address before the Criminal Law Section in 1927 stated that reports regarding judicial councils had come from four states. The California Judicial Council had power to prescribe rules governing the making of the record on appeal in criminal cases; the North Dakota Judicial Council had been given power to organize a bureau of criminal statistics and all state officers were required to cooperate in gathering them; the work of the council was financed by a fund raised from the organized Bar; Rhode Island and Kansas Councils had been created with instructions to study criminal laws and suggest changes.[363]

Thomas Reed Powell, Esq., in a paper given before the Section on Admissions in 1917, set a goal for judicial councils, as follows: A clearing house for activities of all existing agencies for the improvement of law to present results of investigations in such form as would be readily available for practitioners, courts, legislatures and administrative commissions.[364]

As stated above, the judicial council movement was started by the legal profession; from 1923 to 1930, twenty states created judicial councils, and in 1929, the National Conference of Judicial Councils was organized. The American Bar Association should continue to furnish leadership in this important field, and urge all state bar associations to sponsor the passage of a law providing for adequate judicial councils charged with the duty of passing on questions in relation to the improvement of the administration of justice. To make judicial councils effective, the rule-making power should be restored to the courts.[365]

The personnel should include not only members of the Bench and Bar, but also the attorney general of the state, one or two key members of the legislature, and also lay

---

363 Ibid., Vol. 52 (1927), p. 474.

364 Ibid., Vol. 42 (1917), p. 583.

365 The Judicial Council, Report of Committee on Judicial Administration of The Merchants' Association of New York, 1931, pp. 9-10.

members representative of commercial and labor groups. Not only should the council represent a permanent full-time organization, composed of experts working on (1) court procedure, and (2) court personnel, to keep judicial administration effective, up-to-date and adequate, but the council should act (3) as a bureau for the collection of uniform judicial statistics, and it might also give (4) valuable assistance to the bar association committees in the disciplining of unethical lawyers.

Dean Sunderland in his admirable address stated that though the record of the legal profession as concerned the administration of law was bad, yet it could not be denied that the improvement of legal procedure during the long struggle for better administration of justice was due to the eventual, though reluctant, assistance of lawyers.[366]

The American Bar Association through its Journal has declared that effective procedural reform must come through judicial councils, integrated bars, and rule-making power in the courts.[367] All of this reform machinery has been endorsed by the American Bar Association through its Conference of Bar Association Delegates. The Bar Association should continue its pressure to have all three measures adopted in all the states, to the end that effective procedural reform will be realized, for without constant procedural reform, there cannot be an efficient administration of justice.

---

[366] Sunderland, Edson R., Address by, Pennsylvania Bar Association Report, 1935, pp. 396-397.

[367] Report of Merchants' Association of New York, Op. Cit., p. 106.

CHAPTER VII

MODIFYING GROWTH OF ADMINISTRATIVE AGENCIES [1]

"For forms of Government let fools contest,
Whate'er is best administer'd is best."
—Alexander Pope.

A. EARLY POLICIES AND ACTIVITIES.

1. INTERSTATE COMMERCE COMMISSION

During the past two or three years, there has been great emphasis placed on administrative agencies in most discussions of our government and its functions, and the layman is apt to conclude that they are new phenomena. As a matter of fact, they revert to 1887, when the first so-called administrative agency, the Interstate Commerce Commission, was authorized, though it should be noted that the Commission was not so effective until 1906, when its powers were enlarged by the passage of the Hepburn Act. The Bar Association approved the new development through action of the Committee on Commercial Law in 1887, by sponsoring the proposed Act of Congress for the Regulation of Interstate Commerce.[2] In 1916 the Com-

[1] Administrative agencies are agencies in which all three powers of government, legislative, executive and judicial, are combined, or, at least, two are exercised. These agencies represent departures varying in degree and kind from the rigid application of the doctrine of separation of governmental powers.

[2] American Bar Association Report, Vol. 9 (1886), p. 505, and Vol. 10 (1887), pp. 332-354, passim.

merce Committee considered the question of unification of regulation of both interstate and intrastate commerce by one central federal commission, such as the Interstate Commerce Commission. It asked that it be given authorization to submit a full report as to views on both sides, which authorization was granted.[3] In 1917 it reported that hearing on this subject had been held before a Joint Committee from the House and Senate on Interstate and Foreign Commerce, pursuant to Public Joint Resolution 25; that the hearings extended from November 20, 1916, to May 9, 1917, and covered thirteen hundred and sixty pages. The Committee reported that it was convinced that the questions involved were almost exclusively political and economic rather than juristic, and accordingly were not within the purview of the work of the Association.[4]

In 1919 the Committee considered acts to amend and supplement the Interstate Commerce Act. The portion of the legislation which was considered political did not interest the Bar; the portion that pertained to remedy and administration of justice was considered as so interwoven that the Committee considered it advisable to abstain from making any recommendations.[5]

2. FEDERAL TRADE COMMISSION

The Federal Trade Commission was created by Act of September 26, 1914, its decisions being reviewable by the United States Circuit Court of Appeals.[6] The organized Bar early recognized the importance of this new development and problems that might arise therefrom.[7] As early as 1916, its Committee on Commerce, Trade, and Commer-

---

[3] Ibid., Vol. 41 (1916), p. 21, and American Bar Association Journal, Vol. 2 (1916), pp. 385-388.

[4] Ibid., Vol. 3 (1917), p. 545, and American Bar Association Report, Vol. 42 (1917), p. 51.

[5] American Bar Association Journal, Vol. 5 (1919), pp. 365-366.

[6] Ibid., Vol. 5 (1919), p. 369.

[7] Cf. Ibid., June, 1935, p. 376.

cial Law was authorized to report on the practical administration of right and justice by the Federal Trade Commission.[8] The Committee in its report recited and especially commended the action of the Federal Trade Commission in issuing Conference Rulings, Bulletin #1, January 31, 1916.[9] In 1917 the Committee reported that after watching the practical working of the Federal Trade Commission, it was of opinion that the Commission was performing a useful service. The Bar Association Committee was authorized to continue its study of the practical workings of the Commission and also of the United States Shipping Board.[10] In 1918 it reported that it had continued to watch the functioning of the Federal Trade Commission, and again concluded that it was rendering a valuable service. As far as the United States Shipping Board was concerned, it was so occupied in war activities that no conclusions could be accurately formed as to the practical administration of the board in normal times. The Committee considered the act dealing with the subject of production, distribution, and consumption of food and fuel to be of equal importance with the act pertaining to the control of railroads. The Committee was again authorized to continue its work.[11] In 1919 the work of the Federal Trade Commission was again commended, especially the Conference Rulings, and regret was voiced that none had been issued since May 5, 1917, a period of more than two years. Hope was expressed that publication would be resumed at an early date.[12] In presenting its report, the Committee recommended a bill to Congress, which would direct the Commission to make its complaints more definite and certain. The implied criticism and action of the Committee was

---

8 American Bar Association Report, Vol. 41 (1916), pp. 21-22.

9 American Bar Association Journal, Vol. 2 (1916), p. 388.

10 American Bar Association Report, Vol. 42 (1917), pp. 50-52, and American Bar Association Journal, Vol. 3 (1917), p. 546.

11 American Bar Association Report, Vol. 43 (1918), p. 48, also American Bar Association Journal, Vol. 4 (1918), pp. 320-321.

12 American Bar Association Journal, Vol. 5 (1919), pp. 368-369.

criticised, but answer was made that the purpose of the recommendation was to remove serious criticism, which had been advanced on the procedure of the Commission, and to restore confidence to it. In spite of objection, the Committee's report was adopted.[13]

In 1920 the Commerce Committee initiated a policy of endeavoring to climinate some of the uncertainties existing under the anti-trust laws, by giving the Federal Trade Commission power to pass on agreements, and thus avoid penalties under the Sherman Act. The Committee recommended that it be authorized to prepare the first tentative draft of a bill pertaining to the Federal Trade Commission and the administration of the anti-trust laws, to be submitted at the following meeting.[14]

At this meeting in 1921, the Committee branched out in all its activities, and especially in relation to administrative agencies. Of its twenty-three recommendations, seven pertained to these agencies.[15] These resolutions emphasized the public and its rights. The right of intervention before administrative bodies was stressed in the report, and Hon. Elihu Root was quoted as indicating that administrative bodies, which are agencies of regulation, must themselves be regulated. In view of the fact that administrative bodies represent the public, the public should have an affirmative right by statute to intervene. The Federal Trade Commission Act like the Interstate Commerce Act, contained no affirmative provision giving the public the right to intervene, wherefore the Federal Trade Commission Act should be amended to give an affirmative right to the public to intervene. The Clayton Act should also be amended to give the public the right to intervene.[16]

The American Bar Association, through its Committee on Commerce, Trade and Commercial Law, having deter-

---

13 American Bar Association Report, Vol. 44 (1919), pp. 27-29.
14 American Bar Association Journal, Vol. 6 (1920), p. 427.
15 American Bar Association Report, Vcl. 46 (1921), pp. 309-312.
16 Ibid., Vol. 46 (1921), pp. 340-343.

mined and carried through the above policies respecting administrative agencies from 1916 to 1923, remained quiescent until 1931, when the Federal Trade Commission once more loomed into prominence in Bar Association activities because of the Committee's special interest in the administration of the anti-trust laws. After expressing approval of the Trade Practice Conference movement, developed by the Commission, the Committee recommended specific statutory authorization of the Federal Trade Commission to pass in advance on applications of anti-trust laws to particular agreements, inasmuch as the Commission was specifically designed to meet this problem and to further the development of Trade Practice Conferences.[17]

B. LATER POLICIES AND ACTIVITIES

1. ENCROACHMENT BY GOVERNMENT ON DOMAIN OF PRIVATE BUSINESS

In 1932 the Committee on Commerce considered the subject of "Encroachment by Government on the Domain of Private Business." The estimate was submitted that one person out of every nine or ten was a government employee; that the increase in the costs of government, because of regulatory and competitive activities and attendant diversions of citizens from normal status to that of government officials and employees, had created a challenge. The Committee recommended that the American Bar Association express its condemnation of the practices complained of by appropriate resolution, and authorize the Committee to conduct a further study of the questions involved.[18]

---

[17] Ibid., Vol. 48 (1923), p. 340. For further discussion of this, see infra, pp. 289-294.

[18] American Bar Association Report, Vol. 57 (1932), pp. 397-400.

2. STUDY OF FEDERAL LEGISLATION AND POLICIES AS AFFECTING THE RIGHTS AND LIBERTIES OF AMERICAN CITIZENS

In August, 1934, the Executive Committee on unanimous vote of the General Council approved resolution to appoint a Special Committee to Study Federal Legislation and Policies as Affecting the Rights and Liberties of American Citizens, whereupon a committee of eminent men was appointed. This Committee was continued in 1935, but was discharged at the 1936 meeting. The 1936 report, which was signed by four of the seven members of the Committee presented some criticism of the New Deal because of its omission to recognize any obligation to protect the individual citizen or his constitutional rights.[19]

3. FEDERAL FOOD AND DRUG ACT

Through the Committee on Commerce, the Bar Association in 1934 took a stand on the Federal Food and Drugs Act and the Federal Regulation of Stock Exchanges. There was general agreement that the present federal food and drug laws were inadequate and were in need of revision; that the present bill S. 2800 had eliminated many of the more objectionable features of the original so-called Tugwell Bill, and represented considerable concession to objecting parties. While the principal purpose of this law was to protect the consumer from impositions and fraud, the honest and conscientious manufacturer, dealer and advertiser was also protected from unfair competition and trade practice. Some features of the bill were considered by the Committee to be either unnecessary or unreasonable.[20]

---

[19] Ibid., Vol. 59 (1934), p. 153; Ibid., Vol. 61 (1936), pp. 199-201 and 864-877.

[20] Ibid., Vol. 59 (1934), p. 445.

4. FEDERAL REGULATION OF STOCK EXCHANGES

The subject of the Federal Regulation of Stock Exchanges was considered at the Committee's public hearing in 1934.[21] In its report submitted that year, the Committee discussed the National Securities Exchange Act (the Fletcher-Rayburn Bill), passed in 1934. It stated that the act created a Federal Securities and Exchange Commission, and provided in general for regulation of national security exchanges, and also of securities to be traded on exchanges. It further provided for supervision and control of practices of security brokers and dealers, and also certain practices of officers, directors and principal stockholders. The Commerce Committee had carefully considered from time to time problems arising in the field, and also progress of legislation, and it was prepared to make recommendations for certain changes in the bill as originally drafted, and as subsequently revised in Committee. However, since the bill had become law, comments as to provisions that should or should not have been included could serve no useful purpose. The interests of all could probably be best promoted if practical operation of the act was carefully studied, and then, on the basis of experience, necessary or desirable amendments or additions to the Act could be suggested. It was essential to wait until rules and regulations under the Act had been issued, and some opportunity had been afforded to study them through practical operations. The Committee would endeavor to keep in close touch with the operation of the Act, and the rules and regulations thereunder.[22] In 1934-1935, a Committee on Amendments to the Securities Act of 1933 was appointed, which in 1935 recommended simplification of registration forms and certain amendments looking to clarification of the Act.[23] A resolution was offered at the 1936

[21] Ibid., Vol. 59 (1934), pp. 439-441.
[22] Ibid., Vol. 59 (1934), pp. 441-443.
[23] Ibid., Vol. 60 (1935), pp. 224, 539ff.

meeting of the assembly to provide for a Uniform Security Act, which resolution was referred by the Resolutions Committee to the Conference of Commissioners on Uniform State Laws, for such action as it deemed advisable; this action of the Resolutions Committee was approved by the assembly.

5. APPOINTMENT OF COMMITTEE ON ADMINISTRATIVE LAW, AND ADOPTION OF POLICY OF SEGREGATION OF JUDICIAL FUNCTIONS

In 1933, when the movement to organize administrative agencies was so greatly accelerated, a Special Committee on Administrative Law was created at the meeting of the Executive Committee in May, 1933, to study the situation and make recommendations for remedial legislation to cure defects in existing system. Though appointed at such a late date, the Committee presented an exhaustive report at the annual meeting in August, 1933, which report was stated to be only a preliminary survey. This report pointed out that the appointment of such a Committee was justified because of the growing multiplicity of administrative machinery, representing a new orientation in the functions of government. By way of definition of policy, the Committee stated that the time was appropriate to appraise the merits and demerits of various types of administrative machinery as methods for serving the public welfare, and at the same time for providing due process of law and substantial justice to people regulated. Too, the Committee would endeavor to provide a sound basis for reorganization of existing agencies. The purpose of the preliminary report was to suggest appropriate fields of inquiry to which the Committee might address itself. The Committee made certain delimitations, the most important of which was that it would only consider federal administrative agencies, and would exclude state and municipal bodies. The practical operation of the various types of administrative machinery, particularly on the quasi-judicial side, was to be studied, also the various methods of judicial review, to the end that generally recognized defects could be remedied.[24] A report was submitted that Senator Mills M. Logan of Kentucky, formerly Chief Justice of the Kentucky Court of Appeals and a member of the Senate Committee on Judiciary, had introduced three bills, one of which proposed to establish an administrative court of fifteen judges.[25] This idea of an administrative court to consolidate certain of the reviewing agencies, such as the Court of Claims, Court of Customs and Patent Appeals, and certain other special jurisdiction exercised by the Courts of the District of Columbia in mandamus and injunction proceedings, was first proposed by Senator Norris.[26]

After presenting its illuminating and thorough report, the Committee was continued. In 1934 it offered an even more elaborate report with some very definite recommendations. The Committee recognized the tendency of government to extend its scope of operations and regulation and to employ administrative machinery for making detailed rules and initial determinations of controversies. The advantages of administrative agencies were also noted. For example, the employment of a body of experts exercising continuous supervision over subject matter requiring expert or specialized training renders possible technical services in such fields. However, the Committee expressed its opinion that the advantages claimed for the administrative agencies were reflected chiefly in the exercise of legislative functions, such as the formulation of rules and regulations, and that these advantages were greatly exaggerated in relation to judicial functions. Speedy action was obtained, but at the tremendous cost of dispensing with basic safeguards vital to the administration of justice.[27] The disad-

24 Ibid., Vol. 58 (1933), pp. 407-427.
25 Ibid., Vol. 58 (1933), p. 426.
26 American Bar Association Journal, March, 1936, p. 197.
27 Ibid., Vol. 59 (1934), pp. 543-544.

vantages of administrative agencies were also noticed, namely, (1) the resultant uncertainties due to the fact that orders, rules and regulations were not registered at any central office or classified; (2) the obliteration of essential lines of governmental structure, the threefold separation of powers; and (3) the too great delegation of legislative power. The conclusions of the Committee were definite and sweeping:

(1) There should be a segregation of judicial functions.

(2) Independent boards should be abolished, or transferred to one of the ten executive departments of government.

(3) Reform of existing machinery should immediately be undertaken, such as registration of rules and regulations in a central office,[28] publication of decisions, higher and more uniform standards for those practicing before administrative tribunals, and more uniformity in practice and procedure.[29]

It is obvious that the first two represented a long-term program and the third, a short-term program; the first two would eliminate independent administrative agencies, pending which process the third would add to their effectiveness by removing existing uncertainty and confusion.

In support of the above conclusions, especially the first, the evils of combining judicial with executive or legislative power were emphasized, and the fact that when there is such a combination of powers, there is violation of the fundamental maxim that a man should not be permitted to adjudge his own case. Then, too, the tenure of office of administrative judges was insecure, and there was a lack of effective independent review. Review was often limited to questions of law, and as far as the licensing provisions of the National Recovery Act were concerned, there was no provision at all for review.

---

[28] The Commerce Committee sponsored this reform in its 1934 report; see American Bar Association Report, Vol. 59 (1934), p. 439.

[29] Ibid., Vol. 59 (1934), pp. 539-541.

To accomplish the segregation of Judicial functions, a Federal Administrative Court was proposed, patterned to some extent after the French system of Administrative Courts, with branches and divisions and appropriate appellate jurisdiction.[30] If a satisfactory administrative court could not be obtained then the Committee recommended an appropriate number of independent tribunals or combination of tribunals, modeled after the Court of Claims, Board of Tax Appeals, and Court of Customs and Patent Appeals. The Committee recognized the need for limiting its Federal Administrative Court until the proposed court had demonstrated its practicability in taking over judicial functions now exercised by other administrative tribunals, neither so firmly established nor free from criticism.

In making the second recommendation that independent boards and commissions be abolished, the Committee showed alertness to the necessity for concentration of responsibility in government. It stated that there was need for the proper coordination of government activities under a limited number of executives, responsible to the Chief Executive, to avoid confusion resulting from the maintenance of such a vast number of separate agencies, responsible to no one.[31]

The Committee was authorized to confer with appropriate governmental officials and Committees of Congress, and to draft and urge the enactment of legislation in furtherance of Committee's conclusions. This authority was exercised, and in December, 1934, news was forthcoming that a Court of Administrative Justice, composed of fif-

[30] Note the action of the Committee of Jurisprudence and Law Reform in 1929, in relation to a United States Court of Administrative Justice. The Committee had given some attention to S. 5154, introduced by Senator Norris, to establish a United States Court of Administrative Justice, and was favorably impressed with the necessity for legislation to relieve the deplorable complexity and confusion in method of settling claims by or against the United States. The Committee requested the privilege of retaining the subject for further consideration, but apparently nothing further was done by this Committee. American Bar Association Report, Vol. 54 (1929), p. 377.

[31] American Bar Association Report, Vol. 59 (1934), p. 551

teen judges appointed by the President, was planned in legislation taking form in conferences between Senator M. M. Logan, Democrat, of Kentucky, and a Special Committee of the American Bar Association. Also, another bill by Representative David J. Lewis, Democrat, of Maryland, indorsed by the American Bar Association, would require all administrative orders to be filed under seal with the Secretary of State five days before they went into effect. In addition to provisions of accessibility to the public, provision was made that all such decrees must be published, at least once every six months in the same manner as Acts of Congress.[32] On July 26, 1935, Congress enacted the measure requiring the filing of rules and regulations with the Archivist of the United States and making certain requirements with respect to compilation and publication. Mr. Louis G. Caldwell, member of the Washington Bar and Chairman of the Administrative Law Committee from its inception until 1935, stated that this law almost achieved what the Bar Association had recommended.[33]

The recommendation relative to the establishment of a Federal Administrative Court[34] encountered considerable opposition at the 1936 meeting, but recommendation approving in principle the establishment of a Federal Administrative Court was adopted.[35]

---

32 The Philadelphia Inquirer, December 14, 1934, p. 3.

33 Letter received from Mr. Louis G. Caldwell, dated February 10, 1936; also Notice of U. S. Government Printing Office, Office of Superintendent of Documents, Washington, D. C., of publication of Federal Register wherein it is stated: "The Special Committee on Administrative Law of the American Bar Association for 1934 recommended Federal legislation requiring the central filing and publication of every rule, regulation, or order of general applicability and legal effect issued or prescribed by any executive officer or administrative board of the United States." The substance of the Bar Association recommendation formed the basis of the Federal Register Act.

34 American Bar Association Journal, March, 1936, pp. 197-202.

35 American Bar Association Report, Vol. 61 (1936), pp. 216-227, and pp. 232-234. The creation of an Administrative Court System to enforce regulatory laws is listed as a proposed governmental reform. See Philadelphia Inquirer, June 7, 1937, p. 32, for account of Brooking's Institute Report on Governmental Reorganization.

It would appear that policy of the Administrative Law Com-

Emphasis is usually made by lawyers of the danger of delegation of legislative power, and the autocratic Henry VIII Orders are used as illustration. Gilbert H. Montague, Esq., a New York lawyer, has stated that in periods of rapid change as in England in the fifteenth and sixteenth centuries, and Great Britain and the United States in the twentieth century, when social needs have not yet crystallized with enough definiteness to be expressed in the general body of law, new tribunals and lawmaking executives and commissions usually make appearance to supplement the legislature and older courts.[35a] Perhaps, this is the reason that law and administration are, as Carl McFarland says, to some extent antagonistic institutions of government; they represent the old versus the new. According to Mr. McFarland, the one, the judiciary, is interested in regularity and protection of private rights, while the other, the administrative agency, is interested in getting something done and done swiftly and more effectively. In other words, the administrative agency sets action above principles.[36]

It is too soon to criticise or evaluate the policy and activities of the Special Committee on Administrative Law. The Honorable John Dickinson, Assistant Attorney General, and an exponent of Administrative Agencies, considered that the American Bar Association in appointing a Committee on Administrative Law had taken an appropriate and timely step.[37]

---

mittee regarding the establishment of a Federal Administrative Court is about to be abandoned. See Annual Address delivered before Pennsylvania Bar Association June 23, 1937, by Col. O. R. McGuire, Chairman of the Committee on Administrative Law, American Bar Association.

35a Annals, July, 1935, Vol. 180, p. 149, see p. 156.

36 McFarland, Carl, "Administrative Agencies in Government and the Effect thereof of Constitutional Limitations," Prize Winning Essay in Contest conducted by American Bar Association under the terms of the Erskine M. Ross bequest, 1934. See American Bar Association Report, Vol. 59 (1934), pp. 326-347. On limitations of administrative tribunals, see Address of Edson R. Sunderland, Pennsylvania Bar Association Report, 1935, p. 395.

37 Address before Joint Meeting of Conference of Judicial Councils and Committee on Administrative Law, July, 1935.

It would seem that the Special Committee on Administrative Law might accomplish more if it concentrated on its short-term program as embodied in its third recommendation of the 1934 report, namely, a central office for registration of orders, rules, and regulations of administrative agencies (already enacted into law), a publication of decisions, higher standards for practitioners before the agencies, and more uniform practice and procedure. If to this were added a definite campaign to provide for review on all questions of law, it does seem that the chaotic condition complained of could be largely obviated. Through review, a body of legal principles would be built up that would add greatly to order and certainty in the realm of administrative law. It is strange that while the Special Committee complains of the existing lack of review in many cases, it does not, under the existing judicial system, emphasize and recommend review, as one means of gaining a segregation of the judicial from the legislative and executive functions. Most of the questions and problems in the field of administrative law are non-legal in character, and can best be solved, in the first instance, by those who are experts in the field. This would give the desired speed of action. To protect the individual and avoid the feared tyranny of government, the right of review should be available. In addition to giving protection to individual rights, review would be the means of building up a needed body of legal principles in the different fields to give order, stability, and certainty by guiding the administrator and keeping him subject to law.

As for the long-term program of the Committee, it would seem to be rather sweeping. The recommendation of the Administrative Court shows emphasis on concentration of power and responsibility in line with the best thought of experts in government. However, if the Administrative Court is to be effective, it must be organized and continued along the same functional lines as administrative agencies are organized at present. Of course, a long-term program shows vision, and is not amiss, especially in this field. For Dean Roscoe Pound in a 1919 address entitled, "Administrative Application of Legal Standards," intimated that administrative justice represented apparently a permanent phenomenon. He said:

> "In the whirl of change which has gone on in Anglo-American law in the past two decades the rapid rise of executive justice, of administrative adjustment of relations and disposition of controversies through boards and commissions, stands out as a significant and apparently a permanent phenomenon. . . . As we look back, we may now perceive the beginnings of change in the United States, as far back as 1880, and it had made much progress beneath the surface by 1900." [38]

---

[38] American Bar Association Report, Vol. 44 (1910), p. 445.

CHAPTER VIII

RENDERING TECHNICAL AID IN THE DRAFTING AND PASSAGE OF LEGISLATION

"The Law is the last result of human wisdom acting upon human experience for the benefit of the public."—Samuel Johnson.

A. MORE SCIENTIFIC DRAFTING OF LEGISLATION

1. BACKGROUND LEADING UP TO BAR ASSOCIATION'S INTEREST IN SCIENTIFIC DRAFTING OF LEGISLATION

No higher duty rests on the American Bar Association than that of advancing the science of jurisprudence.[1] As the economic and social sciences are sought to furnish principles of legislation on the substantive side, so legal science is expected to furnish such principles for the formal or technical side of legislation.[2] The increasing complication of our industrial, social, and governmental administrative problems has made it imperative that some concern be given to the collection, arrangement, and drafting of material for legislation.[3]

The subject of more scientific drafting of legislation was first brought before the American Bar Association in 1882. In that year, the Committee on Jurisprudence and Law Reform reported in favor of a Committee or Legal

1 American Bar Association Report, Vol. 36 (1911), p. 385.

2 Ibid., Vol. 38 (1913), p. 628.

3 Ibid., Vol. 38 (1913), p. 623.

Board whose duty it should be from time to time to prepare such bills for the legislature as progress of events or consolidation of existing statutes might require. The Committee considered an address by Professor Francis Wayland of Yale on "The Defects of our Method of Making Laws," most helpful, and felt that the making of law should be intrusted to competent and skilled hands. The difficulty was not the presentation of bills, but their presentation in proper form. It was thought that an act authorizing the attorney general to employ, or the legislature to appoint, skilled assistants would provoke little opposition, and might be safely urged by the local councils on the legislatures of the several states.[4]

In 1884 after the presentation of a paper by Mr. Simon Sterne of New York on the subject of "Slipshod Legislation," interest was revived, and the paper was referred to the Committee on Jurisprudence and Law Reform for action. In 1885 the Committee reported on the paper and asked permission and authority to consider legislation on the subject. Authority was given to draft the necessary legislation to be submitted at the following meeting. It was considered that through the machinery of local councils, the matter could then be brought before the legislatures of the different states.[5] Then in 1886, the Committee presented a report and draft of act providing for a simple joint standing committee of the legislature.[6] But report on the bill was never acted on, and the matter laid dormant until it was revived in 1896 by the able report of a Commission appointed under the Act of the General Assembly of New York, of which Commission Mr. Simon Sterne was a member. Certain suggestions in the report were deemed valuable, and it was considered advisable for the American Bar Association to refer the subject again to the Committee, with the request that it report to the Association on

---

[4] Ibid., Vol. 5 (1882), pp. 297-302.
[5] Ibid., Vol. 8 (1885), pp. 23-25.
[6] Ibid., Vol. 9 (1886), pp. 282-286, and Vol. 12 (1889), pp. 343-346.

the best methods of preventing the enactment of hasty and slipshod legislation in general and special law.[7] In 1897 the Committee was granted an extension of time within which to report on this matter.[8] A short report setting forth seven rules to prevent slipshod legislation was made by the Committee in 1902, but no action was taken.[9]

2. POLICY AND ACTIVITIES OF BAR ASSOCIATION IN RELATION TO MORE SCIENTIFIC DRAFTING OF LEGISLATION

In 1911 the matter was revived when the Committee on Jurisprudence and Law Reform was directed to consider and report at the following annual session on whether or not some efficient agency could be inaugurated under the auspices of the Bar Association to promote the scientific and expert supervision of the formulation of laws, to the end that their number might be decreased, and their quality improved, or whether a Special Committee should be appointed to consider and act on the subject.[10] The Committee reported in 1912 that the problem of the expert drafting of legislation could be solved by looking to the Conference of Commissioners on Uniform State Laws, a creation of the American Bar Association, for bills drawn by that body were drawn by experts, and were models of parliamentary writing.[11] The consideration of this important problem culminated in 1912 in the appointment of a Special Committee on Drafting of Legislation. After commenting on the fact that much social legislation was being declared unconstitutional and void, and was thus bringing criticism on the courts, resoluton was adopted that a Special Committee of seven be appointed to consider the problem. This Committee was instructed to report at the following meeting on existing methods of furnishing such assistance in prepara-

7 Ibid., Vol. 19 (1896), p. 41.
8 Ibid., Vol. 20 (1897), p. 67.
9 Ibid., Vol. 25 (1902), p. 398.
10 Ibid., Vol. 36 (1911), p. 384.
11 Ibid., Vol. 37 (1912), pp. 31 and 430.

tion of legislative enactments, with recommendation as to the part which the Association should take in the matter. The work of the Special Committee was to investigate drafting associations and bureaus connected with legislation to ascertain if they were effective in making legislation less slipshod, and whether the Association should encourage the movement to create legislative reference and drafting bureaus.[12]

In 1913 the Special Committee, reporting in the affirmative, stated that the most important existing public agencies for furnishing information and rendering expert assistance in preparation of legislative enactments were existing legislative reference and drafting bureaus. Assistance in framing legislation given by existing agencies fell under two heads: (1) legislative reference service or work of collecting matter throwing light on the subject matter of legislation, and (2) drafting service. Appendix A attached to the report listed eleven reference bureaus and nine reference and drafting bureaus.[13] Committee reported that it seemed practicable to establish permanent agencies, capable of giving expert drafting assistance for all bills introduced, and further urged the Association to place itself on record as favoring such an agency as the most practical means of bringing about scientific methods of legislation. The Committee submitted that the Association should urge the establishment of legislative reference and drafting bureaus in those states which had not already established them. In addition, it recommended the creation of a legislative manual or code, which should include a collection of directions or suggestions to draftsmen as well as model clauses for constantly recurring statutory provisions and problems. Thus, the establishment of drafting bureaus would be appropriately supplemented by giving the work from the start a scientific and uniform direction. The Committee submitted a tentative plan of topics for the manual, and stated

12 Ibid., Vol. 37 (1912), pp. 63-67.
13 Ibid., Vol. 38 (1913), p. 636.

that the American Political Science Association would recommend a similar arrangement of topics. Suggestion was presented that probably directors of existing bureaus would aid in working out some plan. To carry out its conclusions, the Committee offered two resolutions: (1) That the Association favored the establishment of permanent, efficient, central agencies in the several states and Washington to furnish expert legislative drafting and reference service, and (2) That the Committee should prepare a legislative manual or code, if practicable, for a code of model clauses was needed. An appendix to the report listed the Legislative Reference Bureaus and the Legislative Reference and Drafting Bureaus in the different states.[14]

In 1914 report was submitted that since the publication of the 1913 report, official agencies had been created in four additional states, while Congress had appropriated $25,000 for legislative reference work under the direction of the Librarian of Congress.[15] Recommendation was presented that the Committee on Drafting of Legislation be continued and directed to prepare the Manual for submission to the Association. It was added that the ability of the Committee would depend on the financial support which it might obtain from persons or associations interested in the improvement of legislation and simplification of law.[16] Tentative draft of proposed Manual dealing with two subjects had been prepared and submitted.[17]

In 1915 Committee reported that it had addressed a letter to the secretaries of the different bar associations asking what assistance their association had furnished members of the legislature and others in drafting bills. Almost all replies were in the negative with one exception, namely, the Nevada Bar Association. At the annual meeting of the American Bar Association held in 1914, report had been made of the work of the Committee, and also on

---

[14] Ibid., Vol. 38 (1913), pp. 56-58, 622-635.
[15] Ibid., Vol. 39 (1914), p. 631.
[16] Ibid., Vol. 39 (1914), pp. 629-632.
[17] Ibid., Vol. 39 (1914), p. 629.

the establishment of legislative drafting and reference bureaus by the different states. The result of this report was an appropriation of money by the Nevada Bar Association for the purpose of creating an unofficial and voluntary legislative drafting and reference bureau to assist the Nevada legislature. The work of the unofficial bureau created such a favorable impression that it laid a good foundation for the establishment of an official bureau at the following session of the legislature.[18] The Committee was again continued, and directed to prepare legislative manual for submission to the Association, and also to continue its research pertinent to the improvement of the form of statutory law.[19]

In 1916 the Committee reported that since it had been instituted three years before, it had from year to year submitted chapters of the Manual of Legislative Drafting, and that the Committee on Uniform State Laws had cooperated with this work. During the year 1915-1916, the Committee had completed two more topics or chapters of the Legislative Manual, and was seeking the cooperation of the Carnegie Foundation in preparation of the Manual.[20] The Committee was also charged with the promotion of Legislative Drafting Bureaus, but no new legislative drafting bureaus had been created by legislation of 1915 or 1916. Interesting statutory provisions for extension or improvement of work of existing official drafting agencies was set forth.[21] The Committee was again continued to prepare the Manual, to further research pertaining to improvement of form of statutory law, and to report results to the Association.[22]

In 1917 the Committee announced that, though the Carnegie Foundation had not seen its way clear to cooperate, it had received generous financial support from the Executive Committee of the Association to the extent of

---

18 Ibid., Vol. 40 (1915), p. 534-535.
19 Ibid., Vol. 40 (1915), p. 537.
20 Ibid., Vol. 41 (1916), p. 548.
21 American Bar Association Journal, Vol. 2 (1916), p. 455.
22 Ibid., p. 456.

$2,000. Furthermore, preparation of the Manual would require six or seven years unless the Committee could obtain further financial assistance, in the event of which the work could probably be accomplished in two or three years. The Committee also reported that another topic or section had been completed during the previous three months. The Association continued the Committee for another year with instructions to proceed with the Manual on Legislative Drafting.[23] On its aim to encourage the institution of legislative drafting and reference bureaus in the various states, report was submitted of developments in three states: Indiana, New Jersey, and Maine.[24]

In 1918, the Committee reported that in the first year of its existence, an exhaustive report had been presented, in which was included a recommendation that every legislative body should have legal expert assistance in the formulation of policies, not to help to determine what any policy should be, but to give assistance in wording and formulation of that policy. The Committee had prepared for Congress a bill carrying out its recommendation that expert assistance be employed in the formulation of bills.[25] In addition, the Committee had been engaged in the preparation of the manual which had been interrupted by the war. The Committee had recommended to the Committee on Uniform State Laws the preparation of a Uniform Interpretation Act, which would provide for uniformity of existing state acts, by defining the various words and phrases constantly repeated in those acts. The Conference of Commissioners on Uniform State Laws had appointed a Special Committee to take up the subject.[26]

In 1919 for the purpose of receiving suggestions, the Committee published as an appendix to its report a second

---

23 Ibid., Vol. 3 (1917), p. 464, also American Bar Association Report, Vol. 42 (1917), p. 446.

24 American Bar Association Journal, Vol. 3 (1917), pp. 465-466.

25 American Bar Association Report, Vol. 43 (1918), p. 88.

26 Ibid., Vol. 43 (1918), pp. 88-89, and American Bar Association Journal, Vol. 4 (1918), p. 426.

tentative draft of the outline of the Manual. This revised plan or syllabus formed the basis of final report made in 1921.[27]

It was in 1919 that the Federal Act of February 24, Section 1303, providing for Legislative Drafting Service, was passed. The act provided for two draftsmen, one appointed by the House, and one by the Senate, at $5,000 a year. This provision corresponded to the office of Parliamentary Counsel to the Treasury in England, which in turn had been instrumental in raising legislative drafting to a recognized branch of legal science. In the 1921 report, it was noted that the Revenue Act of 1919 was a great improvement over that of 1913.[28]

In 1920 the Committee was directed to prepare final report on the Manual. In submitting the final draft in 1921, the Committee emphasized that the Legislative Drafting Manual was by no means complete, since, with the continuing and growing body of material, exhaustiveness was out of the question. The Committee felt, however, that the collected material should be made available in appropriate form, and the Committee then discharged. Credit for the Manual was given to Professor Ernst Freund of Chicago.[29]

3. INFLUENCE AND CONTRIBUTION

In appointment of the Special Committee on Legislative Drafting, the Association recognized the fact that the Bar of the United States should not only call attention to evils resulting from confused and poorly drawn statutes, but should also help to correct the evil by positive suggestion and constructive action. From the beginning, the Special Committee, unlike the Committee on Jurisprudence and Law Reform, acted to promote scientific legislative drafting; (1) through a study of existing agencies, (2) through the promotion of efficient legislative reference and

---

27 American Bar Association Report, Vol. 46 (1921), p. 410.
28 Ibid., Vol. 46 (1921), pp. 410-414.
29 Ibid., Vol. 46 (1921), pp. 68-69.

drafting bureaus, and (3) by compilation of the Manual.[30] The exhaustive first report of the Committee on Drafting of Legislation, which was presented in 1913, and showed the extent of legislative reference and drafting bureaus, was widely used. In subsequent discussion of the problem of drafting legislation and proposals for established official bureaus, the report was frequently quoted. Proponents of drafting bureaus of Congress and for the Legislature of Virginia also used the reports. Too, the report was practically adopted by a Committee created by the American Political Science Association to study legislative methods.[31] Since the adoption of the resolution authorizing the appointment of the Committee on Drafting of Legislation, one of the duties of the Committee was to urge the establishment of legislative drafting and reference bureaus. A number of bureaus were established, and the action of the Association in each case could be said to be a contributing factor. The Bar Association action also tended to improve the organization of bureaus already established.[32]

While it cannot be said that the work of the Committee was the sole cause of the rapid progress of the movement for legislative drafting and reference bureaus, still it can be said that its work and support were important factors in the steady growth of the movement during the past decade. As to whether the incompleted Manual was ever used, a separate study of subsequent action of the various state legislatures would have to be made to collect the data necessary for a conclusion.

30 Ibid., Vol. 40 (1915), p. 532.
31 Ibid., Vol. 39 (1914), p. 631.
32 Ibid., Vol. 40 (1915), p. 36.

B. ACTIVITY TO PREVENT HASTY DRAFTING AND PASSAGE OF FEDERAL LEGISLATION BY ELIMINATION OF SHORT SESSION OF CONGRESS

1. NEED OF CONSTITUTIONAL AMENDMENT TO CHANGE DATE OF PRESIDENTIAL INAUGURATION AND TO ELIMINATE "LAME DUCK" SESSION OF CONGRESS

The long time which elapsed between the election of the President in November and his inauguration in March was considered a serious weakness. The short three-month session of the old Congress, occurring after the new Congress had been elected, was unsatisfactory. It gave opportunity for partisan activity. Though the intention of the framers of the Constitution clearly indicated that the new Congress elected in November should assemble in December, for reasons of convenience, it was the old Congress that had assembled, and such had been the practice ever since.[33] The inaugural date had originally been fixed by the Continental Congress, and again by the First Congress under the Constitution. Since the inaugural date, March 4, had been recognized by the Twelfth Constitutional Amendment, any change in the inaugural date would necessitate a Constitutional Amendment.[34]

The measure to eliminate the long interval between the date when the President and members of Congress were elected and the date when they began to serve in their respective capacities was considered one of the most vital reforms in government organization before the country.[35] The main purpose of the reform was to eliminate the short session and have two equally long sessions. The so-called long session of Congress, delayed more than a year after

[33] American Bar Association Journal, Vol. 6 (1920), p. 417.

[34] Ibid., p. 418.

[35] American Bar Association Report, Vol. 48 (1923), pp. 116-118 and 461-466.

the general election, found itself heavily burdened with routine and general legislation. The short session that commenced in December and ended March 4 following the general election not only presented an anomaly of legislation by a House and Senate in which many of the members found themselves defeated at the prior election, but ended abruptly on March 4 by Constitutional limitation on the terms of all representatives, and at least of one-third of the Senators. If public business required a further immediate sitting of Congress, it was necessary that all mechanical operation of Congress should be halted, and then resumed de novo by the new Congress with its attendant reorganization. The short session led inevitably to parliamentary situations; for example, deliberation was sacrificed to the necessity of time, and the filibuster was a menace. Two equally long sessions would insure fair deliberation and more prompt conclusion of public legislative business. The filibuster was useless unless there was a time limit on the legislative session.[36]

A situation which existed during the closing days of the Sixty-ninth Congress presented a striking illustration of the difficulty which the arrangement of Sessions of Congress created. Important public supply measures failed of enactment, and during four months of the fiscal year 1926-1927, vital public interests were jeopardized through failure of appropriation of public funds. The inconvenience was greatly felt. For example, in the administration of public justice, failure of deficiency appropriations resulted in substantial abandonment of all grand jury sittings and of jury trials for four months prior to June 30, 1927. Necessity for reform was indicated by the Congressional situation created by the Constitutional limitation, which resulted in substantial suspension of many activities of government among them the orderly conduct of terms of court of the federal judicial system.[37]

---

[36] Ibid., Vol. 50 (1925), pp. 339ff.
[37] Ibid., Vol. 52 (1927), pp. 131 and 240.

The American Bar Association, with William L. Putnam, Esq., as Chairman of its committee, drew attention of the country to the necessity for a change in date of Presidential Inauguration and the elimination of the short session of Congress.[38] The fundamental principle involved and supported was that the President of the United States when elected should take office more promptly, and that Congress should convene by January after the general election, and conduct at least two regular sessions in orderly fashion.[39]

2. SHORT HISTORY OF MOVEMENT AND BAR'S ACTION ON PROBLEM PRESENTED

The Bar Association's interest in the above problem dates back to 1916. In that year, the subject of efficiency of administration was discussed by the President, Hon. Elihu Root, who brought to the attention of the Association the inefficiency of the long-time period which elapsed between the election and inauguration of the President of the United States and also between the election and convening of Congress. In certain cases where a change in administration involved a change of party, this situation was even perilous. Committee on Jurisprudence and Law Reform was instructed to consider and report at the following meeting on the desirability of shortening the period between the election and inauguration of the President of the United States, and also between the election and convening of Congress.[40] A year later, a minority committee reported that the matter should be referred to a Special Committee, which would naturally confer with members of Congress and with Senators, and would endeavor to work out the best solution of the problem. On motion of William L. Putnam, Esq., the Association authorized the appointment of

---

38 Ibid., Vol. 50 (1925), p. 126.

39 Ibid., Vol. 53 (1928), pp. 150-151.

40 Ibid., Vol. 41 (1916), p. 19.

the Special Committee to consider the subject.[41] The Committee was inactive during the war. In 1920 it reported favorably on the proposed change, and the report was approved by the Association. Before the Association had taken any definite action looking to the solution of the problem, however, it found that Senator Ashhurst of Arizona, on December 23, 1920, without any previous communication from the Committee, had introduced in the Senate a resolution providing for change in the Constitution to shorten the time between the election and inauguration of the President, and also providing that the old Congress should not assemble for the short session after the new Congress was elected.[42] Since this Ashhurst resolution followed the Bar Association's recommendation, the Committee felt justified in supporting it. Through the efforts of Mr. Levi Cooke of Washington, a member of the American Bar Association Committee, the Senate subcommittee ordered a hearing on the resolution December 5, 1922. Mr. Cooke and the Chairman of the Committee, Mr. Putnam, were present; they presented the resolution of the Bar Association, made oral arguments in support of it, and also filed a written argument.

On the very day of the hearing on the Ashhurst resolution before the Senate Judiciary Committee, the Committee on Agriculture reported to the Senate a Resolution proposing an amendment to the Constitution in line with Senator Ashhurst's proposal. This resolution became known as the Norris Resolution. The members of the Bar Association Committee had the advantage of consultation with Senator Norris and others concerned with the proposal. The Committee recommended to the Association that it take steps when the Amendment was passed by Congress to secure favorable action by the states, and suggested the appointment of a larger committee of one member from each state to take action to secure passage of the Consti-

[41] Ibid., Vol. 42 (1917), p. 35.
[42] Ibid., Vol. 46 (1921), p. 476.

tutional Amendment, known as the Norris Resolution. The recommendation was adopted.[43] In an effort to aid in the passage of the resolution, the Committee sent a letter to all members of the Senate and also to the President, and enclosed remarks on the subject by Hon. John W. Davis from his Presidential Address of 1923 as well as reprint from records of the Association of the discussion which took place.[44]

The proposed amendment in one form or another was before Congress from 1923 to the date of its passage in 1932. Though the Senate in each of five Congresses had passed the resolution almost unanimously, the House displayed quite a little opposition to the measure, and also quibbled about some of the details included by the Senate, as, for example, the Longworth amendment in the House, which provided that the second session of Congress should be terminated in May.[45]

During all this time, the Bar Association Committee did not participate in the discussion over details, but emphasized that it considered its only function to be adherence to the principle involved; that it did not use stern measures in the way of urging upon the House of Representatives that the Resolution be passed, but persistently and with dignity urged on all members of the House the great principle at stake.[46]

After laboring for fifteen years, the object for which the Special Committee had been appointed was attained, and both Houses of Congress at last adopted the joint resolution proposing to the states an amendment to the Constitution changing the date of the Presidental Inauguration to January 20. This victory was gained in the Seventy-sixth Congress, first session. Since ratification by three-

[43] Ibid., Vol. 48 (1923), pp. 461-464.
[44] Ibid., Vol. 49 (1924), p. 276.
[45] Ibid., Vol. 56 (1931), pp. 129-130.
[46] Ibid., Vol. 51 (1926), p. 125; Vol. 53 (1928), p. 331; Vol. 56 (1931), p. 131.

fourths of the states was necessary, the Special Committee recommended to the Association that an auxiliary committee, consisting of one member of the Association from each state be appointed so that the Special Committee could keep in touch with each state legislature through such auxiliary committeemen and could assist in bringing about ratification of the amendment by the requisite number of states.[47] That the state groups must have been effective is evidenced by the fact that the Twentieth Amendment to the Constitution was ratified by the requisite number of states, and was an accomplished fact by the 1933 meeting. In making its final report, the Committee stated that the work entrusted to the Committee had been successfully completed, and commented that it could not make its final report without taking note of the splendid services rendered by state committees in obtaining ratifications of the amendment, nor could it fail to express its appreciation of the constructive work done by previous committees of the Association in charge of the subject.[48]

3. REFORM ACCOMPLISHED, AND ITS CONTRIBUTION TO EFFICIENCY OF GOVERNMENT AND MORE CAREFUL DRAFTING OF LEGISLATION

The Twentieth Amendment, as finally adopted, provided that the term of the President and Vice-President, now beginning March 4, should begin January 20 at Noon, and that the terms of Senators and Representatives should commence on January 3. The Amendment also provided that Congress should assemble each year on January 3, unless by law a different date was fixed.

It is too soon to venture an opinion as to whether or not the new system will give all the desired results. On the other hand, it is generally agreed that the old system was untenable, and one wonders not that it was changed, but that it could have endured so long.

47 Ibid., Vol. 57 (1932), p. 540.
48 Ibid., Vol. 58 (1933), p. 441.

Certainly, the shortening of the time which elapses between the election and inauguration of the President and the abolition of the short session of the old Congress was a step in the direction of greater efficiency in government and more careful drafting of legislation. Examples from history could probably be multiplied as to dire calamities resulting from the long period between election and inauguration. For example, it was stated at one meeting that the Civil War might have been averted if Lincoln could have assumed the Presidential office in January, 1861, instead of March, 1861, though later this was labeled a doubtful speculation.[49] Hope has been expressed by many leaders of the Bar and country that two equally long sessions of Congress will insure more careful drafting of legislation. Whether the hope is realized or not, it must at least be admitted that the old system led inevitably to parliamentary situations, as suggested above. In the short session, members of Congress or blocs would rush through desired legislation without careful consideration or deliberation, or could hinder the passage of undesired legislation by means of the filibuster.[50]

While other groups or agencies may have contributed something to the adoption of the Twentieth Amendment, still it must be conceded on the evidence presented in the American Bar Association reports that this Association through the work of its Special Committee to Consider the Change of Date of Presidential Inauguration, which carried on its activities from 1917 until 1933 with the aid of state associations, played a potent part in bringing about the reform.

[49] Ibid., Vol. 52 (1927), pp. 131-133.
[50] Ibid., Vol. 50 (1925), p. 341.

C. CONTRIBUTION TO UNIFORMITY OF LAW

1. ORIGIN AND DEVELOPMENT OF MOVEMENT FOR UNIFORMITY OF SUBSTANTIVE LAW

The subject of Uniformity in Judicial Procedure was discussed above; here it is proposed to confine the discussion to Uniformity in Substantive Law. The discussion will not be exhaustive as far as the uniformity movement is concerned,[51] but will rather be limited to the part played by the American Bar Association in its development. Though the Bar Association had taken a stand for uniformity in respect to particular subjects such as authentication of instruments conveying real estate, execution of wills, marriage and divorce,[52] it was not until 1899 that the Association inaugurated a general movement for uniformity of legislation. The adopted resolution proposed that the President of the American Bar Association appoint a Committee consisting of one member from each state, which Committee should meet in convention at time and place fixed by the President to compare and consider laws of the different states relating to the subjects of marriage and divorce, descent and distribution of property, acknowledgment of deeds, execution and probate of wills, and to prepare and report to the Association such recommendations and measures as would bring about the desired uniformity.[53] The Special Committee, which was appointed, concentrated its early efforts on obtaining appropriate legislation providing for the appointment of three commissioners to the Conference of Commissioners on Uniform State Laws. The first Conference was held August, 1892, when only nine

[51] On the development of the whole uniformity movement, see W. Brooke Graves, Uniform State Action (1934).

[52] For details, consult American Bar Association Reports, Vol. 2 (1879), pp. 194-208, Vol. 5 (1882), pp. 283-386, Vol. 9 (1886), pp. 294-319, Vol. 11 (1888), pp. 50-58, 307-321.

[53] Ibid., Vol. 12 (1889), p. 50.

states were represented. By 1912 all states, territories, and the District of Columbia were officially represented.[54] In 1896, when more than half the states had appointed Commissioners, the Conference recommended the Negotiable Instruments Act; thereafter, in addition to reporting on the increase of Commissioners, the Committee presented the uniform laws, adopted by the Conference, together with report of enactments. Meetings of the Conference have always been held at the meeting place of the American Bar Association and immediately before the annual meeting.

The Committee, appointed as above in 1889, reported in 1890 that New York had led the way to the uniformity reform by passing a law that within thirty days after passage of the act, the Governor should appoint, with the consent of the Senate, three Commissioners, styled "Commissioners for Promotion of Uniformity of Legislation in the United States." The American Bar Association Committee recommended the passage of such a law in all the states and the District of Columbia, and also recommended that the Secretary of the Association be instructed to print report and annexed resolution and to send copies to the General Council and Vice-President of the Association as well as to members of the American Bar Association Committees in states and territories and the District of Columbia.[55] In 1891 report was presented that the Chairman of the Committee had sent a circular to each member of the Committee requesting answers to certain inquiries concerning the formation of Commissions on Uniformity and the need for uniformity in substantive law. Answers had been received from most states, also letters from judges of the highest courts and lawyers making a special study of interstate law. The replies had indicated that commissioners on Uniform State Laws had been appointed in six states: New York, Pennsylvania, Massachusetts, Michigan, New Jersey,

---

[54] Ibid., Vol. 45 (1920), p. 540, and Vol. 47 (1922), p. 692.

[55] Ibid., Vol. 13 (1890), p. 336.

and Delaware.[56] Report was accepted and recommendation with amendment adopted, as follows: That the Secretary of the Association transmit copy of report and resolution to the governors of the states and territories, members of the General Council, commissioners of each state on uniformity of legislation, with formal request to members of the General Council to make personal efforts to induce legislatures of respective states to provide for appointment of Commissioners on Uniform State Law, . . . to go in person to the Legislature, if necessary, and urge the matter.[57]

In 1893, in reporting that nineteen states had then created commissions, it was recommended that members of the Committee on Uniform State Laws, vice-presidents and members of local councils of each of the states not yet appointing commissioners be charged with the duty of endeavoring to secure legislation in aid of establishing commissions similar to those existing in the nineteen states; and that officers in all states be urged to promote enactment of measures recommended by the Conference, which recommendation was adopted.[58] In 1894 report was made that twenty-two states had appointed commissioners,[59] which number in 1895 had been increased to a total of twenty-eight states and one territory.[60] The continued cooperation of the Bar Association in the establishment of new commissioners was urged. The increase in commissions continued until by 1896 twenty-nine states were represented. Up to that time, the only act of any length recommended for adoption was the Negotiable Instruments Act, based substantially on the English Act of 1882. Almost the entire week of the session in 1896 had been used to examine the act, section by section, line by line.[61] In

[56] Ibid., Vol. 14 (1891), pp. 365-375.
[57] Ibid., Vol. 14 (1891), p. 51.
[58] Ibid., Vol. 16 (1893), pp. 52-53.
[59] Ibid., Vol. 17 (1894), p. 349.
[60] Ibid., Vol. 18 (1895), pp. 335-336.
[61] Ibid., Vol. 19 (1896), p. 407.

1897, in reporting that thirty states and one territory had appointed commissioners, belief was expressed that the success of the enterprise for uniformity depended on the cooperation of the bar associations of the country.[62] In 1899 the Conference reported thirty-two state commissions with ninety-seven commissioners,[63] while in 1900 there were thirty-five jurisdictions in which commissioners were officially appointed.[64] In 1900 an effort was made to change the Special Committee on Uniform State Laws to a Standing Committee, but after it was pointed out that Standing Committees were composed of five members each, while the Uniform State Law Committee was composed of forty-six members, and that there was practically no difference between Special and Standing Committees, motion was adopted to lay the proposal on the table until the following year.[65]

In 1904 recommendation was submitted that the proceedings of the Conference be published each year in the American Bar Association report,[66] which was done for a number of years, though of late years only certain statistics are published. By 1909, forty-six states, territories, and the District of Columbia reported official Commissions, and only two states, Delaware and Nevada, were not represented. Alaska and Hawaii were the only territories not represented; Porto Rico and the Panama Canal Zone, the only possessions.[67] By 1912, as stated above, all the states, territories, and possessions of the United States were reported as represented in the Conference either by virtue of legislative action or the exercise of the governor's discretion.[68]

---

[62] Ibid., Vol. 20 (1897), p. 407, and also Vol. 21 (1898), p. 331.
[63] Ibid., Vol. 22 (1899), p. 459.
[64] Ibid., Vol. 23 (1900), p. 395.
[65] Ibid., Vol. 23 (1900), p. 33.
[66] Ibid., Vol. 27 (1904), p. 457.
[67] Ibid., Vol. 34 (1909), p. 557.
[68] Ibid., Vol. 37 (1912), p. 491.

binations should be permitted to continue to grow. If so, how should the people be protected from threatened evils; if not, how should their depredations be curbed and their growth limited? If combinations were undesirable, they should be limited by action of the legislatures; Congress, the courts, and the American Bar should act, and the latter should take the lead. The Committee minimized the value of the Sherman Anti-Trust Law because little could be done by directly prohibiting combinations. They must be made unprofitable, but how? Three suggestions were made: (1) Taxation; (2) Pressure to render better and cheaper service; and (3) Governmental competition. The Committee went on record as favoring competition, and concluded that something should be done to stay the progress of modern industrial combinations, though it stated that Committee's purpose was to provoke discussion, as it realized the necessity of mature consideration before any definite action was taken.[102] The report was recommitted for the ensuing year, and the Committee was instructed to report specific remedies in legislative form for any unlawful combination which might threaten commercial intercourse.[103] The Committee in 1904 reported that Congress had by the Act of February 11, 1903, fulfilled the requirements of the Supreme Court in regard to prompt and efficient governmental procedure against illegal commercial combinations, and that additional legislation at present was not necessary.[104]

At the 1905 meeting, the fact was revealed that the report submitted in 1904, to the effect that no legislation was needed, represented not a unanimous but only a majority report, and that the minority report recommended the passage of two specific items of legislation, in accordance with direction of Association in 1903, namely, that the provisions of remedial statutes should be extended to give an equitable as well as a legal remedy, and that the

102 Ibid., Vol. 26 (1903), pp. 23 and 431-448.
103 Ibid., Vol. 26 (1903), pp. 49-50.
104 Ibid., Vol. 27 (1904), p. 392.

fail of accomplishment.[72] And in 1917 Committee stated that while the Commissioners were energetic in their endeavor to enact into law uniform measures proposed by Conference, nevertheless, it was of the greatest importance that members of the Association individually and through their local and state bar associations should exert themselves to give necessary backing to the movement.[73] In addition to the commissioners themselves and the Bar Association Committee of one member from each state, it should be noted that the only mechanism that the Bar Association had to rely on was the vice-president and the local council together with the state bar associations and their committees.

The procedure followed by the Conference in the formulation and passage of uniform laws may be listed thus:

(1) Introduction of resolution for appointment of Committee to report on advisability of considering specific topic. Of late years all proposals of subjects for legislation are referred to the Standing Committee on Scope and Program.

(2) Drafting of legislation, usually with the assistance of expert draftsman, with submission to Conference.

(3) Discussion and report on bill.

(4) Recommitment of bill or tentative draft.

(5) Submission of three or four more tentative drafts. The Conference worked on the Uniform Partnership Act twelve years before it was finally adopted.[74]

(6) Final adoption by Conference and submission to the American Bar Association for adoption.

(7) Enactment by states.[75]

The fact that an expert draftsman is often used by the Conference in the drafting of the Uniform Acts is seen

---

[72] Ibid., Vol. 41 (1916), p. 426.
[73] Ibid., Vol. 42 (1917), p. 347.
[74] Ibid., Vol. 40 (1915), p. 437.
[75] Ibid., Vol. 42 (1917), pp. 77-78; Graves, W. Brooke, Op. Cit., p. 37.

from a consideration of some of the acts formulated. On the Negotiable Instruments Law, the services of Mr. John J. Crawford, of the New York Bar, were secured.[76] The Uniform Sale of Goods Act and the Uniform Law of Certificates of Stock Act were drafted by Professor Samuel Williston, of the Harvard Law School.[77] The Uniform Partnership Act was drafted by Dean James Barr Ames,[78] also of the Harvard Law School. Sometimes, as was the case with the Uniform Sale of Goods Act, printed copies of draft were distributed throughout the United States among members of various benches, bars, law schools, writers on sales, and others, with requests for suggestions as to desirable amendments or changes so that the act might be in the most perfect form possible for adoption.[79] The Stock Transfer Act, prepared in 1906 by Professor Williston, was considered for four years, during which time four separate drafts were prepared before the act was approved by the Conference.[80] A consideration of the Bill of Lading Act gives an idea of the thoroughness of the Conference. The first draft of the bill was submitted in 1906, then sent out to shippers, bankers, and carriers, and also considered at public sessions by the Committee on Commercial Law. The second draft was submitted to the Conference in 1907; a third tentative draft was prepared and distributed in 1908; in April, 1909, a meeting was held in New York City, which was attended by the American Warehousemen's Association, National Board of Trade, Merchants Association of New York City, and others. In 1909 a fourth draft was made, which was adopted by the Conference in August, 1909.[81]

In 1914 report was made to the Bar Association that its Committee had been working twenty-four years, and

[76] American Bar Association Report, Vol. 21 (1898), pp. 319-320.
[77] Ibid., Vol. 26 (1903), p. 501, and Vol. 33 (1908), p. 538.
[78] Ibid., Vol. 29 (1906), p. 592, and Vol. 33 (1908), p. 538.
[79] Ibid., Vol. 27 (1904), p. 456.
[80] Ibid., Vol. 34 (1909), p. 558, and Vol. 35 (1910), p. 562.
[81] Ibid., Vol. 35 (1910), p. 568.

had recommended but eleven laws; of these, the Negotiable Instruments Law had become law in substantially every state, the Warehouse Receipts Law in over half the states, and other acts had progressed proportionately.[82] In 1915, the twenty-fifth year of the work on uniformity, with the adoption of four additional acts, the output was increased to fifteen.[83] It was stated at this meeting that no greater zeal had been employed along the lines of statutory progress than that bestowed by the Conference of Commissioners on Uniform State Laws in cooperation with the Bar Association Committee.[84]

The President of the Conference in 1926, George B. Young, Esq., in an address on the "Function and Methods of Work," stressed that the duty of the Commissioners, appointed under legislative authority, was to present recommendations of the Conference to the legislatures of states and to endeavor to secure enactment. He then added that to attain uniformity, laws should be enacted in the exact form recommended.[85] In addition to this valuable suggestion, the Committee in 1910 secured adoption of a recommendation that any person or organization desiring amendments should submit them first to the Conference.[86]

Even after laws are drafted and enacted into law, only part of the work of uniformity is accomplished; the other part consists in securing a uniform interpretation and construction of law in decisions of the courts. This problem of uniform judicial decisions was also handled by the Conference and Bar Association Committee. In 1913 the Committee suggested that members of the Association call attention of courts to the need for uniformity of decisions in relation to uniform statutes.[87] In 1917

---

[82] Ibid., Vol. 39 (1914), p. 29.
[83] Ibid., Vol. 40 (1915), p. 28.
[84] Ibid., Vol. 40 (1915), p. 28.
[85] Ibid., Vol. 51 (1926), p. 665.
[86] Ibid., Vol. 35 (1910), p. 46.
[87] Ibid., Vol. 38 (1913), pp. 32 and 530.

the Committee reported that to accomplish the end of uniformity of decisions, the Conference had followed two plans:

(1) It had addressed to every court of last resort in the various states communications about the work of the Conference. In particular, it cited that the purpose of the acts was to secure uniformity of law, that interpretation should carry out this aim, and that the response of the Bench in this respect had been gratifying.

(2) The Conference through the Bar Association's Committee on Uniformity of Judicial Decisions had kept and was keeping a card catalogue of all decisions rendered in all states of the union under any of the provisions of the Uniform Acts.[88]

In 1920 the Committee announced that as an aid in promoting uniformity of judicial interpretations of various acts, the Conference had secured through Charles Thaddeus Terry, Esq., of New York, Chairman of the Committee on Uniformity of Judicial Decisions, the various Uniform Acts with full annotations, published in a single volume by Baker, Voorhis and Company, New York City.[89]

3. EVALUATION

The Bar Association has thus developed a trinity of agencies working for uniformity: (1) Conference of Commissioners on Uniform State Laws; (2) Conference of Judges for Uniform Decisions;[90] (3) Committee on Uniform Judicial Procedure.

The Conference has been in existence forty-three years, and in that time has approved 55 acts, embodying 696 enactments.[91] In 1926 it was felt that the movement

---

[88] Ibid., Vol. 42 (1917), p. 78.
[89] Ibid., Vol. 45 (1920), p. 541.
[90] Ibid., Vol. 40 (1915), p. 507.
[91] Ibid., Vol. 60 (1935), p. 733. Cf. Article by Hon. William L. Ransom "Constructive Work of the American Bar Association,"

for uniform state laws had gained in prestige and importance since the organization of the Conference in 1892. President Coolidge was quoted to the effect that we must maintain the proper measure of local self-government while constantly making adjustments to increasing interdependence among political parts. Where uniformity is demanded by exigencies of business and social life, the state must supply the need or otherwise pressure on the national government would be irresistible.[92] Professor W. Brooke Graves agrees that the movement for uniformity in legislation has gained momentum in the last few years, since in 1925 the total number of uniform enactments was less than 400, while in 1932 the number had increased to 600.[93]

In a 1921 address Henry Stockbridge, Esq., then President of the Conference, classified the Conference subjects under three heads: (1) Those which related to carrying on of commercial relations between man and man or corporation and individuals; (2) Those which dealt or attempted to deal with family life or relations under law; and (3) Those which dealt with idealistic legislation by which on a comparatively new subject a model form of legal regulation was attempted to be given. In addition, there had been a limited number of acts of a procedural character. He called attention to the known fact that acts securing the widest adoption were of a commercial nature, such as the Negotiable Instruments Law, Bills of Lading, Warehouse Receipts and Sales Acts.[94] George B. Young, Esq., President of the Conference in 1926, stated that an analysis of approved acts indicated that the Conference was most successful in preparing uniform acts dealing with strictly legal matters and with subjects in which law was

American Bar Association Journal, November, 1935, p. 705, where the number of Uniform Laws approved by the American Bar Association is listed as 57.

[92] Ibid., Vol. 51 (1926), pp. 652-654.

[93] Graves, W. Brooke, Op. Cit., pp. 55-56.

[94] American Bar Association Report, Vol. 46 (1921), p. 718; Graves, W. Brooke, Op. Cit., p. 46.

well settled and well developed. The best work of the Conference was achieved when pioneering and reform were avoided.[95] Whether or not the statutes having most enactments to their credit represent codification of well settled and well developed law, it is apparent that the majority are of a commercial nature.

D. POLICIES AND ACTIVITIES IN THE FIELD OF ANTI-TRUST LEGISLATION

1. EARLY INTEREST IN THE SHERMAN ACT, AND ATTEMPTS TO MAKE MORE CERTAIN AND DEFINITE

The Sherman Anti-trust Act was passed July 2, 1890. The Association showed its almost immediate interest, for as early as 1894, it adopted a resolution that the Committee on Jurisprudence and Law Reform be requested to submit to the Association at the following meeting a report comprising (1) a succinct history of operations to date of the Act of Congress commonly known as the Anti-Trust Law, with such comments on its success and usefulness as seemed pertinent, and (2) recommendation for any additional legislation within the constitutional power of Congress, which would increase the effectiveness of the act or improve modes of procedure under it, with such suggestions as should seem to them advisable on the subject.[96]

The Committee thereupon collated court decisions in an elaborate report. The report was distributed in the hope that it would be made the subject of private study before discussion. Resolution was adopted that Committee be requested to submit to the Bar Association at the following meeting report on the subject of existing laws in reference to trusts and combinations in business.[97]

95 American Bar Association Report, Vol. 51 (1926), pp. 657-658.
96 Ibid., Vol. 17 (1894), pp. 71-72.
97 Ibid., Vol. 20 (1897), pp. 9-11, 72, and 325.

In 1900 the Committee reported that "Trusts and Combinations," was a subject referred to the Committee with directions to make suggestions as to effectual discriminations in law between trusts and combinations injurious to society and those which were not harmful; that the Committee had the subject under consideration but was unable to agree on a report.[98] In 1902 the Committee reported that its duty was not to express an opinion on the wisdom or folly of the legislation, but simply to say whether more effective laws were practicable.[99] In 1903 a resolution was referred to the Committee to inquire whether industrial and commercial enterprises should be amenable to national restrictions against unlawful combinations.[100] On this point, the Committee in 1904 reported that such power contemplated by the resolution should not be delegated by the state to Congress, that is, that Congress should not be given power to regulate state organizations. Report on "Combinations and Trusts," was laid on the table.[101] Thus ended the activity of the Committee on Jurisprudence and Law Reform in this field.

In 1903 the Committee on Commercial Law submitted a report on combinations, which pointed out that during the year it had been wrestling with a question which it considered one of the most important before the Bar of the United States, namely, the effect of modern gigantic commercial combinations upon the commercial jurisprudence. Moreover, the modern combination was entirely industrial and largely commercial, and its primary object was to control trade and commerce in certain articles of production, and substitute more or less perfect monopoly in place of a more or less free competition. Too, the organized Bar had served the community in various capacities, and should grapple with the question whether modern industrial com-

---

98 Ibid., Vol. 23 (1900), p. 11.
99 Ibid., Vol. 25 (1902), p. 400.
100 Ibid., Vol. 26 (1903), p. 106.
101 Ibid., Vol. 27 (1904), pp. 21-29 and 380.

binations should be permitted to continue to grow. If so, how should the people be protected from threatened evils; if not, how should their depredations be curbed and their growth limited? If combinations were undesirable, they should be limited by action of the legislatures; Congress, the courts, and the American Bar should act, and the latter should take the lead. The Committee minimized the value of the Sherman Anti-Trust Law because little could be done by directly prohibiting combinations. They must be made unprofitable, but how? Three suggestions were made: (1) Taxation; (2) Pressure to render better and cheaper service; and (3) Governmental competition. The Committee went on record as favoring competition, and concluded that something should be done to stay the progress of modern industrial combinations, though it stated that Committee's purpose was to provoke discussion, as it realized the necessity of mature consideration before any definite action was taken.[102] The report was recommitted for the ensuing year, and the Committee was instructed to report specific remedies in legislative form for any unlawful combination which might threaten commercial intercourse.[103] The Committee in 1904 reported that Congress had by the Act of February 11, 1903, fulfilled the requirements of the Supreme Court in regard to prompt and efficient governmental procedure against illegal commercial combinations, and that additional legislation at present was not necessary.[104]

At the 1905 meeting, the fact was revealed that the report submitted in 1904, to the effect that no legislation was needed, represented not a unanimous but only a majority report, and that the minority report recommended the passage of two specific items of legislation, in accordance with direction of Association in 1903, namely, that the provisions of remedial statutes should be extended to give an equitable as well as a legal remedy, and that the

---

102 Ibid., Vol. 26 (1903), pp. 23 and 431-448.
103 Ibid., Vol. 26 (1903), pp. 49-50.
104 Ibid., Vol. 27 (1904), p. 392.

franchise tax should be graded up rather than down.[105] A resolution, that these recommendations of the minority report amending the Sherman Act be approved, was lost.[106] The matter was again revived in 1906, but motion to reconsider was tabled.[107]

The matter of anti-trust laws was not again considered until 1919, when the Committee on Commerce, Trade and Commercial Law, formerly the Committee on Commercial Law, suggested that it seemed proper that some group like the Federal Trade Commission should be empowered to predetermine whether a business agreement was reasonable or not under the Sherman law.[108]

In 1920 the Committee was asked to prepare for the following meeting a first tentative draft of bill pertaining to the Federal Trade Commission and the administration of the anti-trust laws.[109] In 1921 the matter of the administration of the anti-trust laws through the Federal Trade Commission, issuing declaratory orders and advisory opinions, was resubmitted to the Committee.[110]

In 1927 the Committee on Commerce, formerly the Committee on Commerce, Trade and Commercial Law, again considered the uncertainty produced in business by the anti-trust laws. The report for that year pointed out that the Sherman Act was not in all respects economically sound as then interpreted. Too, economic conditions had changed since 1890, and since the Sherman Act was economic legislation, it could only be helpful if it was subservient and not in opposition to economic laws. Not only was the Sherman law economically unsound, but its application to individual cases was uncertain. Recent enactments had sought to modify the Sherman Act. Again, the legislature in recent years had indicated that Congress no longer conceived un-

---

105 Ibid., Vol. 28 (1905), pp. 35-75.
106 Ibid., Vol. 28 (1905), p. 76.
107 Ibid., Vol. 29 (1906), p. 21.
108 American Bar Association Journal, Vol. 5 (1919), p. 373.
109 Ibid., Vol. 6 (1920), p. 427.
110 American Bar Association Report, Vol. 46 (1921), p. 312.

restricted competition as necessary in the public interest, and the Federal Trade Commission had been empowered by the Clayton Act, approved October 15, 1914, to regulate competition as to price discrimination, tying contracts, corporate stock ownership, and interlocking directorships. The Commerce Committee considered that the country had outgrown the Sherman law. Further legislation was suggested to establish standards and confer on a Federal Administrative Agency power to determine whether any given agreement restraining trade conformed or violated those standards and was otherwise unlawful. The Committee was of opinion that future amendments to the law should be made in the public interest. However, the Committee had formulated no definite conclusions of its own as to what the amendments should be, but with approval of Association, it would continue its study of the subject. This approval was given by resolution.[111]

In 1928 it was reported that a year's study had confirmed the Committee's view, as reported in 1927, that further legislation was necessary. The present need was an affirmative anti-trust law. Congress had recognized the propriety of the suggestion; the Capper-Volstead Act established an affirmative standard of conduct for those subject to its provisions; likewise the Packers and Stockyards Act was an affirmative, constructive piece of anti-trust legislation. These acts brought business into helpful, hopeful, and forward-looking contact with government through administrative channels that had nothing to do with enforcement of criminal law. The Committee was granted its request that further time be given to study of the anti-trust laws.[112] At the public meeting held in March, 1929, seven members of the Bar and one layman spoke on various aspects of the anti-trust problems. With one exception modification of existing statutes was favored, and some concrete suggestions as to amendments were made.

---

[111] Ibid., Vol. 52 (1927), pp. 248-251 and 99.
[112] Ibid., Vol. 53 (1928), pp. 338 and 373-374.

The Committee in its 1929 report reaffirmed its view as expressed in its reports of 1927 and 1928, and was of opinion that the time had come when appropriate Committees of Congress should be asked to give consideration to amendment of the anti-trust laws. Then, too, there was need for cooperation between government and business; the difficulties under the Sherman Act because of its vague commands could be eliminated by amendment to the Clayton Act, which would confer on existing administrative agencies jurisdiction to determine in advance at the request of industry whether or not a given agreement could take effect without incurring the Sherman Act penalties. A resolution was adopted, which directed the Committee to request appropriate committees of Congress to hold hearings for the purpose of considering and passing on the advisability of amending the anti-trust laws.[113]

The Committee reported work in the field of anti-trust laws as its major activity for the year 1929-1930. After the 1929 annual meeting of the Association, and prior to the April, 1930, committee meeting, a bill with recommendations had been drafted, copies of which bill were sent to interested persons, who spoke on it before the Bar Committee. A number of objections to the bill were advanced on constitutional grounds. The Committee emphasized that the present procedure of enforcing the Sherman Act represented an ex post facto enforcement, because the only standards of judgment were as yet unknown economic standards of the court, which was asked for decision long after the act was done. The Department of Justice had recognized the situation, and engaged in the rather doubtful extra-legal practice of ex parte examinations of proposed agreements affecting interstate commerce. This practice has demonstrated the necessity of establishing an authoritative body of men to whom proposed agreements could be submitted. The Committee recommended that this function of approving or disapproving agreements be given to the

[113] Ibid., Vol. 54 (1929), pp. 308, 310-313.

Federal Trade Commission. No bills were prepared, but hope was expressed that they would be prepared by the 1931 meeting.[114]

The matter of anti-trust laws was discussed at Committee's public meeting in 1931, and revolved mostly around bill drafted by Committee embodying action of the Association in 1929. The Committee indicated its approval of proposal to amend anti-trust laws by conferring on the Federal Trade Commission the power to pass in advance on restraint of trade contracts voluntarily submitted, and by granting immunity to parties to contracts approved by the Commission from criminal, confiscatory, and three-fold damage provisions of the anti-trust laws. The parties who addressed the Committee were unanimous in their view that anti-trust laws should be amended. Revised draft was presented to the annual meeting, and the Committee was authorized to present its views to Congress.[115] In 1932 it was reported that demand for the proposed amendment had grown, as evidenced by the number and scope of bills introduced in Congress. There had been a diversity of opinion on the extent to which amendment should go. Many persons appearing before the Committee had favored the Committee's suggested amendment, and the main objection was that it did not go far enough. The effect of the amendment was as above set forth. Helpful results, which would be obtained from the enactment of Committee's bill, were listed. A copy of the ninth revised draft of Committee's bill was appended to report. The Committee considered that the bill was in a most satisfactory form, and enunciated its purpose to be present at anti-trust law hearings, when held by Committees of Congress, to declare views substantially as expressed in this and preceding reports.[116] Authorization to do this was given.[117]

---

114 Ibid., Vol. 55 (1930), pp. 78 and 321.
115 Ibid., Vol. 56 (1931), pp. 60-61 and 339-341.
116 Ibid., Vol. 57 (1932), pp. 395-397.
117 Ibid., Vol. 57 (1932), pp. 89-95.

The Committee on Commerce also held in 1932 a joint meeting with the Section of Mineral Law for a discussion of the federal anti-trust laws.[118] Among many other matters, the discussion brought out the fact that over 2200 distinct efforts to amend the Sherman Anti-Trust Law had been made; that the Bar Association bill had gone as far in an endeavor to meet the situation as could be expected, and represented a forward step.[119] In presenting its report, the Bar Association through the Chairman of the Committee defined the purpose of the Committee's bill as the relief of business men from fear of criminal prosecution, which now deterred them from entering into contracts, by conferring additional powers upon the Department of Justice and the Federal Trade Commission. The Committee's proposal had a dual aspect; it provided (1) that contracts, voluntarily submitted to Attorney General and filed with the Federal Trade Commission, should become automatically effective unless within sixty days objection was made by the Department of Justice or interested persons, in which event they might be made effective by order of the Commission, but only after hearing; (2) that parties to such contracts were exempt from criminal three-fold damage and confiscatory provisions of the Sherman Act.[120]

At the Executive Committee meeting in May, 1933, Commerce Committee reported that the administration had changed its attitude on amending the anti-trust laws. Therefore, the Committee requested authority to cooperate with the President's advisers in preparation of bill being drawn for purpose of putting the President's program into effect. The Commerce Committee did not consider that it lacked authority to act, but decided, because of necessity for broader legislation than had been indicated in reports in previous years, that special action of the Executive Committee was necessary to justify the Commerce Committee in recommending enactment of legislation, the effect of

[118] Ibid., Vol. 57 (1932), pp. 698-710.
[119] Ibid., Vol. 57 (1932), p. 703.
[120] Ibid., Vol. 57 (1932), pp. 90-91.

which might even be to validate price control agreements. The Commerce Committee received the requested authority.[121] In presenting a report in 1933, the Commerce Committee called the enactment of the National Industrial Recovery Act the outstanding event of the year. It included an anti-trust law modification, which the American Bar Association on recommendation of its Commerce Committee had for years advocated. The price paid for the exemption was considered high, since the only asset acquired by business through the National Recovery Act was the rather limited Sherman Act exemption referred to.[122] Since the Supreme Court has declared the National Recovery Act unconstitutional, the Commerce Committee is once more grappling with the problem of regulated competition, and advocating the adoption of its bill providing for submission of agreements to the Federal Trade Commission.[123]

2. EVALUATION OF POLICIES AND ACTIVITIES, AND RECOMMENDATIONS

The Bar Association in its policies and activities in this field of anti-trust laws was acting true to its general policy of stressing the need for certainty in law. However, it would appear that the emphasis was too strongly placed on the fear of criminal prosecution. It is surprising that so much confidence could be placed by a legal group in an administrative agency. The Bar Association's plan of having trade agreements first passed on by the Federal Trade Commission would have been a constructive development as long as the personnel of the Commission was beyond reproach. But if the personnel degenerated, and agreements, constituting definite monopolies under the Sherman Act, were approved, then no criminal prosecutions could afterwards

---

121 Ibid., Vol. 58 (1933), p. 346.

122 Ibid., Vol. 58 (1933), pp. 128-129.

123 Ibid., Vol. 60 (1935), p. 222; also see Philadelphia Inquirer, June 7, 1937, p. 32, for an account of Brookings Institute Report on Governmental Reorganization.

be brought. Lincoln Steffin in his biography has emphasized that monopoly is inevitable. If this is so, then instead of endeavoring to stem the tide of an inevitable development, would it not be more sensible to concentrate on an adequate system of regulation? With monopoly, regulation is a necessity.

Big business itself seems convinced that unbridled competition is destructive, but has been unable to develop any machinery looking toward self-discipline and self-control. The difficulty is found in drawing a line between what is fair and unfair competition, or fair and unfair trade practices.[124]

The Bar Association, through its Commerce Committee, has consistently taken the stand, and rightly, that the Sherman Act, as interpreted, was satisfactory to no one, and did need and still does need clarification, especially by way of being made more definite and certain.

E. COMMERCIAL ARBITRATION PRINCIPLE ENACTED INTO LAW

1. FORMULATION AND DETERMINATION OF POLICIES AND HOW EXECUTED

The movement to promote special courts of arbitration was initiated in the American Bar Association as early as 1886. In that year, a project for a bill to establish courts of arbitration in connection with federal courts was referred to the Committee on Jurisprudence and Law Reform.[125] A report was presented in 1887 that there then existed in New York a Special Court of Arbitration for the speedy hearing and adjustment of controversies between mer-

---

124 The American Bar Association through its Commerce Committee is again endeavoring to have legislation enacted, which will confer on a federal administrative agency the power to determine the status of specific trade practices. American Bar Association Report, Vol. 60 (1935), p. 223.

125 American Bar Association Report, Vol. 9 (1886), p. 509.

chants. However, suitors and lawyers preferred to trust to the regular course of law. But because of frequent conflicts between labor and capital, the Committee believed the experiment of a court of arbitration worth trying. It accordingly recommended the adoption of a resolution that the project of a bill for an act to establish courts of arbitration as printed in reports of the Association [126] presented a fair and practicable scheme for enlarging powers of courts of the United States in respect to arbitration, and that such a bill was worthy of careful consideration by Congress at the next session.[127] After prolonged discussion, the resolution was recommitted to the Committee.[128]

New York again took the lead in this field when in 1914 the New York State Bar Association created a Committee known as the Committee on Prevention of Unnecessary Litigation. In 1918 this became the Committee on Arbitration of the New York State Bar Association. In January, 1919, the Committee announced that it had become convinced "that the doctrine of revocability of such agreements was a legal anachronism which should be eliminated from the law at the earliest moment, and should induce courts to reverse former rulings as the wisest method of correcting judicial error of long standing." A proposed bill for recognition and enforcement of agreements for abitration of controversies was then submitted. As a result of the work of the three committees of New York State Bar Association, the Arbitration Law of the State of New York was drafted and enacted into law in 1920.[129] Thus, for upwards of three centuries prior to 1920, the accepted law in the United States had been that an agreement to arbitrate a difference out of court was revocable at the pleasure of either party. Not until 1920, when the three Committees of New York State Bar Association together with Committee of Chamber of Commerce of the State of New York procured the en-

[126] Ibid., Vol. 9 (1886), p. 509.
[127] Ibid., Vol. 10 (1887), pp. 322ff.
[128] Ibid., Vol. 10 (1887), pp. 29-50.
[129] N. Y. Laws 1920, Chapter 275.

actment of the New York State Arbitration Law, were agreements to settle by arbitration valid, enforceable, and irrevocable. This law also provided machinery by which agreements were enforced. The New Jersey State Chamber of Commerce and New Jersey State Bar Association, following a like cooperative policy, had a similar statute enacted in 1923. In 1918 the Conference of Bar Association Delegates by adopted resolution urged the Bar Association to encourage the settlement of disputes out of court by arbitration as far as practicable.[130]

Then in 1920, the matter of commercial arbitration was referred to the Committee on Commerce, Trade and Commercial Law. The Committee took up the question of drafting a uniform state act and a federal act on arbitration. In 1921 the Committee submitted a uniform state arbitration act, which it stated was based on the New Jersey bill, drawn by the New Jersey Chamber of Commerce, and modeled on the New York law.

The Committee also submitted a tentative draft of bill pertaining to United States Arbitration of Disputes, which bill had been drafted after repeated consultations with business men.[131] During the year 1921-1922, impetus was given to the movement when Secretary of Commerce Herbert Hoover requested permission to introduce a proposed Federal Arbitration Statute in Congress. Copies of a draft of the federal statute were furnished him by the Bar Association Committee. At public hearings various suggestions for improving the statute were made. The Committee considered all these suggestions, and, with the assistance of Professor Samuel Williston, a much improved draft of the federal statute and uniform state statute had been formulated.[132]

On the international side, at the request of the Committee on Arbitration of the New York State Chamber of

---

[130] American Bar Association Report, Vol. 50 (1925), pp. 356-362.

[131] Ibid., Vol. 46 (1921), pp. 309 and 355-359.

[132] Ibid., Vol. 46 (1921), pp. 355-359, and Vol. 47 (1922), pp. 315-322.

Commerce, a member of this Committee and counsel for the Chamber drew a form of treaty to be negotiated with foreign countries for the purpose of making effective international commercial arbitration agreements. The treaty had been submitted to Secretary of Commerce Hoover, then revised and submitted for the approval of the Association. Resolutions were adopted to approve (1) the Uniform State Arbitration Act, Appendix C, to be referred to the National Conference of Commissioners on Uniform State Laws, (2) the form of treaty to be negotiated with foreign countries for making effective international arbitration in commercial disputes and controversies, and (3) the suggested provisions of the bill for United States Arbitration Act (Appendix B).[133]

Pursuant to the 1922 resolution, the United States Arbitration Statute had been introduced into the Sixty-seventh Congress, Fourth Session,[134] which had been referred to the Committee on Judiciary. Chairman of the American Bar Association Committee and Mr. Julius Henry Cohen had had several conferences with members of the Senate Committee. Mr. Charles L. Bernheimer, Chairman of the Committee on Arbitration of the New York State Chamber of Commerce, appeared before the Committee and several times visited Washington. The bill received the cordial support of the National Association of Credit Men, the New York Chamber of Commerce Committee, and forty-six other commercial organizations.

On the international commercial arbitration treaty, it was reported that Mr. Bernheimer had conferred with Secretary of State Hughes, and further that the subject was receiving the careful consideration of the Economic Committee of the League of Nations.[135]

---

[133] Ibid., Vol. 47 (1922), pp. 289 and 293-294.

[134] S. 4214 and H.R. 13522.

[135] American Bar Association Report, Vol. 48 (1923), pp. 286-287. Note should be made of the fact that in 1923, Wade H. Ellis, Esq., in an address before the Criminal Law Section on "Criminal Law in England and France," made some commendatory remarks of the Bar's policies and activities in the field of arbitration when he stated

Pursuant to 1923 resolution, the Committee had the amended United States Arbitration Statute introduced again in December, 1923.[136] In January, 1924, the subcommittee of the Senate and House Committees on Judiciary held a joint hearing on the bill, and the House Committee on Judiciary made a favorable report.[137] On February 18, 1924, an important decision, Atlantic Fruit Company v. Red Cross Line, was handed down by the Supreme Court. On the same day, the American Bar Association Committee sent a letter to the Chairman of the Judiciary Committees of the Senate and House, stating that the decision had an important bearing on the proposed United States Arbitration Law,[138] prepared by the American Bar Association. The decision went a long way to reverse the ancient error of revocability in arbitration agreements, and removed the last vestige of doubt concerning the making of such agreements valid and enforceable. On March 7, 1924, a letter together with a copy of Committee's resolution was sent to Senator Walsh; the Arbitration Bill, amended to accord with suggestions made in Senator Walsh's letter, was annexed to report as Appendix B. The situation on the Arbitration Bill showed that the House Bill had been favorably reported by Committee on Judiciary, but had not been acted on by the House, and that the Senate Bill was still under consideration by the Committee on Judiciary.[139] The United States Arbitration Bill was again approved by the American Bar Association and enactment urged.[140]

On the international commercial arbitration treaty, it was pointed out that in 1922 Committee had drafted a form

---

that one measure of relief for congestion of courts was that proposed in the plan sponsored by a branch of this Association, to increase the number and widen the scope of arbitral courts for settlement of civil controversies of a commercial nature. Ibid., Vol. 48 (1923), p. 632.

136 S. 1005.

137 On H.B. 96.

138 S. 1005, H.R. 646.

139 American Bar Association Report, Vol. 49 (1924), pp. 281-284.

140 Ibid., Vol. 49 (1924), p. 279.

of treaty,[141] and in 1923 it had submitted a form of arbitration agreement,[142] and a bill had been introduced into the Sixty-seventh Congress to make valid such arbitration agreements. If the American Bar Association could further legislation of the South American countries and encourage treaties, uniform procedure in the law merchant could be secured.[143] Resolution was adopted that the American Bar Association favored negotiation of commercial arbitration treaties between the United States and South American states as the most practical method to reconcile the differences in law merchant of North and South America.[144]

In 1925 the Committee reported that the United States Commercial Arbitration Statute had been enacted into law February 12, 1925. The passage of the act marked the culmination of many years of effort in which the Bar Association and commercial interests had cooperated toward harmonizing the administration of law with the requirements of business. The Bar Association had appeared in support of the measure before subcommittees of the Senate and House Committees on Judiciary at joint hearings January 29, 1924, and credit for bringing about results had been given to the American Bar Association. Due acknowledgment was made by the Bar Association to commercial organizations throughout the United States for the splendid cooperation in support of the bill.[145]

As far as the Uniform State Act was concerned, by 1925 a conflict had developed between the Committee on Commerce, Trade and Commercial Law and the Conference of Commissioners on Uniform State Laws. In considering a recommendation of the Executive Committee which proposed an amendment of by-laws relative to the Committee on Commerce, Trade and Commercial Law, the whole matter of the state arbitration law was reviewed. The subject

---

141 Ibid., Vol. 49 (1924), p. 289.
142 Ibid., Vol. 49 (1924), p. 289.
143 Ibid., Vol. 49 (1924), pp. 289-290.
144 Ibid., Vol. 49 (1924), p. 280.
145 Ibid., Vol. 50 (1925), p. 353.

of arbitration had come before the Committee on Commerce, Trade and Commercial Law in 1920, through and by act of the Association sending it to the Committee as a mandate to draw a federal and a state law. The Committee, pursuant to direction, had discharged the obligation, and had brought back to the Association two acts, the federal act and the state act. It was then directed to introduce the federal act into Congress, and to turn the state act over to the National Conference of Commissioners on Uniform State Laws. The National Conference had subsequently changed the state law in such a way that it was the reverse of the national act in that the Conference bill provided for arbitration by agreement in writing between two or more parties to any controversy existing between them at the time of agreement to submit, whereas the Commerce Committee bill provided for compulsory arbitration of any controversy arising in the future. The proposed amendment was referred back to the Executive Committee.[146] However, the Uniform Arbitration Act was approved by the American Bar Association in 1925,[147] and by 1935 had been adopted in five states.[148]

2. EVALUATION AND RECOMMENDATIONS

Though the Bar Association is conceded credit for the passage of the United States Arbitration Act, there is no doubt that the movement for commercial arbitration was hastened by the conviction of business men that their own trade tribunals were better adapted than the courts to settle commercial disputes. The fact that the Bar Association did play a major role in the development of sentiment for arbitration as well as pressing for the passage of an Arbitration Law should be more definitely noted than it usually is. The Bar Association bill also included a provision for

[146] Ibid., Vol. 50 (1925), pp. 36-64.

[147] Ibid., Vol. 50 (1925), pp. 161-162; for text of the bill, see p. 591.

[148] Ibid., Vol. 60 (1935), p. 733.

the amicable settlement of industrial disputes, but since it was gathered that such provision could not be passed, it was deleted from the bill. Afterwards the Commerce Committee considered this question in a separate bill, but this will be discussed under the next heading.

F. CONTRIBUTION TO THE SOLUTION OF THE LABOR PROBLEM

1. EARLY POLICIES AND ACTIVITIES

Though employer and employee relationships would seem to belong in the realm of economics, and though it was the Bar Association's policy, at least in its earlier days, to avoid all political and economic questions, still because out of employer-employee relationships come many legal problems, it is not surprising that the Bar Association early showed activity in the field. The Association's first attack on the problem was with the troublesome "fellow servant" defense, available to employers to prevent employees from collecting damages for injuries sustained. The Bar Association here, and later, through activities of the Committee on Compensation for Industrial Accidents and their Prevention, took the side of the employee. However, the latter committee's activities were cut short by the contention that after the Committee had accomplished its initial job of drafting a Uniform Compensation Act, it was in the realm of politics when it endeavored to establish particular types of compensation insurance in the several states. Later, when the Bar Association worked, first for coercive industrial courts, and then for voluntary industrial arbitration, it did not take sides, but seemed to have achieved at least the semblance of cooperation among the many conflicting interests in its effort to realize its object of amicable adjustment of industrial strife.

In 1896 a resolution was adopted to refer to the Committee on Jurisprudence and Law Reform the question whether the law in relation to fellow servants should not be so amended as further to protect the laboring men from the results of negligence caused by persons unknown to them and over whom they had no control.[149] Nothing further appears to have been done by this Committee, but in 1910 a policy was initiated to study the question of compensation for industrial accidents and their prevention. In that year, the Executive Committee recommended the following resolution: Resolved, that the President of the Association be authorized to appoint a Committee of five on the subject of "Compensation for Industrial Accidents and their Prevention," and to cooperate with the National Civic Federation in this work.[150] This subject of compensation for industrial accidents and their prevention would include the problem of fellow servant, the common-law defense which usually prevented the plaintiff employee from recovering for injuries sustained. The Committee of the National Civic Federation, after careful and extensive consideration of the subject, had not been able to agree on a uniform act to be adopted in the states, and had postponed action until later. In the interim, report was to be compiled showing progress of the movement toward enactment of compensation acts as well as showing judicial decisions in those states where Acts had already been adopted. The Bar Committee in 1911 reported progress by the National Civic Federation. When proper time arrived for the Bar Committee to cooperate with the National Civic Federation by examining the plan prepared, to either approve or suggest modifications, it would take the matter under consideration and report further to the Association.[151] The Committee was continued with power "to report upon such plan as it might approve in regard to compensation for industrial accidents and their prevention."

---

149 Ibid., Vol. 19 (1896), p. 40.
150 Ibid., Vol. 35 (1910), p. 95.
151 Ibid., Vol. 36 (1911), pp. 484-485.

In 1912 the Committee reported that it had had several meetings during the year, in Washington with the National Civic Federation, in New York with the Compensation Committee, and also had met in conjunction with a similar committee of the Conference of Commissioners on Uniform State Laws. During the year, much had transpired in regard to the adoption of compensation laws, state and federal. Laws had been examined, but the Committee was not prepared to recommend any particular form of adoption. However, the consensus of opinion was that uniform law regarding compensation for industrial accidents should be enacted by all states and the United States. Seven basic principles of the law were listed. The Committee stressed the element of prevention of industrial accidents, and urged that every effort should be made to procure the adoption of uniform laws for the proper safeguarding of industrial employees from accident.[152]

In 1913 it was reported that progress had been made in regard to adoption of compensation laws both state and federal; résumé of such laws was annexed to report. A general public opinion was reported as constantly growing in the country that uniform laws on compensation for industrial accidents should be enacted by all the states and by the United States. Although the seven basic principles were reiterated, the Committee again reported that it was not prepared to report on the particulars of the subject, and desired further time to consider the operation of enacted laws, and to carefully examine those now pending in several of the states. However, the Committee considered that insurance by employers had become a necessary element of any system of compensation for industrial accidents. The Committee considered itself not prepared to recommend any particular system of industrial accident compensation insurance, or to enlarge on details of regulation other than that the insurance plan should in all

[152] Ibid., Vol. 37 (1912), pp. 567-568.

cases provide for sufficiency of reserve to meet all accrued liabilities. Committee again stressed the element of "prevention" of industrial accidents, and urged the adoption of the principle of safeguarding industrial employees from accident; it backed the merit system of premium rating, the premium rating to give economic advantages and disadvantages according to degree of efficiency and carefulness exercised by employer. The Committee asked to be continued to make a report at a future meeting.[153] Upon presentation of the report and consequent discussion, opposition developed. Criticism was offered that the Committee had been originally appointed to cooperate with the National Civic Federation to secure a Uniform Workmen's Compensation Act for adoption in the various states, and that Committee had gone as far as it should attempt to go by procuring active help of the Conference of Commissioners on Uniform State Laws. Furthermore, the Committee had been working on the subject more than two years, and had reported to the Conference a tentative draft of an act, which act had been approved by the Conference. Also, the Committee's present report did not deal with an effort to secure uniformity, but it rather discussed and recommended methods of insuring compensation to workmen and the amount of their compensation. Such matters were deemed more or less political considerations, which the Bar Association ought not to pass on even tentatively. Finally, all that the Association could hope to do was being done by the Committee on Uniform State Laws. A suggestion was presented that unless the Committee on Industrial Accidents had some particular reason for continuing work, it ought to be discharged, for such phrases as were inserted in its report ought not to be cited to legislatures of the country as being expressions of the American Bar Association because they were on such political questions as desirability of a state system of insurance. The Committee

[153] Ibid., Vol. 38 (1913), pp. 605-608.

was discharged from further consideration of the subject.[154] Since Workmen's Compensation Acts are at the present time in need of revision or amendment, it is to be regretted that the Bar Association did not continue its activities in this field.

2. INDUSTRIAL COURT AND ARBITRATION

There appears to have been no further activity on the part of the American Bar Association in the field of industrial problems until 1923, when through its Committee on Commerce, Trade and Commercial Law, it considered the subject of an industrial court. In that year, the Commerce Committee reported that the National Conference of Commissioners on Uniform State Laws had appointed a Committee to draft a Uniform Act, which provided for the establishment of industrial courts in the several states. Too, at a meeting of the Kansas State Bar Association, the Kansas statute providing for such a tribunal had been the subject of an address, "Law and Order in Industrial Disputes," presented by the Honorable Charles Thaddeus Terry.[155] Further time was given to the Commerce Committee to consider the subject.

In 1924 the Committee reported that though the system devised and adopted on the Pennsylvania Railroad had been effective, since over 5,000 cases of disputes had been successfully dealt with by committees or tribunals created by agreement of employees and railroad managers, the most efficient machinery thus far developed was that of the industrial court, established in Kansas in 1919 and composed of thirty sections. The prime purpose of the Kansas act was protection of the public against evils of industrial warfare. The Committee again asked that further time for investigation and action be given, and that it be

---

154 Ibid., Vol. 38 (1913), pp. 21, 50-52.

155 American Bar Association Journal, February, 1923, pp. 115-123.

authorized to cooperate with the Special Committee of the National Conference of Commissioners on Uniform State Laws, which was charged with the duty of drafting a Uniform Industrial Law.[156]

In 1925 the Committee reported on the case of Wolff Packing Company v. Court of Industrial Relations, and considered that while it did not destroy the Kansas Industrial Court, it did limit to some extent activities in which the court or any industrial court might effectively engage. The Committee was again continued.[157]

In 1926 the Committee reversed its policy and took a stand for voluntary industrial arbitration rather than coercive industrial courts, after a public hearing in which the Committee had received valuable suggestions from representatives of employers, employees, and the public, and had considered remedies used for the settlement of industrial disputes, namely, compulsory investigation in Canada and the Industrial Commission in Kansas.[158] In the opinion of the Committee, judicial machinery had broken down in relation to industrial disputes; the Interstate Commerce Commission, the Federal Trade Commission and the Workmen's Compensation Boards, etc., had been established, because of difficulties of ascertaining facts within the realm of the technique of industry. The thought was expressed that the United States Arbitration Law, enacted in February, 1925, providing for a method for settlement of commercial disputes by means of arbitration, could be extended to industrial disputes. The enactment of such a statute would furnish an inducement to collective bargaining between capital and labor. The Parker-Watson Act was reviewed. It represented an act to provide for the prompt disposition of disputes between carriers and their employees. This act represented an extension of principles

[156] American Bar Association Report, Vol. 49 (1924), pp. 279-280, 285-288, and 52-53.
[157] Ibid., Vol. 50 (1925), pp. 86-87, 354, 362.
[158] Ibid., Vol. 51 (1926), pp. 391-394.

applied in the field of commercial arbitration in the United States Arbitration Act, which the Committee had drawn, and which had been enacted into law on appeal to Congress by the Bar Association and organized trade bodies throughout the country. Labor's new attitude was shown by the fact that Donald R. Richberg and Alfred P. Thom, who drew the Parker-Watson Bill, spoke in its support before the House Committee on Interstate and Foreign Commerce. The views of these two men together with those of Mr. Matthew Woll opened the way to cordial relations between the American Federation of Labor and the American Bar Association. The Bar Committee presented its belief that instead of urging the passage of an act for the creation of an industrial court with power of coercion, or adding to penal statutes, the Bar of the country should encourage the movement for dealing with industrial controversy through voluntary agreements by parties themselves, in line with the principles of the Parker-Watson Bill. The Committee expressed the hope that it could soon work out a bill that would save capital and labor the loss of millions suffered every year.[159]

By 1928 a bill providing for the creation of a Federal Industrial Council had been drafted.[160] During 1926-1927, a Special Committee on Industrial Disputes under the Commerce Committee was appointed, which Committee had two or three special sessions in New York City, at which all members of the Special Committee were present.[161] The 1927 report noted a letter received from Mr. William Green, President of the American Federation of Labor, commending the Bar Association for opposing passage of legislation providing for creation of coercive industrial courts, and the report also referred to an expression of Mr. Matthew Woll in favor of voluntary arbitration and collective bargaining. The establishing of cordial relationships between

159 Ibid., Vol. 51 (1926), pp. 394-404, 68.
160 Ibid., Vol. 53 (1928), Appendix A, pp. 376-381.
161 Ibid., Vol. 52 (1927), p. 97.

the American Federation of Labor and the American Bar Association received comment.[162] The Committee was authorized to continue its studies.[163]

On January 30, 1928, the Bar Committee sent out an announcement, in which it reviewed its studies of the previous years, and also stated its desire for the peaceable adjustment of industrial disputes. The Bar Association was eulogized by the press of the country for its stand. The Committee's report included excerpts from the newspapers.[164]

In its 1928 report, the Committee reviewed its activities in the field of commercial and industrial arbitration, and called attention to the fact that the Bill for Commercial Arbitration, sponsored by the Bar Association, originally favored the application of the law to agreements to arbitrate industrial as well as commercial controversies. Moreover, the established policy of the country was to encourage the settlement of industrial disputes by voluntary arbitration and to make awards of arbitrators binding and effective on all parties. Nineteen statutes required mandatory inclusion in agreements to arbitrate a clause accepting prospective decision, and the principle of encouraging the settlement of industrial disputes by voluntary submission to arbitrate were carried forward through boards or commissions in thirty-seven states.[165] The 1928 report also revealed the interesting disclosure that the Committee at its public hearing had listened to all sides, and also to all shades of opinion on the labor side, including, among others, Mr. James A. Emery, Counsel for the National Association of Manufacturers, Mr. Julius Rosenwald, President of Sears, Roebuck Company, Jacob Lit, Mr. Donald Richberg, Mr. William Green, and Mr. William Z. Foster, who represented

---

162 Ibid., Vol. 52 (1927), pp. 246-247.
163 Ibid., Vol. 52 (1927), p. 243.
164 Ibid., Vol. 53 (1928), pp. 344-346.
165 Ibid., Vol. 53 (1928), pp. 349-354.

the left wing of labor.[166] Out of the mass of conflicting opinion, the Committee presented certain items upon which there was a concurrence of opinion:

There should be created a Federal Industrial Council made up of official representatives appointed by the President from the American Bar Association, the American Federation of Labor, the National Chamber of Commerce, the National Association of Manufacturers, three agricultural organizations in the country, and should also include the Secretary of Commerce and Secretary of Labor ex officio. This Federal Industrial Council was not to be a judicial tribunal or an arbitration board, but a representative group sitting continuously and studying problems with the view of recommending to Congress and the public generally from time to time a national industrial policy, which would represent a meeting of minds of various groups.[167] In the field of interstate commerce, permission should be given those in industry to make any kind of agreement they chose by which they would set up machinery for the adjustment of their controversies, without resort to strike or lockout. Agreements when recorded with the Federal Industrial Council should be valid, and those rulings made by such arbitration tribunal should be effective and valid, all of which was embraced in a bill, annexed to the report as Appendix A. By the necessary two-thirds votes of members present, a recommendation was carried that the Committee take steps to have the bill, creating the Federal Industrial Council and making industrial arbitration agreements irrevocable and enforceable, enacted into law.[168]

In 1929 the Committee reported that a number of amendments had been suggested to the bill adopted at the 1928 meeting, and that the Committee proposed to have the bill introduced into Congress at the session in December, 1929. The report of the Executive Council of the

166 Ibid., Vol. 53 (1928), pp. 357-364.
167 Ibid., Vol. 53 (1928), pp. 111-112.
168 Ibid., Vol. 53 (1928), pp. 113, 349-354.

American Federation of Labor to its forty-eighth annual convention on November 19, 1928, had spoken of the American Bar Association's activities with approval, which report had been signed by Matthew Woll, J. P. Frey, and Victor A. Olander. The Committee on Resolutions of the American Federation of Labor had recommended that this section of the report of the Executive Council, dealing with cooperation with the American Bar Association, be approved, and that the American Federation of Labor Committee referred to therein be authorized to proceed along lines indicated in the report, namely, to confer with the American Bar Association. The report was unanimously adopted.

In 1929 the Bar Association readopted the Commerce Committee's 1928 report, and reaffirmed its approval of the proposed bill concerning the settlement of industrial disputes affecting and relating to interstate commerce, and directed the Committee to take steps to have the bill introduced into both houses of Congress.[169]

In 1930 the Commerce Committee reported that though no objections had developed to the bill, it was satisfied that public opinion was not yet ready for the legislation, and that the bill ought not to be pressed actively at that time.[170] The 1928 report was readopted and approval of the proposed bill regarding industrial disputes reaffirmed. However, the Committee desired permission to use its own discretion as to the time the bills were to be presented.[171] Nothing further appears from the records to have been done with the proposed act providing for amicable settlement of industrial disputes. In answer to an inquiry concerning the reason for this, Rush C. Butler, Esq., of the Chicago Bar, and Chairman of the Commerce Committee for eight consecutive years,[172] answered: "Concerning the

169 Ibid., Vol. 54 (1929), pp. 308 and 314-315.
170 Ibid., Vol. 55 (1930), pp. 327-328.
171 Ibid., Vol. 55 (1930), pp. 77 and 320.
172 From 1927 to 1935.

activity of the Committee as to Industrial Arbitration, we had a wonderful experience in working out the bill submitted in the 1928 report. We worked in close cooperation with Matthew Woll, John P. Frey and Victor Olander of the American Federation of Labor, Mr. Woll and Mr. Frey, I believe, being Vice Presidents and Mr. Olander being Secretary of the Illinois Federation of Labor. They came to a perfect agreement with us as to every word and letter in the bill. We agreed not to present it to Congress for enactment until they had endorsement of the bill by their organization. This they were unable to obtain for reasons unknown to me or our Committee. The bill has never been introduced." [173]

3. EVALUATION

It is interesting to note that the Bar Association through its Committee on Commerce concerned itself with the labor problem, and studied and worked in an endeavor to eliminate or diminish industrial disputes and strife. It is cause of regret that the Committee did not continue its labors looking to a solution, or at least a partial solution of the problem with which it was grappling, namely, the amicable settlement of industrial disputes. For, as was stated in the presentation of the 1928 report, the American Bar Association can take neither the side of labor nor of capital. Essentially, a body of lawyers must be neutral and impartial in its treatment of social groups; lawyers are only concerned that the processes of social conflict shall, as far as practicable, be put on the basis of law and order. To the extent that there is an interruption in commerce because of industrial disputes, the Commerce Committee felt bound to submit a constructive program.[174]

The present National Relations Act represents an attempt to solve the problem of employer-employee relation-

[173] Quoted from letter to author, dated February 17, 1936.

[174] American Bar Association Report, Vol. 53 (1928), p. 111.

ships; it differs from the attempt of the Bar Association through its Commerce Committee in that it provides for coercive rather than voluntary machinery.

G. ACTION ON TRANSPORTATION PROBLEMS

1. INTRODUCTORY

In this field, policies were largely initiated and carried through by the Bar Association's Committee on Commerce, Trade and Commercial Law, later the Committee on Commerce. The Committee's early policy from 1914-1922 was to concern itself with particular legal problems revolving around liability of common carriers. The Committee even aspired to a codification of the Law of Common Carriers. Later, from 1924 on, it assumed the responsibility of trying to solve the pressing economic traffic problem with particular reference to motor vehicles.[175]

2. FEDERAL REGULATION OF MOTOR VEHICLES

In 1924 the Committee on Commerce, Trade and Commercial Law undertook a study of the question of federal regulation of motor vehicles, in the interest of reducing automobile accidents and of securing unity of law. Statistics for 1925 showed that 24,000 lives had been sacrificed, and over 600,000 persons had been injured in highway accidents, not to mention $600,000 damage to property.[176] The Committee pointed out that government regulation of motor vehicles involved two important considerations: (1) Reg-

[175] For details see American Bar Association Reports, Vol. 39 (1914), pp. 21, 457, Vol. 40 (1915), pp. 22-24, 382-383 and 386, Vol. 41 (1916), p. 21, Vol. 43 (1918), pp. 47-48, Vol. 46 (1921), p. 310 and Vol. 47 (1922), pp. 288-290, also American Bar Association Journal, Vol. 2 (1916), p. 384, Vol. 3 (1917), p. 545, Vol. 4 (1918), pp. 319-320, Vol. 5 (1919), p. 366, and Vol. 6 (1920), pp. 427, 430-431.

[176] Ibid., Vol. 51 (1926), p. 405.

ulation of the actual physical characteristics and physical operation of motor vehicles used as common carriers, and (2) Regulation of business engaged in by motor vehicle common carriers. In 1933 the Commerce Committee expressed the opinion that the former should be regulated by the state and the latter by the federal government.[177] Since the Committee did not deem it advisable to recommend a particular statute until hearing had been had before leading automobile and traffic associations for cooperation and suggestions, it asked for an extension of time.[178] During the years 1925-1935, the Committee on Commerce, Trade and Commercial Law continued to study the problem especially from the federal viewpoint while the Conference of Commissioners on Uniform State Laws worked on a Uniform Vehicle Code.[179] A series of resolutions were passed, but little action resulted.[180]

3. EVALUATION

Though the American Bar Association had ambitious policies in this field, the problems of uniform traffic signals, uniform traffic regulations and regulation of motor vehicles has not been solved. It would appear that since these are not legal problems, they are not within the purview of the Bar Association. Nevertheless, the Bar Association should be able to make a contribution to the solution of transportation problems by initiating a study of the entire subject of traffic courts and procedure with relation to curbing the toll of accidents. The organized legal

---

[177] Ibid., Vol. 58 (1933), pp. 345-346.

[178] Ibid., Vol. 49 (1924), pp. 295-298, 280.

[179] The Uniform Vehicle Code includes four acts. For details and jurisdictions in which adopted, see Ibid., Vol. 60 (1935), p. 734.

[180] For details, see Ibid., Vol. 50 (1925), pp. 89-92, 354, Vol. 51 (1926), pp. 386, 404-406, 72-81, Vol. 52 (1927), pp. 98, 243, 248, Vol. 53 (1928), pp. 338, 373, Vol. 54 (1929), pp. 309, 319-320, Vol. 55 (1930), pp. 320 and 329-331, Vol. 56 (1931), pp. 342-344 and 337, Vol. 57 (1932), pp. 400-402, 754, Vol. 58 (1933), pp. 345-346, Vol. 59 (1934), pp. 443-445 and Vol. 60 (1935), pp. 220, 439, and 734.

profession might also assist in the drafting of laws and amendments when opinion on the subject becomes crystallized to the point of demanding legislation on the subject.

H. PROBLEMS IN THE FIELD OF RADIO LAW, AND THE BAR ASSOCIATION'S CONTRIBUTION TO SOLUTION

1. MACHINERY DEVELOPED AND EVALUATION

The American Bar Association in sponsoring the Radio Control Act of 1927 did much to minimize confusion, and to clear the way for an orderly and equitable adjustment of problems of radio broadcasting. It is due to the continuous efforts of the American Bar Association from 1920 to 1926, that the passage of the Radio Act of 1927 was accomplished. Thus spoke a lawyer for the lawyers' group.[181] Mr. W. Jefferson Davis also credits to the Bar Association the passage by Congress of the Air Commerce Act of 1926. At the meeting of the Association in 1926, the permanent Committee on Air Law was created, and this Committee had jurisdiction over all law pertaining to aeronautics, radio, and other uses of the air. One of the functions of the Committee working with the Secretary of Commerce was to assist in drafting regulations under the Air Commerce Act. The Committee advised with Congress regarding the law of radio control. In November, 1926, hearings of the Committee were held in Washington with a view to clearing up chaotic conditions then existing in the ether, and it was deemed necessary to look to the early passage of a law to replace the previous Act of 1912.[182]

The Radio Control Act of 1927 was sponsored by the Bar Association, and although it represented a compromise solution and was not completely adequate, still it showed a

[181] Davis, W. Jefferson, "Radio Law," p. 1.
[182] Davis, W. Jefferson, Op. Cit., Chapter 3.

substantial advance over the old law of 1912. The Committee on Air Law was thus an important factor in the solution of problems, and up until 1928, its work included both aviation and radio. In 1928 the work was divided, and a newly created standing committee on radio law began to function with "power to consider and report on all questions pertaining to the laws of Radio." The first meeting of the Radio Law Committee was held December 11, 1928, at Washington, with open and closed sessions. The open session was attended by Senator C. C. Dill of Washington, author of the Senate Bill, Congressman Wallace H. White, author of the House Bill, four members of the Federal Radio Commission, members of the Engineering and Legal Divisions of the Commission, a representative from the Department of Justice, and representatives of organizations interested in radio. A tentative report was submitted to the executive committee of the American Bar Association, and on January 15, 1929, the report was made public.[183]

At the 1929 meeting of the Bar Association, the name of the Radio Law Committee was changed to Committee on Communications. The reason for the change of name is readily seen from a consideration of the Couzens Bill, which provided for a Commission on Communications, and also from a consideration of the many legal, legislative, and international questions, which were common to both wire and wireless transmission of intelligence.

At the 1930 meeting of the Association, the Committee on Communications was authorized (1) to contact appropriate Senate and House Committees, and in the name of the Committee on Communications, but not of the Association, to make available information gathered, conclusions reached, and recommendations agreed on by the Committee on Communications with respect to legislation and treaties governing electrical transmission of intelli-

---

183 American Bar Association Journal, Vol. 15 (1929), p. 173, and American Bar Association Report, Vol. 54 (1929), pp. 406-407.

gence, (2) to send a delegation to the fourth Juridical Congress, and (3) to no longer oppose the Couzens Bill. The same type of resolution authorizing Committee to confer with Congressional Committees was adopted in 1935.[184]

The Association, first through its Committee on Air Law, after through its Committee on Radio Law, and then through its Committee on Communications, maintained an active and continuous study of the problem of electrical communication of intelligence. It has taken a definite stand on all problems raised by the Act of 1927, has consistently opposed the Davis Amendment and the provisions respecting monopoly. It was through its efforts that reforms in procedure were accomplished by the passage of the Act of July 1, 1930. Its position on the Couzens Bill was weak.

The greatest usefulness of the Committee on Communications of the Bar Association would appear to be to provide a source of information. In the present formative state of the law of electrical communications, the Committee's chief opportunity for service lies in the direction of assembling facts and information for lawyers, that is, to provide periodically a source of information; conclusions and recommendations are of secondary importance. Although the law of radio is obviously in its infancy, problems already are so numerous and important, and have so many ramifications that the Committee oftentimes finds it difficult to organize even intelligent discussion. But the time to prevent errors is during the period that radio law is in a formative stage, as later these mistakes may become too firmly imbedded.

---

184 American Bar Association Report, Vol. 55 (1930), pp. 103, 351; Ibid., Vol. 60 (1935), pp. 216-217.

I. SCOPE, NATURE AND TREND OF INFLUENCE IN RELATION TO TAXATION PROBLEMS

1. BRIEF SURVEY OF BAR'S INTEREST IN THE TAX PROBLEM

The statement was made some years ago that the President of the United States looked to the American Bar Association to keep the people properly informed upon the legal phases of all public questions.[185] Since taxation is definitely a public question, it is not surprising to find, in studying the Bar's influence on taxation legislation and on the solution of problems in this field, that there should be a distinct stressing of the legal phase.

The legal group should be a potent group in the field of taxation, if only because of the interests represented. Since the business of the members of this group is to give advice and counsel on the technicalities of the law, lawyers practicing in the field of taxation law should know the problems in that field, because of their close contact with them. The big question is whether or not disinterested advice and aid can be expected from such a group.

It is interesting to note that the Bar's interest in tax problems began with an attempt to solve the intricate one of double or multiple taxation. This interest dates back to 1904, when the Standing Committee on Jurisprudence and Law Reform stated that after studying the question, it could not recommend a resolution submitted to it that state taxation should be upon property actually within the state only; rather, personal property should be taxed under the laws of the state of the residence of the owner. If a state could only tax property actually within the state, it would lead to tax evasion. The purpose of the submission of the tax question to the Committee on Jurisprudence and

185 Ibid., Vol. 28 (1905), p. 123.

Law Reform was to prevent double taxation. As the law was administered at that time, for example, a state in which property was located and where it was used could tax property, and the State of New York could also tax the owner on all his property. Thus, the same property was taxed in the state where located, and also taxed in New York, the domicile of the owner. The intention of the resolution submitted to the Committee was to eliminate double taxation in this respect, and to provide for taxing only in the state where the property was located. After much discussion, it was decided that the question was one of taxing intangible property, and that the Committee was trying to deal with a complicated economic problem perplexing even to economists and growing out of conflicting sovereignties in exercising the law of taxation. The matter was finally referred to the Committee on Uniform State Law to study the question, and to report at the 1905 meeting.[186] At this meeting, the Committee on Uniform State Laws made no report, whereupon an effort was made to so amend the Constitution of the American Bar Association as to include a Standing Committee on Taxation. It was felt that the Committee on Uniform State Laws had too many problems of its own to consider, and that this problem of double or multiple taxation was a sufficiently colossal one to occupy the entire time of a committee. Also, opinion was expressed that if the injustices of double or multiple taxation were to be avoided, and united action on the part of the states in the matter of necessary tax legislation was to be obtained, it was necessary to have a Standing Committee on Taxation. Therefore, an Amendment to Article III of the Constitution was proposed to be acted on at the following meeting of the Association.[187]

At the 1906 meeting, by such an amendment, the Committee on Taxation was duly created. From that time until 1916, with the exception of one year, the Committee con-

---

186 Ibid., Vol. 27 (1904), pp. 15-27.
187 Ibid., Vol. 28 (1905), pp. 13-14, 123, 129-131, 529-530.

centrated on the problem of double or multiple taxation. The one exception was the year 1913-1914, when Professor Ernst Freund was Chairman of the Committee; that year, the Committee on Taxation became active with the passage of the Income Tax Act of 1913, and in its 1914 report it did two things: (1) It listed 20 or more points in which the Income Tax Act of 1913 was ambiguous, and urged the removal of the defects, and (2) It recognized that the entire act should be recast and remodeled so as to be made reasonably intelligible for reference, and effective and consistent in all its parts.[188] Yet, after all this unusual activity under Professor Freund, by 1915 the Committee was inactive and had no report to present. At the 1916 meeting, the Standing Committee on Taxation was abolished.[189]

In 1931, when a Special Committee on Internal Revenue Law and Its Means of Collection was formed, it had its inception in the explicit purpose of protecting lawyers themselves in regard to their practice before the Bureau of Internal Revenue, or as it was expressed, "to further cooperation of members of the Bar and officers of the Treasury Department in the enforcement of the Federal tax laws and regulations issued thereunder, and to urge the adoption of a simpler procedure in the Bureau of Internal Revenue." To carry out this purpose, the Committee was continued as a Special Committee on Federal Taxation, members of which were appointed by the President of the Association after the 1922 meeting. From that time to the present, the Special Committee has concerned itself with a program of relief for taxpayers. It will be seen that the Committee in this phase of its activities has concerned itself with very definite, technical, and particular problems. At the present time, the Special Committee on Taxation has grown so greatly in importance that there is a movement on foot to have it expanded into a Section of the Association.

---

[188] Ibid., Vol. 39 (1914), pp. 14 and 533.
[189] Ibid., Vol. 41 (1916), pp. 7 and 93.

To sum up, it should be noted that the Association in its earlier period concerned itself with more general problems, but in the latter period concentrated on more particular and technical problems in the field of taxation, though, at present, it is once more branching out and considering some of the insolubles. It should be noted, however, that the emphasis is always being made that the Association's influence is exercised particularly in the field of procedure and administration, and that questions of political and economic policy are avoided.

2. PARTICULAR POLICIES IN FIELD OF SUBSTANTIVE LAW

(a) Taxation of Intangibles and Double or Multiple Taxation; American Bar Association Cooperated With Other Groups Working on This Problem

The Constitution and By-Laws were amended at the 1906 meeting to make provision for a Standing Committee on Taxation.[190] This Committee started its work with high hopes and an ambitious program. In a general way, its purpose was to consider the problem of double or multiple taxation, and in particular, to devise methods for obtaining uniform legislation among the different states on the subject of taxation of personal property, especially that of corporations. This emphasis was natural since corporations were more subject to the unjust burdens of double or multiple taxation by reason of different methods of corporate taxation in different states, which methods were based either on place of incorporation, place of carrying on corporate business, or location of personal property of corporation. It was all too apparent to the Committee that the field of inquiry was a vast one, and that much preliminary work was necessary before it could recommend reformatory legislation. The Committee therefore asked for

[190] Ibid., Vol. 29 (1906), p. 42.

authorization to employ necessary help to make an investigation and compilation of laws and decisions of the various states, and also asked the Association to solicit the governors of the various states and territories to appoint delegates to an Interstate Convention or Conference to deliberate and report on the subject of taxation, and more particularly on the subject of corporate taxation.[191] At the following meeting in 1908, it was reported that since the Executive Committee would only allow a $200 appropriation, this amount was not sufficient to commence work. Since the 1907 meeting, the National Tax Association had been organized and was to be concerned with questions of taxation and necessary legislation. The Committee preferred to wait for the work of the National Tax Association to assume more definite form, and if developments were forthcoming, proposed to cooperate in having necessary remedial legislation passed.[192]

In the matter of the Inheritance Tax Laws, the Committee worked with the International Tax Association. An appropriation of $1,000 was made at the 1909 meeting to enable the Committee to make an investigation of inheritance tax laws in cooperation with the International Tax Association. This latter Association was also working on a Model Inheritance Tax Law for the American States, and of its Committee of nine members, three came from the American Bar Association, three from the International Tax Association, and three from the Commissioners on Uniform State Laws. It was stated at this time that the subject of double inheritance tax was of additional importance owing to the probable enactment of a federal corporation tax law and income tax law, whereby the states were driven to inheritance tax as one of the few remaining sources of revenue for state and local purposes.[193]

---

[191] Ibid., Vol. 31 (1907), pp. 76, 670-675.

[192] Ibid., Vol. 33 (1908), pp. 26, 540-541.

[193] Ibid., Vol. 34 (1909), pp. 48, 563-567.

With these auspicious beginnings, one might expect something constructive, but though an appropriation of $1,000 was voted to the Committee in 1909, to permit the compilation and digest of laws of the various states providing for taxation of inheritance, the Executive Committee offered only $250, which was considered too small to do any effective work in this field. Yet, such a study was considered essential before a model inheritance tax law could be framed. Fortunately, the International Tax Association had been busy and had submitted draft of a model inheritance tax law and also a summary of the main provisions of inheritance tax legislation in the several states. In January, 1911, at a Conference on Taxation, the general features of the Model Inheritance Law were approved, and on July 21, 1911, the Model Inheritance Law was adopted in New York state.[194] By 1912, since the problem had grown so large, and definite action and achievements were so insignificant, the matter of continuing or discontinuing the Committee was referred to the Executive Committee of the Association. If the decision should favor the renewal or continuance of the Committee, then Committee asked for a strictly divided and limited problem.[195] In 1913 it was decided, since a subcommittee of the General Committee on Uniform Laws was considering the subject of taxation so far as the situs of real and personal property for purposes of taxation was concerned, and since it would be unwise for the Association to enter the political field of national taxation, that the Committee should be abolished.[196] In 1915 the Committee made no report, and in 1916 the Committee on Taxation, as stated above, was abolished.[197]

Though the Committee on Taxation was revived in 1921, it did not again take up the problem of double or

[194] Ibid., Vol. 36 (1911), pp. 39-42.
[195] Ibid., Vol. 37 (1912), pp. 549-554.
[196] Ibid., Vol. 38 (1913), pp. 30-31.
[197] Ibid., Vol. 41 (1916), pp. 7 and 93.

multiple taxation until 1932-1933, and then it made a federal rather than a state emphasis. The Committee that year undertook to obtain the views of tax practitioners with respect to advisable changes in tax procedure and revenue laws, and among other matters, it recognized a need for a vigorous attempt to harmonize the national and the forty-eight state tax systems, because many of the taxes overlapped. There were income and inheritance taxes by the federal government and most of the states, and in respect to sales taxes, there were serious conflicts existing as to tobacco, beer, gasoline, etc.[198] It was stated that though no adequate governmental machinery existed to accomplish the intricate task, significant efforts were being made to bring about a harmonization. Subcommittees on conflicting taxation in the House (Ways and Means Committee), and in the Senate (Finance Committee), were making a survey of the situation from the standpoint of the federal government. The Interstate Committee on Conflicting Taxation of the Interstate Assembly, organized by the American Legislators Association, composed of delegates sent by both the legislatures and the executives of the various states, was surveying the problem from the standpoint of states. The United States Chamber of Commerce and National Tax Association were taking an active part in the solution of the problem. The American Bar Association recognized these undertakings as much needed, endorsed the objectives of the studies, and resolved to cooperate with all these groups.[199]

In the field of International Double Taxation, the need for the development of tax uniformity was recognized as of importance to international traders and to the different governments. The undertakings of the International Chamber of Commerce and the League of Nations were endorsed, and assistance was offered by the Committee on Federal Taxa-

---

198 Ibid., Vol. 58 (1933), p. 450.

199 Ibid., Vol. 58 (1933), pp. 450-451.

tion in passing on merits of either general principles or particular proposals as they might be formulated.[200]

The inevitable conclusion here must be made that the Bar Association did not of itself accomplish anything tangible in the solution of this problem of double or multiple taxation. The problem is still with us. However, it is worth noting that members of the Bar Association, because of their close relationship with taxpayers, were peculiarly equipped to diagnose the double taxation problem, and render assistance to other groups. Certainly, in the past they have shown their willingness to cooperate and assist in the solution of this difficult situation.

(b) Policy Regarding Estate Tax Relief

As the chairman of the Special Committee on Taxation well stated at the 1933 meeting, one of the most distressing incidents of the depression has been the effect of the federal estate taxes upon decedent's estates. It can readily be seen that the valuation base for determining the federal estate tax has proven too inelastic for just reflection of values in an era of rapidly changing price levels. In many cases, estates, which at the time of the death of the deceased were solvent and well able to pay taxes, were, as a result of the fall in values, entirely confiscated by the federal tax which fell upon them. Some adjustment should be made if the tax was to be non-confiscatory. As early as 1931, the Special Committee on Taxation advocated that rules with respect to valuation of securities and other property, particularly in the case of decedents' estates, be liberalized to take into consideration abnormal rises and falls in market value.[201] At the 1933 meeting, the Bar Association endorsed studies published by the Staff of the Congressional Joint Committee on Internal Revenue Taxation, and recommended to Congress and to the Treasury Depart-

[200] Ibid., Vol. 58 (1933), pp. 451-452.
[201] Ibid., Vol. 56 (1931), p. 63.

ment the development of a system of estate taxes better calculated to reflect price fluctuations in the value of assets in decedents' estates both at time of death and at time tax is paid.[202]

The Bar Association here showed that it was alert to a pressing problem, as it should be since its members are in a position to have first-hand knowledge of the confiscatory results of the present law, but it does seem that, with its technical and practical knowledge regarding estate taxes, it might have made a more constructive contribution than a mere endorsement of the Congressional Joint Committee study and a recommendation for a change. However, this presents an instance of the close connection that exists between the Bar Committee and the Joint Committee, especially the permanent staff of experts.

(c) Endorsement of Mellon Bill, Differentiating Between Earned and Unearned Income

In 1923, because there was a possibility of a revision of the Revenue Act of 1921, a subcommittee of the Special Committee on Taxation was appointed to study the desirability of differentiating between earned and unearned income as a basis for taxation, and to investigate the feasability of incorporating that principle into the federal tax law.[203] At the following meeting of the Association in 1924, the principle of the proposal in the so-called Mellon bill to differentiate earned income arising from wages, salaries, and professional fees from income received from the employment of capital was endorsed by the Committee and Association. It should be noted that this differentiation represents a distinctly partisan matter. Much preliminary work was done by the Committee, and sentiment favoring the differential was demonstrated to the Treasury officials and members of Congress. However, the Committee did not

202 Ibid., Vol. 58 (1933), pp. 112, 452.
203 Ibid., Vol. 48 (1923), p. 440.

attempt to advocate the exact form the differential should take.[204] The 1924 Revenue Act included a differential in favor of earned income, but at the 1925 meeting, the Association put itself on record as being in favor of securing additional legislation by Congress to increase taxpayers' exemptions in computations of income if earned, as distinguished from unearned income. To this end, the Committee asked to have a hearing before the Finance Committee of the Senate and the Ways and Means Committee of the House.[205] Nothing concrete seems to have evolved from this effort. Then in 1931, under the pressure of securing all possible income, the differential in favor of earned income was deleted from the law.

At the 1932 meeting, the Special Committee on Federal Taxation stated its desire to have the differential reinstated, the theory behind such differential being that it was fair as an offset against the allowances for depreciation, obsolescence, and the like, which were allowed to the business man who derived income from the employment of capital.[206] Though the Bar Association failed to secure in the Act of 1932 the retention of the allowance in favor of earned income, the present tax bill of 1934 includes a deduction for earned income.[207]

It is difficult to determine what forces brought about the incorporation of the differential in favor of earned income into the law, but there can be no doubt but that the Bar Association was a factor in bringing it about. Was the differential in favor of earned income a constructive development? If it were merely making a distinction in favor of the man earning a salary as over against the man cutting coupons, the differential would not appear to be constructive, since capital in the latter case is earning income as much as the man in the former case. But if the dis-

[204] Ibid., Vol. 49 (1924), p. 312.
[205] Ibid., Vol. 50 (1925), pp. 81 and 392.
[206] Ibid., Vol. 57 (1932), pp. 129 and 547.
[207] Ibid., Vol. 59 (1934), p. 87.

tinction is based on the theory, as stated by the Committee, that the business man has an opportunity to charge off allowances for depreciation and for obsolescence, a privilege not available to the salaried man, then it does seem that the differential is constructive and justifiable.

(d) Advocated Law That Bankrupt be Discharged From Federal Tax Liability

Another of the many distressing effects of the 1929 depression has been the inability of persons, who have been forced into bankruptcy, to be relieved of the federal tax liability, which is not discharged by the bankruptcy proceeding. At the 1933 meeting of the Association, the Committee drafted and proposed an amendment to the Bankruptcy laws, which would permit discharge from such federal tax liability, as it was felt that there was no reason why the government should not share as other creditors in the losses resulting from bankruptcy, or why the bankrupt should carry the tax burden after his discharge. Such a situation was contrary to the economic rehabilitation spirit of the bankruptcy laws.[208] While the proposal sounds justifiable, nothing definite has been done by way of amending the Bankruptcy Act to relieve the bankrupt from federal tax liability, though the Committee on Commercial Law and Bankruptcy cooperated in backing the proposed amendment.

(e) Policy Regarding Charitable Contributions

Out of the depression grew a consideration of many problems not heretofore even suggested. One of these was the relaxation of the limitation on reduction for contributions to charitable organizations, which proposal aimed to allow a one hundred per cent deduction against income if contributions were made to charities dispensing the neces-

[208] Ibid., Vol. 58 (1933), pp. 114-115, 457-458.

sities of life to the poor and indigent. It was thought that this provision would greatly accelerate and increase amounts of gifts made to charitable organizations. While it might reduce government income in a measure, it would ultimately effect a double saving by reducing the requirement of government public assistance.[209] In opposition, one of the Committee stated that the Committee was here delving into a problem for which no data could be marshalled for proof of contentions, and therefore little could be accomplished. Certainly, the Bar Association Committee should not consider such highly controversial matters.

Another problem in this field concerned the computation of the fifteen per cent reduction, the question being whether or not the taxpayer was allowed to include capital gains and losses in the basis of deduction for charitable contributions. Because of certain decisions, much confusion had arisen, and to eliminate this confusion, the Committee drafted a law which would correct the present situation by definitely stating that such capital gains and losses should be included.

In this field of substantive tax law, while the Bar Association has been alive to the problems involved, it does not appear to have been successful in accomplishing many concrete results. While legislation has been drafted, and pressure exerted in most of the above fields, only the provision regarding the differential between earned and unearned income seems to have been adopted into law.

---

[209] Ibid., Vol. 58 (1933), pp. 113, 453-454.

J. POLICIES AND ACTIVITIES RESPECTING DEBTOR-CREDITOR RELATIONSHIPS

1. BANKRUPTCY

(a) Sponsored the National Bankruptcy Act, Later Sponsored Particular Amendments, and Opposed Repeal

At a time when there is great concern about debtor-creditor relationships and the disproportion between the value of wealth and the debt structure, it is interesting to note what has been and is being done by the American Bar Association in this field. The subject of debtor-creditor relations, especially as it concerns debt release or bankruptcy, is highly technical, but the subject is so closely connected with business and industrial conditions of the country that it should be considered.

Activities in this field were largely carried on through the Committee on Commercial Law, changed in 1915 to the Committee on Commerce, Trade and Commercial Law, which in 1926 was divided, and the division thereafter known as the Committee on Commercial Law and Bankruptcy was authorized to assume jurisdiction of debtor-creditor relations. The earliest action of the Commercial Law Committee was to advocate a national bankruptcy act. After the passage of the act in 1898, the Committees to the present date have supported the law, at times have suggested particular amendments, but have consistently opposed drastic changes or repeal.

As early as 1886, the American Bar Association adopted a resolution that the Committee on Commercial Law be requested to consider and report at the following meeting on the question of the desirability of enactment by Congress of a national bankruptcy law. If such a law was considered desirable, the Committee should suggest what should be its general character, and what method should be adopted by the legal profession to secure its enactment.[210] In reporting in 1887, the Committee submitted an elaborate report, in which it recommended a national bankruptcy law, and stated that periods under the administration of a bankruptcy law in the United States had been from 1800 to 1801, from 1841 to 1843, and from 1867 to 1878, or a period of only fourteen years. If report was approved, then the Committee recommended that the Bar Association should take such action as would bring the subject before the people of the country so that Congress might know of the pressing need of the business community for relief and protection. The Committee appended a draft of a bankruptcy bill. Report was laid over for a year.[211] Nothing further was done until 1897, when report was presented that the Chairman had written to each member of the Committee, and requested submission in writing of suggestions for reform in the law governing commercial transactions. Mr. Walter S. Logan forwarded a paper, entitled "A Broader Basis of Credit," which discussed the necessity for some legislation to further protect creditors. While the Committee recognized that certain evils did exist, it stated that it was not prepared to recommend a remedy, but suggested that report and paper be submitted to Commerce Committee to report the following year what if any legislation was necessary, and to submit bill or bills deemed advisable.[212] In 1898 the Committee announced the passage of the Bankruptcy Act on July 1, 1898, which to a great extent provided remedies for many of the evils pointed out in Mr. Logan's paper. The Commerce Committee asked that an appropriate Committee inquire into the practical working of the bankruptcy law, and report advisable changes at the following meeting.[213]

---

[210] American Bar Association Report, Vol. 9 (1886), p. 79. It should be noted that in 1886, the Committee on Jurisprudence and Law Reform reported on Relief of Simple Contract Creditor Against Frauds of Insolvent Debtor. Ibid., Vol. 9 (1886), p. 275.

[211] Ibid., Vol. 10 (1887), pp. 332, 344-353.

[212] Ibid., Vol. 20 (1897), pp. 65 and 414.

[213] Ibid., Vol. 21 (1898), pp. 14 and 410-411.

After this, the Committee on Commercial Law included this important question of debtor-creditor relations on its agenda each year. In 1899 the Committee reported a summary of its conclusions, as follows: (1) That the bankrupt law was wise and beneficent legislation; (2) That the general features of the present law should have the approval and support of the bar and commercial community, (3) That amendments should provide better protection to creditor against fraud in bankruptcy proceedings; (4) That amendments as to involuntary bankruptcy should be along the lines of better protection to creditor for fraud; and (5) That the ideal bankrupt law would give the debtor a speedy discharge, the creditor a complete remedy for fraud, and would punish fraud on the part of debtors or creditors. The Committee early invited cooperation of mercantile bodies and members of the American Bar Association. Members of both Houses of Congress asked Committee to continue its work, and accorded recommendations of Committee the highest consideration.[214] It is thus seen that the early stress by the Bar Association Committee was on creditors' rather than debtors' rights.[215]

In 1900 the Committee submitted a fourteen-page report in which it asked permission of the Association to sponsor certain amendments to the Bankruptcy Act of 1898. The Committee reported in 1901 that it had obeyed instructions, and had urged Congress personally, and in writing, to pass amendment to the Bankruptcy Act. No action, however, was taken by Congress. Committee also reported that it had observed the workings of the bankruptcy law during the year, and that its opinion of the wisdom of the proposed amendments was strengthened.[216] The Committee's report was accepted and approved, and it was authorized to continue its work of perfecting the bankruptcy law.

---

214 Ibid., Vol. 22 (1899), pp. 25-27 and 414-416.
215 Ibid., Vol. 22 (1899), pp. 26-27.
216 Ibid., Vol. 24 (1901), pp. 421-423.

In pursuance of a mandate from the Association, the Committee reported in 1902 that it had gone on with previous work in connection with bankruptcy legislation, and had urged the Judiciary Committee of both Houses of Congress to pass the Ray Bill amending the present bankrupt law. The Ray Bill in substantially the form in which it had met the approval of the American Bar Association, had passed the House by an overwhelming majority. Though it did not reach the Senate in time to be acted on, it was expected that it would pass the next Session, be approved by the President, and become law. The members of the Judiciary Committee of both Houses and the Attorney General of the United States had expressed appreciation of the work of the Committee and the stand taken by the Association on the subject. The Committee expressed its conviction that the bankruptcy law would remain a permanent part of American jurisprudence, as the sentiment of the Bar and the people were overwhelmingly in its favor. The report had been printed and distributed in advance of meeting of Association. The wisdom of thus distributing the report beforehand was shown by the fact that it had reached fifteen hundred or more members of the Association instead of only one hundred and fifty or less, who were present at the meeting. The Association had taken a strong stand for several years in favor of the general principles of a Bankruptcy Law, which should not only relieve debtors but should enable creditors to protect their interests. The Committee believed that the bankruptcy law contained too great emphasis on the discharge of the debtor, whereas the administration of estate under the bankruptcy law should have only one main object, namely, the fair and equitable distribution of assets. One of the Committee's recommendations was that the bankruptcy court should have jurisdiction over estates of deceased insolvents as well as over living insolvents. The Committee's report was approved and adopted, and the Committee was authorized and directed to advocate and urge Congress to pass legislation recommended in report.[217]

In 1903 the Committee reported that armed with the endorsement and approval of its 1902 report by the Bar Association, the Committee turned its batteries on Congress, and with representatives of interested commercial bodies, appeared repeatedly before the Judiciary Committees of the Senate and House to urge the legislation to which the Association stood committed. Report was submitted that success crowned its efforts, for a bill amending the bankruptcy law was passed February 5, 1903, and contained the essential features of Committee's recommendations. It was further reported that in discussions of the subject before Committees of Congress, the Bar Association Committee had taken a leading part and that the Chairman of the Bar Committee was present, at the request of the Chairman of the Senate Judiciary Committee, when the bill was finally reported and passed. The adoption of the Ray Bill seemed to give general satisfaction to the legal and commercial community. In the presentation of its report, the Committee stated that it had for several years been wrestling with bankruptcy questions, and had made reports from year to year, which reports advocated certain remedial amendments to the bankruptcy law. These amendments had been substantially adopted, largely by reason of the endorsement of the American Bar Association. The bankruptcy law, as amended, was practically the work of the Bar Association. Although not perfect, it represented the best bankruptcy law that had ever been adopted by any nation in Christendom. In accordance with its own recommendation, the Committee was instructed to keep in touch with all proposed legislation on bankruptcy questions, and whenever the opportunity occurred, to enforce views and principles heretofore expressed and adopted.[218]

---

[217] Ibid., Vol. 25 (1902), pp. 408-518, 11-14.

[218] Ibid., Vol. 26 (1903), pp. 12, 42, 429-431, and Vol. 28 (1905), pp. 427-33.

In 1905 in presenting its eighth report on the subject of bankruptcy, the Committee initiated its policy of opposing repeal of the National Bankruptcy Act. It pointed out that its reports had to a large extent been embodied in the jurisprudence of the country; that it was general opinion that the bankruptcy law had been very much improved through work of the Association. A bill was then pending in Congress to repeal the bankruptcy law, which bill had been vigorously opposed by the Committee. The Association approved resolutions endorsing the bankruptcy law, opposing repeal, authorizing the Committee to appear before Congressional Committees, requesting cooperation of Association members, and providing that the Secretary send copies of resolutions to members.[219]

In 1906 it was reported that pursuant to directions, the Secretary had sent copy of resolutions to each member of the Association, and that this had resulted in considerable correspondence between members of the Association and various members of Congress. When Congress met, the Committee took steps to oppose the passage of the proposed act repealing the bankruptcy law, and was effectively reinforced and assisted by efforts of different members of the Association. Commercial bodies also joined in an effort to oppose the repeal act. These activities brought success, as no repeal act was passed. The sentiment of the Bar and the general public was thoroughly tested, and sentiment seemed to be generally opposed to such repeal. The Committee reiterated its belief in the National Bankruptcy Law and its opposition to repeal.[220]

During the year 1906-1907, Committee gave attention to the course of Congressional legislation in order to oppose actively any attempt to repeal the Bankruptcy Act or to amend its provisions in such a way as to impair its efficiency. The Committee submitted as part of its report a proposed bill embodying suggested changes in the Bank-

219 Ibid., Vol. 28 (1905), pp. 34 and 432.
220 Ibid., Vol. 29 (1906), pp. 19-21 and 502.

ruptcy Act. In view of the frequently declared policy of the Bar Association, the Committee was again instructed to oppose any effort to repeal present law.[221]

During 1907-1908, the Committee again followed the course of legislation concerning the Bankruptcy Act, and reported no change, though various bills had been introduced, some proposing repeal, others providing for amendments. The Committee had, however, on February 25, 1908, attended a public hearing before a subcommittee of the Judiciary Committee of the House, and submitted and discussed recommendations of the Association concerning bankruptcy legislation. A proposed enlargement of definition of insolvency met no favor with the subcommittee of House. The panic of October, 1907, had crystallized sentiment against such definition; therefore, the Committee recommended that further efforts to procure such amendment be abandoned. The Committee renewed its recommendations on two other proposed amendments. The Committee also asked that for the ensuing year it be instructed to oppose all efforts at repeal as well as to oppose amendments, which restricted the field of operation or impaired the efficiency of the bankruptcy law. In addition, the Committee asked for power to confer with Judiciary Committees of Congress on proposed changes.[222]

In 1909 it was reported that the Sherley Bill, providing for certain amendments, had been adopted by the House, but had failed of passage in the Senate. The Committee was again given the same authorization as in 1908.[223] In 1910 a report was presented that the Sherley Bill had been enacted into law thus greatly strengthening the Bankruptcy Act. Furthermore, the Committee had received suggestions for other amendments, but before making any definite recommendation, the Committee considered it necessary to

---

221 Ibid., Vol. 37 (1907), pp. 601-603.
222 Ibid., Vol. 33 (1908), pp. 507-509.
223 Ibid., Vol. 34 (1909), p. 523.

hold public meetings, and invite lawyers, bankers, credit and business men to give information on those subjects on which suggestions had been made.[224]

In 1911 Committee reported that on June 15, 1911, first session, Sixty-second Congress, a bill [225] had been introduced to repeal the Bankruptcy Act, and that every effort should be made to defeat the measure. It recommended an amendment respecting receiverships, and asked for further time to consider amendments regarding uniform exemptions and distribution of partnership and individual assets.[226] In 1912 it was reported that on December 4, 1911, the Sims Act to repeal the Bankruptcy Act had been introduced. Committee again advised that every effort should be made to prevent enactment of the bill. As to the amendment regarding receiverships, the Committee, after consultation with members of Congress, concluded that it would be inadvisable to urge at that time any measure looking to amendment of the National Bankruptcy Act. The Committee, however, was still of opinion that passage of amendment would improve the act. As to amendments respecting Uniform Exemptions and Distribution of Partnership and Individual Assets, the Committee requested further time. As to Act Fixing Time Vesting Title to Realty in Trustee, the Committee recommended that the Association exert its influence against the adoption of the bill by Congress.[227]

In 1913 it was reported that three bills to repeal and four to amend the Bankruptcy Act had been considered in the first session of the Sixty-third Congress. The Committee was empowered to oppose any attempt to repeal the Bankruptcy Act, and was given further time to consider the four bills of amendment.[228] In 1914 the foregoing seven bills were still pending, and had not been acted on by the

---

[224] Ibid., Vol. 35 (1910), pp. 511-518.
[225] H.R. 11,662.
[226] American Bar Association Report, Vol. 36 (1911), pp. 392-393.
[227] Ibid., Vol. 37 (1912), pp. 437 and 439.
[228] Ibid., Vol. 38 (1913), pp. 477-479.

House Judiciary Committee to which they had been referred. Five additional bills, three to repeal and two to amend the Bankruptcy Act, had been introduced. The Committee secured approval of its resolution that the American Bar Association recommend the continuance of the National Bankruptcy Act, that the various bills pending to repeal the act be defeated, and that consideration of various bills pending to amend the act be postponed to future date.[229] In 1915, the Committee reported that when the Sixty-third Congress ended, six bills to repeal and eight to amend the National Bankruptcy Act died. The Committee felt that other bills would again be introduced to repeal or amend the Bankruptcy Act, and bent its efforts with success in securing a resolution that the American Bar Association renew its adherence to the bankruptcy statute, and authorize the Committee to oppose any repeal measure introduced in the Sixty-fourth Congress.[230] In 1916 the Bar Association reported the introduction of five bills to repeal the Bankruptcy Act. The Association consistently continued its policy of opposing such bills, and authorized its Committee to work for their defeat. Another bill, introduced to amend the Bankruptcy Act and provide for prevention of discharge of bankrupt for liability incurred for breach of promise of marriage accompanied by seduction, was favored by the Committee and was carried by the necessary two-thirds vote.[231]

In 1917 policy was somewhat changed, and in addition to opposing repeal of the Bankruptcy Law, opposition to other than vital amendments was also declared. Two bills to repeal and four to amend the bankruptcy law were reported, and the stand of the Committee against all the bills was adopted.[232] Again, in 1918, the Committee re-

[229] Ibid., Vol. 39 (1914), pp. 448-449 and 456.

[230] Ibid., Vol. 40 (1915), pp. 382, 386, and 20.

[231] Ibid., Vol. 41 (1916), pp. 21-22, and American Bar Association Journal, Vol. 2 (1916), p. 389.

[232] American Bar Association Report, Vol. 42 (1917), pp. 51-52; American Bar Association Journal, Vol. 3 (1917), p. 544.

ported six House bills, two bills to repeal and four to amend, introduced in the Second Session. The Association again renewed its adherence to the National Bankruptcy Act, voiced its opposition to pending repeal bills, and authorized Committee to oppose passage.[233] In 1919 the Committee reported its consistent opposition to repeal, and its approval of amendments only when in the interests of furthering and expediting the administration of right and justice. The Committee recommended endorsing and urging passage of the Mott Bill,[234] supplementing Section 25 of the National Bankruptcy Act.[235] In 1920 the Committee turned about face and disapproved of the Mott Bill, but secured authorization to prepare for the following meeting draft of bill containing such amendments to the act as Committee considered should be made.[236]

In 1921 Committee again resumed a policy of advocating certain amendments; a tentative draft of proposed amendments was submitted. The Committee held a public hearing on April 26 to 29, 1920, and on the basis of information thus garnered, organized its first tentative draft. It then asked for suggestions and criticisms, after which the Committee prepared a second tentative draft, which was printed in full in the April, 1921, Journal, at pages 204-205. The second tentative draft thus reached twelve thousand members. The Committee in public meeting May 3, 1921, gave full consideration to the second draft, and received written and oral suggestions. Adoption was secured for resolution approving the bill submitted by the Committee to amend the Bankruptcy Act.[237] In 1922 resolution was adopted, thus approving amendment of Section 22 (a) of the Bankruptcy Act.[238]

---

233 American Bar Association Report, Vol. 43 (1918), p. 48; American Bar Association Journal, Vol. 4 (1918), p. 319.

234 H.B. 402.

235 American Bar Association Journal, Vol. 5 (1919), p. 364.

236 American Bar Association Journal, Vol. 6 (1920), p. 427.

237 American Bar Association Report, Vol. 46 (1921), pp. 311 and 361.

238 Ibid., Vol. 47 (1922), pp. 53, 289, and 295.

In 1923 the Committee considered the matter of the solicitation of claims in bankruptcy, which topic was presented pro and con, and adoption of rule by district court recommended.[239]

In 1924 the Committee turned its attention to the administration of bankrupt estates, and presented a rather full report, advocating the appointment of official receivers. On the general subject of the administration of bankruptcy law, the Committee submitted that there had been much study and consideration given to the matter by various organizations, professional and otherwise.[240] The Bar Committee considered that the Bar was properly chargeable with the responsibility for the proper administration of law by the courts, and that the administration of bankrupt estates was not a private function, dependent for effective operation on the good will of those especially interested, but was a public function, now committed to courts. The Committee recommended official receivers in accordance with the English method. Since no bill was submitted to provide for official receivers, the recommendation was ruled out of order, and hence was not carried.[241]

The Committee on Jurisprudence and Law Reform in 1924 showed some activity in the field of bankruptcy administration when it was instructed to inquire and report as to the adequacy of accommodations for referees in bankruptcy. A subcommittee sent questionnaires to all referees in bankruptcy in the United States, replies to which showed that such accommodations were inadequate. The subcommittee report was sent to the Chief Justice of the United States, the chairman of the Committee on Practice in Bankruptcy matters of the American Bar Association, the Chairman of Committee on Bankruptcy of the Federal Judicial

239 Ibid., Vol. 48 (1923), pp. 285 and 294.

240 In particular, the Committee mentioned the report of the Merchants Association Committee representing 103 pages with 14 pages of statistical matter. Official receivers were commended.

241 American Bar Association Report, Vol. 49 (1924), pp. 53, 280, 290-295.

Council, and the Chairman of the Committee on Bankruptcy, Commercial Law League of America. This laudable movement did not progress beyond the stage of an adopted resolution that the federal government make suitable provision for the transaction of the bankruptcy law business, and that the subject be referred to the Bar Association's Committee on Practice in Bankruptcy matters, with power to draft bill providing for adequate accommodations for the bankruptcy business.[242]

The 1925 report of the Committee on Commerce, Trade and Commercial Law submitted three acts introduced in Congress embodying amendments to the Bankruptcy Act, its administration, and rules of procedure and practice thereunder. Through the courtesy of Mr. William Randolph Montgomery, a comparative statement of the various provisions was formulated for the purpose of endeavoring to bring about concurrence of view between the American Bar Association, the Merchants Association of New York, the National Association of Credit Men, the Commercial Law League of America, and the Association of the Bar of the City of New York. Because the analysis would be helpful to Association members, it was attached to report as Appendix A, and the provision for official receivers was attached as Appendix B. The Committee reiterated its opinion, expressed in its 1924 report, that the solution of much of the difficulty in bankruptcy practice would be eliminated by the appointment of official receivers.

By 1926 a new Committee on Commercial Law and Bankruptcy had been authorized by amendment of Article IV of the Constitution.[243] Thereafter, the new Committee concerned itself with the items included in its name, "Commercial Law," and "Bankruptcy," and followed the policy of its predecessor, the Committee on Commerce, Trade and Commercial Law by holding a three-day public hearing, which was attended by a large number of persons including

---

[242] Ibid., Vol. 49 (1924), p. 74.
[243] Ibid., Vol. 51 (1926), p. 355.

members of the federal judiciary and the Association of Referees in Bankruptcy as well as representatives from large financial institutions, business organizations, colleges, and law offices. These experts presented facts, arguments, constructive criticisms and helpful recommendations on matters included in the agenda. On the substantive side, the Committee recommended that the American Bar Association recommend to all state and local bar associations that they use their best efforts to procure the adoption in their respective states of uniform legislation on commercial subjects. The Committee also considered the practice of commercial law, which was also under consideration by the Special Committee on Supplements to Canons of Ethics, and stated that it would report simultaneously with this latter Committee. Too, the practice in bankruptcy matters was considered, and also certain amendments to the bankrupt law, which the Committee deemed advisable. The Association adopted a resolution that the Committee investigate the causes of commercial fraud and recommend remedies.[244]

After public hearing in 1928, from the mass of testimony, the Committee obtained certain facts, which were expressed in a report.[245] On the subject of bankruptcy, the Committee recommended successfully that the Association commend to the country the more general acceptance and timely use of bankruptcy law, and also that an official receiver for handling the administration of bankrupt estates valued at between $5,000 and $10,000 be approved in principle.[246]

A suggested reform in bankruptcy procedure was also made by the Committee on Jurisprudence and Law Reform in 1928, namely, a modification in present practice, by which judgment and execution at law with return of nulla bona is a necessary prerequisite to maintenance of a creditor's

---

[244] Ibid., Vol. 52 (1927), pp. 254-261 and 100-101.
[245] Ibid., Vol. 53 (1928), pp. 114-117.
[246] Ibid., Vol. 53 (1928), pp. 114 and 386-391.

bill. The Committee felt that the Supreme Court of the United States could make a rule in equity which would substantially incorporate the provisions of a statute, and recommended that the matter be submitted to the Supreme Court.[247]

The Committee on Commercial Law and Bankruptcy in 1929 held its accustomed public meeting, which was attended by a representative group of experts. In 1929 the Committee presented five recommendations for adoption, which epitomized very definitely the work of the Committee for the year 1928-1929: (1) That in the matter of professional ethics, no action be taken directly affecting the interests of commercial law until the Special Committee on Supplements to Canons should have concluded its work and deliberations; (2) That nothing be done in reference to bankruptcy practice until official investigation of bankruptcy practice in New York, instituted at the instance of the Association of the Bar of the City of New York, the New York County Lawyers Association, and the Bronx County Bar Association, acting on behalf of the public, had been concluded; that the Committee's 1924 report would show that Bar Committee had forecast the explosion which had occurred in New York in bankruptcy circles; (3) That the bankruptcy law be again commended; (4) That uniformity be considered the major subject of importance in bankruptcy practice, and that recommendation be made to the Bench and Referees for a more uniform application of bankruptcy general law and procedural rules; that the Referees Association, which met with the Bar Association, and tendered its services and counsel, the Association of Credit Men and the Commercial Law League, be commended on their cooperation in the enterprise for uniformity; (5) That the practice of selecting receivers on the basis of friendship or patronage be condemned.[248]

---

[247] Ibid., Vol. 53 (1928), pp. 419 and 428.

[248] Ibid., Vol. 54 (1929), pp. 329-338, 73-77, and 110-111.

In its 1930 report, the Committee reviewed the activities of the New York investigation of bankruptcy matters. In addition to the judicial inquiry into bankruptcy practice in New York, Colonel Donovan and associates, through means of questionnaires and searching correspondence, had expanded the compass of inquiries in order to reach into every district of the country to gather facts, data, and opinions from judges, referees, lawyers, and others, whose pursuits and relationships brought them into contacts of intimacy with these subjects. One conclusion of the Donovan report was that the policy of creditor control in the administration of bankrupt estates had proven a failure. The Committee called attention to the fact that the American Bar Association had been advocating for years the curbing and restraining of activities of proxy solicitation. It recited that, after the joint Conference held early in 1924 by representative commercial groups, the Special Committee on Bankruptcy of the American Bar Association, the forerunner of the present Committee, had recommended to the Supreme Court a rule of practice which was subsequently adopted by a number of districts as a local rule. This rule practically eliminated control of estates through proxy solicitation. Pending a nation-wide investigation of bankruptcy administration and the suspension of action for an official receiver, the Committee recommended that the present system of suppressing proxy solicitation be applied. The Committee also made recommendations regarding certain legislation, which were adopted as follows: (1) A bill to vest control in receivers of property within United States outside territorial limits wherein receiver was appointed;[249] (2) A bill to enable a receiver to sue in the United States court in any jurisdiction and to the same extent as owner

[249] Ibid., Vol. 55 (1930), p. 84. Note should be made of the fact that the Committee on Jurisprudence and Law Reform had under consideration in 1931 the question of equity receiverships and the unification thereof to eliminate ancillary receivers in other circuits and save expense. Majority report opposing legislation on the subject was adopted by a majority of the Committee. Ibid., Vol. 56 (1931), pp. 405-408.

of estates;[250] (3) Defeat of a bill, amending Bankruptcy Code, to add boarding-house keepers to the list of those entitled to priority;[251] (4) Principle involved in a bill fixing a time limit for United States, state, political, or administrative subdivision to file tax claims.[252]

In 1931, because of economic and industrial conditions, the subject of bankruptcy received unusual attention. A nation-wide survey and investigation of conditions of practice in bankruptcy was then being made by the Department of Justice with the Department of Commerce on the recommendation of the President of the United States. The Committee submitted that its report would be withheld until the survey was completed, but offered its cooperation and assistance in the achievement of objectives. Furthermore, it had conferred with the Solicitor General and had called and sponsored, before the Bar Association annual meeting, a Joint Conference of Committees from interested organizations, at which Conference the subject of investigation and survey received major attention. Other groups attending the Conference included the National Association of Referees in Bankruptcy, the Commercial Law League of America, the National Association of Credit Men and the Association of Retail Credit Men. The Committee reported that it would continue cooperation and study of facts and recommendations. Since the matter would probably come before Committees of Congress, the Bar Association Committees would keep in close contact with Executive Committee of the Bar Association during the interval between meetings.[253]

Following its annual Conference May 2 and 3, 1932, the Committee appeared before the Executive Committee of the Association, and submitted an oral report, which consisted of a discussion of pending revision of legislation.

---

250 Ibid., Vol. 55 (1930), p. 85.
251 Ibid., Vol. 55 (1930), p. 86.
252 Ibid., Vol. 55 (1930), pp. 87 and 338-349.
253 Ibid., Vol. 56 (1931), pp. 66-67 and 346.

and recommended that the Committee be authorized to appear before Committees of Congress in opposition to this pending legislation. It based its opposition on the conclusion that the recommended legislation was not amendatory, but constituted an entirely new bankruptcy system, and was, therefore, unsound and impracticable. Moreover, the proposed legislation sought to eliminate judicial control or supervision of bankruptcy administration, to substitute creditor control, and to increase compensation of existing bankruptcy officials as well as to create new officials. The Executive Committee by resolution authorized opposition. On May 4 and 5, 1932, the Committee appeared before representatives of the subcommittee of the Judiciary Committee of the Senate and House, where opposition was expressed, and also amendments to existing law were suggested. The Committee was thereupon requested by the joint subcommittee of Congress to prepare and submit at a later time amendments and changes to existing law, and to express its views for needed improvement in procedure. The Committee prepared a tentative draft of amendatory bill, which was attached to the 1932 report. Though the suggested amendments were not final, they represented results of numerous conferences and studies of the Committee with representatives of widely diversified groups of experts. Its purpose was to accumulate before the next Congress the composite sentiment of the country on some measures, which all people, and not special interests only, considered wise. The following recommendations were submitted:

(1) The Committee continue opposition to the bill of the Attorney General. This was adopted.

(2) A tentative bill, filed with report, should have the approval of the Association, and Committee should cause the same to be introduced and supported. This was approved.

(3) The Committee be authorized to continue studies, conferences, and exchange of views with public officials

and other interested persons or groups for formulation of bankruptcy changes in present bankruptcy law and procedure. This was adopted with an amendment that the Committee hold at least one public hearing before adopting any recommendation to be presented to the Executive Committee.[254]

In furtherance of powers and instructions, the Committee continued contacts in its effort to formulate and agree on further changes in the bankruptcy law; it kept itself informed of contents, objectives, and progress of various bills offered in Congress. During the month of January, 1933, increasing pressure of the country toward governmental relief from debt burdens began to be manifested in the Judiciary Committees of both Senate and House. This resulted in the speeding up and passage of various suggested emergency bankruptcy and moratorium measures. Plans and schemes of various forms for debt elimination were brought forward. The President and Secretary of the American Bar Association made themselves available for conference work. Two members of the Committee joined them as well as representatives of the National Association of Referees in Bankruptcy, the Commercial Law League of America, and other interested organizations, which freely gave of their services to Committees of Congress. During the closing week of the session ending March 4, 1933, the Chairman, in conjunction with representatives of the United States Chamber of Commerce, the American Bankers Association and others, was similarly engaged in Washington.

During the period April 29 to May 3, 1933, the Committee joined in an extensive conference composed of conferees from every section of the country, and representing perhaps the widest diversity of bankruptcy experts ever assembled. Proposed amendatory drafts of the American Bar Association and various other organizations and persons

[254] Ibid., Vol. 57 (1932), pp. 408-412 and 161-170.

were compared and codified. From May 20 to 22, 1933, the labors of the Conference were committed to writing by a Drafting Committee; final draft of amendments thus prepared represented an enormous amount of research, exchange of experience and views.

The 1933 report pointed out that the bankruptcy legislation enacted and pending showed that the Seventy-third Congress was relief conscious; the administration recognized that the aggregate liabilities of the country were disproportionately high as compared to value of assets, and consequently evolved a five-point program for relief of debts:

(1) Provision for Relief of Debtors Act. This combines moratorium for distressed individual debtors and discharge for those unable to compose obligations with creditors.

(2) Agricultural Compositions and Extensions Act.

(3) Reorganization of railroads engaged in interstate commerce. This aimed to hold creditors at bay and keep railroads in operation.

(4) General Corporation Reorganization Act.

(5) Relief of cities and other taxable districts.

The Committee reported that the first three bills had been enacted. It also reported to the Executive meeting in May, 1933, its opposition to the principle of municipal bankruptcy, and received authority to oppose it. The Committee then registered its opposition before Committees of Congress. The Bar Committee also expressed its purpose of recommending as soon as economic and financial conditions improved the introduction into Congress of a comprehensive, conservative amendment for the improvement of bankruptcy law, both substantive and procedural. Exhaustive study then would enable the Committee to take action later. The Bankruptcy Committee also cooperated with the Taxation Committee in sponsoring an amendment to the bankruptcy law, which would provide for the discharge of bankrupts from tax liabilities as well as debts.[255]

This progress report was approved with the exception of the provision regarding corporate reorganization by federal law, which provision the Association disapproved in principle.[256] The second recommendation, that the Committee continue its studies and activities, was adopted.[257]

The Committee presented an elaborate report of its activities for the year 1933-1934, which included a comprehensive account of the administration's five-point program and its adoption. It reported that the Act providing for relief of cities and other taxable districts had been enacted into law May 24, 1934, though the measure had been actively opposed by the Committee, both on constitutional grounds and also on grounds of sound economy and political policy, and though the Committee's views had been accepted by a minority of the Judiciary Committee of the Senate, composed of four of the five members of the subcommittee before whom the hearings were conducted. This act was, however, a temporary measure, its duration being limited to two years. The Corporate Reorganization Act, also enacted into law June 7, 1934, was not a temporary measure; this measure had also been opposed by the Committee. This new bankruptcy policy differed radically from that of the old. Under the old policy liquidation and debt reduction were the chief objects, while composition was incidental and reorganization rare. Under the new policy composition and reorganization were the chief objects, while debt reduction was only incidental. The Committee deemed that the acts did meet an emergency, and would as time passed make a contribution to the subjects of composition, extension, and rearrangement among creditors and debtors. But none of the acts would make a significant contribution

255 Supra, p. 328.

256 American Bar Association Report, Vol. 58 (1933), pp. 123-126.

257 Ibid., Vol. 58 (1933), pp. 348-354 and 126.

to the subject of debt reduction, the sine qua non of release and recovery. Only receiverships (bankruptcy) and mortgage foreclosures would function to reduce the debt burden.

The Committee also reported on the general Bankruptcy Conference, which, as reported for the two previous years, had continued its labors and studies with a view to improving the entire system of bankruptcy law and procedure. The Committee added that the fourth tentative draft, suggesting amendments and delivered to conferees, was not prompted by emergencies of economic depression, but was designed to formulate a better system of bankruptcy administration for permanent use. Factual studies of the Department of Justice under the direction of the Solicitor General in 1931 and 1932, together with vast quantities of material assembled before Committees of Congress, had made available the truth concerning conditions and results of present and former methods of practice in every district of the country. Since the facts of experience and proposed changes in law, thus being considered in conference by groups of lawyers, referees, instructors, and authors of bankruptcy law, represented every shade of opinion and point of view, the final product, which was to be concluded before the next Session of Congress, would represent the most thoroughly studied work of the kind yet produced.[258]

The American Bar Association through its Committees has done a great amount of research and study of problems in the field of bankruptcy, and has worked to clarify the national bankruptcy law, and to eliminate certain abuses which had developed. Its stand on recent legislation has been tolerant, though it has tended to make the deflationary bankruptcy emphasis regardless of hardship entailed. Its whole policy and activity shows a realization of the difficult problems involved, the great amount of work necessary for solution and the need for a long-term program to attain results.

---

[258] Ibid., Vol. 59 (1934), pp. 450-461 and 90-96.

2. INTEREST ON CLAIMS AND JUDGMENTS AGAINST THE GOVERNMENT

When the government is the debtor it seems natural that it should have the advantage. The Bar Association, true to its policy of protecting the individual as against the government, undertook to sponsor a bill providing for payment of interest on judgments against the United States. As long ago as 1915, a report was submitted that among three matters referred to the Committee on Jurisprudence and Law Reform was the matter of interest on claims and judgments against the United States as incorporated in a bill to amend Section 177 of the Judicial Code.[259] The Committee recommended that instead of six per cent, the rate should be not less than three per cent, nor more than four per cent. This recommendation of a lower interest rate was lost, and the rate of six per cent was approved.[260]

In 1921 a resolution was referred to the Committee on Commerce, Trade and Commercial Law, that it consider a bill then pending in Congress,[261] to provide for payment of interest on judgments against the United States, and report conclusions and recommendations at the following annual meeting.[262] The Committee in 1922 reported in favor of the bill.[263] In 1923 the Committee reported that it had urged the passage of the bill, but that it had failed of passage because of the shortness of the session. The Committee had been informed, however, that it would be reintroduced at the following session of Congress.[264] In 1925 it again failed of passage, and Committee again recommended reintroduction of the bill.[265] In 1926 the bill in

259 Ibid., Vol. 40 (1915), p. 374.
260 Ibid., Vol. 40 (1915), pp. 16-19.
261 S. 77.
262 Ibid., Vol. 46 (1921), p. 54.
263 Ibid., Vol. 47 (1922), pp. 289 and 290.
264 Ibid., Vol. 48 (1923), pp. 284 and 290.
265 Ibid., Vol. 50 (1925), pp. 355 and 368.

modified form was readopted and approved; the interest rate was changed from six per cent to four per cent.[266] In 1927 the bill was again approved, and the Committee was directed to cause the introduction of said bill at the following session of Congress.[267] In 1928 it was reported that the bill had been introduced into the Sixty-ninth Congress, but because of congestion had never been reported out of Committee. Through the effort of the Commerce Committee, the bill on the subject had been put in such form as to be in harmony with the Judiciary Committee's views, and had again been introduced into the present Congress.[268] In 1929 it was reported that though the bill had been introduced in several successive Congresses and had had active and powerful support, it had been opposed by Former Director of the Budget, General Lord. Since Clarence W. DeKnight, Esq., Washington, D. C., had given much time and effort to the matter, he proposed to have it reintroduced at the December session.[269] In 1930 it was reported that much work had been done in the Seventieth Congress in an effort to get the bill passed; that it had been referred to the Committee on Judiciary of the House, and submitted to subcommittee No. 1 for consideration. Different government bureaus issued copious reports showing the number of cases unsettled in which the question of interest would be of great importance. Since there was no report by the subcommittee, the bill never got beyond the Committee. After the adjournment of Congress, plans were formulated to have the bill reintroduced in the Seventy-first Congress. This was done early in the session. On January 28, 1930, the bill was referred by the Committee on Judiciary of the House to the Attorney General of the United States for an expression of views. The Attorney General, in turn, referred the bill to various bureaus for report on previous

---

266 Ibid., Vol. 51 (1926), pp. 386, 390, and 70-71.

267 Ibid., Vol. 52 (1927), pp. 98, 242, and 245.

268 Ibid., Vol. 53 (1928), pp. 337 and 343.

269 Ibid., Vol. 54 (1929), pp. 309 and 316.

expressions of views by the former Attorney General as well as additional information. Consequent delay was due to congestion in the Attorney General's office. Clarence W. DeKnight, Esq., of Washington, D. C., endeavored to have the Attorney General's report compiled and submitted. The Committee was advised that, while data had been assembled for the Attorney General's report, no report had been made, and that the bill would not be considered in that session of Congress.[270] In 1931 it was reported that it would be impossible to obtain favorable consideration of bill until approved by the Attorney General of the United States, and that he had not up to that time submitted his report.[271] However, by the 1932 meeting, the report of the Attorney General had been made under date of February 15, 1932. In reference to statistics in the Attorney General's report, and the present status of the proposed legislation, Mr. DeKnight, in report dated June 17, 1932, said, inter alia, "Endorsement of the Bill by your Committee and the American Bar Association will have material weight with the Judiciary Committees of the House and Senate in connection with consideration of Bill when Congress reconvenes in December next." A bill to amend Section 177 of the Judicial Code, to provide for the payment of interest, was annexed to the 1932 report.[272]

Nothing further appears to have been done. Mr. DeKnight in an interview April 4, 1936, stated that the matter had not been pressed in Congress because, under the existent depression and emphasis on economy, the President would have vetoed the bill. The enormous amount of work done by the Committee and other interested persons to get this bill passed gives some suggestion of the manner in which bills are pressed for passage.

---

[270] Ibid., Vol. 55 (1930), p. 328, also p. 454, for similar action by the Committee on Jurisprudence and Law Reform.

[271] Ibid., Vol. 56 (1931), pp. 339 and 342.

[272] Ibid., Vol. 57 (1932), pp. 394, 402-404, 88.

Chapter IX

TECHNIQUE AND PROCEDURE USED FOR EXECUTION OF POLICIES

"Thought is parent of the deed."—Carlyle.

A. Policies Formerly Determined by the Executive Committee, Now by the House of Delegates

The Executive Committee was formerly the policy-determining body of the American Bar Association, because it had power to act in the interim between annual meetings. During the annual meeting, the membership present could, by a majority vote, or where legislation was involved by a two-thirds vote, adopt such measures as it considered expedient. Since the adoption of the New Constitution in 1936, power of determining policies is vested in the representative House of Delegates.

After policies are determined, then follows execution. Policies were first executed by Committees, and subsequently, after Sections were organized, by Committees and Sections. Sections represent subsidiary, semi-autonomous organizations of experts in a particular field such as Public Utility Law, Insurance, etc., each Section having its own officers, General Council and committees. Members of Committees also represent experts in the particular field in which they function.

Policies involving problems of national scope can be handled by the National Association itself. However, many of the problems considered by the American Bar Association related to states or counties, and these had to be carried through with the aid of state and local bar associations. The National Bar Association early used the only machinery it had, the Vice-President for each state, the Local Council of five, and the member of the General Council, to contact the state and local bar associations. This was not always effective as ascertained by the Citizenship Committee when it endeavored to carry through its policy of developing knowledge and respect for the Constitution. The Citizenship Committee showed its efficiency by initiating its own machinery of an American Bar Association Committee in each state, when it found that working through state bar association committees did not give the desired results.[1] After 1916, when the Conference of Bar Association Delegates was organized, another point of contact between the national, state, and county units was developed. Since the national organization still found its connection with state and local groups much too loose for effective action, in 1933 it adopted its National Bar Program. A change was also made from a Vice-President for each state to ten Vice-Presidents, one for each judicial circuit.

After these changes, as dissatisfaction with the type of organization still prevailed, a dynamic movement was initiated, which culminated in 1936 in the adoption of the New Plan of organization, which proposed to make the American Bar Association more representative of the lawyers of the country, especially by way of giving the stay-at-home member some voice in the selection of the policy-determining body, and also to promote greater cohesion within its own organization and more effective coordination without.

---

[1] Supra, p. 119.

1. SECTIONS AND COMMITTEES AUTHORIZED TO ACT THROUGH RESOLUTIONS

How do the Sections and Committees get power to act? Authorization to act formerly was obtained through resolution of so much of the membership as was present at annual meetings, or by resolution of the Executive Committee between annual meetings. Resolutions were adopted by a majority of the membership at annual meetings except when resolutions involved the sponsoring of specific legislation, when a two-thirds vote was required.

Since the adoption of the New Plan of organization in August, 1936, resolutions may be introduced in the Assembly, which are referred to the Resolutions Committee. The Resolutions Committee after hearings and due consideration report back to the Assembly. If the resolution is approved by the Resolutions Committee, and such procedure is adopted by the Assembly, then the Resolution is referred to the House of Delegates. If the House should reject a Resolution of the Assembly, provision is made for referendum to the membership. Section and Committee resolutions are submitted to the House of Delegates for action.

2. SECTIONS AND COMMITTEES EXECUTE POLICIES THROUGH RESEARCH, CORRESPONDENCE, QUESTIONNAIRES AND CONFERENCES

From the reports, it is seen that committee and section personnel are on the whole expert in the fields in which they are functioning. They proceed to study the question or problem referred to them by gathering data through correspondence, questionnaires, and conferences with other experts in the field.

For example, when information was desired in relation to legal qualifications for admission to the Bar in the different states, resort was had to correspondence with Vice-Presidents and Local Councils; a circular of inquiry was also sent to the chief justice of each state. With respect to legal education in foreign countries, the Bar Association was instrumental in having the Commissioner of Education send to all foreign countries lists of questions prepared by the Committee on Legal Education and Admissions to the Bar.[2] Letters requesting views on legal education were also sent to educators, and law school catalogues were collected. The Committee on Admissions also addressed a communication to the Honorable Elihu Root, then Secretary of State, asking that the Department secure, through diplomatic officers of the United States abroad, information concerning legal education and rules governing admission to the Bar in foreign countries. The Department issued such a circular, and information from thirty-five countries was obtained.[3]

The Legal Aid Committee also gathered much data through correspondence when it directed a letter to the secretary of every bar association in the country to determine how far the organized Bar had given support to legal aid.[4]

The effective Judicial Recall Committee, concentrating efforts in Arizona and North Dakota, sent twenty-five thousand copies of speeches of various senators, representatives, and other public men to the entire electorate of Arizona. It carried on its campaign in North Dakota through correspondence and personal interviews with members of the bar, which resulted in discussion opposing judicial recall.[5]

To ascertain law respecting detention of innocent witnesses, letters of inquiry were sent to general councils and replies were received from forty-eight states.[6] The Committee on the Federal Code of Criminal Procedure obtained information on necessary changes in criminal procedure

---

2 Supra, pp. 42-45.
3 Supra, pp. 51-52.
4 Supra, p. 104.
5 Supra, p. 146.
6 Supra, p. 184.

through correspondence with district attorneys of the United States.[7] On its policy of accelerating the organization of Legislative Drafting and Reference Bureaus for the more scientific drafting of legislation, a letter was sent to all secretaries of state associations relative to the assistance which bar associations had furnished members of legislatures and others in drafting bills.[8]

The method of obtaining information through questionnaires was resorted to on many occasions. Questions were sent out by the Secretary of the Association regarding the usefulness of bar associations in various states, with special reference to standards of admission to the Bar.[9] When the 1921 standards for admission were in process of being formulated, questionnaires were sent to deans of every resident law school in the United States, to every Committee on Legal Education of a State or Local Bar Association, to every State Board of Bar Examiners, and to members of the Bar, whose names were obtained by state Vice-Presidents of the American Bar Association and other sources. From the replies much valuable information was obtained.[10] The Council of Legal Education later in 1928-1929 resorted to questionnaires to all law schools, approved and unapproved, to obtain a fair picture of the character of each school. Replies were furnished by all but six schools.[11]

In 1931 and 1932 the Committee on Unlawful Practice of the Law sent a letter and questionnaire to all bar Associations to obtain desired information on unlawful practice.[12]

The Committee on Citizenship, when it desired to obtain data on the extent to which the Constitution was taught in colleges and universities, sent questionnaires to

---

7 Supra, p. 186.
8 Supra, p. 264.
9 Supra, p. 47.
10 Supra, p. 63.
11 Supra, p. 71.
12 Supra, p. 95.

which three hundred and thirty-six replies were made, showing that such teaching was a mere incident.[12a]

In carrying out the National Bar Program relative to criminal law enforcement, questionnaire was sent to thirteen hundred bar associations, to which large response was made, and on which resolutions of 1934 were based.[13]

At the request of the American Bar Association Committee on Uniform Judicial Procedure, the Vice-Presidents sent questionnaires to Senators and Congressmen to obtain their stand on the bill giving the Supreme Court the rule-making power on the law side. Though desired information was forthcoming, effective action on the bill was not obtained until it was supported by the Attorney General and the Administration. In the formulation and drafting of the Rules, the Bar and the Court have cooperated to an extent probably never realized before.

Public hearings have proven so effective in obtaining information for the Commerce Committee and the Committee on Commercial Law and Bankruptcy that other committees are in process of copying this procedure. At these public hearings, anyone can testify before the Committee on the subject assigned. As a matter of fact, those who appear on any given subject are usually outstanding experts in the field. For example, at one of the public hearings of the Committee on Commercial Law and Bankruptcy, there were present members of the Federal Judiciary, Referees in Bankruptcy, college professors and representatives of large financial organizations.[14]

3. AMERICAN BAR ASSOCIATION HAS EXECUTED CERTAIN POLICIES THROUGH ORGANIZATION OF OTHER GROUPS

To carry out many of its policies, the American Bar Association has been instrumental in organizing other groups; for example, in 1892 the Conference of Commis-

[12a] Supra, p. 120.
[13] Supra, p. 205.
[14] Supra, pp. 341-342.

sioners on Uniform State Laws, through which organization uniform laws are drafted and passed; in 1900 the Association of American Law Schools, through which organization the Bar Association has worked to raise standards of legal education; in 1931 the Conference of Bar Examiners, through which it has endeavored to raise standards of admission to the Bar. In 1923 the Association played some part in the organization of the American Law Institute, engaged at present in organizing and publishing a Restatement of the Law.

4. LEGISLATIVE ACTIVITIES

(a) Preparation and Draft of Bills, and Appearance Before Congressional Committees

Many of the resolutions proposed by Sections and Committees and adopted by the American Bar Association embody legislation which is urged for passage. The Bar Association, through its Committees, has prepared and drafted many bills, for example, the Poor Litigants Statute, the purpose of which was to insure to each person a day in court, the Federal Declaratory Judgments Act, the Federal Commercial Arbitration Act, the act providing for a Federal Industrial Council in 1928, proposed amendments to the bankruptcy law, not to mention the long list of uniform laws, drafted by the Conference of Commissioners on Uniform State Laws, and listed in the American Bar Association reports each year. In drafting these laws, Committees often held public hearings to obtain suggestions for improving drafts. For example, this was done in the case of the Federal Commercial Arbitration Statute.[15] The Committee on Commerce did not consider itself sufficiently advised to draft a statute regarding motor vehicles until it had had hearings with the leading automobile and traffic associations.[16]

---

15 Supra, p. 297.
16 Supra, p. 314.

The Bar Association has not only initiated legislation by drafting bills and having them introduced, but it has also watched legislation. For example, the Committee on Commercial Law and Bankruptcy successfully opposed repeal of the Bankruptcy Act, as well as sponsored and opposed amendments. The Committee on Jurisprudence and Law Reform also opposed as well as sponsored much legislation, not always successfully, as witness the passage of the Johnson Bill abridging jurisdiction of the federal courts. The Committee also interviews those in charge of legislation, and appears before Congressional Committees, especially the Judiciary Committees of the Senate and House, since the Bar Association has been deeply interested in Judicial Administration and Procedure. In the case of the Federal Commercial Arbitration Act, the Commerce Committee had conferences with members of the Senate Committee; it sent a letter to Senator Walsh, a prominent member of the American Bar Association, with its recommendations, and appeared at hearings on the bill.[17] On the Federal Declaratory Judgments Act, the Committee on Jurisprudence and Law Reform testified at hearings, submitted briefs, and communicated at length with members of Congress.[18] In the matter of judicial recall, the Special Committee that opposed the measure concentrated on state legislatures as being the strategic place at which to use pressure.

Does the American Bar Association maintain a lobby? The Committee on Jurisprudence and Law Reform stated in one of its reports that it could consider a great volume of legislation because it had on its committee a man who was permanently in Washington.[19] However, when the Committee on Jurisprudence and Law Reform proposed in 1929 such a change in policy as would make more effective the Association's influence on legislation by having a per-

---

17 Supra, p. 299.
18 Supra, pp. 172-176.
19 Supra, p. 177.

manent staff located at Washington, it was not successful with its proposal though it endeavored to show the value and unselfishness of the Bar in its legislative activities.

(b) Contact With Administrative Departments

Since administrative departments are instrumental in getting much legislation drafted and passed, the Bar Association by means of its contacts with some of these departments may be said to influence legislation in this way. Note that in the highly technical field of radio, the Radio Committee of the Association at one of its meetings was able to have present members of the Federal Radio Commission, a representative from the Department of Justice and others from organizations interested in radio as well as Senator C. C. Dill and Congressman Wallace H. White.[20] The Committee on Federal Taxation is in constant touch with the Treasury Department as well as the Permanent Staff of the Congressional Joint Committee on Internal Revenue Taxation.[21]

(c) Contact With Other Interest Groups

The Bar Association works constantly with other interest groups for the passage of legislation. This is evidenced from the foregoing survey, particularly in the fields of Legal Education and Admission to the Bar, Legal Aid, the United States Constitution, Criminal Law, Uniformity, Commercial Arbitration and Labor Problems.

5. CONTACT WITH JUDGES

The American Bar Association through its Judicial Section as well as its contact with the National Conference of Judicial Councils is well able to make its policies known to Judges. That is probably one reason that the Bar Asso-

---

20 Supra, p. 316.

21 American Bar Association Report, Vol. 59 (1934), pp. 612-619.

ciation considers that if bar admissions and practice and procedure were governed by rules of court rather than by statutes, quicker action could be had looking toward higher standards for admission to the Bar and more efficient administration of justice. In effecting the division of the eighth circuit, it was found that quicker action was obtained after the judges of the eighth circuit had been consulted on proposed change and had approved it.[22] On the uniformity problem, every court of last resort in the various states was approached and requested to hand down decisions on Uniform Acts.[23]

6. DISTRIBUTION OF PAMPHLETS

In carrying through many of its policies, the American Bar Association resorted to pamphlets. To raise standards of legal education, it distributed 50,000 copies of the pamphlet on "Law as a Career" to high and preparatory schools.[24] A pamphlet on "Unauthorized Practice" was widely distributed to curb that evil. In spreading its propaganda in relation to the Constitution, the Committee on Citizenship distributed many pamphlets, in particular, the "Story of the Constitution."[25] The Judicial Recall Committee resorted to this method of developing opposition to judicial recall; 350,000 pamphlets were distributed, speakers and debaters were furnished, and prizes awarded for essays.[26]

7. PUBLICATIONS

The main publication of the American Bar Association in addition to its Year Books is its monthly magazine, the American Bar Association Journal. Many of the Bar Asso-

22 Supra, pp. 134-136.
23 Supra, pp. 283-284.
24 Supra, pp. 72-73.
25 Supra, p. 125.
26 Supra, p. 150.

ciation's subsidiary groups also have publications. The Council of Legal Education and the Conference of Bar Examiners both issue a Bulletin. State bar associations also publish reports and journals. A Legislative Manual has been published, which is supposed to act as a guide in the drafting of scientific legislation.

Radio has been resorted to on occasions, notably by the Committee on Citizenship in its stress on developing knowledge of the Constitution. Fifty-five broadcasting stations contributed facilities free of charge. The series of fifteen addresses on "The Lawyer and the Public" should also be noted.

Referendum has also been used; for example, by the Committee on Federal Taxation, through the January, 1928, Journal of the Association, and in 1937 on the President's proposal regarding the federal courts.[27]

The social aspect of pressure has not been traced or discussed, since the significance of social functions cannot be estimated or measured in any way.

The American Bar Association, with its personnel including as it does many of the Presidents of the United States, Senators and Representatives, the Chief Justice plus the whole judiciary, occupies an important position to develop a completely adequate and efficient administration of justice. Aside from training in the field of government and law, the legal profession because of its contacts can readily enter into negotiations with the Chief Executive, administrators, congressmen, judges, or other persons of high and influential position. From a study of the reports, it would seem that though the organized Bar has done a great amount of work by way of study, research, and investigation in reference to various governmental and legal problems, fruitful activity has been limited, though it must be conceded that it has made definite contributions to a more efficient administration of justice.

---

[27] American Bar Association Journal, January, 1928, p. 54; Ibid., April, 1937.

CHAPTER X

EVALUATION OF EFFECTIVENESS OF BAR'S INFLUENCE AND TECHNIQUE, AND RECOMMENDATIONS

"By their fruits ye shall know them."—Matt. 7:20.

1. In evaluating the effectiveness of the Bar's influence and its machinery for the execution of policies, it is realized that there is no recognized technique for measuring the influence of various groups. In the absence of a recognized measuring rod, the criteria of judgment will be actual accomplishments or results obtained in the various fields where the Bar Association was active.

A survey of the sixty annual reports of the American Bar Association, the American Bar Association Journal, Opinions of the American Bar Association Committee on Professional Ethics and Grievances as well as other relevant legal periodicals, shows that government and legal problems of the past and present are not easy of solution. Such an empirical approach develops a sense of perspective and a suspicion of quick solutions or panaceas. It is wrong to look for simple unified solutions where none is possible. A study of the policies and activities of the American Bar Association demonstrates little that is spectacular, but rather shows functions of necessity limited and contributions in a comparatively narrow, special field. Reforms in government and more particularly in the field of judicial administration and procedure are complex and difficult of solution, demanding a need for competency. Problems can only be solved by hard thinking, a clear understanding of the problem and the forces that begot it followed by clean-cut action. Wishful thinking is useless.

2. The American Bar Association, though organized with the idea of maintaining a close connection with all other bar associations, represented a loose organization, both with reference to its own internal organization and also in relation to other Bar Association groups, state and local, down to 1936. From the time of its organization in 1878, there has been almost continuous effort, with spasmodic concentration, to establish closer relations between the different units, but without success until the adoption of the New Plan of organization in August, 1936. The problem of greater cohesion within its own organization and coordination with the state and local units was one of the important problems before the American Bar Association. In the past, the Association functioned and carried through its policies through state and local bar associations. Because such functioning did not often survive the pragmatic test, the National Bar Program was developed to strengthen contacts among Bar groups to the end that their functioning would bring about the desired results. Having served its purpose, the National Bar Program was merged in the New Plan of organization, the next step looking toward a federated bar.

The New Plan is commended in so far as it represents an attempt to give more representation to the stay-at-home member, and to grant state and local associations some part in choosing representatives to the policy-determining body. It is conceded that a step in the right direction has been taken to eliminate apparent looseness within the bar organization between sections, committees and the governing body, and to develop great coordination between the national, state and local bar associations, to the end that greater cohesion within and coordination without might be promoted.

To solve the problem of membership, emphasis on service would give results, because if the Bar Association would perform a service for its members, then there would be the extra incentive to join the organization. Every lawyer should feel the necessity of becoming a member of all three units of Bar organization, the local, state, and national.

3. It will be observed from a study of the American Bar Association's policies and activities in the field of professional efficiency that the Bar Association always has taken a stand for high professional standards. The question might well be asked, "Have they been high enough?" At the time of organization in 1878, the Association showed great foresight, in an age when law office training was the rule, by taking a stand for law school training.[1] Thereafter, in adopting a policy of improving the existing law schools, the Bar Association is also deserving of praise for its stress on a broad, general preparatory education, as well as legal training with an appropriate curriculum.[2] Criticism, however, should be given because more attention was not paid by the Bar and the law schools to curriculum. The social emphasis should be more clear cut, since law is a public calling. The public service aspect of the profession should be made by the law schools, boards of law examiners, bar associations, and all other agencies interested in high standards of legal education and a high type of bar personnel. Legal training should not be purely legal in character but should include a wider cultural background as well as training in the sciences of economics and politics, with some emphasis on law reform.

It is cause for regret that the Bar Association, after it sponsored the Association of American Law Schools in 1900, did not thereafter maintain a close relationship with it. Though the two groups had a joint meeting in 1913, it

---

[1] Supra, p. 42.
[2] Supra, pp. 49-52.

was not until 1920 that the American Bar Association and the Association of American Law Schools entered on their unified policy of raising bar standards.

Regret must also be expressed at the anomaly of a Committee and a Section of Legal Education, both working for the same object of raising professional standards, and it is cause for rejoicing that a conflict between the two groups in the formulation of the Standard Rules produced the more effective organization of a Council of Legal Education, which functioned under the Section of Legal Education.[3] While it may be granted that the Council of Legal Education has obtained results, still it should be recognized that pressure used on the official state groups to raise the official standards of admission to the Bar would be much more effective than pressure used on law schools, for law schools that did not conform to state requirements, and enable students to pass the state examination, would be forced out of business. Let the official standards be high, and law schools will be compelled to follow.

Though the two-year preparatory requirement was proposed as long ago as 1904, it was not adopted officially by the American Bar Association until 1921, and is still in process of being adopted and endorsed by the states. It is recommended that to further emphasize the need for the highest standards of admission to practice law, the standards should be raised to require a minimum of four years of college training, three years of law school training in an approved law school, and one year further study in a law office or law clinic. Thus the legal profession could emphasize the need for discipline and training for governmental office in a democracy.

The American Bar Association has furnished leadership in this important matter of maintaining standards, but since their enforcement is really the job of the state bar associations, there is need of strong state associations.

---

[3] Supra, pp. 57-60.

What constitutes a strong state association? A study might well be made of the different types of state bar associations, namely, the voluntary, affiliated, and integrated associations to ascertain, on the basis of facts and experience, which type of organization is most effective in maintaining standards of professional excellence, as well as other matters which are the special province and job of state bar associations.[4]

4. The American Bar Association furnished leadership in the movement to develop standards for those already in the profession and a basis for expulsion for those who ignored them, when it drafted and promulgated the Canons of Ethics in 1908. Opinions of the Committee on Ethics and Grievances, now numbering about one hundred and twenty, form an important reference as to what is or is not permitted. However, the enforcement of the Canons is dependent also on strong state and local bar associations, and their adoption as Rules of Court. The survey of present methods of disciplinary procedure in the various localities should prove valuable, and the American Bar Association should again furnish leadership in a movement to promote uniformity of such methods as will most effectively eliminate the shyster. By purging the profession of undesirables, standards of professional excellence can be maintained and public confidence won.

---

[4] Several surveys of state bar associations are in process of being made. A survey of the legal profession was suggested by Dean Clark in presidential address before the American Law School Association December, 1934. Surveys in Wisconsin and Idaho were noted as in process of being made in January, 1935. (American Bar Association Journal, January, 1935, p. 66.) The February, 1935, Journal noted a symposium of "Bar Surveys" at the meeting of the Association of American Law Schools, at which Dean Lloyd K. Garrison, of the University of Wisconsin Law School, who planned and directed the Wisconsin survey, spoke. (American Bar Association Journal, February, 1935, p. 68.) The Wisconsin survey was financed chiefly by government funds (C.W.A.). When funds were exhausted in March, 1934, it was financed by the state bar and the Milwaukee Bar Associations. American Bar Association Journal, May, 1935, p. 264. Recently, the New York County Lawyers Association has completed a survey, which has not as yet been published.

5. The American Bar Association also furnished leadership in endeavoring to eliminate unauthorized practice of the law, but here again enforcement is dependent on strong state and local bar associations. Evaluation of activities of the local groups cannot be made until a factual study has been completed. According to Charles E. Beardsley, Esq., of the California Bar, the integrated Bar of his state has been more effective by way of actual results that the former voluntary Bar Association in suppressing unauthorized practice of the law.

6. Lawyers at Bar Association meetings emphasize service to the public. Do they render such service and how adequate or inadequate is it? Because of the complexity of our legal system and consequent expense of seeking redress in the courts, many worthy poor persons are excluded from their legal rights. This is apt to cause unnecessary unrest and dissatisfaction with the administration of justice. Though the Bar Association came late into the field of legal aid, it is evident that it did accelerate to some extent the organization of Legal Aid Bureaus. It has fallen far short, however, of what it could do in making available to the poorest an adequate remedy at law. In developing favorable public relations, the Bar has been rather slow. By assuming the responsibility of organizing well-staffed and adequate Legal Aid Bureaus in every community of the country, and simplifying legal process, particularly with reference to small claims, wages, etc., the organized Bar could render a service in a field which is its own particular responsibility, and also at the same time build up favorable public relations.

Campaigns of propaganda via newspaper, radio, etc., are useless for most organizations and causes in building up favorable public relations, but for the Bar are worse than useless. Mere talk will not suffice to interpret the lawyer to the public; efficient and adequate service available to all should be given. The subject of Legal Aid should be emphasized to a greater degree, not only because it represents a vital local problem, but because its effective operation would promote healthy public relations.

7. The Citizenship Committee in its campaign to develop reverence for the Constitution encountered the lack of a functional coordination between the national and state bar associations. When the Committee found that it could not carry out its policies through the existing structure, it initiated its own new plan and had the national association appoint state committees to carry out policies in the states. Under the new plan of operation, state laws requiring the teaching of the Constitution were passed in forty-three states, and all under the direction of the Committees of the National Association. In addition, the Bar Association organized Conferences on the Constitution at colleges, forced the teaching of the Constitution at law schools through its pressure on state boards of law examiners, organized Americanization committees, had national holidays celebrated, distributed pamphlets and cartoons on the Constitution, cooperated in arranging oratorical contests in the senior high schools, and planned radio addresses. It is to be doubted whether speeches on the Constitution would have much influence; interesting dramatic presentations would, doubtless, have more. In the light of present-day operations of the American Liberty League in the matter of pamphlet distribution, the activities of the Bar Association in this respect seem infinitesimal; it might be noted that pamphlets to be effective must be read and digested and radio addresses must be heard.

It would seem that the Committee did accomplish what it started out to do, namely, to have state laws passed requiring the teaching of the Constitution in the public schools. The Bar's activity in this respect of having the necessary laws passed in the states providing for the teaching of the Constitution in the public schools is creditable, though the mere passing of the law does not necessarily mean that the Constitution was adequately taught.

The Constitution, with its amendments and decisions rendered thereunder, represents the basic law of the country, and it should be known and respected. This is essential for stability. A certain degree of flexibility is also requisite if the constitutional machinery is to remain adequate for the solution of current problems. The Honorable Newton D. Baker, in an address before the Philadelphia Bar Association on December 18, 1935, stated that it was necessary and wise to amend the Constitution, but that such amending should not be done in a fit of absent-mindedness.

The organized Bar with its training in government and law has shown something of its capacity to furnish necessary leadership in drafting and passage of legislation. Why should it not furnish leadership in the matter of constitutional amendments, necessary to make the fundamental law adequate to the needs of the people, commensurate to the solution of problems, and thus impervious to attack. The Bar did give leadership in pressing for the passage of the Twentieth Amendment, conceded to have added to the effectiveness of governmental machinery. Why not have a continuing committee to study and draft necessary and appropriate amendments and oppose iniquitous amendments. With profit, such a Committee might study the question as to whether the Constitution should be amended to expand regulatory powers of the federal government, or why pressure at times is brought to curb powers of the United States Supreme Court.

8. Aside from regimentation and discipline of members, the best work of the American Bar Association has been done in the field of judicial procedure. In this extremely technical field the Bar Association has had a measure of success in inaugurating reforms in court organization, court personnel and court practice and procedure. From its inception, the Bar Association has labored continuously to rid the legal system of delays, technicalities and uncertainties as well as to decrease the expense of litigation. It has been shown that it was through the efforts

of the American Bar Association that the Circuit Court of Appeals was organized, the Eighth Judicial Circuit was divided, and the Board of Tax Appeals organized, all conducing to a lessening of court congestion. Through an effective campaign of opposition, it succeeded in crushing the judicial recall movement, so strong and popular in 1912.

With regard to its activities in the field of selection of judges, though the problem is largely a state and local one, nevertheless the American Bar Association should furnish necessary leadership if any reform is to be obtained. The Bar Association's activities in this field have been insufficient. Since selection of judges represents largely a state and county problem, there is need for a scientific study of the different methods of selecting judges, and how such methods work before any definite stand can be taken. The federal court personnel may appear to be superior to that of the state and local courts, but this apparent superiority may not be due so much to the method of selection as to the fact that higher type men are available, and the tenure is for good behavior. The late George W. Wickersham contended that the method of selection was unimportant; the important factor was long tenure, to give security and independence.

It has become the fashion in legal circles to cry "wolf" at popular election of judges, and to go to the other extreme and sponsor appointment, with varying ramifications. Though an independent judiciary is indispensable to the proper administration of justice, the danger of having the judiciary too far removed from the electorate might well be considered. Also, the advisability of having the electorate make selection of judges from a list submitted by some group such as the judicial council, should be studied. The type of men serving on the Bench is a matter of first importance.

The history of the Bar organization in the field of practice and procedure shows the difficulty of obtaining adequate legislation to make judicial administration speedy, inexpensive and effective. The field is such a highly technical one that it is difficult even for courts and lawyers to grapple with such problems. It is little wonder then that members of the legislature are loath to struggle with questions of practice and procedure, for there is nothing here that is spectacular or provocative of votes. The one remedy for getting an efficient administration of justice would appear to be through judicial councils, and through a restoration to the Court of its ancient power of rule-making. Bar associations have done fine work in getting judicial councils organized in twenty states, but should continue until the task is completed not only in organizing judicial councils in all the states but in continuing to check on the efficient functioning of these councils.[5] If power and responsibility for adequate rules of practice and procedure are concentrated in the courts and the bar, this concentration will force such necessary reforms in judicial procedure as will develop a competent administration of justice.

9. In the matter of administrative agencies, the American Bar Association showed alertness to the development of the new phenomena by considering the Interstate Commerce Commission Act and possible amendments thereto. However, under an early policy of only considering legal as opposed to political and economic questions, the Bar Association definitely limited its activities. A study of the Federal Trade Commission resulted in the conclusion that the Commission was performing a useful function. The Association also commended the filing of the Conference rulings showing even at an early date its insistence on certainty. With the appointment of the Special Committee on Administrative Law in 1933, the Association took a definite stand against further extension of administrative

---

[5] Pennsylvania is listed as having a judicial council, but all it has is a Conference of Supreme Court Judges. The Pennsylvania Bar Association in June, 1935, appointed a Committee to study judicial councils.

agencies and for the segregation of judicial from legislative and executive functions, the placing of independent boards or commissions under one of the ten departments of government, and reform of existing administrative machinery. While the policies of the Bar Association through its Special Committee are somewhat sweeping, they are true to its tradition of emphasizing certainty in law, and protection of the rights of the individual as over against the government, through proper separation of governmental functions and the right of review.

11. In the field of substantive law, the American Bar Association through its Committees has rendered a distinct service in the drafting if not the passage of legislation. Many of its committees are permanent research groups interested in the problems in a particular field, for example, uniformity, commerce, bankruptcy, etc. Through its promotion of Legislative Reference Bureaus, it has conduced to the more careful drafting of legislation. This result was also obtained by the successful campaign for the Twentieth Amendment, which provided for change of date of Presidential Inauguration and two equally long sessions of Congress. Legislation drafted by the Conference of Commissioners on Uniform State Laws, a group which owes its existence to the American Bar Association, has been cited as the best drafted and most scientific legislation existent. True, in the field of uniformity, results have been mostly in the field of commercial rather than in that of social legislation.

The Bar's activities in the field of anti-trust laws showed its consistent emphasis on certainty, though it has not been able thus far to obtain passage of desired legislation. The whole emphasis in arbitration is to decrease litigation. Transportation, radio and taxation problems are intricate, and here the Bar should definitely confine itself to the legal aspects, with particular reference to judicial procedure in the way of a speedy, fair and adequate remedy for protection of legal rights.

It should be noted that the American Bar Association took a stand for a national bankruptcy law even before such a law had been enacted, and has consistently adhered to this policy in its opposition to repeal or drastic amendments. At first, its policy tended to emphasize creditors' rights, though later it did take a stand against creditor control when it advocated official receivers. In 1931 through its Committee on Commercial Law and Bankruptcy, it called and sponsored a Joint Conference of Committees, representative of various interested organizations, before the Bar Association annual meeting, which Conference is at present working on a long-term program for the betterment of bankruptcy law and procedure.

11. The American Bar Association has performed a service through its organization of many groups, such as the Conference of Commissioners for Uniform State Laws, charged with the duty of developing necessary uniformity in the law, Association of American Law Schools, with the purpose of developing the highest standards of legal education, and the Conference of Bar Examiners, also interested in raising standards of admission to the Bar. The Bar Association also contributed to the organization of the American Law Institute, engaged in a Restatement of the Law conducing to necessary simplification of the common law. The Bar Association has shown its capacity to work in cooperation with other groups. Many conflicts have developed within the Bar Association group, and this is to be expected since the legal profession may be said to represent a cross section of the country, and thus bar association members are what may be called past-masters at eliminating conflicts, and a need does exist for an interpreter among different groups. In the field of capital and labor as well as that of criminal law, the Bar Association has shown its potentiality in developing cooperation and reconciling conflicting interests.

12. The American Bar Association differs from groups heretofore surveyed and studied such as the Anti-Saloon

League, a reform group, the United States Chamber of Commerce, the business group, and the American Federation of Labor, the labor group, in at least three particulars:

(1) The Bar Association represents a professional group, and draws its membership from the legal profession, which for centuries has had high and definite standards for admission to practice law. Canons of Ethics represent standards to be adhered to if membership in the profession is to be retained. A certain amount of self-regulation and self-discipline has always characterized the legal profession.

(2) The membership of the legal profession from which the American Bar Association draws its members represents a semi-official body, since lawyers are officers of the court, the third branch of government.

(3) While the groups heretofore studied maintain permanent staffs at Washington, sometimes called "lobbies," to press for or hinder passage of legislation, the American Bar Association does not maintain such a staff.

13. When the Bar Association confines itself to its own field, namely, that of the administration of justice, it has been fairly successful in carrying out its policies.

14. This study is not exhaustive, but is meant to be suggestive only. Need of many other studies is apparent, not only of the other bar association groups, state and local, and special problems such as selection of judges, but also of other groups that play any part in developing efficiency in government. While early Bar policies showed a decided inclination to limit activities to strictly legal matters, there has been a recent tendency to participate in all governmental problems. On the legislative side, Bar activities show something of the way laws are drafted and passed, that they do not spring full-armed as did Minerva from the brain of Jupiter; it is only by intensive work that laws are drafted and passed, and such laws usually represent a compromise, the best obtainable under all the cir-

cumstances. The Bar Association did practically nothing in the field of civil service, nor has it appeared, from written records, to have a contact with political parties or leaders, but it has made its chief contribution in the field of judicial administration.

15. To one who believes in the democratic process and desires that it should be able to meet the pragmatic test, the conclusion is irresistible that if democratic government is to endure, it should not only include its own expert service but a utilization of the work of outside trained groups. The American Bar Association has opened a door to good legislation, administration and interpretation. What law can accomplish depends, in large measure, on the state of public opinion, which, in turn, is largely the product of individual and cooperative effort. The Bar Association has made its contribution in this field.

It has often been pointed out that there are, at least, two weaknesses in our laws: (1) Uncertainty, and (2) Complexity. Movements to eliminate both of these imperfections have been attacked by the Bar Association, namely, through the organization of the National Conference of Commissioners on Uniform State Laws in 1892, through its assistance in the organization of the American Law Institute in 1923, through the above mentioned acceleration of the movement for Legislative Reference and Drafting Bureaus, through the passage of the Twentieth Amendment, etc. Always the emphasis of the Bar Association has been on certainty, accuracy, and simplification.

The American Bar Association has developed and shown a method for the careful drafting of legislation, namely, that such drafting must be done by or under the advice of those who are trained, for even with training, the drafting of legislation presents a difficult task. Then, in addition to the careful drafting and passage of legislation, the Bar Association has shown its realization of the problem of administration and interpretation. Though the judiciary is, at present, under criticism, still any student of government will admit that the judiciary is the one branch of our government where some training for the office is required and found; it is the one branch of government that gives stability to a democracy enfeebled because of the paucity of trained leaders and workers in its service. A great burden has been placed on the courts because of slipshod and carelessly drawn legislation. But the burden and responsibility would be heavy, in any event, in a country where the common law prevails. The organized Bar should recognize and assume even more definitely its responsibility of organizing the judiciary on the highest plane of training and accomplishment.

Because of the innate instinct of self-preservation, it is quite likely that we shall always have real pressure groups, such as the great reform groups, the farmers, labor and business groups, working for their own specific objects and ends, without regard to accuracy or long-term results. Their emphasis is on the passage of legislation often without regard to its constitutionality, problems of administration incident thereto, or other effects. The history of the American Bar Association shows that it had a realization of the need in a democracy for stability, certainty and confidence. To attain these, laws should be not only carefully drawn but provision should be made for adequate, efficient machinery for their execution and interpretation. With its continued insistence on training for entrance into its own ranks, its emphasis on certainty in the law to insure stability and confidence, and its efforts to have laws written and administered with some degree of efficiency, the American Bar Association would seem to have pointed the way to the devising of a modus operandi by which our constitutional, democratic government may serve and survive. It would appear that this survival is conditioned on the utilization of the available specialized knowledge, discipline and training of individuals and groups. This includes not only a trained civil service in all units and departments of government and the marshalling of the contributions of trained groups such as the Bar Association, but a definite educational policy to greatly increase the supply of trained, key people in all fields of service.

16. There is much current armchair philosophy which is both eulogistic and derogatory of lawyers and the Bar. Some of this ranting would aim to convince the public that lawyers are reactionary, while much of it essays to prove the contrary, that they are progressive. Sometimes one point of view is dominant; sometimes the other. Both are false and untrue. The foregoing study represents a scientific piece of work written with no pre-conceived ideas or prejudices, and this study shows clearly and conclusively from data collected definite benefits derived by the public through the efforts of the legal profession. Legal aid was initiated by a lawyer, and the whole movement has been largely directed and financed by lawyers and bar associations. Constitutional government has always been supported by the lawyer group; judicial administration has been and is being simplified and improved. Merely "passing a law" is not going to cure all ills, social, economic and political; there must be efficient administration of good laws. In this era of panaceas and a return to a belief in wishful thinking, a study of the American Bar Association and its influence on Public Opinion and Legislation is valuable to show the work and effort necessary for constructive reform.

BIBLIOGRAPHY

PRIMARY SOURCES

American Bar Association Reports, Volumes 1-61 (1878-1936).

American Bar Association Journals, Volumes 1-20 (1915-1934).

American Bar Association Journal, January, 1935, to December, 1936.

American Law Institute Proceedings, Volumes 1-12.

American Judicature Society Journal, Volumes 1-18 (1917-1935).

Carnegie Foundation for the Advancement of Teaching, Bulletin No. 15, Training for the Public Profession of the Law, by Alfred Z. Reed (1921).

Bulletin No. 21, Present-Day Law Schools in the United States and Canada (1928).

Annual Review of Legal Education (1930, 1931, 1932, 1933, 1934).

Federal Trade Commission Reports.

Handbook of the National Conference of Commissioners on Uniform State Laws:

Proceedings (1911-1919).

Handbook (1920-1935).

Proceedings 1892-1911, from American Bar Association Reports.

Interstate Commerce Commission Reports.

"Judicial Council," Report of Committee on Judicial Administration. Merchants Association of New York (1931).

Opinions of Committee on Professional Ethics and Grievances of American Bar Association, August, 1922-March, 1934, Opinions 1-109.

Pennsylvania Bar Association Reports, 1-42 (1895-1936).

Philadelphia Bar Association Minutes.

Philadelphia Law Association Centennial, 1802-1903 (1906).

SECONDARY SOURCES

Bentley, A. F., "The Process of Government," University of Chicago Press (1908).

Borchard, E. M., "Declaratory Judgments" (1934).

Child, Harwood Lawrence, "Labor and Capital in National Politics," Ohio State University Press (1930).

Codel, Martin, "Radio and its Future," Harpers (1930).

Davis, W. Jefferson, Radio Law, Parker, Stone & Baird Company, Los Angeles (1929).

Dickinson, John, "Administrative Justice and the Supremacy of Law in the United States," Cambridge, Harvard University Press (1927).

Elliott, W. Y., "Pragmatic Revolt in Politics," Macmillan (1928).

Follett, M. P., "The New State," Longmans, Green and Company (1925).

Freund, Ernst, "Administrative Powers Over Persons and Property," University of Chicago Press (1928).

Graves, W. Brooke, "Readings in Public Opinion," Appleton (1928).
"Uniform State Laws," Chapel Hill (1934).

Herring, E. P., "Group Representation Before Congress," Institute for Government Research (1929).

Kent, F. R., "The Great Game of Politics," Doubleday, Page and Company (1922).

Laski, H. J., "Grammar of Politics," Yale University Press (1925).
"Studies in Law and Politics," Yale University Press (1932).
"Politics," J. B. Lippincott Company (1931).

Logan, E. B., "Lobbying," Supplement, Annals of the American Academy of Political and Social Science, Vol. CXLIV, July, 1929.

McBain, H. L., "The Living Constitution," Macmillan (1927).

McFarland, Carl, "Administrative Agencies in Government and the Effect thereof of Constitutional Limitations," Prize Winning Essay in contest conducted by American Bar Association under the terms of the Erskine M. Ross bequest (1934).

Merriam, C. E., "American Political Ideas," Macmillan (1920).
"The American Party System," Macmillan (1922).
"New Aspects of Politics," University of Chicago Press (1925).

Merriam, C. E., and Barnes, H. E., "A History of Political Theories—Recent Times," Macmillan (1924).

Mill, J. S., "Considerations on Representative Government," Harper and Brothers (1867).

Munro, W. B., "The Invisible Government," Macmillan Company (1928).

Odegard, P. J., "Pressure Politics, The Story of the Anti-Saloon League," Columbia University Press (1928).

Ogburn, W. F., "Social Change," Viking Press (1927).

Pound, Roscoe, "The Spirit of the Common Law," Dartmouth College (1921).

Rogers, James Grafton, "American Bar Leaders," American Bar Association (1932).

Smith, Reginald Heber, "Justice to the Poor," Carnegie Foundation, Bulletin No. 13 (3d Edition, 1924).

Warren, Charles A., "History of the American Bar," Little, Brown and Company (1911).

White, L. D., "Public Administration," Macmillan (1926).

Wickser, P. J., "Bar Associations," Reprint from Cornell Law Quarterly, Vol. XV, No. 3, April, 1930.

Willoughby, William F., "Principles of Public Administration," John Hopkins Press (1927).

PERIODICALS

Annals American Academy of Political and Social Science, Vol. CXXIV, March, 1926, "Legal Aid Work."

Annals, March, 1928, Vol. CXXXVI, "Progress in the Law."
January, 1930, Vol. CXLVII, "Anti Trust Laws of the United States."
July, 1935, Vol. 180, "Socialism, Fascism and Democracy."

Commercial Law Journal, December, 1935.

Harvard Business Review, July, 1931, Article by Dr. J. M. Herring, "Equalization of Broadcasting Facilities within the United States."

Legal Intelligencer, Philadelphia.

Missouri Bar Journal, May, 1932.

National Income Tax Magazine, October, 1927.

United States Daily, February 11, 1930; July 23, 1930.

INDEX